Red

'Gripping and authoritative. Family men, circus
performers, solicitors, communists and reactionaries
all fought together and shed blood for their country – a
true and moving story of war' Andy McNab

'Riveting. Impeccably researched. Authoritative.
Urban reveals the Red Devils in all their glory, as they
forged the path for airborne forces to follow in World War II.
Full of daring action, standout characters and cutting-edge
operations, this is unputdownable' Damien Lewis

'A detailed, fast-paced history of these remarkable
men that reads like a thriller. Brilliantly researched
and brilliantly told' Julia Boyd

'I couldn't put Red Devils down' Amanda Foreman

'Excellent . . . Mark Urban has brought an old soldier's insights
and a fine journalist's clarity to tell this story resoundingly
well, mixing superb accounts of the battles with a deep
understanding of personalities, service politics and the
paratrooper ethos' Patrick Bishop, Daily Telegraph

'If you want to get under the skin of the pioneers of airborne
soldiering, this is it . . . fast-paced, well written and attention-
grabbing from start to finish' Adrian Weale, Mail Plus

'Masterful . . . Mark Urban paints a colourful picture of
the officers and men who volunteered for what in 1940 was
a leap into the unknown' Paul de Zulueta, Spectator

'Does not disappoint . . . A story of courage and adversity,
Red Devils is a must-read' Who Do You Think You Are? Magazine

ABOUT THE AUTHOR

Mark Urban is Diplomatic Editor of BBC's *Newsnight* programme and was previously the defence correspondent for the *Independent*. He formerly served in the British Army, both in the Royal Tank Regiment and in the Territorial Army. He is the author of books such as *Rifles*, *The Skripal Files* and *Task Force Black,* a *Sunday Times* number one bestseller.

Red Devils

The Trailblazers of the Paras in World War Two: An Authorized History of the Parachute Regiment

MARK URBAN

PENGUIN BOOKS

PENGUIN BOOKS

UK | USA | Canada | Ireland | Australia
India | New Zealand | South Africa

Penguin Books is part of the Penguin Random House group of companies
whose addresses can be found at global.penguinrandomhouse.com.

First published by Viking 2022
Published in Penguin Books 2023
005

Copyright © Mark Urban, 2022

The moral right of the author has been asserted

Maps by Evolution Design
Typeset by Jouve (UK), Milton Keynes
Printed and bound in Great Britain by Clays Ltd, Elcograf S.p.A.

The authorized representative in the EEA is Penguin Random House Ireland,
Morrison Chambers, 32 Nassau Street, Dublin D02 YH68

A CIP catalogue record for this book is available from the British Library

ISBN: 978-0-241-99522-8

www.greenpenguin.co.uk

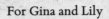
For Gina and Lily

Contents

Contents

Illustrations

15. Wing Commander Charles Pickard, who led the formation of Whitley bombers to the Bruneval drop, with men of the 2nd Battalion and a trophy of the raid.

16. One of the many 'synthetic' training devices adopted to prepare men for their first drop and make up for the shortage of suitable aircraft was the 'fan trainer', which allowed practice landings at different speeds.

17. At Hardwick Hall, would-be recruits to the Parachute Regiment were put through extensive physical training, both on the assault course and with repeated route marches.

18. Having passed Hardwick, aspirant paratroopers were sent to No. 1 Parachute School at Ringway, near Manchester, where they practised all aspects of jumping before making their first drop from a balloon.

19. Another view of training at Ringway: 'knees together, elbows in', students learn how to land without injury.

20. A pre-deployment tea with (left to right) Arthur 'Chalky' White, Maud Selman, her son Fred Selman, and Mike 'Lou' Lewis.

21. Officers from A Company of the 2nd Battalion after the Oudna debacle: Captain Ronald Stark, Lieutenant Desmond 'Slapsey' Brayley and Major Dick Ashford, who sports a non-regulation beret picked up from French stores.

22. The arduous Tunisian campaign exposed the men to the rigours of a North African winter while moving to one threatened sector after another to thwart enemy advances. This photo features the 1st Parachute Battalion.

23. This aqueduct in the Tamera valley provided a landmark in the Tunisian landscape and a rallying point for these 1st Battalion men after a night patrol.

24. General Dwight Eisenhower visits the 1st Parachute Brigade in May 1943, soon after its return from the Tunisian front. Airborne forces figured prominently in his plans for the next stage of the war.

25. The Tunisian campaign was distinguished by several battles between British and German paratroopers, who here had captured Private Gavin Cadden, a veteran of Dunkirk and Bruneval whose luck ran out at Oudna.

26. After posting to the Army Film and Photographic Unit, Mike Lewis put up sergeant's stripes and was here pictured by a memorial to those, including so many of his friends, who had fallen in the Tunisian battles.

27. Containers for dropping stores by parachute being prepared in the run-up to 1st Airborne Division's operations in Sicily.

28. A model maker puts finishing touches to a diorama used for briefing the men of 1st Parachute Brigade about their target in Sicily, the Primosole Bridge.

29. General 'Windy' Gale in full flow, giving 6th Airborne Division a pep talk prior to D-Day.

30. Men of the 22nd Independent Parachute Company synchronize their watches prior to taking off from RAF Harwell in Oxfordshire.

31. Members of the 225th Parachute Field Ambulance, crammed into a Stirling bomber on their way to Normandy.

32. Gliders and their Stirling tugs at RAF Tarrant Rushton.

33. Drop Zone N became Landing Zone N as scores of gliders landed there on 6 June 1944, there being 355 of them dispatched in support of 6th Airborne Division, mostly carrying heavy equipment and stores.

34. Critical to the success of Operation Tonga, was the landing of a *coup de main* party on the night of 5/6 June adjacent to the bridges over the Orne and the nearby canal. Four of the six assigned Horsas landed close to their targets, deploying assault troops.

35. Passengers on a Horsa dubbed 'Charlie's Aunt' wasted no time unloading the jeep and cargo trailer on board.

36. Troops crossing the canal bridge at Bénouville. Once taken by airborne forces, it became an important asset for moving men and equipment within the Allied bridgehead.

37. Another jeep-and-trailer combination speeds into action, this heavily laden vehicle belonging to 6th Airborne Division's Royal Army Service Corps company, which delivered supplies.

38. A pair from the 6th Airborne Division's provost (or military police) company guarding a junction near Ranville in the airborne bridgehead.

39. Men of No. 4 Commando linking up with paratroops from the 7th Battalion in Bénouville on 6 June 1944.

40. Panzer IVs of the 21st Panzer Division were used to launch a number of counter-attacks against 6th Airborne Division.

41. Men of 6th Airlanding Brigade pictured a few days after the Normandy landings in nearby Bénouville.

42. Many of the fallen were initially interred in Normandy graveyards, in this case three men of the 7th Parachute Battalion and a member of the Royal Engineers.

43. The sky full of aircraft and parachutes above the Dutch countryside on 17 September 1944, as Operation Market Garden got underway. This remarkable image was captured by a reconnaissance Spitfire.

44. Men of the 1st Battalion, the Border Regiment, one of the airlanded battalions that arrived to the west of Arnhem on the first day of the operation.

45. Sergeant Mike Lewis captured film of Dutch locals greeting their liberators. This still shows members of 21st Independent Parachute Company (including the sergeant, who jumped with his arm in plaster) and one 3rd Battalion man.

46. A party of German prisoners captured soon after the landings being escorted near the Wolfheze asylum, about ten kilometres north-west of Arnhem.

47. An aerial view showing the elevated roadway leading off the main bridge at Arnhem with the burnt-out remnants of the SS column that was ambushed there on the morning of 18 September 1944.

48. A German photographer in Arnhem snapped these captured British paratroopers being led away.

49. A 3-inch mortar team in action during the Cauldron battle on 21 September 1944. Mike Lewis's AFPU colleague Sergeant Dennis Smith captured many dramatic images of this fight.

50. Another image from Sergeant Smith, men of the 1st Parachute Battalion trying to fight their way into Arnhem on 17 September. They did not succeed, so the 2nd Battalion remained isolated.

51. Many of those pressed into action during the Cauldron battle were not infantrymen by training: here two glider pilots hunt for a sniper in Oosterbeek on 21 September.

52. Major General Robert 'Roy' Urquhart outside his HQ at the Hartenstein Hotel. Although Sergeant Lewis, who filmed him, and Sergeant Smith, who took this image, tried to make him look like a man in charge, poor communications and a period spent hiding from the Germans at the outset meant his role was limited.

53. Allied forces did eventually liberate Arnhem, but not until April 1945 when this image of an unknown paratrooper's grave was taken near the bridge defended by the 2nd Battalion.

54. Shortly after being appointed Colonel Commandant of the Parachute Regiment, Field Marshal Montgomery, sporting a maroon-red beret, visited its troops in the Ardennes to confer awards. Among them, right behind the man with a Sten gun, is Sergeant Sid Cornell.

55. The Ardennes battles of December 1944 and January 1945 were bitterly cold as well as costly for the 13th Battalion. This image of an airborne sniper team in action shows the snow suits adopted at this time.

56. An airborne view of the Operation Varsity Rhine-crossing operation gives some idea of the smoke that obscured many landing and drop zones. Some came from burning buildings, but the Allies also deployed smoke generators to cover the river assault itself.

57. A 6-pounder anti-tank gun flown in to Hamminkeln during Operation Varsity.

58. Lieutenant Colonel Pine-Coffin (right) pictured during a roadside rest on 30 April 1945. The facial wound he suffered the previous month is still fresh.

59. Men of the 6th Airborne Division marching across northern Germany in April 1945.

Illustration Acknowledgements

Images 1, 3, 4, 6, 7, 8, 9, 10, 11, 12, 13, 14, 15, 16, 17, 18, 19, 21, 22, 23, 24, 25, 26, 27, 28, 29, 33, 34, 36, 43, 44, 45, 46, 47, 49, 50, 51, 52, 53, 54, 55, 56, 58: Airborne Assault Museum, Imperial War Museum Duxford

2. Courtesy of John Grayburn
5. Courtesy of Michael Pine-Coffin
20. Courtesy of Dr Helen Lewis, Lewis Archive
30. © IWM/Getty Images
31. © Imperial War Museums CH 13304
32. © Imperial War Museums CL 26
35. © Imperial War Museums B 5200
37. © Imperial War Museums B 5205
38. © Imperial War Museums B 5291
39. © Imperial War Museums B 5058
40. Bundesarchiv, Bild 101I-493-3356-07 / photographer: Siedel
41. © Imperial War Museums B 5585
42. © Imperial War Museums B 5432
48. Bundesarchiv, Bild 101I-497-3526-09A / photographer: Erich Wenzel
57. © Imperial War Museums BU 2304
59. © Imperial War Museums BU 3231

Maps

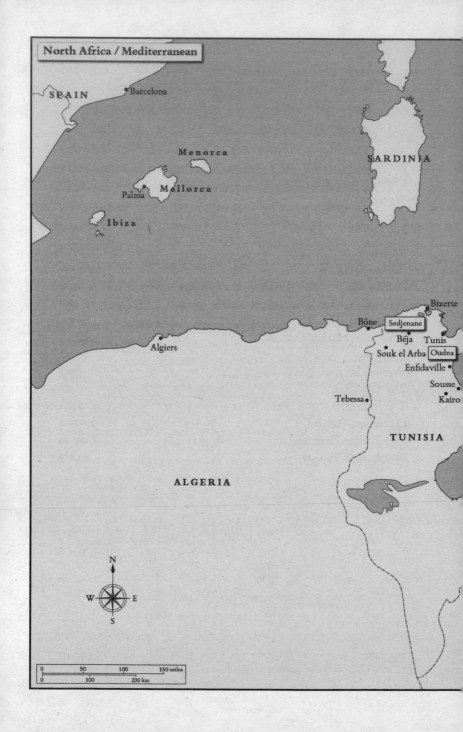

North Africa / Mediterranean

SPAIN
Barcelona

Menorca

Mallorca
Palma

Ibiza

SARDINIA

Bizerte

Bône   Sedjenane
Béja   Tunis
Souk el Arba   Oudna
Enfidaville
Sousse
Kairo

Algiers

Tebessa

TUNISIA

ALGERIA

N
W—E
S

0   50   100   150 miles
0   100   200 km

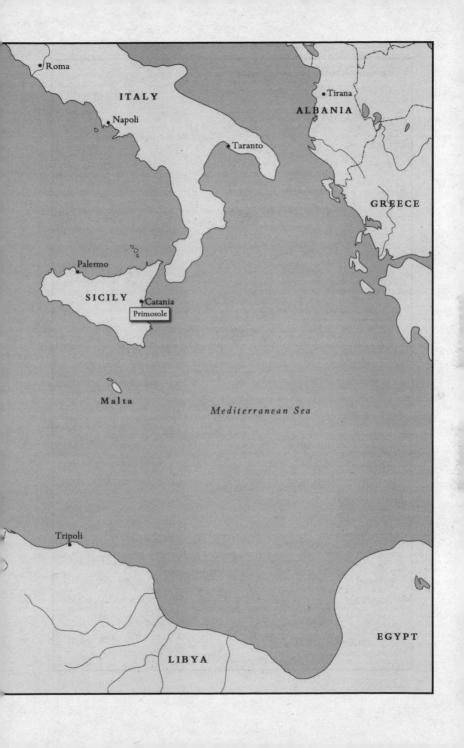

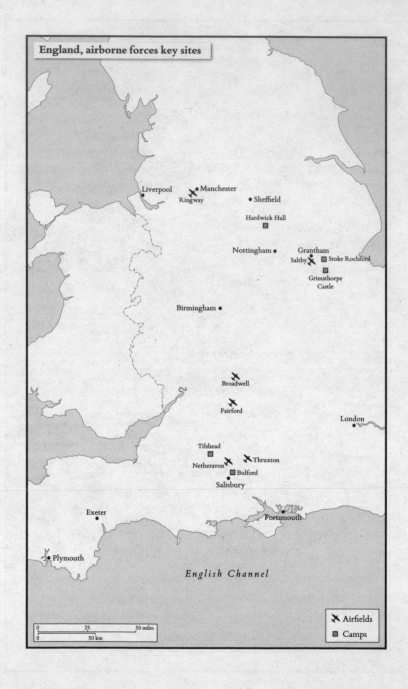

England, airborne forces key sites

Liverpool
Manchester
Ringway
Sheffield
Hardwick Hall
Nottingham
Grantham
Saltby
Stoke Rochford
Grimsthorpe
Castle
Birmingham
Broadwell
Fairford
London
Tilshead
Netheravon
Thruxton
Bulford
Salisbury
Exeter
Portsmouth
Plymouth

English Channel

| 0 | 25 | 50 miles |
| 0 | 50 km | |

✗ Airfields
■ Camps

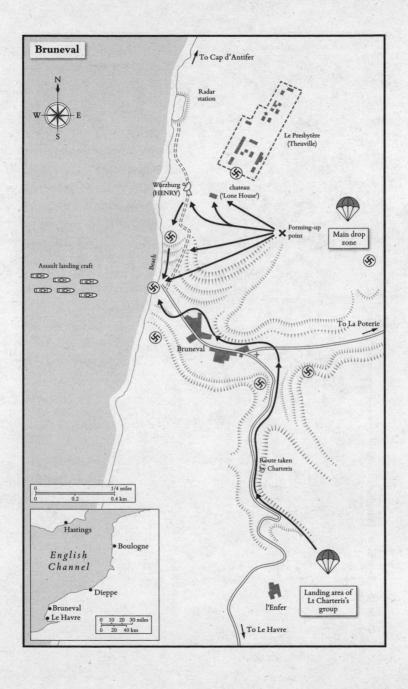

Bruneval

To Cap d'Antifer

N
W—E
S

Radar station

Le Presbytère (Theuville)

Würzburg (HENRY)

chateau ('Lone House')

Forming-up point

Main drop zone

Assault landing craft

Beach

To La Poterie

Bruneval

Route taken by Charteris

0 ___ 1/4 miles
0 ___ 0.2 ___ 0.4 km

Hastings

Boulogne

English Channel

Dieppe

Bruneval
Le Havre

l'Enfer

Landing area of Lt Charteris's group

To Le Havre

0 10 20 30 miles
0 20 40 km

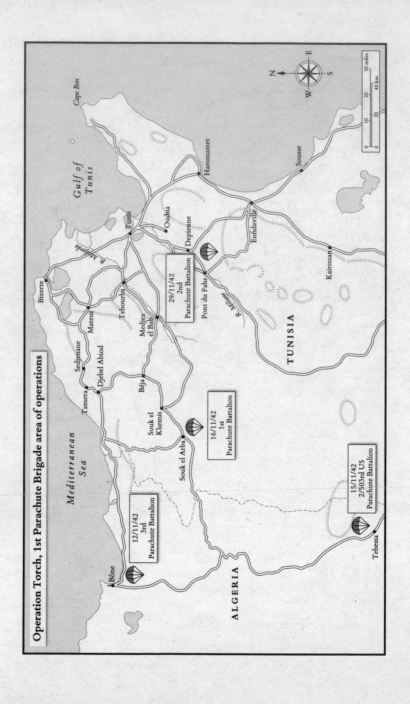

Operation Torch, 1st Parachute Brigade area of operations

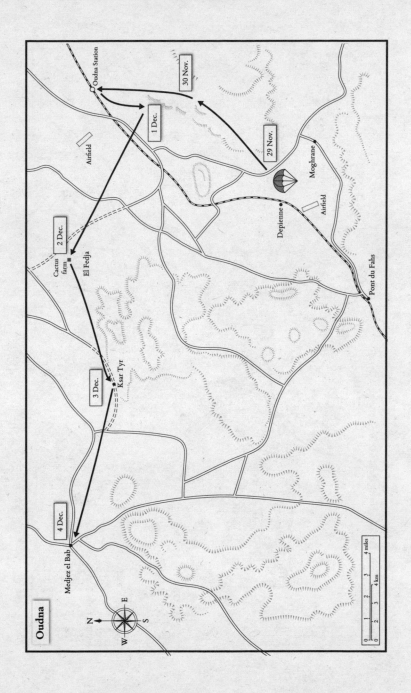

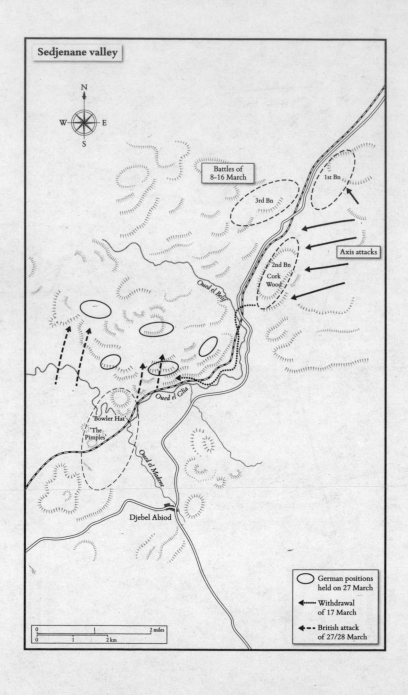

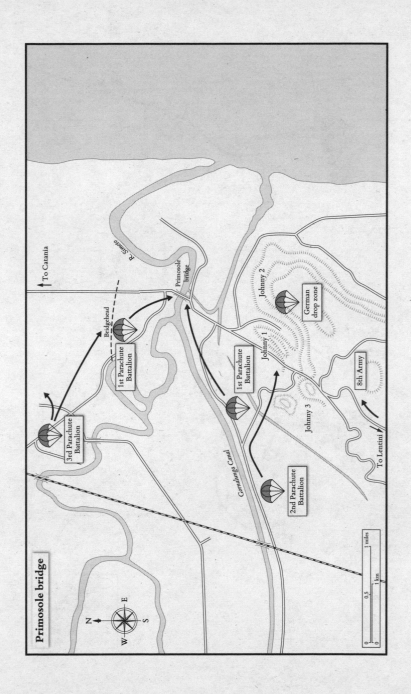

Primosole bridge

To Catania

R. Simeto

Primosole bridge

Bridgehead

3rd Parachute Battalion

1st Parachute Battalion

1st Parachute Battalion

2nd Parachute Battalion

Gornalunga Canal

Johnny 1

Johnny 2

German drop zone

Johnny 3

8th Army

To Lentini

N
E
S
W

0   0.5   1 miles
0   1 km

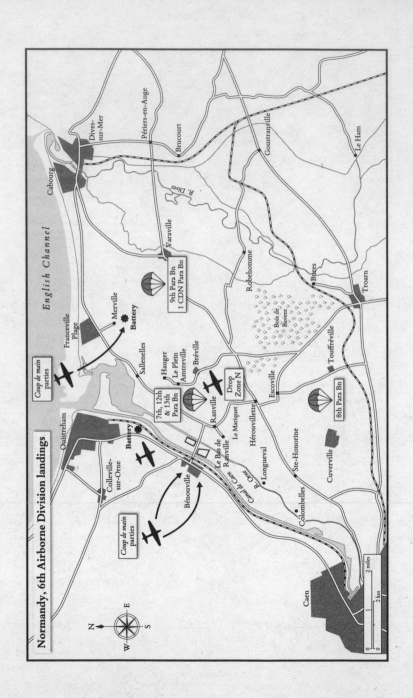

Normandy, 6th Airborne Division landings

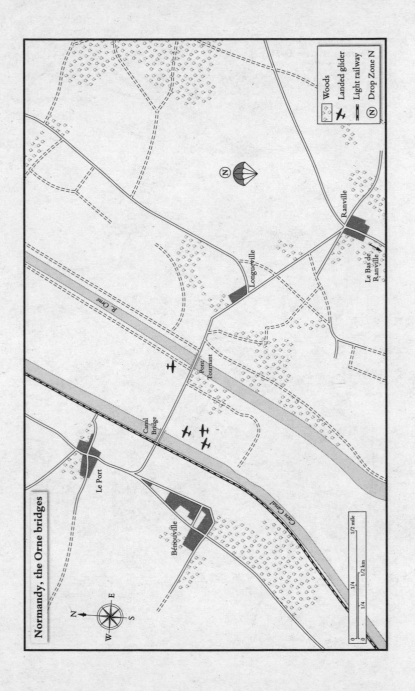

Normandy, the Orne bridges

Woods
Landed glider
Light railway
Drop Zone N

N — Drop Zone N

R. Orne

Ranville

Le Bas de Ranville

Longueville

Pont Tournant

Canal Bridge

Le Port

Bénouville

Caen Canal

N
W   E
S

0   1/4   1/2 mile
0   1/4   1/2 km

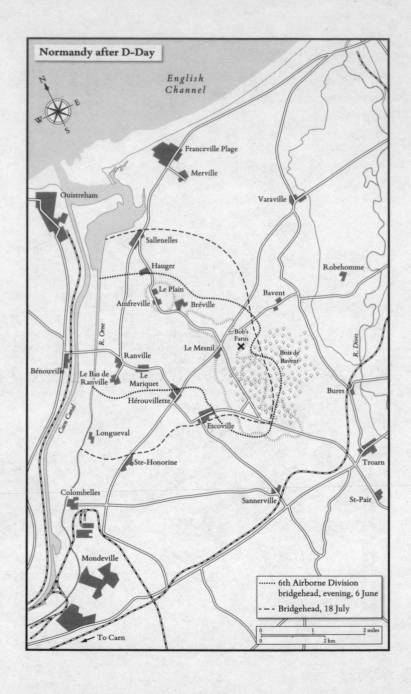

Normandy after D-Day

English Channel

N
W E
S

Franceville Plage
Merville
Ouistreham
Varaville
Sallenelles
Hauger
Robehomme
Le Plain
Bréville
Bavent
Amfreville
R. Orne
Bob's Farm
Le Mesnil
Ranville
Bois de Bavent
R. Dives
Bénouville
Le Bas de Ranville
Le Mariquet
Hérouvillette
Bures
Caen Canal
Longueval
Escoville
Ste-Honorine
Troarn
Colombelles
Sannerville
St-Pair
Mondeville

To Caen

······ 6th Airborne Division
        bridgehead, evening, 6 June

- - - Bridgehead, 18 July

0   1   2 miles
0   2 km

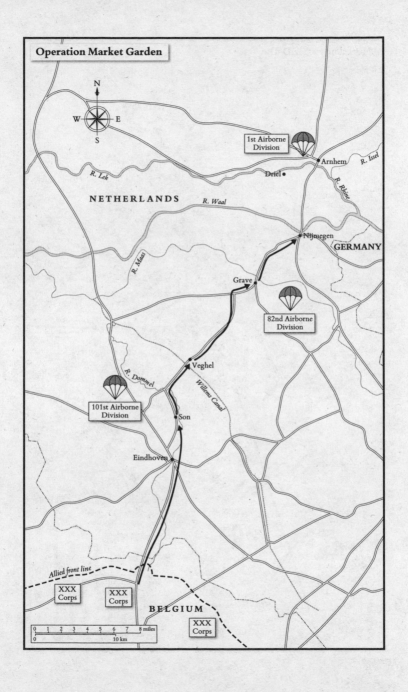

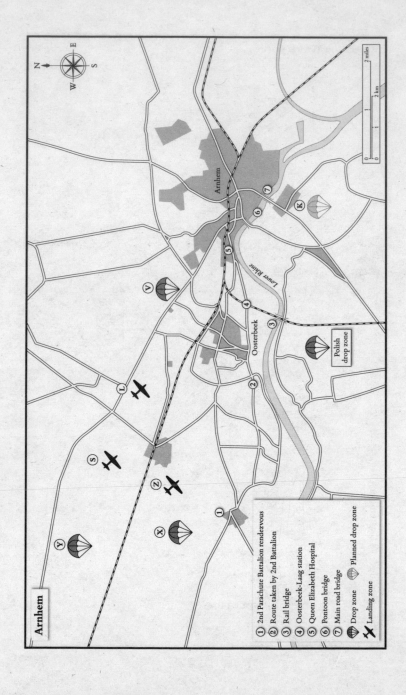

Arnhem

Legend:
1. 2nd Parachute Battalion rendezvous
2. Route taken by 2nd Battalion
3. Rail bridge
4. Oosterbeek-Laag station
5. Queen Elizabeth Hospital
6. Pontoon bridge
7. Main road bridge

Drop zone
Planned drop zone
Landing zone

Arnhem

Oosterbeek

Lower Rhine

Polish drop zone

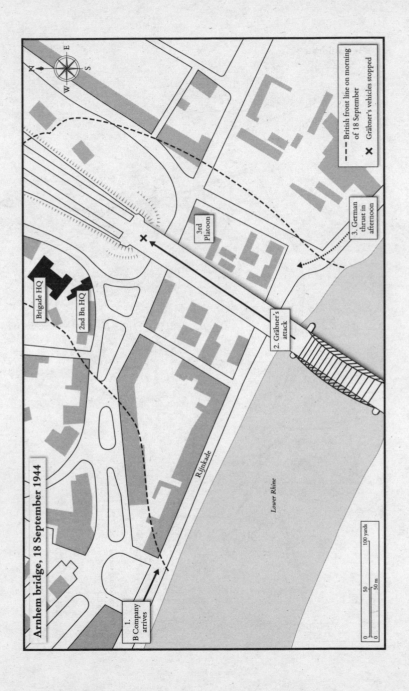

Arnhem bridge, 18 September 1944

Brigade HQ

2nd Bn HQ

3rd Platoon

1. B Company arrives

2. Gräbner's attack

3. German thrust in afternoon

Rijnkade

Lower Rhine

- - - British front line on morning of 18 September

✕ Gräbner's vehicles stopped

N E S W

0   50   100 yards
0   50 m

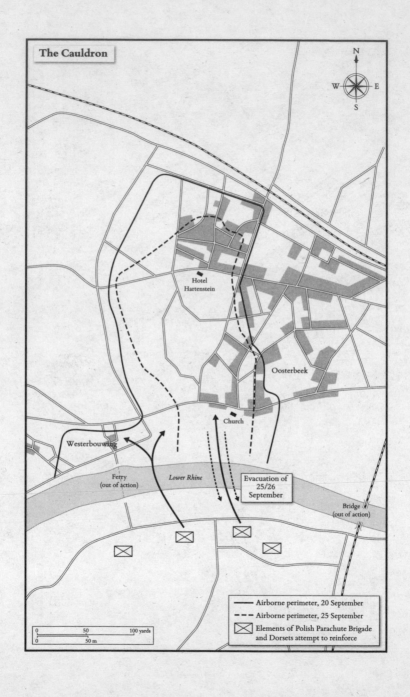

The Cauldron

N
W   E
S

Hotel
Hartenstein

Oosterbeek

Church

Westerbouwing

Ferry
(out of action)

Lower Rhine

Evacuation of
25/26
September

Bridge
(out of action)

| 0 | 50 | 100 yards |
| 0 | 50 m | |

——— Airborne perimeter, 20 September

- - - - Airborne perimeter, 25 September

☒ Elements of Polish Parachute Brigade
and Dorsets attempt to reinforce

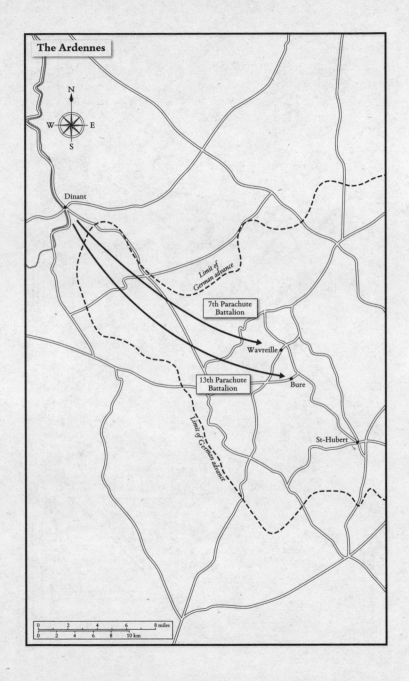

The Ardennes

N
W E
S

Dinant

Limit of German advance

7th Parachute Battalion

Wavreille

13th Parachute Battalion

Bure

St-Hubert

Limit of German advance

0   2   4   6   8 miles
0 2 4 6 8   10 km

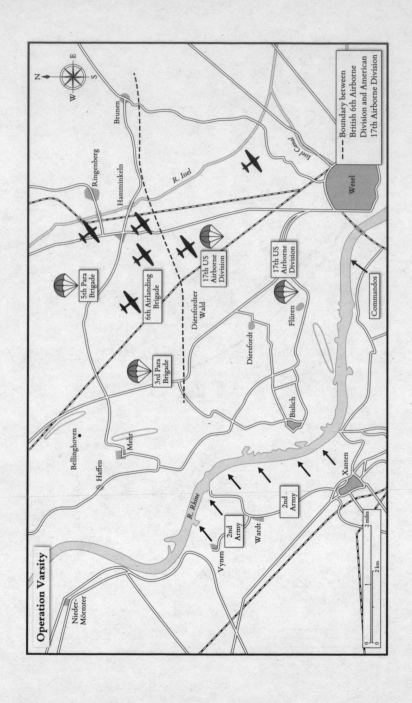

Operation Varsity

Boundary between
British 6th Airborne
Division and American
17th Airborne Division

Wesel

Commandos

17th US
Airborne
Division

Flüren

17th US
Airborne
Division

Diersfordt

Bislich

Diersfordter
Wald

3rd Para
Brigade

6th Airlanding
Brigade

5th Para
Brigade

Ringenberg

Hamminkeln

Brunen

R. Issel

Issel Canal

Bellinghoven

Haffen

Mehr

Xanten

2nd
Army

Wardt

2nd
Army

Vynen

R. Rhine

Nieder-
Mörmter

0   1   2 miles
0   1   2 km

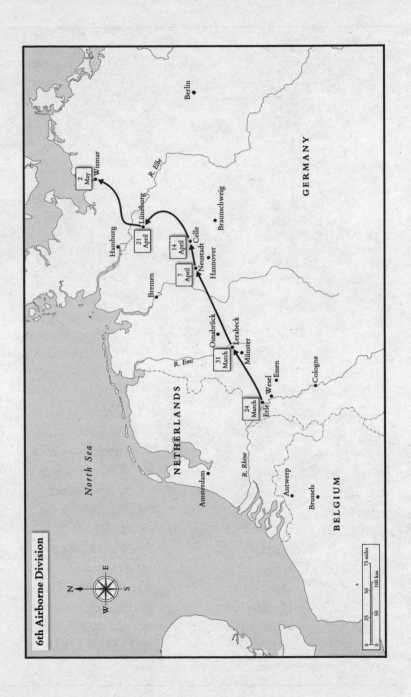

6th Airborne Division

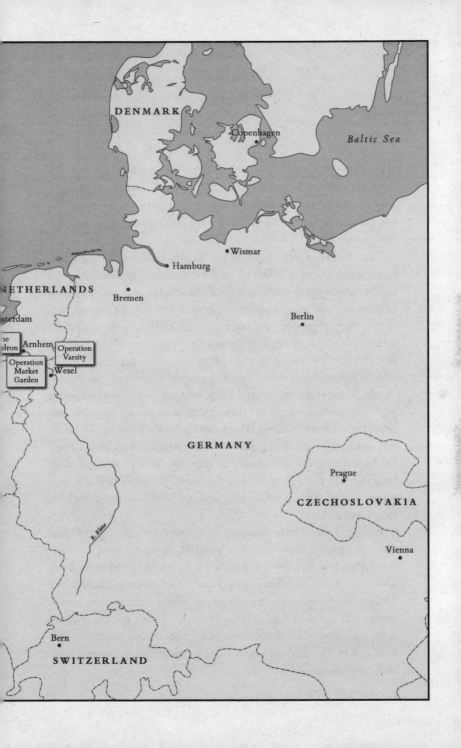

Preface

A new regiment, with a new way of getting to war, is a start-up story for military historians. It is about whose ideas won through, how the doubters were routed and how that instinctively conservative institution that is the military went from grudging acceptance to full embrace.

This challenge was made all the harder because Britain was a late entrant into the airborne warfare business. In Germany and the Soviet Union large numbers of parachutists had been trained in the 1930s and many exercises conducted to try out new tactics. It was the best part of two years after the outbreak of war before serious preparations began in Great Britain and the call went out to find the first few thousand volunteers.

Many have commented upon the tribal nature of the British Army. Those who would establish a new regiment must endow it with the symbols, rites and ethos that bind its people together and bring them success in battle. That story forms a big part of this book.

I don't think it matters whether the person telling such a story has been a member of the tribe in question. Although I did serve long ago and for a short time in the army, it wasn't in the Rifles, whose origin story I told in a previous book, or the Parachute Regiment either.

Indeed, I didn't have much to do with 'Paras' during my Cold War soldiering experience decades back, though I have encountered them in quite a few operational situations as a journalist – from Kosovo to Iraq and Afghanistan. I have tried to set to one side the modern stereotype of 'the Paras' as rapid deployment shock troops imbued with 'airborne aggression'. That's got more to do with recent worldwide conflict, particularly the Northern Ireland and Falklands campaigns and the experience of a generation of professionals.

The wartime founders of this clan were also volunteers, but from an army largely stocked by conscripted soldiers. That meant they were very diverse, coming from all over, embracing a wide range of professional backgrounds and religious beliefs. They also spanned the political schisms of that time, suffused as they were with class antagonism.

So, we find a gravedigger and a docker sharing a trench in Tunisia under the command of an assistant manager at Marks & Spencer. There are communists and reactionary Tories shoulder to shoulder on that same hillside. Their fellowship resulted not just from a common enemy, but from common experience of the ordeals of airborne training.

Indeed, the wartime national service system brought some quite extraordinary people into airborne forces. If you want to discover, for example, how it came to be that 140 unarmed pacifists parachuted into Normandy with the 6th Airborne Division, read on.

Although the struggle to field large units of paratroopers went on for years, once they were ready for action they were swiftly committed to a series of campaigns in arenas ranging from North Africa to Italy and from Normandy to the Rhineland. Along the way there were terrible operational miscalculations as well as heroics.

This story about the soldiers forming a new regiment inevitably centres on those who fought and shed their blood. But I didn't want to write the type of book that simply quotes lengthy chunks of later veteran accounts. Instead, I wanted to place particular emphasis on letters or journals written at the time rather than post-war reminiscences, although I have, of course, drawn extensively on those and various types of authentic record.

While telling the story of a group of men at the outset of a conflict, bound together through trials and tribulations, was the treatment adopted in my books *Rifles*, *Fusiliers* and *The Tank War*, it would prove a little more complex to deliver in the case of the Parachute Regiment. My wartime armoured corps story was able to focus on one of many battalions of the Royal Tank Regiment (the 5th), because, being representative of the bigger story, it had been in all the key battles that needed to be covered. In the case of airborne forces that isn't possible. So instead of trying to tell every unit's story in one volume, a treatment that would produce a book both lengthy and superficial because of its need to tell a little of everyone's story, I have opted for a more focused approach that allows the bonds and rivalries of a small number to be followed through all of the regiment's key wartime moments. As with those previous books, you will meet half a dozen near the start whose individual fates span the gamut of the regiment's wider war: hard fighting, wounding, capture, death and decoration.

So the 2nd Parachute Battalion (as part of the 1st Airborne Division) provides the main focus for weaving together personal stories for much of this book, but if I had simply told its story I would have left an enormous amount uncovered. The formation of a second division in England in 1943–44 (confusingly, the 6th Airborne, so named as a deception measure) provided forces for many of the regiment's most important wartime actions, from Normandy to the Rhine Crossing. Clearly, I had to find a way to relate their experiences also.

This account therefore takes the formation of one of the first units, the 2nd Battalion, and links the stories of men who served in it. Several were subsequently carried by the tides of war to other places, allowing the reader to follow their trajectory. Indeed, one of those we find early on in the story goes on to lead the 7th Parachute Battalion, part of that 6th Airborne Division, and becomes our guide, via copious papers he left to posterity, through those episodes in 1944–45 in which the 2nd Battalion played no part.

Similarly, while the focus of this account is the Parachute Regiment rather than the wider supporting cast of 'enablers' that made up the airborne forces as a whole, the careers of some of those we first find messing together in the 2nd Battalion take us to other elements, such as signallers and medical orderlies who effectively became part of parachute units on operations, although they wore different badges on their maroon-red berets.

As will become apparent, the question of how to define the ethos and tactics of the new regiment produced different answers in the 1st and 6th Airborne Divisions. Returning to the start-up analogy, it is almost as if there were rival teams trying to prevail.

I would make one more point about my approach to these 'organizational biographies'. While the testimony of those fighting within a unit is critical to such a narrative, the assessment of those whose lives have depended upon each other in battle is quite understandably conditioned by mutual loyalty and solidarity. Unless you want to write hagiography, it is necessary to check those views regularly and ask what their higher commanders, other units and, of course, the enemy thought of a particular battalion's performance in action. That's an approach I've taken with all the books of this kind that I've written. After all, it was enemies of the Parachute Regiment who dubbed them the Red Devils.

1. First Blood

It was night, early in 1942 and a formation of twelve bombers was reaching its cruising altitude over the Channel. Being February, it was freezing. The aircraft were heading south, towards the coast of German-occupied France, and the pilots knew it would not be long before they were picked up on German radar. They were on course for Le Havre, but not to deliver the air raid their enemy might have expected.

In the bays beneath the aircraft were containers rather than bombs, steel tubes full of weapons, ammunition and other kit. Nestling in the fuselage of each aeroplane were soldiers, men tasked with mounting the biggest parachute assault yet attempted by Britain in the war. An enormous amount was riding on the success of their mission, not least because the war up to that point had seen the army brought low by a series of defeats from Norway to Dunkirk and Singapore.

The officer commanding those men was lost in thought as he huddled for warmth under a blanket, rehearsing the details of their secret mission in his mind. Major J. D. Frost, Johnny Frost to his brother officers, had been given the task of leading the raid. A solidly built six-footer, the twenty-nine-year-old had squeezed himself into the aircraft, half hoping the mission might be called off; there was just so much a stake it was nerve-wracking.

Frost, like most of C Company, was a proud Scot. As the men had filed up to the planes before take-off, he had ordered a piper to play the marches of their various regiments.

That night the hopes of an entire corps of men, elite volunteers to the cause of airborne warfare, rested on his shoulders. There were enemies below, who would soon be trying to kill them, and then there was the foe back home, those in Whitehall who wanted to throttle the whole parachute experiment, something they considered one of Winston Churchill's mad hobby horses.

The omens were hardly auspicious. One year earlier, the first British parachute raid of the war, Operation Colossus, had ended in failure in Italy. All thirty-five men had been captured and the submarine sent to evacuate them failed to arrive. Operation Squatter, in November 1941, featuring L Detachment of the Special Air Service, was another disaster: only twenty-one of the fifty-five men dropped had returned.

Like many of the soldiers flying on that February night over the dark waters of the Channel, Frost had been tested in combat before. Born in India into an army family, he had led Arab levies in Iraq the previous year, surviving numerous skirmishes, and was hardly a man to let the mere business of getting shot at unnerve him. During breaks in his military duties, he had also managed to ride to hounds with a Baghdad hunt and pot many a game bird with his shotgun.

Under pressure, Frost often displayed a mordant wit and an outward indifference to danger. But inwardly, bumping along in the turbulent night skies, the wheels were turning in his mind: would they reach their objective? How many of them would die? And could he contain an unbearably full bladder, the result of too much tea before take-off, for long enough to get down to terra firma without wetting himself?

As their planes neared the French coast the men sang 'Lulu', 'Annie Laurie' and 'The Rose of Tralee' to the throb of the bombers' twin engines. The flak would start soon and they all knew that casualties were highly likely. Given what had happened on the previous missions, it was quite possible that none of them would be going home.

Paratroopers called these planes, which were Whitley bombers, 'flying coffins'. 'The windowless fuselage of a bomber is oppressive, dark and lowering to the morale of most men,' wrote one corporal who volunteered early for the new regiment. 'No smoking can be permitted, no movement is possible . . . men are huddled in cramped positions on the floor, unable to stretch their legs, unable to relieve themselves . . . and unable to see what is going on outside.'

If that wasn't bad enough, the men of C Company of the 2nd Parachute Battalion were trussed up in their parachute harnesses with Sten guns, ammunition pouches, explosives and all manner of other equipment strapped to them. In short, it was so grim that when the red lights blinked on, one by one, announcing they were close to their drop zone, many of them couldn't wait to escape the aircraft's confines.

A Royal Air Force crewman got up and opened the hatch in the floor, admitting a blast of icy air into the fuselage and allowing those sitting nearest to glimpse the snow-blanketed Normandy landscape below. Frost inched forward until he was sitting with his legs dangling into the void, awaiting the green lamp. In another Whitley, the interior was briefly lit with flashes from the German flak trying to shoot them down.

Their mission had been codenamed Operation Biting. In Frost's secret orders, marked 'Not to be taken in aircraft', their target was referred to as HENRY. The objects of that night's raid were: 'to capture various parts of HENRY'; to take prisoners who had been in charge of HENRY; and to gather 'any documents referring to him' found in a nearby 'Lone House'. In fact, they were there not to dismember a person, rather to attack a German height-finding Würzburg radar station and remove its key components and operators to a nearby beach for recovery by the Royal Navy to the south coast of England. The low-UHF band Würzburg radar had emerged as a key element in an air defence system that was taking a rising toll in Royal Air Force bombers, so the boffins wanted to unravel its mysteries.

The moment came – green light; a little early in a couple of the leading bombers – and the paratroopers started dropping through the hatches. For each one, a second or two of falling, gripped by the icy slipstream, before the crack of an opening chute and the reassuring tug in the harness as their silk canopy filled with air.

When exiting the planes, speed was of the essence, for a few seconds' delay could add a hundred yards to the separation between two men reaching the ground. It was a drill they had practised many times, repeated until it became second nature. For Frost, who'd studied their objective for hours on end, as well as planning C Company's mission rehearsals, the opening of his chute was followed by a welcome panorama as he gazed below: 'I was able to recognize the ground as being identical with that depicted by the model, maps and photographs.'

As he landed, there was the soft crunch of snow underfoot. Frost collapsed his parachute and then, before proceeding to any other business, opened his flies and took a pee, 'it had become essential and was also a gesture of defiance'. Seeing their leader anointing French soil, many of the other paratroopers did likewise.

Then, taking other matters in hand, they moved about the drop zone, pinpointing the containers that had been parachuted down with them and breaking out weapons, explosives and all the other paraphernalia necessary to their mission. Under the plan presented to Frost as a fait accompli by the Combined Operations people, his 120 men were divided into five parties, each one named after a famous admiral.

Happily for those planning the mission, one Würzburg station sat on a clifftop in Normandy within striking distance of raiding forces. The radar unit was emplaced just to seaward (and west) of a chateau, the 'Lone House' in Frost's orders, in turn close to a presbytery with a group of buildings where soldiers guarding the area were stationed. These facilities on the upland were about one kilometre to the north of a village, Bruneval, which, set in a deep draw or ravine, gave access to a beach. That was where the paratroopers would be picked up by a group of landing craft standing offshore.

As the groups gathered themselves in the drop zone they soon realized that some people and equipment seemed to be missing. Two 'sticks', or groups of paratroops (twenty men in all), had been dropped too early, landing a couple of kilometres to the south. And for those who had made it to the correct area, a few hundred metres inland of HENRY, atop the same upland, there was another unwelcome discovery. The container holding a radio needed to contact the Royal Navy had also gone astray. But neither mishap could be allowed to stop the mission.

Standing facing west, towards the coastal clifftop and their objective, Major Frost gathered the main strike force, sixteen men in the party that he was to lead to the radar installation itself, with another twenty to take the chateau and quell any local resistance. The party included an RAF radar technician who would identify and remove its key parts, a linguist who would interrogate prisoners, and a group of Royal Engineers who would help to transport the key components to the beach. Another group of men, codenamed Nelson, were to set off down the slope into the Bruneval draw in order to secure their line of withdrawal to the beach, where the Germans had placed coastal defences including strongpoints dominating the route to and from the sea. These would have to be put out of action. The third main group of soldiers, codenamed Rodney, would take up a central position on the upland, able to act as a reserve should Frost's men or the beach party get into difficulties. As things turned out, there was one more group moving across the snowy countryside that night: the men who had been dropped south of Bruneval had immediately orientated themselves in order to move north under the leadership of a twenty-year-old second lieutenant named Euan Charteris.

While their leader may have been so callow that his nickname was 'Junior', there was plenty of experience in the small group of men that moved with him across the frozen Norman countryside. Two were veterans of fighting on the North-West Frontier in India and one had fought in the Spanish Civil War.

Even before Frost led his soldiers off from the main forming-up point, at around 1.15 a.m., a German patrol from the local defence force, the 1st Kompanie Infanterie-Regiment 685, had radioed in that an enemy landing appeared to be underway. Canopies from Charteris's group had been spotted as they floated down.

Although the local German troops had been conducting an exercise that evening, the raiders were able to move into position close to their objective undetected. As the main assault party crunched forward, one of the Rodney group lay on the snow with his Bren gun levelled at the presbytery. He listened to a small group of Germans, 'going away from the camp and [they] were in a laughing mood'. He held his fire.

Frost led his men swiftly to the chateau and, seeing that another team was ready to take the nearby Würzburg, blew his whistle, the signal for the mayhem to commence. Entering the building, they found only one defender there, who was swiftly cut down with sub-machine-gun fire.

At the Würzburg, grenades and Stens were used to gain control, another three Germans being killed in the violence. 'In a matter of minutes the apparatus was dismantled, packed into special protective bags,' one of the officers present noted. While that vital work was going on, a couple of other men went chasing after a Luftwaffe technician who had fled the assault. Running in a blind panic away from the attack, he went over the cliff edge, just managing to grab a handhold as he fell. Sergeant Gregor McKenzie, at thirty-nine probably the oldest man in C Company, hence his nickname 'Father', managed to haul the German back to safety. Frost's men had captured their technician. McKenzie relieved the prisoner of his watch, insisting it was a gift for saving him.

To the south, another German soldier had died in a moment of black comedy. Lost in the dark after being sent out in a patrol to investigate reports of parachutists dropping in the area, Adolf Schmitz tagged onto the rear of a group moving through woods near Bruneval. When Schmitz struck up conversation with the rearmost, that man, one of Second Lieutenant Charteris's group, exclaimed, 'Oh my God, it's a bloody German!' Schmitz unslung his weapon but was instantly shot by the paratroopers who had turned to face him.

The night sky was echoing to gunfire in several different places, adding to the defenders' confusion and indeed Frost's. He couldn't account for the shots coming from the direction of Charteris's party because he had no idea where they were. But as the German non-commissioned officers barked orders, their resistance began to coalesce. Several defenders in the presbytery started firing with light machine guns towards the Würzburg emplacement and chateau, where one of Frost's men was killed as he emerged from the building.

Down near the beach, the defenders were holding their own against the Nelson party sent down to clear the way. The heavy firing was echoing around the Bruneval ravine as Frost hurried his men away from the radar station and chateau, towards the beach.

Having photographed the interior of the Würzburg control cabin and removed its signal generating and processing equipment, Frost's men set explosive charges and moved off. The seized components were placed in a two-wheeled trolley parachuted in for the purpose in a weapons container. It was manhandled down a path towards the beach, accompanied by much swearing as the icy way became steeper and the soldiers continually lost their footing.

An hour after dropping, the mission was approaching a kind of crisis. There was effective fire from several enemy strongpoints, one of which directly obstructed Frost's path south to the pick-up point. His sergeant major had been seriously wounded by machine-gun fire here, having taken three shots to the stomach. The Nelson group, meanwhile, was still having difficulty overcoming defensive positions that dominated their way to the beach. Opening up with their Bren guns and Enfield rifles, they were giving as good as they got. This impasse was broken when, to the surprise of British and Germans alike, Charteris led his men to attack the defenders from the south just as the Nelson group renewed its assault from the north. A further German prisoner was taken on the outskirts of Bruneval. The fighting to clear the way down to the beach had taken more than an hour.

By about 3.15 a.m., Frost's men had successfully fought their way down to the shingle. They had the trolley with its precious radar parts, and a couple of prisoners. But several of their own men were missing. Some had been dropped off target, others separated during the fighting. The defenders had been neutralized, but Frost knew this was a temporary state of affairs, since the Germans could bring far greater numbers to bear and would soon organize once it was light. They also had unlimited supplies of ammunition, unlike the raiders. C Company needed to get the Navy in to pick them up as soon as possible. But the Senior Service couldn't be reached.

One vital radio needed to contact the flotilla of landing craft and gunboats offshore had been lost. The other sets they had with them had failed to work throughout the raid. The communications plan gave two back-up modes of communication: a signal lamp and flares fired from a Very pistol. A signaller using a lamp flashed away without receiving an answer. One flare after another had been shot into the sky, also ineffectually.

Looking up from the beach to the steep cliffs that rose on each side of the Bruneval draw, Frost knew that once the Germans were on the crests, firing down onto the tiny beach, his men wouldn't last long. 'The job was done,' one of the officers observed. 'The longer you stayed the more you were going to be in trouble.' Indeed, every minute now counted against the parachutists, helping the enemy bring more troops into play, bringing the dawn light closer and with an ebb tide making things harder for their Navy rescuers, if they ever appeared.

'With a sinking heart', Frost would later note, 'I moved off the beach with my officers to rearrange our defences in the entrance of the village and on the shoulders of the cliff. It looked as though we were going to be left high and dry once more and the thought was hard to bear.'

He could only forestall the danger for a short while. Once the Germans had taken the clifftops, the beaches could be raked with fire and his men massacred.

But then there was a cry from one of his men. About an hour after they had first cleared their way down to the water, the Royal Navy had been sighted. 'God bless the ruddy navy, sir!' one of Frost's signallers shouted. The first of their six landing craft made its way in to the pick-up point.

One by one, Frost's men fell back to the beach from the defensive positions they had taken. Officers and sergeants tried to do it with some semblance of order, reassembling the different groups sent on the mission. But several men were missing and a gun battle between British soldiers on the incoming landing craft and Germans lining the clifftops was growing in volume and intensity.

Stepping into the icy water, Frost supervised the loading of the injured and the radar parts onto the first landing craft as others carried wounded men down. But the firefight was building, and some Germans began lobbing grenades down onto the shoreline. At the same time, the ebb tide was exposing rocks, giving those piloting the landing craft a trickier channel to navigate. 'Our evacuation plan went by the board,' Frost recalled, and as the first couple of loaded craft headed out to sea, he realized that, while the mission's objective might now have been met, he didn't know exactly how many men had got away, or how many were still unaccounted for and might be left behind. All he knew was that nobody, least of all the Royal Navy, wanted to hang about as the cliffs echoed to gunfire.

By this time the last of the escape vessels was loading, and a thirty-year-old sergeant, Macleod Forsyth, was having to take charge of it. Forsyth, a miner's son from Stirling, could hear German machine-gun bullets ricocheting across off the metal sides of the craft he'd just dragged himself onto. Tracer rounds were buzzing over their heads as the parachutists flattened themselves against the protection of its steel flanks. The coxswain gunned the craft's engine, trying to pull it back from the shingle and out to sea. But nothing happened. They were stuck fast on a rock exposed by the tide. Forsyth could feel the weight of fire increasing and felt sure that they were about to die or be taken by the enemy.

The coxswain turned to Forsyth and told him the only hope lay in lifting the craft free.

Wading into the water, Forsyth got a handhold under the vessel, calling to his fellow soldiers, 'Christ! Lift this or we're prisoners!' Some others dropped into the surf to help him. That lightened the landing craft somewhat, and with a concerted heave, the parachutists got it free of the rocks and piled back in. Opening the throttle the coxswain, 'sped off much too quickly before the ramp was closed and we were in water nearly up to our knees'.

As it finally pulled away from the coast, the Germans treated

Forsyth's boat to a final blast of machine-gun fire, but none of those crouching inside was hit. As soon as they were out of range, they began bailing out the water with their helmets, working at it with all the frenzied energy generated by their deliverance. Picking up speed, the craft headed out. A couple of soldiers spotted flashing torches on the beach and assumed it must be some of those left behind signalling, poor bastards.

2. Lap of Honour

The Bruneval raid was over. Major Frost's force had spent just over three hours in France, successfully removing key parts of the Würzburg radar, taking two prisoners and generally sowing mayhem in that small corner of Normandy. As they headed out to sea and the dawn light grew on the horizon, Frost did not know exactly how many men had been left behind. But once the tally was done it would reach eight: two killed and six who hadn't made it to the landing craft and had fallen into the hands of the enemy.

Out at sea, Frost and others transferred to motor gunboats (MGBs) able to speed them across the Channel at thirty knots. There was euphoria aboard, backs were slapped and mugs of rum taken. They heard the sailors' side of the mission too – about how they had dodged German torpedo boats on their way in.

When the flotilla was close to the south coast, a flight of Spitfires flew low over them, dipping their wings in homage. And once the lead MGB got into the Solent at around 10 a.m. a cacophony began. 'Every vessel in port clanged their bells and sounded their fog sirens as our convoy moved in,' one officer recorded. As they tied up in Gosport, 'Land of Hope and Glory' was playing over one of the warships' speakers. The festive mood was such that even the two German prisoners were handed a beer as they came up the MGB's gangway. Six wounded men were stretchered off gingerly, with ambulances on the quayside waiting to take them to the town's Haslar Royal Naval Hospital.

If the welcome for C Company of the 2nd Battalion was ecstatic on that bright, freezing, February morning in 1942 it was because the nation was sorely in need of something to celebrate. Just a fortnight before, two German battleships had successfully forced a passage though the Channel, leading *The Times* to thunder about the worst humiliation of British sea power for centuries. At almost the same moment, the army had suffered a grievous blow with the fall of Singapore to the Japanese. Over 80,000 had been taken prisoner, along with a huge loss of materiel. 'These are black days!' the Chief of the Imperial General Staff had confided to his diary.

Such was the need of a tale of heroism to lift public spirits that the BBC broke news of the Bruneval raid even before the last gunboats had tied up in Gosport. Hours later, the London *Evening Standard* splashed with banner headlines 'Army, Navy and RAF Raid N. France in the Dark'.

'I expect the scientists wanted the radar,' concluded Sergeant Forsyth, 'but it was a big morale booster because at that time, my God, we were losing everywhere.' The sergeant had taken part in the first full-scale parachute course, organized at Manchester's Ringway aerodrome, the previous November. As a regular army non-commissioned officer (NCO) who'd joined up in 1933, serving with the Argyll and Sutherland Highlanders before volunteering as a parachutist, he was very much the sort of man Major Frost hoped could instil grit and professionalism among the younger recruits, many of whom had been conscripted.

Forsyth, however, was nobody's idea of a lackey for the army hierarchy or the officers set over him. His father, who'd been a trade union organizer in the mines, had been dismissed from one job after another by colliery bosses. Young Macleod's dad had supported his decision to join up if doing so meant he escaped a life of back-breaking toil down the pits. Once in uniform, Forsyth had soon realized he had little tolerance for barrack-room bull – the spit, polish and parade-ground drill that characterized so much of garrison life – and hungered for action. Hence, he had volunteered for special service, becoming a paratrooper.

Following their return, Forsyth and the others had been taken by lorry to Tilshead Camp on Salisbury Plain, the place they'd gone to during the final phase of preparations for Operation Biting. On one hand, he was bemused by the joyous reception they received, having only seriously worried for his own fate at the moment his landing craft was stuck aground. But on the other he could take pride in what they had achieved. As parachutists they were all volunteers, inculcated with the belief that they were the elite of the army. Until then, the sergeant reflected, too many people had felt, after Dunkirk and all the other setbacks, that the Germans were ten feet tall, but now his fellow citizens understood, 'they weren't so clever, we caught them with their trousers down around their ankles, they hadn't a clue'.

Only a minority of the 2nd Battalion's 570 men had taken part in the raid. As news of it broke, A Company had been involved in exercises up north and other men were on courses at Ringway or doing duty at the regiment's main base near Chesterfield. One sergeant in A Company noted that factory workers cheered them as they came back from training: 'We basked in the reflected glory.' Another found that in the pubs, '[we] could have had any amount of free beer'. When that soldier protested that his men hadn't taken part in the raid, a generous punter tapped his nose, remarking, 'We know you can't talk.'

The importance of the moment and public hunger for information were such that censorship restrictions were relaxed to a degree, Major Frost's name and photograph appearing in newspapers as well as other details about Britain's airborne forces. Interest went worldwide. The French newspaper *Le Figaro* gave its readers a breathless account, while in the south of France another paper announced, 'British Parachutists Launch a Raid on the French Coast' on its front page. Even the *New York Times* carried an inside photospread on what it described as a 'successful foray' into occupied France. The interest derived not just from the fact that the British had a rare bit of good news to impart but also from the method chosen for the raid: airborne operations were a novelty, a thing hitherto associated with the Nazis' Blitzkrieg victories rather than the plodding operations of their foes.

One write-up they were not able to read at the time was the one penned by the Wehrmacht commander in Bruneval. In his own report, Frost had stated, 'German casualties are estimated at a minimum of 40 killed.' When eventually obtained, the enemy after-action report would state that in fact two Wehrmacht and three Luftwaffe personnel had been killed during the raid. Even so, the German assessment of Operation Biting would have brought great satisfaction to those conducting the debrief in England, had they been able to read it.

'The operation of the British commandos was well planned and was executed with great daring,' the German officer had written, adding that 'the British displayed exemplary discipline when under fire'. Lessons drummed into the parachutists about the limited supply of ammunition that an airborne soldier could carry into action had clearly been learned, for the enemy commander noted that one group of the raiders had been under German fire for half an hour without returning a shot.

In Britain, sufficient details had been trumpeted publicly for soldiers who had joined what were, by March 1942, the army's four parachute battalions to find themselves the subject of intense public curiosity. As the new regiment grew, its volunteers, sporting the uniforms and insignia of their many different parent units, had added the marks of airborne distinction.

The first to be sewn onto their khaki battledress were the 'wings' awarded to those who'd completed seven training jumps at Ringway. By the time the public was devouring news of Bruneval, further markings had been added below the wings sewn at the top of the right sleeve: a square patch of maroon cloth with an image of Bellerophon riding his winged horse Pegasus embroidered upon it and a rectangular one with the word 'Airborne' on it. The men retained the distinctive headgear of their many regiments and corps, as well as some of the other distinctions of dress – Major Frost, for example, was loath to be parted from the tartan trousers, or truibhs, of his Cameronian Rifles. Within C Company, the object of so much national attention at that moment, the headgear was far from uniform, there being Highland bonnets of various kinds and glengarries, reflecting the different traditions of the Scottish regiments. Sergeant Forsyth noted that 'there were Seaforths, Camerons, Black Watch, Argylls, KOSBs and Pontius Pilate's Bodyguard – the Royal Scots – and the CSM was a Black Watch man'.

Lance Corporal Arthur Maybury from B Company noted that when he went out publicly in uniform, 'one felt like something out of Madame Tussaud's, so great was the curiosity'. Wearing wings caused strangers to 'forget their British restraint', bombarding the travelling soldier with questions, and was 'a certain method of ensuring free drinks and bus-rides'. Maybury, a twenty-eight-year-old from Wanstead in east London, had been a freelance journalist before the war and, a slim 5ft 9in tall, found that he defied outsiders' expectations that recruits to the new corps would be hulking bruisers.

Maybury's father had been a professional soldier, killed in the First World War. As an only child, Arthur therefore carried his mother Edith's hopes and welfare on his shoulders. A man of vivid imagination, Maybury hungered for adventure, and there must have been some conflict between the risks he took to find it and his sense of obligation to his mother.

What kind of men had volunteered? A lot of the early cadre of what was briefly called 2nd Commando, then the 11th Special Air Service Battalion before it became the 1st Parachute Battalion of the new Army Air Corps, were, in the words of one of its officers, 'what you call Soldiers of Fortune who wanted to get into the war at any cost'.

'It was really a mercenary battalion,' another early arrival in the 1st Battalion concurred. 'We had a high proportion of public schoolboys in the ranks . . . men who'd fought in the Spanish [civil] war and one or two from the Foreign Legion.' During the summer of 1941 there had been a good deal of weeding out of those early members, with men who failed to keep up with long route marches or skill at arms tests returned to unit, or RTU'd, a fate dreaded by many.

The expansion of this single unit to three battalions, begun in September 1941, had brought in a wider cross-section of volunteers and soon enough a 4th Battalion began forming also. Appeals posted in garrisons across the length and breadth of the army yielded thousands. A desire to escape the boredom of barrackroom life, thirst for action and the appeal of an extra two shillings a day in parachute pay were factors that proved dominant in recruitment.

Those who answered the call were initially sent to Hardwick Hall, an Elizabethan stately home in Derbyshire. Like many grand houses taken over by the army, its grounds were soon filled with Nissen huts, where the uncertain volunteers stayed while being subjected to intense physical training.

One soldier from the Essex Regiment who appeared there early in 1942 recorded that they spent five weeks at Hardwick. After three days of medical and other tests, they were taken on a ten-mile forced march. Each week the loads carried during these outings were increased. Of nineteen volunteers from the Essex Regiment who arrived in his batch, only ten made it through and onto the next stage of training.

Among those sharing Nissen huts in the grounds was an array of backgrounds that enthralled Lance Corporal Maybury: 'ex-clerks, insurance agents, salesmen, labourers, farm-hands . . . artists, musicians, dustmen, policemen, students and theatrical folk'. Most amusing to him, with his writer's eye, was a recruit who had been part of a 'Strong Jaw Act', a circus performer who had toured Europe hanging from a trapeze by his teeth. 'One would walk into a barrack-room or office', Maybury wrote, 'and be startled by a pair of boots dangling at eye level.' It was the strong-jaw man suspended from one of the rafters.

Along with the diversity of regiments and origins came a variety of beliefs. While many professed a mainstream Church of England credo, there were all manner of others from Irish Catholics to Scottish Presbyterians and Welsh Methodists. There were a good many atheists too, including communists, such as two members of Forsyth's company who had fought in the Spanish Civil War, one with the International Brigade. The adventurers and ardent anti-fascists hungered to take the fight to the Nazis. There was a similar motivation among dozens of Jews who had joined the new regiment.

Michael Lewis, who'd grown up as Colman Michael Weisenberg, was the son of Yiddish-speaking immigrant parents who worked the East End rag trade. He'd changed his name before the war because he found it easier to get work as a clerk that way. Lewis's beliefs tended towards socialism and he rejected religion, regarding it as the source of many of the world's problems. Others, though, still chose to define him that way.

Lewis got through Hardwick and made his way to the next stage of training, the parachute course at Ringway aerodrome near Manchester. While there, he'd overheard fellow recruits in his hut betting that 'the Jew' wouldn't make it through – but then listened to some of his messmates take the wager, insisting that 'Lou' was as tough as the rest. He knew he could not fail them.

Like so many of those who passed through this training, Lewis found it was the initial jumps from a platform hanging beneath a tethered barrage balloon that proved the hardest. When the cable between the dirigible and the ground was unwound the balloon might climb to anything between 200 and 300 metres above the airfield. Once the brake was applied, the instructor would open a hatch in the floor of the platform hanging beneath the balloon and invite the first of the four or five recruits it usually carried to take the plunge.

As if the prospect of dropping through the air for a second or two before the static line tugged the parachute out wasn't terrifying enough, the stillness of being that high without any of the sensory distractions of being in an aircraft unnerved many. Stupidly, Lewis, who was first up, ignored advice not to look down through the hatch, 'I was lost, the whole world was filled with the noise of my heart in my ears and my chest and then the instructor roared out "Number One!"'

He dropped, feeling that dramatic acceleration before the crack of his canopy opening and the tightening of the harness around his body confirmed that he was not going to die. Once he'd landed, Lewis felt euphoric and made a beeline for the Naafi and a cup of sweet tea. But, like many, he found his second drop even harder because then he knew what to expect.

The balloon jumps were followed by leaps from an aircraft, usually a Whitley, the men dropping down through the hatch in its floor. Some recruits baulked even at this stage, finding the stress of repeatedly hurling themselves into the void was just too much, but not Lewis.

Swelling with pride when he passed out of Ringway and sewed parachute wings on his battledress, Private Lewis had realized, 'we were being blended . . . made into a cohesive new unit, sharing this coming danger, this common experience'. At that point, only C Company, among the 2nd Battalion troops, had faced the enemy; but for many of them the training was hazard enough.

While Lewis completed his course at Ringway late in 1941 without injury, many others were less fortunate. Both Major Frost and Sergeant Forsyth had picked up bad sprains on landing, causing them to have to finish their qualifying jumps on later courses. Lance Corporal Maybury had found great pleasure leaping out of planes – until breaking his leg on his final descent at Ringway just before Christmas 1941.

The qualifying process and the risks it involved became important factors in mitigating differences of class as well as of religion, politics or cap badge. After all, the vast majority of people in Britain at the time had never been in an aeroplane, far less leapt out of one mid-flight.

Their experience was so rare, and so relatively dangerous, that graduating from parachute training became a defining moment for these soldiers. The hard physical conditioning of Hardwick Hall eliminated some, then the business of jumping, initially a couple of times from the unnerving stillness of a barrage balloon and then from a 'flying coffin', separated those who had the nerve from those who did not.

As often with intense shared experiences, those who had been through it marked their bond with the adoption of their own slang: the 'Roman candle' was a chute that had failed to open, usually resulting in death; 'ringing the bell' was hitting your head or face on the side of a bomber's floor hatch as you exited; and 'jibbing' was refusing to jump. Even among many of those who passed the Ringway course, a fear remained that at some future point their nerve might go and they would be cast back into that great sea of otherness that formed the rest of the army. As events would transpire, parachuting into battle would prove rather a rare experience, even among the pioneers. But for those joining the Bruneval boys early in 1942 there was a hunger not just for action, but for the kind of daring jump that had just been performed in France.

Both Lewis and Maybury (once his leg had healed) were posted to B Company in the 2nd Battalion. Their boss at the time was an officer who rejoiced in the name Major Richard Geoffrey Pine-Coffin. He didn't use that first name, so hereafter is referred to as Geoffrey. The younger son of a landed Devon family with generations of service to the Crown, Pine-Coffin, like Frost, was another pre-war regular army officer in a unit where the exigencies of war had already made such men an endangered species.

By the time of Bruneval, Pine-Coffin had already been an army officer for fourteen years. He had tasted the bitter defeat of the Dunkirk campaign along the way. Although one might have expected a 'blimp' or caricature of the officer class, Pine-Coffin was something of an original, defying easy characterization. But coming from a clan with such long traditions of service, the army had become a surrogate family, one in which he was deeply aware of his responsibility to those under his command.

'Tall, lean and tough, with long-nosed, quizzical, features, he was the quintessential military leader,' wrote one of the officers who served under him. 'He had been one of the earliest officers to volunteer for parachute duties and was a man of extraordinary bravery, but still a caring, wise commander, whose planning always took in the welfare of his men. Quiet-spoken and almost gentle in his manner, there was no tough-guy swagger about Geoffrey Pine-Coffin.'

Thirteen months prior to Bruneval, Pine-Coffin's wife had died, leaving him with a three-year-old son, Peter, to bring up. The conditions of war and service life were such that he was unable to parent the boy personally, relying on a cousin and, later, boarding school, but the knowledge that Peter would become an orphan if his father were to die in action undoubtedly weighed upon him.

Pine-Coffin, Lewis and Maybury had been members of the

same stick during training jumps, the military gentleman of impeccable pedigree along with the son of Jewish East End tailors and the Wanstead boy who lived by his wits. 'Even men of very high rank indeed', Maybury realized, 'become human and conversational under the influence of fuselage camaraderie.' The stress of waiting to leap into thin air was a great leveller, Johnny Frost would have agreed, writing later about, 'the learner parachutists' smile, which has no joy or humour in it'.

During one of their training jumps, Private Lewis had watched Pine-Coffin drift – narrowly avoiding being impaled on a church steeple – before being delivered, of all places, to a graveyard. It just was too good for the men, buoyed up by the gallows humour of jump school, who christened their leader 'Wooden Box'. As for the major himself, he shared the joke, returning to the graveyard at Durweston in Dorset to take a photograph for his album.

In the 2nd Battalion's March return of twenty-four officers Frost and Pine-Coffin were two of the four regulars, with all of the experience and training that implied. The rest were graded 'War Service' or had come via the Territorial Army. As the months went on, that regular cadre would fall even lower, often to just one or two leaders. In the Sergeants' Mess it was much the same story. Even as they drank to the success at Bruneval, men like Sergeant Forsyth, NCOs with the age and maturity to correct a national service soldier in the regulation manner, were in a minority.

This question of how to meld men from so many disparate backgrounds together while harnessing their volunteer enthusiasm would prove one of the great challenges for Frost and others in positions of command. As a small minority among the citizen soldiers who had flooded in, the regulars of the 1930s would have to deal with it. And their task was all the harder because, in establishing a new form of warfare, the ethos of this new warband was being defined as they went along.

Initially, officers in the new regiment fell back on the army's well-established principle of banding men from different parts of the country together to strengthen camaraderie. In the 2nd Battalion, this meant sending cockneys to A Company, northerners to B and Scots to C. However, this principle was soon compromised, with a detachment of Irish going to A Company and Londoners like Lewis or Maybury to B.

As for the rest of the army, they regarded the airborne experiment with a mixture of curiosity, disdain and envy. There were plenty of COs – commanding officers – who had packed off the parachute volunteers of 1941 to Hardwick Hall, telling them they were mad. Some had exploited the trawl for men to get rid of undesirables from their own units.

Then there were the War Office types who suspected that the whole experiment would be slowly throttled by the Royal Air Force, which had better things to do with its bombers. And, indeed, RAF resistance, among other things, had seen to it that the whole airborne project had advanced with glacial slowness.

Nineteen months had elapsed between Prime Minister Winston Churchill's fiat in June 1940, ordering 'we must have a corps of at least 5,000 troops', and the use of just 120 of them in France. The PM's initial order, just weeks after taking office, was one of a clutch of ideas he had to take the war to the enemy following the expulsion of the British Expeditionary Force from France.

A few weeks after giving the order for the formation of an airborne arm, Churchill had signed off on the creation of the Special Operations Executive, with the directive to 'set Europe ablaze' by the organization of resistance groups in occupied countries. His initial thoughts about parachute troops were linked in part to this idea of spreading mayhem at a time when the strategic situation banished his country from regular military operations on the Continent. Thus, SOE agents trained alongside the early airborne recruits at Ringway and French resistance members had played an important role in the preparation of Bruneval.

For the more restive types among those staring out to sea on the Kent coast, in their second year of utter boredom awaiting a German invasion or marching browned-off recruits around a parade square in Catterick, wondering how they might possibly do something more worthwhile, the idea of taking part in secret operations of this kind held a natural appeal. Trudging back to his billet after a day's bitterly cold training in Northern Ireland, Lieutenant Jack Grayburn of the Oxfordshire and Buckinghamshire Light Infantry was one of them. A keen amateur rugby player who had left his job at a bank to sign up, Grayburn wrote in his journal, 'the news almost exclusively with the all-services raid on a radio location plant on the coast of France . . . most successful too'.

Some weeks later Grayburn impatiently recorded, 'I feel that the best part of this war is over and now there only remains intense boredom with very occasional excitement attached.' It would take a while longer for him to find the path to the action he craved.

The fortunes of these six men were now linked: Forsyth, who knew he was as good as any man set over him by the privilege of rank; Lewis, who had escaped the ghetto to find a new family; Maybury, for whom the characters he met day to day provided the richest writer's material he could ever have dreamt of; Grayburn, who yearned for battle; and Frost and Pine-Coffin, whose service to the king also provided the route for their personal ambitions. During the three years that followed Bruneval all of them would shed blood for their country. They would earn many decorations on the battlefield, but two of the six would not survive and one would face disgrace in the regiment.

On 2 March 1942, though, the atmosphere was one of celebration combined with anticipation. Given that millions of people were serving the war effort, the actions of just one company of paratroopers had created a remarkable effect. For the apostles of this new form of warfare it was a moment to be seized. So it was that a staff car was sent around to the Officers' Mess at Tilshead to collect Major Frost. He had run a bath in the expectation of a quiet evening in the Mess. Instead, he digested the news brought to him by an officer from divisional headquarters. Frost had been summoned to brief Churchill in person and to take part in his next battle, the one against the enemies of airborne forces in Whitehall.

3.   Whitehall Warriors

Darkness had long since fallen by the time Major Frost's staff car reached the outskirts of London. On the way up he had passed countless signs of a nation at war. Military convoys choked the roads, uniformed figures thronged the pavements, hundreds of barrage balloons floated over the capital. The streets were pocked with bomb sites, shells of great buildings tumbled during the Blitz.

Having received the summons to brief the War Cabinet, Frost had donned the uniform of the Cameronian Rifles, smartening himself up as best he could in the short time available. He cut a fine figure, well over six feet in his regimental headgear, his dark moustache and hair trimmed neatly.

On the ride up he was a little uneasy. He had not yet been able to debrief everyone on the raid, and probably worried that some eagle-eyed minister or even Churchill himself might ask a question to which he did not know the answer. Frost could not have been unaware of the tensions over airborne operations that divided the chiefs of staff.

The recent disasters in Singapore and the Channel had left the army and navy with much to prove. However, thanks to the Royal Air Force's success in the Battle of Britain the threat of heavy bombing and invasion had by the spring of 1942 lifted in the British Isles. As a consequence, Frost found the RAF 'almost unbearably cocky', and army officers were feeling like second-class citizens.

More widely, following their invasion of the Soviet Union the previous summer, Adolf Hitler's armies were still writing off huge numbers of Red Army troops, even if their initial progress had slowed. In the North African desert, meanwhile, the progress of the war ebbed and flowed. While the strategists had already realized that large airborne forces might be needed for the liberation of Europe, even the most optimistically minded of them did not think that would happen any time soon.

Frost's car pulled up outside an address in Birdcage Walk. He got out and passed through a sandbagged entrance that would admit him to the heart of wartime government. It was in this building's underground sanctum that the military and political leadership came together to chart the course of a worldwide struggle. Arriving in the briefing room, bathed in yellowish light, Frost saw that someone had brought to London the Bruneval model that he had used in Tilshead Camp to brief his officers before Operation Biting.

The first of the principals to arrive was Clement Attlee, the Labour Party leader and a member of the national unity government directing the war. He led Frost into a gentle conversation, under the mistaken assumption he was simply a briefing officer, only to be startled when the tall Scot revealed he had led the raid. It was not often that those actually fighting the war briefed the top brass in person.

Filing into the room came the service chiefs: Admiral Sir Dudley Pound, First Sea Lord; General Sir Alan Brooke, Chief of the General Staff; Air Chief Marshal Sir Charles Portal, Chief of the Air Staff; and the PM's military secretary, Major General Sir Hastings Ismay. The political leadership was represented by the three armed services ministers, as well as those for information, the Home Office, the Colonies and India. Senior civil servants were standing in for their bosses from the Treasury and Foreign Office.

At last, the prime minister himself joined them. Glimpsing him for the first time, Major Frost was not disappointed. Meeting late at night as they were, Churchill wore one of his distinctive 'siren suits' – overalls made of velvet – and clutched a large cigar.

This assembly discussed the course of a global struggle involving millions under arms, from those hunting U-Boats in the North Atlantic to the footsloggers hacking their way through Burmese jungles. It also had to consider a wide variety of political matters, and not least a constitutional crisis in India that was requiring the government to adopt positions about the post-war future of its greatest colony and taking up a great deal of Cabinet time.

However, just as this body came together to coalesce around common positions, it also served as a cockpit for the simmering differences between those fighting the war. Those in navy or light blue or khaki were there to represent their service interests as well as execute the common will. So when Major General Frederick 'Boy' Browning, commander of the Airborne Division, joined them, everyone would have understood that there were reasons why the supreme national council of war, arbiter of the fate of millions, was hearing from a lowly major about the outcome of a raid involving a mere 120 parachutists. To add heft to the briefing, Vice Admiral Lord Louis Mountbatten, the Chief of Combined Operations, was there too.

Frost, to his relief, found that his role became secondary as Mountbatten provided the strategic context for the raid. What they knew was that the future development of air assault forces would depend upon the cooperation of Air Chief Marshal Portal, and that, in his view, 'the bombing of German industry was an incomparably greater contribution to the war than the training and constant availability of an airborne division'.

Portal was a formidable antagonist. He had risen from the ranks during the First World War, arriving at the top of the RAF in his late forties after a short spell in charge of Bomber Command. Since the air offensive against Germany remained the main national effort at this time, and the dropping of parachutists or towing of gliders for airlanding diverted aircraft like the Whitley away from that task, his views on the subject were hardly a surprise.

The Chief of the Air Staff was at the time engaged in a separate argument over the production of bombers, trying to face down those who believed the nation's manufacturing capability was being switched too fast away from making more fighters. As far as he was concerned, accepting the assignment of more Whitleys or

Albemarles to dropping paratroops would simply undermine his wider advocacy about the primacy of the offensive air campaign against Germany.

It wasn't simply a matter of scarce airframes, either. The RAF's foot-dragging over airborne warfare also concerned the supply of pilots trained to fly bigger, multi-engined aircraft. How else to explain the service's failure to acquire around a hundred civilian airliners, American-made Douglas DC-3s, including many from the Dutch carrier KLM, that had ended up in the UK as the Germans occupied Europe? As events would demonstrate, this type of aircraft (also known by its US military designation, C-47, and its British one, Dakota) would become the perfect carrier for large numbers of parachutists, yet nothing had been done to obtain and repurpose the scores of aircraft available.

Having launched the idea of a parachute force, Churchill had been so beset by the wider concerns of fighting the war that he often had no attention left to give. When, from time to time, he was able to re-engage, he couldn't escape the impression that in an attempt to find a path of least resistance between the army's enthusiasm to make something – anything – happen and the air force's reluctance to assign any significant number of aircraft to doing it, things were hardly moving forward at all. In September 1940, realizing that a blueprint he'd been sent for a new airborne brigade would involve just 500 parachutists, or one seventh of the planned force (the rest having to go to war by glider), Churchill observed, 'Are we not in danger of being fobbed off?'

Attending a demonstration in April 1941, he had watched six Whitley bombers drop an airborne force of just sixty men and the landing of a single glider – hardly the stuff to tip the scales of war. The capability had doubled by the time of Bruneval, but the levels of effort being made by the army and RAF were still completely out of kilter. And the notion that the embryo parachute force was really just for small-scale raids was by this time holding back the whole venture.

Indeed, the success of Frost's mission a few nights before had shown the way ahead as far as Portal was concerned. An operation involving a dozen Whitleys and a company of men was an acceptable level of effort, particularly since the objective of Operation Biting had been to find out more about the impact of German radar on the bomber offensive. Portal believed, at least at this stage of the war, that parachutists should be used only 'for raiding purposes and for assisting in minor operations'.

General Brooke and Lord Mountbatten had very different ideas. Just as Germany had employed thousands of paratroopers during the invasions of the Low Countries and Norway in 1940, and Greece in 1941, they believed that an airborne division, a force of several thousand troops, must now be prepared for the moment when the Allies could take the strategic offensive in North Africa. Major General Browning had been appointed the previous autumn precisely to bring this vision to fruition. They also believed that the prime minister, from his June 1940 order establishing airborne forces onwards, endorsed such a plan.

In that Cabinet briefing room, however, were two of the most articulate advocates that Frost and his soldiers could ever have hoped for. Lord Mountbatten was a member of European royalty, both driven and highly connected. Browning, who always cut a sharp figure in his immaculately tailored uniforms, had arrived at his command via Eton and the Grenadier Guards. He had garnered a network of military ties that was second to none. But if the proponents of this new form of warfare had hoped that evening's Bruneval post-mortem might bring matters to a head, they were to be disappointed. The RAF had been dragging its feet on the matter for well over a year despite receiving a number of explicit instructions from Churchill.

After the formal briefing, as senior officers stood chatting, General Brooke advanced on Portal, flanked by Mountbatten and Browning, saying they needed 'more aircraft, more aircraft, more aircraft'. Frost watched as the air chief 'raised his arms and fists in mock defence and backed slowly and smilingly from the room'. Evidently Portal felt confident enough of his position to brush it off as a joke.

Having witnessed at the highest level this contest for resources,

Frost took the staff car for the journey to his London club, where he finally took the bath he had been looking forward to all day.

Major General Browning, meanwhile, directed his own driver to take him up the A1, towards the house he shared with one of the most remarkable women of his time and the next stage of his battle to get his division training and ready for action.

4. Mad About the Boy

It was the early hours of the morning before Major General Browning reached Langley's End, a neoclassical pile near Hitchin that he was renting as temporary accommodation for his family. While Boy Browning was in many respects the archetypal 1930s senior army officer, his marriage to the novelist Daphne du Maurier placed him in a very unusual category for his time.

While reading her novel *The Loving Spirit*, Browning had become fascinated both with its depiction of the Cornish coast and with the writer herself. A keen sailor, he had taken his yacht down to that coastline in 1931 and, discovering the author to be in residence nearby, invited her to sail with him. They had married the following year, and were by now raising two young daughters and a son.

Marriage to a literary celebrity allowed Browning to add an artistic circle to his formidable array of political and military contacts. His father, a wealthy wine merchant, had packed young Frederick off to Eton, where he became friends with several future politicians, including three ministers, as well as military figures such as Oliver Leese, who had in 1941 been appointed to command the newly created Guards Armoured Division.

Boy Browning had cut his teeth as an officer in the Grenadier Guards during the Great War, serving for a time with Winston Churchill and establishing his reputation in 1917 as a twenty-year-old lieutenant with the award of a Distinguished Service Order. That was quite an achievement, given the decoration for feats of command was usually granted to those higher up the ladder.

During the interwar years, Browning gained notoriety within the army as adjutant of the Royal Military Academy at Sandhurst, commanded the 2nd Battalion of Grenadiers and in general continued his seemingly effortless rise while garnering contacts left, right and centre, including in the Royal Household. One officer who accompanied him on a later visit to Gibraltar observed a little wearily that, 'as usual, the admiral, the Governor-General and everyone else of consequence had been to school with, played polo with, sailed with or fought in World War I with Browning'.

There can be little doubt though that in an age where the army's leaders went by public school or regimental nicknames like 'Fatty', 'Pug' and 'Windy', placing the 'Boy' at the head of airborne forces was an inspired move by the army's head, General Sir Alan Brooke. As Chief of the Imperial General Staff, Brooke knew when he assigned the command of 1st Airborne Division in October 1941 that Browning had the necessary drive and would be uniquely placed to beg, steal or borrow the resources – in army circles, at least – needed to make it a reality.

On that evening in March 1942, Boy returned to Langley's End profoundly exhausted. Having attended the War Cabinet that night, he was taking his first leave in the five months since assuming control of the airborne venture. One of his staff noted that nothing had been easy about the creation of the new force, 'month in, month out, he worked for this, but always against resistance'. Browning was forty-five years old by this point, his moustache and hair contained flecks of grey and he was living on his nerves. His constant absences, travelling to Hardwick Hall, Ringway, Whitehall, Salisbury Plain and who knows where else, had put a strain on his marriage. Indeed, unbeknown to the general, it was at this time that du Maurier began an affair with their landlord at Hitchin.

Once Browning's leave was up, he returned to the task in hand. During the early months, Browning and the small group around him had occupied the basement of a War Office building in London, becoming known as the Dungeon Party. It was a tight-knit team that thought highly of its general. 'One was given a job to do and left to get on with it,' Colonel Gordon Walch, Browning's chief staff officer noted, adding, 'It leads to a very happy, confident, staff.' While Browning won the esteem of his military 'family', regularly spending his own money (for example, when buying motorbikes from a civilian dealership) to make his staff's life easier, those under his command often formed a different view. Given his class, Guards background and age, it was hardly surprising that Browning was a stickler for standards of dress and drill, but many serving under him felt that his background also made him aloof and distant. One referred memorably to Browning's persona when in charge as one of 'mannered arrogance'.

The work of his airborne forces staff had started the previous November, when, having assumed command of a few hundred trained parachutists, Browning must have realized what a mountain he would have to climb in order to create an 'airborne division' with ten times that number.

By early 1942 the headquarters had moved to Syrencot House, near Netheravon on Salisbury Plain. The 2nd Battalion, after Bruneval, had briefly reconvened at Hardwick Hall before shifting to Bulford Camp in Wiltshire. Shortly after arriving there, Major Frost heard that Major General Browning was coming over to inspect C Company. 'I was dreading this visit as I knew well what his views on turnout were,' he later wrote. The major general was suitably unimpressed, telling Frost, 'I have never seen such a dirty company in all my life.' Browning's definition of 'turnout' was broader than simply having polished boots or spotless uniforms. It included clipped, clean fingernails, short hair and generally carrying oneself like a soldier. So the major had to add the procurement of new uniforms and regular checks on his soldiers' appearance to his other myriad duties in the new camp.

It was at Bulford that, with its two sister battalions, the 2nd Battalion formed part of the 1st Parachute Brigade, at that time comprising something like 1,800 trained soldiers. The division designed by Browning and the Dungeon Party would require the formation later that summer of a second parachute brigade and one of airlanded or glider troops.

Each of these steps required the training of new cohorts, and it didn't stop at the six parachute and three airlanded infantry battalions that would be needed for the new formation. A parachute brigade of three or four battalions also had its headquarters element, a signal squadron and one of engineers. That spring they were just about getting there with the 1st Parachute Brigade, but knew they would have to do it all over again for the 2nd. Regiments of both field and anti-tank artillery would also have to be formed if the division was to have real firepower, as well as reconnaissance units.

Their study of German operations had convinced the architects of Britain's airborne forces that an airlanded force, carried in gliders, would be essential to the wider venture. Paratroopers could be dropped with arms or ammunition canisters but there was only so much a man could carry. Gliders could be filled with weapons too heavy to drop by parachute or manhandle, such as howitzers, anti-tank guns and heavy mortars along with tonnes of ammunition, as well as reinforcing infantry.

That spring, Browning and his team had also hit upon an American light utility vehicle, the jeep, as a way of moving these items across the battlefield. Each solution in this process was apt to throw up new challenges though. The Hotspur, an eight-man glider that had been used to train pilots and practise airlanding tactics, was too small for such loads. By early 1942, however, an altogether more impressive machine, the Airspeed Horsa, made largely from wood and canvas, was undergoing trials. With a length of twenty-two metres, it could carry a jeep and a light artillery piece with crew, or twenty-five men, the best part of an airlanding platoon, putting them down in one place rather than scattering them about the landscape as often happened with parachutists. The army ordered 440 Horsas and they would become a key part of the airborne force from late that summer.

Some of the 2nd Battalion men, sharing airfields with their glider brethren, strolled over to inspect their craft. Lance Corporal Arthur Maybury peered into a Hotspur. 'My first impression was that it had been knocked together in his spare time by some fretwork enthusiast.' Among his comrades the opinion soon formed that, 'if to go into action by parachute is worth two shillings a day extra pay, then to go into action in a glider is worth four!'

Just as equipment choices had knock-on effects with the organization of units or choice of the Horsa, so factors like adopting a new glider design had their own consequences. The Glider Pilot Regiment, the special unit selected, like the parachute battalions, from volunteers across the army, had to be expanded, and bigger sailplanes required larger, more powerful bombers to tow them, which in turn produced fresh tensions with the RAF.

The spring months of 1942 involved a frenzy of perpetual motion, both for the men of the parachute battalions and for Browning himself. Whether heading off to the ranges, back from a parachute jump or simply killing time, men from the battalions were marched from pillar to post. The standard they maintained was being able to cover fifty miles during twenty-four hours, or thirty miles during a typical day, with rest. Coming back from one scheme in the New Forest, the 2nd Battalion walked in stages over two days eighty miles back to Bulford Camp.

It was not simply about physical conditioning. A series of lectures was laid on to underscore what was at stake, the 2nd Battalion hearing talks about 'Hitler's Racial Myth', German war production methods and an account of concentration camps from a German Jewish member of the brigade intelligence staff.

The months of spring and early summer were a time when Major Johnny Frost felt there was 'a solid welding together of officers, NCOs and men and it was soon very obvious that a very fine instrument of war was being prepared'. These were times when bonds flourished between the soldiers.

Private 'Lou' Lewis had found the new family he had yearned for, becoming firm friends with Fred Selman, one of those who'd rooted for him on his parachute course, whose parents lived near their camp, and Arthur 'Chalky' White, a big South African boxer. 'If there was any happiness to be found in war, the days I was happiest in, comparatively, were those in the group of men I found myself with,' Lewis felt.

While Frost remained in command of C Company, the constant expansion of the airborne arm produced many changes.

Sergeant Macleod Forsyth was transferred to A Company and, following the promotion of the 2nd Battalion's CO to lead their brigade, majors' commands were reassigned, leaving Geoffrey Pine-Coffin to become second in command of the unit.

During spring, a shortage of aircraft continued to hamper jump training. The battalion occasionally resorted to balloon drops, there being a general feeling that it wasn't wise to let too long a gap develop since a man's nerve might falter. As 1942 wore on, though, the availability of planes improved, a result of battles being fought at the highest level by Browning.

On 16 April Churchill, accompanied by General George C. Marshall, Chief of Staff of the US Army, had watched a demonstration by the 1st Parachute Battalion and a group of Hotspur gliders. Boy Browning hosted King George VI and Queen Elizabeth for a similar spectacle the following month. Displays were laid on for factories producing their kit and other members of the top brass too. Browning's aim with all of this was to garner support in Whitehall while keeping the new organization in the public eye.

To anyone watching these demonstrations, however, the wrinkle in Browning's plans was all too evident. Where his network succeeded, for example in achieving the allocation of more soldiers or the acquisition of equipment modified for airborne operations, everything came together very smartly. But when people such as those in the Air Staff were immune to his charms, or had different interests, things moved at a snail's pace. Vice Admiral Lord Mountbatten had in April tried to stir the chiefs of staff to action, urging those who'd been at the Bruneval briefing to see 'the desirability of employing airborne forces in larger numbers than hitherto for raids'.

During the demonstration of 16 April just twelve Whitleys had dropped paratroops and nine older bombers had been used as glider tugs. And this was essentially the entire air component dedicated to supporting the airborne forces, a total hardly improved from one year before, much to Churchill's annoyance. Once again, the PM had the sense that he was being 'fobbed off' by the service chiefs, and in particular those in light blue.

Training men to jump from the newer Wellington bombers, something that had begun that same month, could considerably expand the number of planes available for a specific operation, but simply exacerbated the tensions between Browning's people and those who believed these planes should be entirely devoted to dropping high explosives on the Reich.

On 6 May Churchill tried to break the impasse, chairing a meeting at which Browning once more addressed the chiefs of staff, asking for ninety-six bombers to be dedicated to working with his division, a three-fold increase. The PM followed up with a memo telling Air Chief Marshal Portal, 'we cannot go on with 10,000 men and only 32 aircraft at their disposal'. Given that each Whitley could drop only ten parachutists the situation was manifestly absurd.

Portal, faced with this bulldozing by Churchill, had to give ground, even if he was still far from reconciled to Browning's plans. The arrival in service of the powerful four-engined Lancaster was in any case changing perspectives in Bomber Command, where it was now recognized that the Whitley was becoming obsolete. So, the Chief of the Air Staff yielded, agreeing to allocate eighty-three Whitleys to the airborne forces that summer, adding in ten Halifax aircraft for good measure. The Halifaxes, like the Lancaster powered by four engines, would be needed to tow the largest of the gliders, the Hamilcar, a sailplane so big that it could even bring in light armoured vehicles.

This was all very well, but as COs trained their men that April and May, there was a lingering sense of uncertainty about what exactly a British airborne division was for. The business of alarming the enemy in occupied Europe could be done with small raids like Bruneval. With regard to waging war further afield, an argument had been made in relation to the Far East that the large distances and poor transport infrastructure there meant an airborne brigade able to drop into action or simply be landed to respond to crises as a 'fire brigade' force could be most useful.

This led to the formation of the 50th (Indian) Parachute Brigade in the autumn of 1941. It combined a single battalion of British volunteers from units across the Raj, with two of local troops. The challenge of finding suitable aircraft for training was even more vexed in India, and in its early months the brigade remained an air-portable force of picked troops rather than one that could have carried out a parachute assault.

But when it came to the force taking shape on Salisbury Plain, the other sorts of missions that were anticipated, such as seizing enemy airfields or bridges, implied a large-scale advance, and at that moment it was unclear where this might happen. Many of those at the chiefs-of-staff meetings would have accepted General Brooke's formulation that 'for the defeat of Germany it will sooner or later be necessary for our armies to invade the continent', and that 'the employment of airborne forces in the rear may offer the only means' of taking heavily defended beaches. But they countered that such a campaign might be years away and that in the meantime there were countless more urgent priorities.

There was, however, one argument that Brooke deployed that would prove difficult for the RAF to dismiss as the months ticked by. In his paper setting out the possible use of airborne troops the Chief of the Imperial General Staff noted that the appearance of such forces in Occupied Europe would, 'compel [the enemy] to defend a relatively vast area'. They all knew well enough from their preparations to resist any German descent on the British Isles that the requirement to defend all manner of potential targets against a possible airdrop on one of them could soon tie down hundreds of thousands of troops.

Seen this way, an investment in 10,000 or even 20,000 soldiers able to drop from the sky with little warning, in an almost limitless variety of places, could be a very good way to tax the German war machine. The possibility of seaborne or airborne invasion would lead the enemy to maintain dozens of divisions in an arc from Norway through the Low Countries to France. And the larger your airborne force, the worse these defensive dilemmas became for the enemy.

Faced with this logic, the RAF's best course was to emphasize the zero-sum nature of its offensive air campaign against Hitler.

Portal's arguments were fed by Air Marshal Arthur 'Bomber' Harris. Reacting to Brooke's paper he argued: it would require the entire strength of Bomber Command to be taken off operations for four to six weeks in order to prepare for a division-sized airborne operation; that there could be heavy losses of his aircraft during such a mission; that resources being used to train hundreds of army glider pilots were being used at the expense of RAF aircrew instruction; and that the vast hangars needed to accommodate hundreds of gliders were also a waste of resources.

Harris completed his rhetorical fire-bombing by writing, 'I find it hard to resist the conclusion that the raising of the airborne division was undertaken without adequate appreciation of how it could be transported or where and when it might be employed with any prospect of material contribution to victory.'

Harris's critique laid bare the fact that, acting in the spirit of Winston Churchill's order of June 1940, the army, principally through the agency of generals Brooke and Browning, had, by the summer of 1942, given the airborne project such impetus that the existence of their division was driving a search for plausible missions rather than the other way round. Browning, as a major general, was too senior to command the 1st Parachute Brigade, the only element of his force that might soon get into action. If he were to lead his 1st Airborne Division onto some battlefield at an unspecified future moment, more aircraft would have to be found – as indeed would operational uses for the paratroopers and gliders. The RAF continued to fight back throughout the summer and autumn of 1942, but the strategic climate was beginning to move Browning's way.

In June, the US Army 2nd Battalion, 503rd Parachute Infantry Regiment, had arrived in southern England. It quickly established close ties with its British cousins. One of the Bruneval raid lieutenants was sent across to act as liaison officer with the Americans. The US Army Air Forces had flown in dozens of C-47s to England to support their battalion. The British were now able to familiarize themselves with an aircraft that could carry more than double the number of parachutists than the bombers they'd so far trained on, and do so in far greater comfort. There were some differences of approach to be overcome, from the Americans' ideas about ideal dropping altitudes (higher than those favoured by the RAF) to the methods for attaching the static lines needed to pull the chutes open, but none of this was too daunting.

The RAF had its own DC-3s – Dakotas – on order, but these were coming through very slowly. However, now that the US airborne battalion and its supporting aircraft were training so closely with their UK counterparts it was becoming clear that American airpower might provide a way to jettison into the Whitehall slipstream the long argument over the allocation of RAF bombers. A new type of aircraft, specifically designed to transport troops, was coming into the equation in large numbers courtesy of Uncle Sam. Churchill's May diktat to the RAF was also beginning to deliver results.

On 10 June half of the 2nd Battalion was dropped on exercise by Wellington and Whitley bombers. Twelve days later, in drills watched by General Brooke, the 3rd Battalion made the British airborne arm's first battalion-scale drop – more than 500 men – from fifty-six RAF bombers. And at levels far above the men reliving their descents over tea in the Bulford Camp Naafi, discussions of great moment about the course of the war were being held.

The United States was, by July 1942, moving towards the decision to commit a large army to action. These divisions would form the bulk of what would be called the Allied Expeditionary Force, and, because of that, command would be given to an American.

On the 10th of that month, General Brooke's Deputy Chief of the Imperial General Staff brought a visitor down to 1st Airborne Division HQ at Netheravon. They were holding a divisional command exercise and their guest, Lieutenant General Dwight Eisenhower, was keen to see how it was working out. At that moment Eisenhower, who had received his third general's star just three days earlier, simply carried the title of Commander in the European Theater of Operations. But those in the know discovered during the following weeks exactly what Eisenhower was there to do.

As British generals began to speculate about the target of the coming 'big show', Browning sought to ensure that his parachute brigade was ready for action. The pace of training picked up, as did the comings and goings of the headquarters staff at Syrencot House.

Boy Browning's yearning to perfect his new force reached an even higher pitch. Then, one morning, as his staff car drove across the Netheravon airfield, he noticed something that outraged him.

5.   Thirsting for Action

It was the late summer of 1942 and A Company of the 2nd Battalion was due to make a parachute drop. The men had been formed up, ready to board a dozen Whitleys at Netheravon airfield. As so often in army life, where the maxim 'hurry up and wait' prevailed, the soldiers had been brought there but, for reasons not explained, there had been a delay. The men were standing about smoking and chatting as the general's staff car cruised through the aerodrome, passing 2 Platoon. Moments later there was a screech of brakes and an irate Major General Browning emerged from the vehicle.

The general quickly fixed on Sergeant Eddie Hancock, a twenty-one-year-old Londoner who that morning was in charge of 2 Platoon. Why, asked the general, had the platoon not been brought to attention in order to salute him? Sergeant Hancock recorded that he was subjected to 'a fierce verbal onslaught', in which 'General Browning has expressed his disgust at the indolence of my platoon'.

Browning swiftly reported the matter to the CO and soon afterwards the sergeant found himself tapping the boards in front of the 2nd Battalion's adjutant. The matter was so serious, this officer implied, that the battalion might not embark on the overseas service they had all been expecting. As punishment, the platoon would have to parade early each morning for one week, practising its saluting drill for an hour before continuing with the rest of its programme for the day.

When Hancock got back to the platoon's hut and gave the men the bad news, the place was in a state of uproar: 'indignation reigned, expletives and comments abounded'.

Among the paratroopers, their general was often referred to as 'Bullshit Browning' or 'Bastard Browning'. As Sergeant Hancock tried to calm them, the men insisted they would refuse to accept the punishment. He knew them well enough to understand that the cockneys of 2 Platoon were, to use an army phrase, 'bolshie' or militant in defence of their rights, as they saw them, and it would take careful persuasion on his part to carry them along. Eventually, Private Joe Goldsmith, whom Hancock called the platoon's 'shop steward', relented, saying, 'We'll do it for you, Eddie.'

This was no isolated case. Another sergeant recorded an incident that summer where soldiers, fed up with parade-ground drill and kit inspections, had marched on the A Company office with home-made protest placards. He summarized the message of this brief demonstration as 'too much bullshit – we joined for action'.

Those placed in command of parachute battalions often seemed uncertain about how to deal with their soldiers' raucous enthusiasm. The Browning prescription, that men who had volunteered from many different units had to be drilled until they achieved a unity, evidently caused deep resentment. Sergeant Hancock condemned Browning as a martinet who, 'as a result of his Guards background', thought that 'hard line, mindless, Regular Army techniques should be applied to men who were, at heart, civilians in uniform'. The key, in the view of this young sergeant, was to recognize that those volunteering for such dangerous duty in times of war 'were extremely individualistic and didn't take kindly to traditional Regular Army doctrines'.

Messages the soldiers had received about the particular nature of their new service fuelled resentment of parade-ground marching, spit and polish. 'The general feeling about this was that we were not training to beat the Germans in a drill competition,' was how Lance Corporal Maybury of B Company summed up the soldiers' mood, adding, 'it came as a psychological blow to us, who had expected to be treated as men in a higher drawer than the "ordinary" soldier, being, as we had learned in the Press a *corps d'elite*'.

The attitude of younger commanders, officers like Johnny Frost, was that the bridge between the traditionally defined standards set by the hierarchy and the wild enthusiasm of the paratroopers had to be built by non-commissioned officers, the sergeants and corporals, leaders at the troop level, who were such an important part of the British Army's historical formula for success. Because of the chaos often encountered after a drop, the parachute units had in fact been staffed with more sergeants than was usual in the infantry. A parachute platoon (typically at this time around thirty men under a junior officer) was meant to include four sergeants, three corporals and three lance corporals, whereas in a similar-sized element of infantry there was just a single sergeant plus the corporals and lance corporals.

Steady, experienced men like Macleod Forsyth, over thirty years old and with many years of service, were the answer, at least in the view of traditionally minded officers. But in a national service army where the regulars had been swamped, there were too few old-school sergeants and corporals to go round. As a wartime soldier in his early twenties, Sergeant Hancock tired of hearing his maturity questioned. For his part, Frost reckoned that 'our greatest problem in those early days was the lack of good reliable NCOs . . . it was more by accident than design that some of them wore sergeant's stripes'.

Frost seemed quite unable to understand the wayward tendencies of some of his men. As a son of an officer in the Indian Army who'd spent much of his life abroad, he expected soldiers to take pride in their turnout, executing orders diligently and respectfully. He had great admiration for the Arabs in the Iraq Levies he'd served with, opining, 'I never had the privilege of leading better men.' But the volunteers for airborne forces were outspoken and more independently minded. And if he hoped that sergeants like Macleod Forsyth would impose the standards of the 1930s regular army, he was heading for disappointment, because that coal miner's son cared little for most officers and was as intolerant of petty military restrictions as most of the privates.

Browning responded in various ways to these challenges. He tried to encourage more sergeants and sergeant majors from the Guards to volunteer for airborne duty. Regimental Sergeant Major John Lord, who served in the Grenadiers in the 1930s, became a policeman and then returned to the colours on the outbreak of war and was sent to the 3rd Parachute Battalion, was the archetype Browning had in mind. Ramrod straight, moustach-ioed, his words of command carried across a parade ground, no matter how large.

The supply of such men, however, was limited and in sending them in with a mission to impose high standards of discipline and turnout the general created untold friction. While some, particu-larly officers, later wrote admiringly of Lord's adherence to the rulebook, an NCO in the 2nd Battalion claimed, 'the men univer-sally hated him'. Young sergeants like Eddie Hancock simply felt that Guards standards of drill or turnout, intended after all for public duties such as parading outside Buckingham Palace, had no place in a wartime regiment of volunteers training hard for special missions.

The persistence of old-fashioned army principles took other forms also. A couple of the young B Company men, Mike Lewis and Fred Selman, tired at the falsification of the scores each time they went down to shoot at the ranges. They felt the results were being deliberately skewed to make the regular army NCOs look good. So the two conspired, Selman being the company clerk, to post the true results on the noticeboard one day. When people saw the real scores there was consternation, their major tearing down the sheets, which showed the old soldiers hadn't aimed any straighter than the national service ones.

General Browning also tried to soothe these tensions by using positive methods to boost the esprit de corps of his new branch. On passing their training, the men were given Airborne Division ethos cards setting out six rules for their behaviour. The first was: 'You are the elite of the British Army', and urged: 'You must be better disciplined and smarter in your turnout than any other troops.' By this measure he expected them even to outdo the Guards in the matter of parade ground 'bull'.

As well as exhortation to adopt high values, he launched a benevolent fund for airborne forces as a whole, and in August 1942 the creation of the Parachute Regiment was approved by the army (hitherto these had been parachute battalions of the Army Air

Corps). Having produced the distinctive maroon-red shoulder patches for his troops, Browning that summer began issuing them with matching berets. These, worn by glider pilots and members of the parachute battalions, bore an eagle badge, the emblem of the Army Air Corps. Those in airlanding battalions or the supporting units wore the beret with their original cap badge.

Initially, the new headgear received a mixed reaction and indeed there were different opinions about how best to describe its colour. 'I look very swell in my purple hat,' one newly qualified airborne officer wrote, full of pride, in a letter home to his parents. And why shouldn't such a mark of distinction be entirely welcome?

One private in the 2nd Battalion's C Company noted, 'quite a few chaps didn't like wearing them', considering the colour garish. His subaltern, a poet named Richard 'Dicky' Spender (a distant relative of the celebrated writer Stephen), refused, as a matter of aesthetics, to discard his Royal Ulster Rifles caubeen, a dark green Irish hat similar to but more voluminous than the bonnets worn by Highland regiments. Spender would prove a larger-than-life character in many respects and he claimed that, *Beau Geste* style, he had volunteered for the paratroops because his girlfriend's parents had rebuffed his proposal of marriage.

Johnny Frost also proved a lagging convert to the maroon beret. In photographs of King George VI's visit in May 1942, he is wearing his Cameronian bonnet and was still doing so when pictured one year later while receiving General Eisenhower. Many others retained dress from parent regiments, from the dark shirts of the Guards to Highland tartans (kilts and truibhs) and the distinctive black belts of rifle regiments, while adopting the airborne forces' sleeve distinctions. The refusal to relinquish these marks of their former tribes reminded everyone that they were the pick of the army, the crème de la crème, volunteers willing not just to embrace danger but to seek it out.

During those months of hard training in 1942, the paratroopers' wild atavism had become apparent to publicans across the land. Forsyth allowed, 'we used to drink like fish'. It was generally good natured, producing many a late-night sing-song, but when they bumped up against men from other units there was often brawling. The 2nd Battalion wore yellow lanyards as a distinction on their battledress (the wartime 1st had khaki green and the 3rd red ones), leading the landlord who banned them from a pub near Hardwick Hall to condemn the 2nd as 'them yellow bastards'.

Following an exercise in Devon, pubs in Minehead and Barnstaple had been smashed up by men from the battalion, leading to the court-martialling and return to unit of one lance corporal. In another incident, so serious that it ended up in a civilian court, two sergeants managed to escape conviction on charges that they had vandalized a restaurant in Salisbury. There were xenophobic overtones in this case, the establishment's owners being Italian, and the men were lucky to get off, one sergeant noting that the charges had been levelled 'probably not unjustly'.

'Respectable folk might have been excused for believing that we had been recruited from jails and razor gangs,' one 2nd Battalion lance corporal wrote, 'and for closing dance-halls and public-houses against us, as happened for a period.'

A couple of weeks after the incident at Netheravon aerodrome, Browning came to inspect the 2nd Battalion. He soon homed in on 2 Platoon, where a tense Eddie Hancock stood to attention with his men. Browning fixed one of the soldiers in his gaze and then asked him to take his boots off. Was he simply looking for something to find fault with, a way of catching them out?

Hancock had made sure to ask some regular army men about the tricks of the inspection trade, then schooled the platoon in them. He watched as Browning scrutinized 'eleven studs in each sole, clean feet, [and] washed socks which had been properly darned'. Everything had been immaculately prepared. Browning said, 'Good turnout,' turned and went on to the next platoon.

This summer of training, with its intense physical exertion, the thrill of parachuting and a sense that they had become celebrated by the nation, produced many memorable moments for the men. But all understood, as September waned, that an order to head overseas might soon be forthcoming.

In the first days of autumn Private Fred Selman, Mike Lewis's particular friend from Ringway days, asked him and another soldier, Chalky White, to tea at his home not far away. Chalky had come through Ringway on the following course. He was a big South African, athletically built, who had been a semi-professional fighter and was one of the men who fitted the public image of the gorilla-sized paratrooper.

They borrowed three bicycles and set out across the rolling Wiltshire countryside, heading for Melksham, where Fred's parents Herbert and Florence and his sister Maud lived. In the sunshine, Lewis found their journey across that green land quite intoxicating. And when they arrived they saw that Florence 'had laid out a magnificent spread; cakes and bread and butter, jam and other goodies. We were rationed . . . and she'd obviously saved it up for Fred and his friends and we were treated like royalty.'

Fred introduced his new 'brothers', his two mates who'd already come through so much with him and who now faced God knew what. They talked and ate, neighbours came in to meet Fred's new pals, then some beers were shared. Lewis thought it had been the perfect day. Time wore on, and before they left Fred's dad took their photo on the porch. The three soldiers, in their shapeless khaki battledress, were all six foot or over. In the photograph, Fred's head is thick with curls, Lewis has crossed his arms and Chalky – suitably blond, given his nickname – allows himself the hint of a smile. We can assume it was Herbert Selman who clicked the shutter.

On 9 October 1942, a group of dignitaries gathered in the fields near Figheldean, a Wiltshire village a mile or so south of Netheravon. A fleet of aircraft had taken to the sky there and senior officers were waiting in the drop zone to watch a most important demonstration.

During August and September members of the 1st Parachute Brigade had stepped up their training to be ready for the type of operations they might be asked to perform. There were night drops, drills where they practised securing landing zones for gliders, and joint schemes with the American 2/503rd Parachute Battalion. Those in command knew that the US Army paratroopers would soon deploy as the fourth battalion in a British airborne brigade.

As this Allied cooperation intensified, British soldiers had been introduced to jumping from the American C-47 transport aircraft. It had come as a revelation to them. Sticks of twenty paratroops had been carried aloft in comfort, seated down the two sides of the fuselage, with windows to look out of and plenty of room to move about. When the green light had come on, instead of hurling themselves through a hatch in the floor, as they'd done with RAF bombers, they exited through proper doors at the back of the cabin. Compared to the Whitley, 'it was a Rolls Royce', thought one soldier. 'Pure luxury', wrote another, who likened it to sitting on a London Underground train.

However, the Americans did things differently, there were hazards. They flew in low and fast, then climbed to dropping height, a manoeuvre that saw the nose lift and rear drop in such a way that a man exiting the rear doors could strike the tailplane. Early drops were also made using American cotton parachutes rather than the British silk ones.

So when the aircraft appeared, flying towards the Figheldean drop zone that autumn morning, there was both excitement and trepidation. On board, 270 members of the 2nd Parachute Battalion prepared to jump. American planes provided a way of lessening dependence on the RAF, and all the spats that went with it. Orders to deploy overseas had been received during a visit by their brigadier to the War Office in London on 26 September. That message, although secret from most of the rank and file, had produced an unmistakable increase in the intensity of training.

It didn't take long for canopies to begin blossoming over the Wiltshire countryside, and on the ground the excited chatter soon gave way to the first expressions of concern on the faces of those watching through binoculars. One soldier had suffered a Roman candle, the static line fastened to the aircraft had become unclipped as he dived out, streaming behind him until he smacked into the ground with a sickening thud. In a couple of cases parachute panels tore open as they deployed. And then another fatal problem. One man exiting a C-47 had collided with another who had got caught on the tail as the aircraft pulled up for dropping, both soldiers plummeting, 'desperately trying to shake their chutes loose', to their deaths. Three men from the 2nd Battalion died that day.

On the ground, gathering up his canopy, Sergeant Hancock watched in horror as Private Joe Goldsmith, the platoon's outspokenly bolshie 'shop steward', strode furiously towards their brigade commander. Goldsmith's parachute was one of several whose cotton panels had torn, making for a dangerously fast descent. He shouted at the brigadier, cursing the quality of the chute and blaming it for killing soldiers. To Hancock's relief, the complaint was heard politely and without consequences.

Frost, who had by this point left C Company to become second in command of the unit, had been among the jumpers. He was phlegmatic about that day's mishaps. 'We all knew that the difficulties would soon be resolved, for resolved they had to be.'

In the days that followed that ill-fated demonstration, the camp at Bulford was a scene of bustle and focus. Weapons containers were packed, personal arms oiled and zeroed and in mid-October much of the battalion was given a few days' leave prior to embarking on overseas operations.

All the tensions of the previous months' training were being overtaken by the expectation that they were soon to be fighting for their lives. The entire parachute brigade was like a pack of wild beasts, straining at the leash. 'We were all thirsting for action,' wrote Frost, 'whatever might be the cost.'

6.   Oudna

Early morning on 13 November 1942 and dozens of paratroopers gathered on the decks of SS *Strathmore*. Ahead, as they glimpsed the port of Algiers, looming over the Mediterranean, Private Lewis took in what he called 'a blazing city in the distance'. The white facades of many buildings caught the early morning sunlight and the domes, spires and steeples that surmounted them reinforced the impression of oriental mystery. One other ranker in the 1st Battalion thought it 'a romantic picture . . . like an illustration of a biblical scene'.

The beauty of the setting, as disembarkation began, could not disguise its dangers. Occasional German aircraft attacked the harbour and there was uncertainty bordering on apprehension about how local people would receive them. In the summer of 1940 the British had bombed the French fleet in Algeria, killing 1,300 sailors. The French colony had come under the control of the collaborationist Vichy government and it was feared they would regard the British as enemies.

Men were formed up on the dockside, keeping a wary eye on the unsmiling locals who looked on. The paratroopers' baggage was loaded onto ancient steam-powered lorries that puffed and hissed their way up into the city. The 2nd Battalion marched behind, towards billets at a girls' school in a suburb of Algiers.

The impressions formed by the soldiers reflected in many cases the prejudices of their time. Derogatory epithets were often used for the Arab population, and, for their part, many locals returned the soldiers' hostility and condescension.

'I think it evil smelling and poverty stricken,' was one young officer's initial impressions of Algiers in a letter home to his aunts. 'It is obviously a place where the French have made money with no regard towards the good of the natives, although there are fine

schools – in one of which I am billeted, for the native children.'
Writing to his brother a couple of days earlier, the same 2nd Parachute Battalion lieutenant had added some details that he would spare his aunts: 'The Arabs smell like sewage plants and the women (French) make very poor prostitutes. But then what can one expect for the equivalent of 2/6!'

Three days before their disembarkation, Operation Torch, the descent of the Allied Expeditionary Force (AEF) under the command of Lieutenant General Eisenhower on the North African coast, had started. A couple of weeks had passed since the 1st Parachute Brigade had left Bulford Camp but the dynamic of the desert war had changed dramatically. Following victory against Erwin Rommel's Deutsche Afrika Korps at El Alamein, the 8th Army had pursued Axis forces, clearing them from Egypt, then racing hundreds of miles into Libya.

On 8 November the Italo-German armies, falling back towards their logistics bases in Libya and Tunisia, suddenly met with a new threat to their rear. The Torch landings in Morocco and Algeria threatened to cut off their supply lines, and indeed their exit route from North Africa, catching the Axis forces in the vice of the 8th Army approaching from the east and Eisenhower's AEF from the west. This new factor in the desert war came as a shock in Berlin, but, rather than concede defeat, Adolf Hitler had started to reinforce the garrison, sending additional divisions and Luftwaffe squadrons to meet the new threat.

For the disembarking army, time was of the essence. Tunisia lay hundreds of miles east of the Operation Torch landing beaches, so Allied commanders were keen to cover that distance as quickly as possible in order to press home their advantage of surprise. This was where the 1st Parachute Brigade came in. Having yearned so long for action, its soldiers and leaders now faced commitment to battle as their commanders tried to turn this state of flux in their favour.

While the Americans had sent dozens of C-47s/Dakotas to support the airborne force, this was barely sufficient to lift even one of its four battalions. So instead of launching the entire brigade (around 2,500 troops) at one target its three British battalions and one US battalion would go into action singly. Immediately after arriving, those battalion commanders found themselves engaged in an intense but usually unspoken competition to achieve the greatest success in this evolving battle.

Exploring the school that November evening in Maison Carrée, a prosperous suburb of Algiers, Johnny Frost started the business of readying his men for battle. The wheel of fortune had moved in his favour as they set sail from Greenock in Scotland, the CO having succumbed to a flare-up of an old medical complaint. Their brigade commander swiftly put the second in command, Frost, in charge and so, barely eight months after his battle debut at Bruneval as a company commander, he was given the management of the entire 2nd Parachute Battalion. But fate had turned for Lieutenant Colonel Geoffrey Pine-Coffin also, and after the summer months when he and Frost had switched back and forth between the second-in-command posts of the 2nd and 3rd Battalions, it was Pine-Coffin who had been confirmed CO of the 3rd, then given the plum role in this operation.

Flying from Cornwall to Gibraltar, then on to Algiers, the bulk of the 3rd Battalion had been the only element of the brigade to deploy as airborne warriors imagined they would. Leaving England on 9 November, they overtook their comrades at sea and dropped into action three days later. Pine-Coffin's objective was an airfield at Bône, in eastern Algeria, about fifty kilometres from the Tunisian border. It was a classic *coup de main* operation of the type they had long trained for, a daring thrust in the emerging battle. So well chosen was their objective, close to a port as it was, that the Germans had had the same idea, planning their own operation to take the aerodrome that day.

Pine-Coffin's force, soldiers of his battalion with some signallers, sappers and medics attached (a total of 359 carried by twenty-eight aircraft), would have to wait for days before a ground column reached them. There were enormous uncertainties in this mission, not least whether Vichy French troops garrisoning Bône would attack them as they landed. Pine-Coffin, a man of dry wit, also pointed out that 'the aircraft were Dakotas straight from America . . . we had never jumped from Dakotas and the pilots had never dropped parachutists either'. In fact, not only were they ingénues in the matter of airdrops but, despite being experienced commercially, the pilots were almost unable to find their way in uncharted skies (having relied in their civilian flying on an American system of navigational radio beams).

Be that as it may, only a single soldier died in the drop, and the battalion was unopposed when it took the airfield on the afternoon of 12 November. In a pattern that was to be repeated in the coming weeks, far from being hostile, the French were quickly recruited to the Allied cause. The Germans, realizing they had been beaten to it, scrubbed their own operation, instead mounting air attacks on the British force.

By the time the men of the 2nd Battalion were settling into their temporary billets, Pine-Coffin's were already committed and plans were being discussed for a mission by the 1st Battalion. Germany's rapid reinforcement of its North African garrison meant the mission prepared by the 1st during their sea voyage, a drop to secure the main airfield outside Tunis, had been abandoned and a new plan was being prepared for that battalion.

Frost's men, meanwhile, would go third. Setting to work in the way deployed soldiers do, they marked out bed spaces, swept dusty classrooms, established a parade ground on the playground and set a guard on the perimeter.

During their twelve-day sea voyage, the soldiers of the 2nd had discovered the first unwelcome fact about travelling under American command: drinking was banned and the bars of the *Strathmore*, which was originally a P&O ocean liner, placed out of bounds. Some of the soldiers, feeling parched after their sea journey, wanted to explore Algiers, but strolling out of the school gates held various dangers: officious US Military Police had started to patrol the city; it was still unclear whether French or Arab Algerians would attack them; and the local wine was to prove rather too potent for some of the men.

On their first evening in Maison Carrée, two men from A Company had returned to the school blind drunk. Because of the threat of violence in the town, both were carrying pistols, which were drawn as soldiers guarding the school gate tried to detain them. Sergeant Eddie Hancock, coming across the noisy fracas, managed to overpower and disarm one of them, none other than Joe Goldsmith, his 2 Platoon 'shop steward'. But the other man, shouting and swaying in the street outside, proved harder to waylay.

It was at this point that the battalion orderly officer, Lieutenant Desmond Brayley, appeared on the scene. Brayley was an extraordinary type, even among the cast of outsize characters found in the battalion. The son of a Pontypridd café owner, he had started the war in the ranks of the Royal Artillery before being commissioned and volunteering for parachute training. According to legend, Brayley had been either a professional wrestler or boxer before the war, and he soon earned the nickname 'Slapsey' among the cockneys of A Company. Brayley was a man utterly determined to distinguish himself, both in the field and more generally as an officer. This combination of unstoppable temperament and physical power led Sergeant Hancock to call him 'the gorilla'.

Surveying the scene at the gate, the powerfully built Brayley, who was of medium height, strode towards the drunken soldier and knocked him out with a single punch. Some of the paratroopers admired Brayley for his courage and no-nonsense methods. But others despised him for violating the accepted rules of military conduct, where the consequences, if the roles had been reversed and an enlisted man had struck an officer, could be dire indeed. 'He tended to solve disciplinary problems physically', Sergeant Hancock wrote, 'which sometimes verged on brutality.'

In the days that followed this rowdy arrival, those running the battalion tried to focus on fitness and preparation for a forthcoming jump. Although they had been conducting 'minute mills', an inter-platoon boxing competition, on the trip down, this had not involved most soldiers, and Frost's officers were keen to get the men back into training.

Frost, meanwhile, wanted to divine what the headquarters of

the 1st Army, under whose command they served, might have in store for them. Day to day, though, it was far from clear that HQ knew.

The 1st Army commander was keen to hurl them as far forward as possible, to secure routes through Tunisia's hilly border with Algeria so that ground columns might link up and, ideally, fight their way into Tunis before the Axis command had got properly organized. But their enemy was also bringing in troops by air, quickly forming ad hoc fighting groups with the intention of securing the frontier, so denying the Allies any rapid entry into Tunisia. The Luftwaffe was also using Stukas and fighters that it had hurriedly flown across the Mediterranean to harry the AEF.

For parachute officers, going up to 1st Army HQ in search of briefings about what lay ahead, the uncertainty about the whereabouts of troops – enemy and even their own – and emphasis on speed began to cause concern. 'Operations made most difficult', the 1st Parachute Brigade staff recorded, 'by lack of time, air photos, maps and transport.'

On 15 November, soldiers up at the Maison Blanche airfield waved off an assault force from the 1st Battalion, only to see the aircraft return four hours later with the men still on board. Their commander had aborted the drop. The same afternoon, after the aircraft had been refuelled, they took off again, this time dropping the US parachute battalion at a place called Tebessa.

The following day, the bulk of 1st Battalion parachuted into Souk el Arba, the site of an airfield about twenty kilometres inside Tunisia. They rapidly advanced, sending one company all the way to Medjez el Bab, literally the 'key to the door', the suitably named town that was a gateway through the hills to the plain of northern Tunisia. The 1st Battalion men reached it on 19 November and swiftly turned the local Vichy French to the Allied cause. In peacetime, Medjez el Bab was little more than an hour's drive from Tunis.

As the days ticked by, and with every other battalion in the brigade committed, Frost confessed, 'we feared that we might never get our parachute operation'. Pine-Coffin had even returned from

Bône, having handed over to a sea-landed force of commandos, and was now looking for a second mission.

Given the lack of good information about the enemy, Frost did not demur when he was asked to perform aircraft reconnaissance, flying hundreds of miles east with vague instructions to look for a possible drop zone near the Tunisian port of Sousse. The following day he was sent up again, the 1st Army having changed its mind, this time heading for Enfidaville, another town south of Tunis, dodging enemy fighters as they went.

This idea of flying over enemy-held territory to peer at possible landing zones struck him as entirely amateurish, but, having recently been placed in command, Frost did not want to question his orders or appear reluctant to commit his battalion to action. He also found himself unsettled by the growing disciplinary problems at night. As Maison Carrée became home to more contingents, bar-room disagreements between the 2nd Battalion 'delinquents' and French or US soldiers were increasingly being 'settled with savagery'.

Frost was ashamed of this disorder and felt that the inexperience of so many of his NCOs meant they were incapable of imposing their will on wayward soldiers. Indeed, many of the corporals and sergeants joined in the bar brawls. This left him quite uncertain about how to curb his men, feeling that many of his subordinates did not share his ideas on discipline. Both A and B companies were commanded by officers promoted from the ranks, and the officer commanding (OC) of the former, Major Dick Ashford, was a socialist to boot (as indeed was his 2 Platoon commander, Slapsey Brayley).

Fortunately for the nocturnal peace of Algiers, a fortnight after their arrival, an operation finally began to take shape. The staff at 1st Army HQ reckoned there was a chance for 2nd Battalion to seize a series of airstrips at Pont du Fahs, Depienne and Oudna. They would then be relieved by an armoured column a day or two later. For the generals, this idea offered multiple possibilities of destroying whatever aircraft and stores they found, denying some airfields to the enemy while leapfrogging ahead of ground troops, speeding up the drive on Tunis. For Frost, it was a chance to enter the lists, committing his restive battalion to war.

His brother officers were coming to realize that the tall Scot was able to wear the mask of command, that mysterious quality of leadership in which uncertainties or fears are cloaked and the assurance of success projected to those all around. One lieutenant in the 2nd Battalion penned this vivid portrait of their leader:

> He was a dreamer of battles to be fought and to be won. There was no such thing as defeat in his dreams, dreams which became a reality. Johnny Frost had a mystical magic – no need for him to write high sounding messages to his junior commanders or to address the men whom he led with words of inspiration – here was the man himself – the very epitome of inspiration, such was the aura which surrounded him. He was sentimental, sometimes ruthless when he had to be, sometimes aloof, but always calm.

As his men gathered at the Maison Blanche airfield on 29 November, Frost concealed his uneasiness about what lay ahead. And how could he not be worried? At the last moment, headquarters had told him to forget about Pont du Fahs, the first of three airfields they were going to raid: the enemy had moved on. But Frost, who tugged on his moustache at moments of tension like this, knew that there were no aerial photographs of their new drop zone, at Depienne. Nobody could tell him whether the enemy was there either. As he summoned the officers about him it came down to this: Frost would be the first jumper in the lead aircraft. He would survey the landing zone from the doorway and make a snap judgement about whether to go. Everyone should keep an eye on the lead Dakota: if the CO jumped then they all would; if he stepped back, then they would all be returning to Algiers.

The officers raced back to their companies, as the engines of forty-four Dakotas roared into life. Most of the soldiers didn't even know about the change of plan. Instead, they dealt with confusion about which weapons containers and sticks went on which plane, then started to get on board.

Before leaving Bulford each of them had drawn what the army

1. Lieutenant Colonel Johnny Frost, while he was CO of the 2nd Battalion.

2. Lieutenant Jack Grayburn longed for action through most of the war and found it in the 2nd Parachute Battalion.

3. Sergeant Major Macleod 'Maxie' Forsyth, one of the pre-war regular NCOs who joined the fledgling airborne forces.

4. Corporal Arthur Maybury, a pioneer member of the 2nd Battalion who later went into intelligence work.

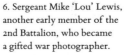

5. Lieutenant Colonel Richard Geoffrey Pine-Coffin, on the day in 1945 that he took his son to Buckingham Palace.

6. Sergeant Mike 'Lou' Lewis, another early member of the 2nd Battalion, who became a gifted war photographer.

7. Sidney Cornell was decorated and promoted for his bravery in Normandy fighting with the 7th Parachute Battalion.

8. Lieutenant Richard 'Dicky' Spender, a poet who discovered that he relished war while fighting with the 2nd Battalion in Tunisia.

9. Major General Richard 'Windy' Gale was instrumental in defining the command culture of the new regiment.

10. Brigadier Gerald Lathbury commanded the 1st Parachute Brigade in Sicily and at Arnhem.

11. Probably the most storied wartime commander in the Parachute Regiment, Alastair Pearson was awarded the Distinguished Service Order four times.

12. Midwife to the Parachute Regiment and Airborne Forces more widely, Lieutenant General Frederick 'Boy' Browning had a network of military and political contacts second to none.

13. This low-level photograph taken by Flight Lieutenant Tony Hill revealed the Würzburg radar and nearby chateau, providing the start point for Operation Biting.

14. Quayside crowds in Portsmouth greeting Johnny Frost's returning men after the Bruneval raid.

15. Wing Commander Charles Pickard, who led the formation of Whitley bombers to the Bruneval drop, with men of the 2nd Battalion and a trophy of the raid.

16. One of the many 'synthetic' training devices adopted to prepare men for their first drop and make up for the shortage of suitable aircraft was the 'fan trainer', which allowed practice landings at different speeds.

17. At Hardwick Hall, would-be recruits to the Parachute Regiment were put through extensive physical training, both on the assault course and with repeated route marches.

18. Having passed Hardwick, aspirant paratroopers were sent to No. 1 Parachute School at Ringway, near Manchester, where they practised all aspects of jumping before making their first drop from a balloon.

19. Another view of training at Ringway: 'knees together, elbows in', students learn how to land without injury.

20. The calm before the storm. A pre-deployment tea with (*left to right*) Arthur 'Chalky' White, Maud Selman, her son Fred Selman, and Mike 'Lou' Lewis.

21. Officers from A Company of the 2nd Battalion after the Oudna debacle: Captain Ronald Stark, Lieutenant Desmond 'Slapsey' Brayley and Major Dick Ashford, who sports a non-regulation beret picked up from French stores.

22. The arduous Tunisian campaign exposed the men to the rigours of a North African winter while moving to one threatened sector after another to thwart enemy advances. This photo features the 1st Parachute Battalion.

23. This aqueduct in the Tamera valley provided a landmark in the Tunisian landscape and a rallying point for these 1st Battalion men after a night patrol.

24. General Dwight Eisenhower visits the 1st Parachute Brigade in May 1943, soon after its return from the Tunisian front. Airborne forces figured prominently in his plans for the next stage of the war.

25. The Tunisian campaign was distinguished by several battles between British and German paratroopers, who here had captured Private Gavin Cadden, a veteran of Dunkirk and Bruneval whose luck ran out at Oudna.

26. After posting to the Army Film and Photographic Unit, Mike Lewis put up sergeant's stripes and was here pictured by a memorial to those, including so many of his friends, who had fallen in the Tunisian battles.

27. Containers for dropping stores by parachute being prepared in the run-up to 1st Airborne Division's operations in Sicily.

28. A model maker puts finishing touches to a diorama used for briefing the men of 1st Parachute Brigade about their target in Sicily, the Primosole Bridge.

called G1098 kit: first-aid dressings that went into back pockets of their trousers or put by some into their jumping smocks; small yellow scarfs for recognition purposes; face net; gloves, silk gloves; string vest; fifty rounds of ammunition; compass; escape compass; forty-eight hours' rations; a clasp knife on a lanyard; and garrotte wires.

The food in the ration packs included tins of bully beef, cheese (also tinned), oatmeal biscuits, chocolate and boiled sweets. Of course, they carried plenty of tea and sugar too, with the aim of brewing up on their small field stoves when the opportunity allowed. And if this avalanche of kit wasn't enough to take the young soldiers' minds off their favourite subject, they'd been given condoms too, producing much ribaldry about who would liberate the first brothel in Tunis.

That morning this bewildering array of stores had been supplemented by extra ammunition, cigarettes and, of course, the weapons carried on their person – pistols and Sten guns, the larger firearms being in the containers. Underneath their para smocks they wore shirts and vests, but not the woollen battledress blouson that was part of their usual uniform, a decision they would later rue.

The first Dakotas lifted off at 11.30, and one by one the others roared after them. The lead aircraft had been circling for an hour before the whole formation headed east towards Tunisia. Through the windows they could see Hurricane and Lightning fighters weaving about, flying over and above, shepherding the vulnerable aircraft through the Algerian skies. Frequently, their aircraft bounced in turbulence, causing many of the men to vomit.

During the two and a quarter hours that followed they had an opportunity to study Algeria. If any of them had thought they were about to parachute into a *Desert Song* landscape of shifting sand dunes studded with oases and wandering camels, the sight of the snow-capped Atlas mountains soon disabused them.

The rolling hill county below, as they crossed the unseen border into Tunisian airspace, received a good deal of rain in autumn and winter, enough to sustain plenty of farms where the French *colons* grew all manner of produce. In the border country the *djebels* or larger hills were typically 100–200 metres high. While these uplands were generally rocky and bare, in places there were groves of trees. Road and rail lines tended to run in the valleys below these heights, where most of the cultivation and small towns were also found.

As for the temperature, they had all been freezing since soon after take-off. Those who had seen the newsreels of the 8th Army boys frying eggs on the glowing surfaces of their tanks understood all too well by this point what winter meant in these parts.

When the red light blinked on in the lead aircraft, Frost got up and peered out of the open rear door. He could see ploughed fields down below. No sign of parked aircraft, or indeed any other enemy. That would do. It was time to step into the slipstream, leading his men into Lord knew what.

Streams of parachutists blossomed behind the aircraft, more than 530 troops, each one getting the shock of freezing air for a second or two before the reassuring crack of an opening canopy. As they landed with a thump on the damp earth, Arabs from the nearby village gathered to watch. It didn't take long before some of them started to dispute with Frost's men the possession of collapsed parachutes, voluminous silk shrouds that had each cost the British taxpayer £65 (equivalent to more than £3,000 at the time of writing).

Relations with the locals worsened when the British went in search of vehicles to commandeer (there were none), donkeys and carts. The tone had been set to a degree by the local ruler, the bey of Tunis, who had sided with the Axis forces, but Frost's men may have compounded this. Their plan required them to move dozens of kilometres with far more stores than the individual soldiers could carry. The paratroopers had French money to pay for these beasts of burden, but that hardly improved the mood when Frost's men led their animals away.

A little more than one hour after the battalion had landed, a troop of British armoured cars appeared. They were the advanced reconnaissance element of the division approaching from the south-west. These crewmen exchanged greetings with the para-troopers, returning after exploring a few miles up the road ahead, promising to see them again soon. So far, so good.

Orders were given for a march over the hills, northwards for twelve miles, towards Oudna, where they would rest up for a few hours before attacking that objective. They set out just after mid-night and not long after four in the morning trudged up to the hilltops selected for them to bed down briefly before entering bat-tle. Their 'rest' lasted little more than ninety minutes, the men huddling together for warmth on the freezing hillsides.

Frost issued orders for a move down towards Oudna that morn-ing. They would take the airstrip, clear the small neighbouring hamlet and await their relief by the approaching ground forces. As the sun came up, B Company in the lead, they came over a ridge that revealed both Oudna and, lying beyond it twenty-five kilo-metres away, the city of Tunis.

It was already clear that they were overloaded. Private Lewis, carrying a haversack of rifle-launched grenades on top of all his other kit, felt the straps cutting into his shoulders as he climbed the hillsides. His platoon sergeant urged Lewis to ditch the gre-nades, saying it wasn't worth bringing them, but he struggled on, focusing one step at a time on the way ahead.

Even the donkeys they'd commandeered to carry ammunition and their 3-inch mortars seemed to be having a hard time of it. The sight of this column with its pack animals, carts and laden paratroopers tottering along, caused Lance Corporal Fred Berry-man, an archetypal A Company cockney, to shout, 'We look more like a fucking travelling circus than a parachute battalion!' prompt-ing a chorus of laughter.

In the middle of the day, orders were given for A Company to assault the airstrip and push on to a railway station beyond it. It was already quite clear, overlooking the area, that there were no Luftwaffe planes using the place, just one wrecked dive-bomber that must have made a hard landing earlier. As Major Ashford shook his company into battle formation, 1 Platoon (which had Macleod Forsyth, perhaps inevitably nicknamed 'Maxie' by the

Londoners, as its platoon sergeant) and 2 Platoon (under Lieutenant Brayley, with Hancock as platoon sergeant) took the lead, with
3 Platoon in reserve.

As they came down the forward slope towards the inhabited
part of Oudna, they were completely exposed and, unsurprisingly
perhaps, having waited until they were only a few hundred metres
away, the enemy opened up. The paratroopers went to ground
immediately, but not quickly enough for some. 'The Germans
were dead on target', Sergeant Hancock noted and within moments
two of the three section commanders in his platoon were hit, one
fatally. As the men hugged the earth under this shower of incoming bullets, they were receiving a hideous baptism in the firepower
of German light machine guns, properly called MG34s, but more
often referred to by British soldiers as Spandaus.

Someone had to get the soldiers moving forward again, and in
this moment of mortal danger it was Major Ashford and Sergeant
Forsyth who rose to that challenge. Ashford, rifle in one hand, yellow recognition flag in the other, stood and bellowed at the men,
'come on the Cockney boys!' Hancock and a handful of the others
answered the major's call, getting back on their feet, 'I would have
followed him to hell and back.'

The two leading platoons made it down to the station buildings
and cleared them with Stens and grenades. Finding some spent
bullet cases in one of them, they concluded that a German MG34
team must have bugged out shortly before. Both platoons were
now well below half strength. Some men had been instantly killed
by the initial salvos, others wounded, lying on the damp earth,
with a few comrades going to their aid. Somehow Ashford had to
reunite his company, or what remained of it, which was now
strung out over half a kilometre. One thing was clear at least: there
was no significant enemy supply dump or presence left at Oudna,
if there'd ever been one. But finding that out had come at a significant cost.

As 1 Platoon cleared the station, destroying its telegraph set, a
big German eight-wheeled armoured car had passed just metres
away. Enemy aircraft were also appearing. Ashford decided to fall

back towards Frost and the rest of the battalion, his men coming under sporadic fire as they went.

The battalion's situation was becoming more complicated by the minute. Enemy tanks had been sighted in the distance, and, as A Company fell back, a flight of Bf-109 Messerschmitts roared into view, strafing the British on the hillside. In their wake it wasn't long before six German dive-bombers began to circle overhead: Ju-87 Stukas, one of the hallmark components of the Blitzkrieg. Frost's men celebrated inwardly when they flew off without dropping their bombs. The CO now determined to fall back to positions close to where they'd started the day, the site of a well called Prise d'Eau, where he posted the companies on hilltops, the better to defend themselves the following day.

On the morning of the mission's third day, 1 December, Lieutenant Colonel Frost managed to make radio contact with his higher headquarters. What they had to say came as a bombshell. The push north to link up with them had been abandoned. The 2nd Battalion was more than fifty kilometres away from friendly forces and the enemy was massing. 'This made my position untenable,' Frost recorded. It was one of those moments when his ability to digest the awful gravity of this situation, while projecting an exterior calm, distinguished him.

At around 11 a.m. battle came on in ways that none of the British had expected. Enemy armour had already been spotted rumbling towards them from the north, but when a couple of armoured cars approached from the south showing airborne yellow recognition flags, some men were deceived for long enough to be captured. One of these men was then sent to Frost with the message that the British were surrounded and should surrender.

Frost ordered his men to move to a new position a couple of hours' march away, which would allow them to escape the encirclement. However, doing so meant abandoning some wounded paratroopers who had been gathered close to the site of their drop zone at Depienne.

It was not long after occupying this second set of hilltops, at around 3 p.m., that fresh attacks started. Mortar shells dropped among them, the men frantically trying to dig scrapes to protect themselves from flying shrapnel. They could see groups of lorries and light armour to the east and west. Groups of infantry approached from north and south. The 2nd Battalion was being hemmed in. Then the ground onslaught began in earnest, armoured vehicles moving towards C Company, cutting down several of the Bruneval men.

Lance Corporal Berryman began picking off the advancing enemy with his sniper rifle. Each time he dropped one, he turned to his comrades, flashing them a smile with a glint from his gold teeth. Like many who had trained for so long, he relished the battle, but what answer did they have to the enemy armoured vehicles?

The battalion still had several Boys anti-tank rifles. Carried with some difficulty by one man, the weapon could send a large bullet (13.9mm in calibre) hundreds of metres. It was powerful enough to punch a hole in one of the approaching armoured cars or Italian light tracked guns, but against a proper tank it was a popgun. They had some rifle-fired grenades too, like the ones Lou Lewis was lugging. They could fly up to seventy-five metres, and with luck you might land one in an open-topped vehicle. If it came down to throwing range, they could use Gammon bombs, explosive charges with a contact fuse.

These, then, were the options at their disposal as a group of armoured cars with infantry trotting behind them approached B Company's hilltop. Lewis put one of the grenades he had hefted about for the previous two days into the cup on his rifle muzzle that held it.

The lead armoured car, about a hundred metres away, was lacing their positions with machine-gun fire. Fixing it in his gaze, Lewis pulled the trigger. The grenade popped on its way, dropping short with a puff of smoke. He lay in cover, reloading. They were a little closer now. *Pop*, the second grenade flew on its way, this time a little too far. Now the infantry, seeing they were being bracketed by these blasts went to ground, but still the armoured car came on.

Then Private Wilkinson appeared, lugging a Boys anti-tank rifle, Lieutenant Doug Crawley following just behind. They were going to take on the armoured car. But as Wilkinson struggled with the unwieldy weapon, it was clear he couldn't position it at the right angle to engage. The armoured car was higher than this gaggle of paratroopers and he didn't have the strength to raise the muzzle to that height.

Lewis was applied to the task. Lying on his back, he lifted the muzzle of the Boys so that Wilkinson could take his shot. But the armoured car crew had spotted them and didn't hesitate, opening up on them with bursts of machine-gun fire.

'For God's sake you're too long in the aim, fire it!' Lewis shouted at Wilkinson. And still nothing. Lewis shouted again. Then a simultaneous explosion – from the Boys and from a light cannon shell fired by the armoured car.

Wilkinson 'had been cleft wide open from neck to legs and all the inside of him, all that blood and all that tissue and all the horror of it, right next to me'. Lewis had been hit by fragments of metal too – his trousers were smoking – and so had Lieutenant Crawley.

The armoured car crunched into reverse, its crew having registered the hit on their vehicle. Lewis attended to the stinging wounds in his leg and another officer came to the aid of Crawley, who had been blinded in the explosion. This bitter fight, at quarters close enough for them to have called out to the Germans and Italians who attacked them, went on and Frost calculated they had to stand until nightfall, somehow, so that they could escape under cover of darkness.

A couple of hours after battle had been joined, a pair of Messerschmitts reappeared. Perhaps this was why the enemy hadn't pressed home the attack. The planes dropped down towards the hills, banking into their attack run.

With the scream of engines and the clatter of machine-gun fire the aircraft rained their destruction down on the hillside. But fortunately for Frost and his men, the Luftwaffe had erred at the moment of crisis: the Messerschmitts were strafing their own men.

None of the 2nd Battalion were hit by their fire. As night finally delivered its protection, their enemy pulled back, unwilling to suffer the risk of further casualties from the air.

After nightfall, wounds were treated and checks made to see which of their mates had come through the day's fight. Frost issued orders for them to move: it was now a matter of trying to escape to the east, anything between fifty and eighty kilometres to where the nearest Allied troops could be found, though nobody knew quite where that would be. It would take two or three marches under cover of darkness and, fixing a rendezvous point for the end of the first, the CO split his companies up so as to improve the chances of at least some of them making it through the encirclement.

Frost gave them the signal to leave by blowing a hunting horn, a treasured gift from the Royal Exodus hunt in Iraq that he had found to be a useful device for rallying his men. They headed out into the darkness in a north-easterly direction (on a bearing of 312 degrees, according to the War Diary), walking down from their hilltops into the cultivated lands below, trying not to stumble or turn an ankle on the heavy clods of earth that their feet found in the darkness. It was a wretched march for men who'd had little sleep for forty-eight hours or more and hardly anything to eat.

'I do not exaggerate when I talk about "the agony" of stumbling over those endless stretches of ploughland and vineyard,' recalled one sergeant in A Company. 'It was like marching over a coal heap.' To add to their misery, it was cold and a freezing drizzle fell. All the time Major Ashford murmured encouragement to the stragglers: 'Keep it up, lad, keep going.' Maxie Forsyth 'was a tower of strength' to his company commander as he nursed the men through the night. It took more than words of encouragement to get some men moving after their hourly rest stop, blows and boots being resorted to.

Lewis, meanwhile, had set off in a small party with the B Company second in command, a captain who placed the sightless Lieutenant Crawley's hand on his shoulder, leading him forward step by step through the Tunisian night. The company sergeant major was in their group too, but Lewis noticed him slowly drift away during that march, perhaps having calculated that his chances might be better without the wounded officer.

These disparate groups had managed by the early hours to reach a place called El Fedja, where there were a few French farmsteads. These were places where the colonists had built up successful holdings producing grapes, olives and cereals. Arriving just before first light, the bedraggled paratroopers received a friendly welcome and were urged to hide themselves in the outbuildings. (The companies each arrived at a different farmstead, and initially they weren't even aware of the others' presence.)

About seventy men of A Company, all that remained by that point, had hidden themselves in a barn belonging to the Rebourg family.

Not long after daybreak, while some men lay in the straw snoozing, those who stood guard at the door heard a motorcycle approaching. The machine laboured its way up the low hill where the farmstead lay, until it appeared in the yard just in front of Sergeant Allan Johnstone, who stood guard with his Sten, watching through a crack in the barn door. Some local children capered about the farmyard, excited by the new arrival.

It was a motorcycle-sidecar combination and there could be no mistaking its passengers: three German Fallschirmjäger (paratroopers). One of the men – the hushed watchers readily realized it was an officer – went to ask whether they'd seen any sign of the British. The farmer's daughter, Geneviève, had come out to talk to the *Leutnant*, but did not give them away.

As this conversation went on, another German, the one who'd been riding pillion on the motorbike, stretched his limbs and then ambled towards them. He'd left his rifle on the sidecar but was armed with a pistol. He was moving towards the barn, but it soon became clear that the German was going around the side to relieve himself. Johnstone and another man holding a Bren gun levelled their weapons while trying to remain concealed in the doorway. And then Johnstone's stare met the German's eyes as he walked back to the sidecar. There could be no doubt that he'd seen them, and, just to prove it, he nodded at them. But as the officer returned from talking to the French family, the young motorcyclist mounted up behind the rider, who kicked the machine into life.

Opening up the throttle, the enemy paratroopers moved off. The young one riding pillion had evidently not told his officer that the British were hiding just feet away. Or would he wait until they were at a safe distance to do so? That soldier's name was Hans Teske, an eighteen-year-old lance corporal from Pomerania, and as he sat on his machine, bumping down the farm track, he was wondering what he should do.

7.   In the Enemy Camp

The group of Germans who had investigated the farm rode away for a kilometre or two, linking up with several others who were mounted in the same fashion, forming a fast-moving motorcycle search group that hunted Frost's 2nd Parachute Battalion.

Hans Teske had kept his secret as the different search parties linked up. He felt that the British soldiers hiding in the barn had evidently spared him, and that they had enough trouble on their hands anyway. Teske's discretion, however, did little to alter the matter, because later that day an Arab boy at the farm had come down to reveal the British presence. The Fallschirmjäger commanders soon put together a plan to attack two farms in the area.

Those who had gone through Hardwick Hall and Ringway during the previous couple of years had spent a good deal of time studying Hitler's airborne arm. It had been held up as something of a pattern to be emulated, from the design of its uniforms to the tactics employed and even certain aspects of its ethos.

Jump smocks worn early on by Frost's men had been patterned on the German *Knochensack*, or 'bag of bones', a garment designed to withstand the forces of leaping into the slipstream. Initially the British too used a 'step-in' one, joined at the crotch, but both nations later adopted smocks that could be put on like a normal combat jacket but had a flap or tail that pulled under the crotch and fastened to the front of the smock in order to stop it filling with air or riding up during a descent. After trying a prototype helmet with a rear protrusion, the British had adopted the Helmet Steel, Airborne Troops, a rounded and brimless (unlike the standard infantry 'battle bowler') model closer in pattern to the German one, with the aim of eliminating any projection that could hit an aircraft hatch or wrench the head back in the airflow.

German arrangements for dropping men and kit had also been

copied. The Ju-52 aircraft they used was an impressive transporter but also had a bomb bay. The Fallschirmjäger's weapons were put in canisters in this bay, each with its own parachute, and the soldier dropped only with a pistol or sub-machine gun. As the British had already discovered, the prospect of men getting separated from rifles, machine guns and heavier weapons was an unwelcome by-product of adopting Luftwaffe practice.

The man appointed to command those forces, General Kurt Student, had set out 'Ten Commandments' designed to guide his soldiers' behaviour. Student combined experience as a pilot in the First World War with army and staff duties before being appointed to command the airborne arm in 1938. He had also led them in battle as the commander of the 7th Flieger (Air) Division during operations in the Netherlands. In many ways the German airborne commander had enjoyed the type of career that Boy Browning aspired to.

Student's formation later became the 1st Fallschirmjäger Division, and following their early successes additional paratrooper regiments were raised. Now the opposing paratroopers were coming face to face, both in combat and following the capture of growing numbers of Frost's men.

In the aftermath of the Operation Torch landings, Berlin had dispatched reinforcements, aiming to close off the entry into Tunisia as quickly as possible. Teske's Fallschirmjäger Regiment, the 5th, had been summoned from training in France and Germany, packed off by train to southern Italy, then flown across to Tunis within five days. On 20 November they had their first contact with the enemy, fighting the British 1st Parachute Battalion near Medjez el Bab.

When Frost's men dropped near Depienne, a small German patrol had been in the village. They witnessed the operation before escaping in Arab clothing to report back to their commanders. The commander of Teske's regiment, Oberstleutnant (Lieutenant Colonel) Walter Koch, was the man organizing the hunt for the British landing force.

Koch, who was thirty-two at this time, exemplified the battle experience of the German airborne arm. He had fought under Student during the assaults of Belgium and France in 1940, earning the Knight's Cross of the Iron Cross. During Unternehmen Merkur (Operation Mercury), the assault on the Greek island of Crete in May 1941, he was wounded while serving as a battalion commander leading a glider-borne assault.

Crete became a high-water mark for Hitler's airborne forces. More than 600 transport aircraft had been massed – in Germany's set-up the paratroopers were part and parcel of the air force, avoiding much of the inter-service rivalry that dogged Britain's early efforts – in order to insert 15,000 troops by a combination of parachute, glider and landing by plane at captured airfields. But thousands of paratroops had become casualties and nearly one third of the transport aircraft taking part were destroyed.

After Crete, the Führer scotched the idea of further large-scale airborne assaults. The commitment of large numbers of transport aircraft to the Russian front further limited this possibility.

By 1942, the German airborne force was being used largely as a 'fire brigade'; a highly mobile force of elite troops that could be deployed rapidly to key points. They had been used as such in Russia and this was how they had been committed to North Africa. In order to overcome the lack of mobility suffered by airborne units, the motorcycle-sidecar combinations from their reconnaissance company were carried underneath the Junkers Ju-52 planes that brought them over the Mediterranean.

Koch had two battalions of his own regiment, a company of armoured cars from the 10th Panzer Division, an Italian self-propelled artillery group (about a dozen vehicles, erroneously reported as tanks by the British) and a company (about a hundred) of lorry-borne Italian infantry under his command, probably about 1,700 men in all, more than three times the size of Frost's force but spread over a considerable area.

The initial Axis response to Operation Torch had also included pressing several 'replacement' or 'march' battalions into action. These were units of draftees being sent out to replace losses in the

Afrika Korps that were only battalions at all in the sense of being parties a few hundred men strong that were travelling out together from Italy to the battlefront in Libya, where they would be parcelled out to the regiments that needed them. Instead, some of these units were diverted to Tunisia, given the necessary equipment to operate as a combat unit and told to hold various key points.

Some of these newly arrived soldiers were also assigned to Koch as he hunted Frost's men. The ability to add thousands of soldiers to the defence of Tunisia by hijacking these march battalions was a sign of the dynamism of the German staff. It also demonstrated – and this would happen again following British airborne operations – the degree to which, literally within days, a military response could be drawn together from second-line or non-combat units largely overlooked by Allied planners.

Additionally, that November, the German colonel had a good deal of air support. Around a hundred Stukas and Messerschmitts had been hurriedly flown to Tunisia after Eisenhower's initial landings. Koch had already used these aircraft to strike the British and they were highly useful for spotting people moving across the bare hills. Indeed the air threat was such that Frost's men were very reluctant to do it in daylight.

The German airborne had soon captured the injured as well as a platoon of C Company left behind at Depienne, and each day more troops fell into their hands. Some of the German and Italian commanders favoured swiftly shooting them. The Supreme Command in Berlin had in October issued the Kommandobefehl or Commando Order, which dictated that Allied raiding forces were to be 'annihilated to the last man'. How far, however, this secret edict had filtered down to junior officers at the Tunisian front by December 1942 is unclear; rather, it may be that some took it upon themselves to deal with Frost's captured men as saboteurs.

Oberstleutnant Koch was aware of and opposed to such a policy, at least as far as British parachutists were concerned. Chancing upon a group of German soldiers who had lined up fourteen captured men from C Company taken at Depienne ready to be shot, he flew into a rage. Slapping the soldier in charge of this firing squad, Koch bellowed, 'British paratroopers will be treated as prisoners of war!'

General Student's 'Ten Commandments' dictated, firstly, 'You are the chosen ones of the German army', underlining their elite status (and echoed in the British ethos card). The sixth point urged them never to surrender. Their ninth 'commandment' instructed, 'against an open foe, fight with chivalry, but against partisans, extend no quarter'. This last injunction was to prove the operative one in this case.

With Frost's men, honourable behaviour was deemed appropriate. The soaked, exhausted prisoners from the Depienne drop were offered cigarettes, food and some measure of sympathy. After all, they were the chosen ones of the British Army. But the same German soldiers had shown no mercy to Cretan guerrillas, nor would they to Italian partisans.

In the couple of days after the abortive attack on Oudna, scores of 2nd Battalion soldiers had been taken. Some, like Sergeant Eddie Hancock (whose platoon had got into trouble for failing to salute Browning a few months earlier), had bullet wounds, so had fallen into the bag. His platoon 'shop steward', Private Joe Goldsmith, suffered similar wounds at Oudna and was also taken. Others got lost or collapsed during the night marches that followed. Teske recorded, 'we picked up one or two fast asleep'.

Shut up in a schoolroom at Depienne, Sergeant Hancock started to plot his escape. He'd taken a shot through the leg but still reckoned he might get away. To his surprise, one of the young privates he approached refused to try it; 'he quoted his wife and child as the reason'. Hancock would try three times to get away, but was foiled at every turn.

The spirits of these captured men varied widely, as Hancock had discovered. Some, angry about being parachuted into such a debacle, were cooperative with their captors. One of Koch's battalion commanders noted, 'my adjutant . . . soon had the very depressed prisoners talking'. The Germans quickly learned both that Frost, whose celebrity from Bruneval was known to them, was in charge and the direction of his planned withdrawal. Koch also benefited from the hostility of the local Tunisians to this British invasion, Teske noting the 'running commentary from the Arabs who told us exactly where the British were'.

Other prisoners, particularly some of the officers, proved rather more awkward guests. There were many escape attempts, and the 2nd Battalion's surgeon even managed to set fire to an aircraft that flew him and others to Italy. Frost's adjutant, Captain Jock Short, chatted amiably with Teske's company commander, and even exchanged addresses with him, after being captured in the early hours of 2 December. But, travelling down the prisoner-of-war pipeline whereby those taken by any Axis forces were handed over to the Italians for incarceration in their country, Short was later shot dead during an escape bid.

The canny Joe Goldsmith from 2 Platoon waited for his wounds to heal and an opportune moment to arise almost one year later. He escaped a prisoner-of-war camp, successfully making his way to Switzerland, where he was interned until near the end of the war.

One day after Goldsmith's capture, during the early afternoon of 2 December, acting on intelligence gained during the early part of the day, Koch ordered an attack on the farm where Frost's group was sheltering. The attackers didn't immediately realize it, but the A Company men, understanding their location had been compromised that morning, had moved across to the same location as their CO and his party.

In planning their attack that afternoon the Germans sought to surround the farmsteads where they knew the British were sheltering, evidently wanting to cut off any line of withdrawal. From about 3 p.m. they started shooting up the farm buildings.

German airborne troops relied heavily on the power of light machine guns with fearsome rates of fire. Each Fallschirmjäger section (ten or so men) had two belt-fed Spandaus (MG34 or MG42 machine guns). The MG42 threw out bullets so fast (up to twenty-five a second) that its bursts had a distinctive ripping sound. British sections, by contrast, had a single Bren gun fed by thirty-round magazines and with a rate of fire slow enough for soldiers to count the rounds in a short burst. Their doctrine favoured accuracy rather than weight of fire.

The German airborne also deployed many mortars, far lighter than field artillery pieces and therefore more easily air transportable. Both types of weapon were brought into action that afternoon, the Tunisian hills echoing to the crump of mortar rounds and bursts from Spandaus.

Teske and the others in the motorcycle column manoeuvred up onto a ridge where the MG34s mounted on their sidecars could get a good angle onto the farms where the British lurked.

Initially, there was little return fire. Frost had ordered his people to conserve ammunition, for, among their other problems, many men had only a few rounds left. But once the German paratroopers approached the farmsteads, using the hedgerow-like banks of cactuses as cover, an ugly, close-range fight began with grenades being lobbed and bursts of sub-machine-gun fire exchanged.

Frost's men knew that, once more, they just had to hold on until nightfall. Before that afternoon's battle had been joined, he had dispatched Lieutenant Euan 'Junior' Charteris, who had distinguished himself at Bruneval, with two soldiers for his protection (one being Lance Corporal Berryman, the A Company sniper) in the hope that they could link up with Allied forces to the northwest, bringing help to the rest of the battalion. But this small party, moving in daylight across the hills, had soon been spotted and surrounded. After refusing to surrender, all three had been killed.

Of course, Frost was unaware of their fate as the battle took on a close-range nature that afternoon. But what he had noticed was that the German dispositions in the direction they wanted to head had thinned out somewhat as the attack started. But he still had to stand firm until it was dark.

The Fallschirmjäger commanders, having initially been confident that they could smash the British stragglers between their forces advancing from the east and stop groups to the west, started to have doubts as the light dwindled. Tracer rounds from their

Spandaus had set fire to some hayricks and thatch and the smoke this produced was adding to their uncertainty. A lieutenant and several men had been killed in the initial attempt to assault the farms and, having treated them to a good deal more mortar fire, a second attack was making only slow progress.

Perhaps the German paratroopers also understood that end-of-day heroics were hardly worth the risk if their commanders intended to halt their assault at nightfall. And as darkness finally came on, Teske and the others close to the farms at El Fedja heard something new, a strange melody above the crackling of burning haystacks and occasional gunshots. It was Johnny Frost signalling with his hunting horn. They were making another break towards Allied lines – it was their last chance of escape.

8.   *Sauve Qui Peut*

Dawn on 3 December 1942 and two men rode across the Tunisian hillsides on local Arab ponies. They had started out before first light, heading west in search of Allied lines. With nothing heard from Lieutenant Charteris, Lieutenant Colonel Frost had sent another party in search of help. The 2 Platoon commander, Lieutenant 'Slapsey' Brayley, and Sergeant Allan Johnstone, a wry Aberdonian, had been furnished with their mounts by French farmers at a village called Ksar Tyr, and had headed off in the dead of night.

With their para smocks, helmets attached to the pommels of their saddles and Stens slung across their backs, Johnstone thought they looked like medieval crossbowmen, or perhaps Don Quixote and Sancho Panza. 'We were quite vague about where we would find 1st Army,' Johnstone recorded. But that didn't deter Brayley, who had already demonstrated a talent for survival and, unlike the rest of their battalion, or what was left of it, these two had been mounted and given official blessing to head west as quickly as possible.

Frost and the bulk of the others, around a hundred men, had set out a little later on foot. Having split his men up on the night of the 1st, the CO had decided it was better to keep the survivors together at this point. Some were out of ammunition, and few had much of it, so better not to get picked off in ones and twos. That said, during those early hours of the fifth day of their ill-fated mission, there were dozens of others who were not part of this main group and they knew all too well that their enemy was hunting them. It had become a matter of *sauve qui peut*, or devil take the hindmost.

The district of Goubellat that Brayley and Johnstone rode into as they headed towards what they hoped would be salvation lay just to the south of Medjez el Bab, the market town and gateway through the hill country. Goubellat is a fertile and well-farmed area, and the two mounted paratroopers found quite a few French *colons* out about their business that morning. Stopping from time to time to seek information in pidgin French, they ascertained that, yes, indeed, the Allies were not far away: at Medjez el Bab, to be exact. At one farm they were even treated to glasses of red wine and something to eat.

For Frost and the others, rations were more meagre. They had stopped to rest at 4 a.m., but, given the desperate nature of their plight and closer proximity to Allied lines, Frost decided to resume movement in daylight. The men were suffering from 'extreme fatigue', so, before getting them moving again, everyone was encouraged to brew up and eat a piece of processed cheese on an oatmeal biscuit, or whatever else they had left in the way of rations.

It was coming up for twelve hours after they'd set out that Brayley and Johnstone, rounding a corner, encountered a couple of tanks. They knew 'there was no escape if they were not ours'. A beret-wearing head appeared in the commander's hatch of the leading vehicle and Slapsey called out, 'Lieutenant Brayley, 2nd Parachute Battalion!'

'Oh, we've been wondering about you', came the laconic reply.

They were the first to make it. But it was not long after that, and a few kilometres to the north, that Frost and the main column came across some troops with half-tracks. They were Americans. 'You should have heard the cheer that went up from us when they turned out to be Yanks,' one of those who trudged behind the CO wrote home to his wife. They had not quite finished their odyssey, for Medjez el Bab lay a few kilometres further west, and dusk was falling by the time they got in, 'hardly able to put one foot in front of another'.

By the map, they had walked more than eighty kilometres since dropping on Depienne five days before, but some reckoned it could have been twice that, given the need to skirt enemy locations and the blundering about in the dark. Lieutenant Crawley had been guided to safety, despite being blinded on the 1st; so had

Private Lou Lewis. Sergeant Maxie Forsyth had proved indomitable on the march, carrying on stoically despite the loss of his subaltern (captured during the action at El Fedja the previous evening) and much of their platoon. Forsyth had become so exhausted and dehydrated during the night marches that he had suffered hallucinations.

Around 140 men assembled in some disused storerooms on the outskirts of Medjez el Bab that evening, out of the 530 who had dropped. A few dozen more came in during the days that followed, but the stark truth remained: Frost had lost more than half of his force killed or captured. Among them were the second in command, the adjutant, the padre and several other officers. Many of the sergeants and corporals, including a good many Bruneval veterans, were also now guests of the Führer. There was no disguising the scale of this setback.

Of the more than 200 members of the 2nd Battalion who never returned from Tunisia, thirty-six had been killed during the operation and the remainder taken prisoner. When a phalanx of them were later marched down to the docks at Tunis, for shipping over to PoW camps in Italy, the paratroopers had sung 'Land of Hope and Glory' and 'Jerusalem' as they arrived quayside. There were ruder ditties too, belted out as they boarded ships that would have to run the gauntlet of British planes and submarines scouring the Mediterranean.

A few days after their arrival in Medjez el Bab, the remaining fighting strength of the 2nd Battalion, formed into a composite company, was sent up to assist Geoffrey Pine-Coffin's 3rd Battalion on the front line. Frost remained behind, weighed down by ruminations about what would happen and whether his battalion might be scrapped.

'My main reaction to having had the battalion cut to pieces on such a useless venture was astonishment,' he wrote, later describing it as, 'the most disgracefully mounted operation of the entire war'. While maintaining his outward composure and keeping his anger from the surviving officers, Frost was evidently furious with

1st Army HQ and Edwin Flavell, the commander of 1st Parachute Brigade, who showed little understanding or sympathy.

Frost did not spare himself from this lacerating analysis. It was he, after all, who made the decision to leap while flying over Depienne. He would not have been the first CO in his brigade to scrub a mission and tell the pilots to set a course back to Algiers. Thinking back to their take-off on 29 November and the decision to jump, he would write, 'many of us chose that day to be particularly stupid'. The loss of so many picked men, volunteers trained over the previous two years to a high pitch of military efficiency, weighed deeply upon him.

Aware of the responsibilities of command as he was, Frost could hardly vent these feelings of guilt and anger within his own battalion. He discovered a uniquely sympathetic listener in Alastair Pearson, a fellow Scot with whom he would sink too many whiskies to count. Pearson, just twenty-seven and a baker before the war, had not long before assumed command of the 1st Battalion. The precocious lieutenant colonel, whose guttural Glaswegian accent defeated many a Sassenach ear, had already demonstrated a battlefield presence so forceful and oblivious to danger that his soldiers called him 'the Mad Jock'.

Facing the results of the Oudna disaster, Frost struggled to see how things could be remedied. The ordinary infantry replacements were not trained parachutists, and in any case the COs of other units jealously guarded them. People held on to their rations and stores as well, the 2nd Battalion initially having to fall back on French support both for food and in furnishing a colourful array of replacement clothing. His men just had the kit they'd walked in with. This scrounging from others focused on fighting their own wars all seemed to add to their humiliation.

Wandering about the border towns, trying to find his stragglers, feed the men and gain some idea of what might come next, Frost watched all manner of forces arriving at the front. There were the American regimental combat teams with their extravagant quantities of armour and motor transport, British columns of the 6th Armoured and 78th Divisions and a number of French units representing the remnants of the colonial army that had rallied to the Allied cause.

As a keen horseman, Frost was fascinated by the Sipahi, blue-jacketed North African cavalry, trotting alongside the roads. Some Goumiers, Moroccan light infantry, also arrived, cloaked in striped robes and with a reputation for dealing summarily with prisoners.

Something similar was happening on the other side too, as add-itional German and Italian reinforcements went up to the front. What these new arrivals heralded was a slowing down of the cam-paign as more troops were now available, leading the lines between the two sides to stabilize. The scope for dashing forward by air-drop or armoured car was diminishing by the day, as chains of outposts became established atop the border hills and the numbers defending Tunisia's frontiers multiplied.

If Frost and his two fellow commanders of British paratroop battalions had been able to have their way, they would have with-drawn their units. This is what happened to their American brethren, whose battalion was removed from the control of 1st Parachute Brigade. But the number of fighting troops available to their generals, coming up lines of communication that stretched several hundred kilometres back into Algeria, was still very limited, and the frontier long. So it was apparent from the day after the 2nd Battalion returned from Oudna, when the few dozen remnants were temporarily given a task defending an airfield, that they would be committed to the fight that was gathering intensity along the border.

While it had become inevitable that they would be drawn into this battle along the hilly frontier, the parachute battalion com-manders felt they would be doing so at a disadvantage because of the way their units had been designed. They were intended for swift, raiding missions of a few days' duration, and so did not have the numbers or support to sustain prolonged attritional fighting.

Regular infantry brigades had battalions with four elements at each level, but the parachute brigade was essentially 'triangular' in its organization: its three battalions each had three rifle companies, with the same number of platoons in each company. Thus, Frost's battalion had nine rifle platoons whereas a battalion in another (line) infantry unit would have sixteen. With three of these smaller companies, and a correspondingly reduced support company and headquarters elements, their battalions could take less punishment: losing 200 casualties in a few days would evidently have a greater impact on a parachute battalion of around 550 men than a regular infantry one of more than 800. The paratroopers were also bereft of support elements such as an anti-tank gun platoon, or one of armoured universal carriers, light tracked vehicles usually called Bren carriers, very useful both as a platform for those machine guns and for tasks such as moving ammunition or casualties.

At around this time, and with this weakness in mind, platoons of Vickers machine guns and 3-inch mortars were established within the parachute battalions. This did not add greatly to their size in terms of numbers, but allowed them to employ this fire-power in a better organized way. The simple reality, though, was that the units led by Pearson, Frost and Pine-Coffin would enter these Tunisian battles at a considerable disadvantage in numbers, placing even more of a premium on the steadiness and fighting qualities of their men.

Three weeks after the 2nd Battalion's return from Oudna, Frost and Geoffrey Pine-Coffin found themselves summoned to lunch by their brigadier. Flavell's HQ was in Béja at the time, another market town at a crossroads thirty kilometres west of Medjez al Bab. It can't have been easy for Frost, since his anger was such in the wake of the recent disaster that he found it hard to be civil to his boss. Pine-Coffin, while he had been more successful in keeping the 3rd Battalion intact, had just been briefed about a forthcoming attack that caused him the gravest doubts.

It was one of those days, though, when the mask of command had to be worn, not just in front of those they led but also because their superiors had summoned them and expected their enthusiastic obedience. Sitting at the table, immaculate as ever, was Major General Boy Browning, along with Brigadier Flavell and some members of the general's staff. Browning had flown out on a tour of inspection, racing about the North African theatre on aircraft furnished by Lieutenant General Eisenhower.

Browning, as always, had his own agenda. With the RAF still trying to stymie the development of airborne forces back in Whitehall, he wanted to make sure that the high-ups in North Africa could still see a role for his troops during the remainder of the campaign and beyond. On this, all of the officers around the lunch table in Béja that day could heartily agree – as they could with Browning's suggestion that the missteps to date had been due to a woeful misunderstanding of airborne forces at their higher headquarters. If the generals flung paratroopers into action in such a cavalier way, was it surprising that even the best soldiers could suffer grievous setbacks?

As for the best way to employ the parachute battalions at their disposal, that was a more delicate question. Frost had come to the view, ever since Bruneval, that relatively small-scale raids or *coup de main* operations at company level (100–150 troops typically) were highly effective, and, if mounted often, could force an enemy to tie down thousands of soldiers in defensive arrangements. Browning was interested in what senior officers at the time often termed the 'big party', not penny-packet operations. Having created an airborne division of more than 10,000 men, he wanted to lead it into action. And if the aircraft were lacking for such scale, and the strategic situation was not yet ripe (the invasion of Italy would soon come onto the agenda), then of course Browning and Flavell could agree that these operations should be at the brigade level.

What to do with the 1st Parachute Brigade, though? Now reduced to three battalions because the Americans had taken theirs back, and light on both manning and equipment, it could not muster more than 1,500 men, or 1,800 when its battalions were restored to strength. The lack of assets such as anti-tank guns was rather important when additional panzers, including the dreaded new Tigers, were being unloaded in Tunis. Their commander at 1st Army could certainly see a use for the brigade – as crack assault troops or to plug gaps in the line. But it was a 'quite suicidal' plan for the 3rd Battalion to attack a German-held hilltop on 24 December that preoccupied Pine-Coffin at lunch on the 22nd.

What Pine-Coffin understood was that the scope for questioning orders in war was decidedly limited. If he refused to lead the attack, dismissal from command was highly likely. Something similar would happen to the 2nd Battalion CO a few weeks later in a place they bitterly referred to as Happy Valley: an invitation to hazard his depleted unit over a large frontage against a huge expected enemy attack, with a court martial or sacking as his only options other than accepting the mission. If Frost understood the near impossibility of refusing such orders, he had just learned to his bitter regret the cost of obeying instructions to embark on an ill-thought-out mission. Such was the weight of command.

Christmas came early that year for both of the battalion commanders. Driving rain caused 1st Army to postpone the 3rd Battalion's assault, and, over lunch, Browning reassured Frost that his battalion would be restored to strength. He would see to it that replacements were found. There was no question of its relinquishing the parachute role either.

The following day, Browning toured the brigade's units, hearing about their experiences, digesting lessons for the future. Frost could at least now begin rebuilding his command, even if questions remained about where the men would come from.

Appropriately enough, it was Christmas Day when an officer, six NCOs and forty-five other ranks, arrived at the 2nd Battalion. These were fully trained airborne reinforcements who had been through the system and, sent out from Bulford Camp weeks before, survived the torpedoing of their troopship. However, these prized drafts were followed by scores of men from anti-aircraft batteries: good for making up numbers but often quite bewildered by the reception they received in an elite branch like the Parachute Regiment.

The new men soon found themselves negotiating the tricky atmosphere that develops in a unit that has emerged from a trauma like Oudna. There were those who shared the experience and those who didn't. So it was that one of the reinforcements who reached the 2nd Battalion on Christmas Day would recall, 'we took all the bluff and bullshit from older members'. If it was wearisome for him, as a trained paratrooper, imagine the treatment awaiting the Royal Artillery men drafted in.

Following another influx of trained men from the UK a few weeks later, one of the A Company platoon commanders noticed a particularly bad relationship had developed between a recently arrived private and an experienced corporal. The latter was refusing to speak to the new man, even though they shared a trench, telling him, 'get some hours in under shellfire before you talk to me'. It struck the lieutenant as utterly petty, particularly in hindsight, since neither man was destined to survive the trial that awaited the 2nd Battalion that March.

As the new drafts came in there were moves and promotions among the veteran cadre of the battalion. Sergeant Macleod Forsyth was elevated to warrant officer rank, becoming the company sergeant major (CSM) of A Company, a position of considerable clout in terms of the management of that element. Forsyth brought his hard eye to the new task and particularly to the officers he had to work with.

In the weeks that followed Browning's visit, all three battalions of parachutists were in action, often individually, occasionally together, as the generals moved them back and forth along the frontier, plugging gaps. With the density of troops still low in many sectors of the frontier, the paratroopers were often employed in patrolling. Apart from the engagements that occasionally became quite severe, the discomforts and the cold, they were able to perform this service without too many casualties, enjoying the challenge.

Lieutenant Dicky Spender, one of those who'd joined the battalion at Christmas, was given a platoon to command in C Company. Writing to one of his former teachers, he reviewed his first month's soldiering: 'I have lived in a sewer, a hayrick, a tent, a bivouac, a tent, nothing and a railway truck since I began moving about.' As for the North African winter, 'rain here is not rain, but the sea picked up and put down again in and around my shivering body'.

As for the brigade's sense of achievement during these miscellaneous fights in the border hill country, sent in when others had failed, Lieutenant Spender summed up their growing pride:

> The equation is roughly
> 1 American Div = 1 Guards Bttn
> 1 Guards Bttn = 2 parachutists
> Therefore Parachutists = all dirty work

The 2nd Battalion suffered a blow early in February when two of its majors (including Dick Ashford, who'd been decorated for his leadership of A Company at Oudna) were killed by a mine. For Macleod Forsyth, this loss, prompting the appointment of a new major, John Lane, in charge of A Company, would require him to build a new relationship. The rapport between CSM and OC was key to the effective running of any company.

For many of Frost's people the repeated actions of January and February, moving up and down the border, underlined the intensity of battle and the likelihood of their own injury or death. Spender had, in his early letters home, made light of the danger, insisting he was at no risk. But one cold February night, having had some of the local liquor and facing the prospect of combat the next day, he was overcome with melancholy and a sense that he would never see them nor his sweetheart (whom he nicknamed 'Bobby') again. He tried to break this to his parents gently:

> It is ten minutes to midnight. It is proposed to hold a party tomorrow. My boys are just finishing off the decorations. I am writing this now so that if I slide under the table and become incapable of further drinking or writing, you will always have this . . . give my bestest and mostest love to Bobby and to your own two dear selves . . . good night dear things and don't get sorry about anything. It's all v simple this snuffing out and moreover it's inevitable.

Spender, twenty-one at the time, not only survived the action but also cemented his reputation in C Company as a fearless young officer. Like so many of them, he had the face he showed his comrades and the private side, of dark fears, that he had confided in his letter home. Perhaps it had served as a catharsis also, a surrender to the inevitability of falling in battle helping him to face the trials that lay ahead of them.

The Axis high command, meanwhile, did not want to accept the slowing down of things on the Tunisian front. Pressured from the east by the 8th Army, which entered Tripoli on 23 January 1943 and reached Libya's border with Tunisia a few weeks later, it sought to drive the Allies back in the west. While the German and Italian generals faced a severe handicap in terms of numbers, they exploited the advantages of being able to switch troops between their front against the 8th Army and that facing the 1st.

In mid-February they launched Unternehmen Frühlingswind (Operation Spring Wind), a large-scale assault aimed at forcing the Allies back from Tunisia's western borders. Six days later they reached the Kasserine Pass, having smashed American forces standing in their way. A few days on, in the last week of February, they launched further thrusts, including a concerted attempt to take Medjez el Bab and an advance to the north, close to the Mediterranean, along the Sedjenane valley, towards a town called Tamera.

So it was that in the middle of the day on 3 March, the 1st Parachute Brigade received orders to redeploy to the Sedjenane valley with all due speed. The enemy was making rapid progress and the situation was in the balance. Their journey north, around eighty kilometres as the crow flies, but considerably further by road, would be accomplished in a fleet of troop-carrying vehicles whistled up by the 1st Army. The paratroopers were to head up there and place themselves under the command of the hard-pressed British force, the 46th Division.

What none of them realized, as they bounced along, singing in the lorries, was that the trials awaiting them would prove so severe. For they were about to enter a desperate battle against their toughest foe – indeed, those whose standards they had striven to emulate: the German Fallschirmjäger.

9.   Cork Wood

In the early hours of 8 March 1943, paratroopers of the 2nd Battalion found themselves trudging uphill in the dark. They had already done this a couple of times since moving into the northern sector, and, although they were expecting enemy resistance on the previous couple of occasions, they hadn't found it. This time they had been told that they would be relieving soldiers from the Lincolnshire Regiment, who'd been hard-pressed and were going to be pulled back.

Sergeant Major Maxie Forsyth, stepped up the incline, Sten gun at the ready, growling occasionally at the men, trying to keep their formation. Once they had got off the lowland, with its main road, railway and farms, heading east and up, the ground became stonier and the ordered cultivation yielded to groves of small oaks. Straining their eyes in the dark to see the crown of the hill known as Djebel Diss, they reached the top at about 3 a.m. and, A Company being in the lead, they had started to look about for the Lincolns. Ideally, the newcomers could occupy their trenches, which they hoped would at least be facing the enemy.

After whispered calls received no reply, Forsyth and his major conferred. Were they in the right place? What had become of the Lincolns? They had no idea how far away the enemy was, and therefore how much noise they could make or light they could show, but eventually the decision was taken to start calling out to them.

At length, a voice piped up, 'We're over here, sorry we thought you were the Germans'. Realizing that the Lincolns had escaped detection because they had pulled gas capes over their trenches and collectively gone to sleep, Major Lane 'went absolutely bananas', cursing their prowess as soldiers and telling them to clear off.

Since it was still dark, one of the A Company sergeants asked a corporal in the Lincolns for help orientating himself. Where was the enemy? 'He gave a thin tired smile and said that this was where they had finished up the day before and that was about all he knew.' They started to occupy the trenches already dug and made a start on a few of their own, wondering what dawn would bring.

That night the 2nd Battalion had taken up positions on Djebel Diss in the forest of Sedjenane. It became known within the unit as Cork Wood. Behind them, running north-north-east was the valley of the same name, with road and rail links to Tamera, these roughly parallel to the Mediterranean coast about ten kilometres away. The mission of the 1st Parachute Brigade was to hold a line of hilltops just east of that road, preventing further advances by Axis forces in the area.

It was a mission that had been given to the brigade as a whole, with the 1st Battalion taking up similar positions to the north-east of the 2nd, while the 3rd Battalion remained behind them on the low ground, just west of the road, able to reinforce the other two.

As the first glimmer of light appeared ahead of them, some of the more tactically aware members of A Company began to get an uncomfortable feeling. They could see higher ground to their front, which meant they in turn could be seen from there. In military terms, they were on the 'forward slope' whereas the rest of the battalion, a hundred or so metres further back, were either on the crown of this low hill or on the reverse slope, and better covered by cork trees. One of the paratroopers felt that 'being in the front trench of the battalion, it was rather worrying'. A couple of men sharing a trench were pointing ahead. It seemed to them that there was a radio aerial about 500 metres to their front.

Their OC decided to send out a dawn patrol Sergeant Stan Howard and three others readied their kit and walked gingerly past their comrades' trenches, where the men were finishing an early morning brew and chomping on rations. 'If you don't come back, can I have your pudding?' one wag asked Howard.

How many minutes passed? No more than five. Then, 'the early morning quietness was pierced by the vicious chatter of a Spandau'.

Tracer rounds zipped above their heads or kicked up the earth around them as more German machine gunners joined in. The intensity of it was breathtaking.

It didn't take long for some of the rounds to start striking flesh, cries to go up, and for many of them to realize the awful vulnerability of their forward-slope position. A few men leapt out of their trenches, racing back towards the ridgeline. One young officer 'ran past Company HQ so fast he nearly burnt us', said Forsyth.

With gunfire raging, those who peered out of their trenches saw one of Sergeant Howard's patrol come crawling back towards their positions. He had been shot and had dragged himself back to friendly lines. Those who patched him up with dressings heard the sorry tale of how the sergeant's patrol had walked into an ambush mounted by soldiers creeping up on their position.

As the morning wore on, small parties of German troops inched forward, using folds of the ground and the oak groves to cover themselves from view. With close-range firefights erupting into C Company's positions behind them, there was a growing fear that A Company, or what was left of it, had been surrounded and was about to be overwhelmed.

Realizing that the men had to be steadied, and feeling none of the company's officers were quite up to the task, Sergeant Major Forsyth left his cover, moving onto the forward slope, and shouted to those who crouched in their trenches, 'Come on boys, the bastards are more frightened of you than you are of them!'

Men raised themselves, opening up with Brens, Stens and Enfields on the enemy to their front and flanks. And for a few hours that was enough. In the afternoon the attack slackened, but not for good reasons. The attackers were expecting help from the air and wanted, if possible, to get to a safe distance.

What followed was a terrifying demonstration by Ju-87 Stuka bombers. Wheeling over the battlefield, they began their screeching attacks on the 2nd Battalion's hilltop. 'A flight of Stukas dived on A Company', Frost wrote, 'and dropped their bombs among them, making huge craters and smashing acres of trees, with a numbing and bewildering effect.' The concussion from explosions that size left ears ringing and bodies winded. Even so, as the sound of the Stukas died away, the day's fight was not yet over.

The survivors of A Company had heard a cry. It was Sergeant Howard. He had been captured by the enemy that morning and now was calling out to his comrades: 'The Germans want you to surrender; if you do they'll look after you because you've fought well today.' It was evident to all who heard it that Howard and his captors were close. In fact, he was near a point that they had been taking intense machine-gun fire from.

Considering this situation, Lieutenant John Timothy, commanding one of A Company's platoons, realized that if they remained passive they would probably all die or be taken prisoner the next day. Timothy was a veteran of the Bruneval raid, an assistant manager at Marks & Spencer before the war who had demonstrated a fearsome talent for fighting.

As the light began to fade, Timothy led a section of eight men forward. They carried a couple of Bren guns, Stens and grenades, as they moved in an arc to the left, where the gap between the 2nd and 1st Battalions had been used by the Germans themselves to infiltrate earlier, to sneak round to the flank of the German machine-gun position. They moved down the slope, through shredded oaks, until they were approaching from its side the shallow trench where their enemy was digging in, intending to consolidate the day's advance.

When Timothy led his boys forward in a rush, the issue was resolved in seconds and without gunfire. The eight occupants raised their hands. Stan Howard, lying nearby, outside the trench, in a pool of blood with a bandaged thigh, called out to the stormers, 'Go easy on them, they've fed me and given me water.'

Timothy surveyed the trench: there was an MG42 machine gun mounted on a tripod and an MG34 nearby. The paratroopers took possession of both weapons along with eight prisoners and helped their wounded sergeant back up the slope to their own lines. Aggression had paid an astonishing dividend.

Evacuation was not yet possible for Howard and the others

wounded that day. For as long as there was a glimmer of light their position was being raked with fire: it was just too unsafe. The wounded men were laid down in the lee of trenches or fallen trees and their comrades just willed the night to come. Even then, there was a horrible surprise.

Frost's adjutant had put together a resupply party, several men who would lead mules laden with ammunition and food up from the valley behind them as soon as it was dark. They could then begin the evacuation of the wounded as well. But, as the supply train was close to the hilltop, a salvo of enemy mortar shells fell among them. As soon as the barrage was over, Forsyth raced back to help the survivors, only to find a scene of carnage, men and beasts blown apart, their remains mingled: 'What a bloody mess,' he remembered. Finding one of the victims groaning and limbless on the ground, Forsyth collected some syrettes of morphine and helped him on his way into the next world.

It didn't stop there; a stretcher party carrying back one of that day's wounded trod on a mine, and that produced another four casualties. So ended a wretched day for the battalion, and for A Company in particular. Nine men had been killed and dozens wounded.

The following day, 9 March, there were intermittent stonks from enemy mortar. Several men were wounded, but they considered that a good day. The 1st Parachute Brigade, supported by 70th Field Regiment, Royal Artillery, returned this fire with interest. The soldiers of the 1st and 2nd Battalions carried on digging in, trying to carve some more depth in the holes dug by the Lincolns, or get some new positions in to face the likely infiltration routes.

They had also started thinking in practical terms about how to neutralize the crushing fire that the German Spandaus could bring to bear. The two machine guns brought in by Lieutenant Timothy's raid would help, but more needed to be done. The Bren, the British Army's standard light machine gun, was highly accurate and the paratroopers had already used it to suppress MG42s or

MG34s on occasion. However, the men in A Company came up with another tactic on Djebel Diss.

Sergeant Frank Lyoness had tired of the enemy's light machine guns raking their position, and after another failed attempt to silence one vowed, 'I'll get the bastard somehow.' He decided to use a Boys anti-tank rifle against enemy Spandau crews. It was a fearsome weapon to employ against another person, but Lyoness, one of the original A Company fighting Irish, didn't care too much about that. With a mass more than four times that of the rounds fired by their Brens and rifles, the Boys' 13.9mm bullet could penetrate an earthen parapet or sandbag and take a man's limb or head off.

That afternoon Lyoness spotted a four-man Spandau team moving up to a new position several hundred metres to their front. He drew a bead on one of them, and, with an ear-splitting crack, let fly. He pushed the bolt forward again and fired a second time. Then again. Three of the four enemy soldiers had been felled and were quite still. That night a patrol was sent out, successfully recovering their Spandau and some belts of ammunition.

After a couple of days in the position, A Company had added another light machine gun to their stash, giving a total of four Spandaus with which to face the enemy. Having taken these weapons, the company was no longer at a disadvantage in firepower. 'We were like a fortress with those machine guns,' one member of the company recalled.

The following day, after a timeout to reconsider tactics and reorganize, there was another concerted attempt to take the 1st Parachute Brigade's positions. That morning, the British were heavily shelled by mortars and field guns. Crouching in their trenches as the shells burst, sending red-hot metal fragments zizzing through the air, the paratroopers longed for it to stop but knew that, when it did, another assault would come in.

They were occupying their trenches for the third day, and the reddish soil had thoroughly rubbed off on their clothes and flesh. Some of their foxholes were beginning to get waterlogged too, as the freezing rain made their lives even more uncomfortable. Any activity such as cooking, or leaving a trench to defecate, became highly dangerous during the hours of daylight.

Around 1 p.m. the fire slackened and groups of enemy troops were spotted moving through the trees and along the gullies, coming towards them. The soldiers thrown against them came from the Fallschirm-Pionier Abteilung and Fallschirm-Regiment Barenthin, two airborne units of the Luftwaffe. The combat engineer unit was led by none other than Rudolf Witzig, a hero of the Eben-Emael raid, where a few dozen of his men had overwhelmed an allegedly impregnable Belgian fortress in 1940, and the Barenthin regiment was an amalgam of paratroopers and other picked men.

These soldiers pressed home their attacks against the 1st and 2nd Battalions with vigour and skill, but the assaults were broken up by the use of artillery and machine-gun fire. By nightfall the situation had stabilized, although the enemy had managed to push forward in the gap between the two battalions and had caused significant losses to the British. The 2nd Battalion had seven men killed and twenty-six wounded that day, another heavy blow.

The brigade commander, Edwin Flavell, had been growing increasingly nervous during the day, feeling his troops were too stretched out and were slowly but surely being ground down. His mood was not helped by his own HQ being shelled. Flavell had visited their divisional commander in the morning, 'to represent the seriousness of their situation', and by evening was telling him by radio that, 'unless more troops were provided, a general withdrawal . . . would become necessary'.

Flavell had been feeding troops from Pine-Coffin's 3rd Battalion up onto the hills in support of his other two units, but that evening much larger numbers became available as another brigade was effectively put under his command.

Forsyth and the rest of A Company were holding on, just about. They received some help from an unexpected quarter also that day. A second Stuka strike went in, but hit the lines of the German attackers, causing significant casualties. The attackers had received an ugly lesson in the mixed blessing of air support.

Early on the 11th a troop of four Churchill tanks from the North Irish Horse advanced up the hill, onto Djebel Diss and then into the gap to the 2nd Battalion's left, strafing the troopers from the Barenthin regiment with machine-gun fire. The tanks had some success in pushing back the Germans from the tongue of ground they had taken between Flavell's two forward parachute battalions.

Even so, the extended nature of the 1st Parachute Brigade's front and the thinning out of its units through casualties meant that at night small parties of Germans could infiltrate the British line, exploring behind it and down into the Sedjenane valley. This produced many strange encounters in the darkness.

One member of A Company, trudging back down the slope behind their positions to get a bullet wound treated at the regimental aid post, noticed a group of nine men moving back up from the valley. As he strained his eyes in the darkness he realized they were enemy. Although they were close enough to talk to him, they let him pass, a single wounded man, without anything being said, let alone any violence. A little later the wounded paratrooper passed a mule team going up to resupply the 2nd Battalion, telling them to keep their eyes peeled for Germans. Minutes later there was a clatter of fire as the two parties moving through the night engaged one another.

Reinforced by some regular infantry battalions, tanks and French troops, the parachute brigade managed to hold on to the line of hills day after day. Life in their trenches was utterly wretched, a daily round of sudden death, wet feet, cold food and red mud. Rooted to the ground in this hellish routine, the paratroopers were treated to petty injunctions from brigade headquarters.

Shortly before going into the position, orders from brigade had been passed down to them, including, 'particular attention will be paid to saluting both in and out of the line'. Rules had also been set about headgear, saying that steel helmets must be worn during daylight, not 'cap comforters', the woolly lids that they often preferred, or berets turned inside out. The soldiers avoided drawing attention to themselves in daytime by wearing their red berets inside out; having the black liner facing outwards was less conspicuous and a good deal more comfortable.

This was against regulations, but 'Officers and men alike were "Bolshy" because the alternative head-wear was the parachute helmet and to ask them to wear those throughout the twelve hours of daylight was unreasonable,' an officer of the 3rd Battalion remembered. 'We were all very angry at this stupidity.' In this battalion matters were exacerbated by their RSM, John Lord, who 'was a stickler for Guards style discipline'.

Lord's practice of carrying out kit inspections even in the midst of the Tunisian battles rankled. 'The men considered themselves to be fighting soldiers not parade ground types,' an NCO from the 2nd Battalion recalled. 'Consequently there was always friction.' On one of these occasions a grenade dropped in front of RSM Lord and everyone dived for cover. After an agonizing few seconds it became clear the pin was still in, and that someone wanted to send their regimental sergeant major a message.

For his counterpart Forsyth in their sister battalion it was a different bit of small-minded officialdom that rankled. Each night he oversaw the resupply of the company and removal of its casualties. The dead men were carried down in their issued blankets, remaining wrapped in them as they were lowered into graves. But Forsyth was told to recover these unconventional shrouds: 'We said, "We'll use a blanket. If he's not worth a blanket then what's the use of fighting?" We just ignored it.' Forsyth despised those who had issued the order.

As the days wore on, A Company was whittled away. Around a hundred men had gone into the line on 8 March, but a week later they were down to forty. Some sections had only a couple of men left. Slapsey Brayley found himself in acting command after Major Lane joined the casualty list. It was Forsyth, though, who remained the steely backbone among that band of survivors.

Private Lou Lewis had been suffering with the rest of B Company, just to the rear of A. 'It felt then as if the world had never been anything else but mud and shellfire, gunfire, standing in the cold. This terrible tension about whether you were going to be hit and if you were hit whether it would be clean or nasty.' All thoughts of escaping his East End origins had given way to the overwhelming imperative of survival.

On 16 March neighbouring units sighted enemy troop-carrying lorries moving up in the distance. This was the harbinger of assaults the following day. With the expectation of a further trial, Lieutenant Spender crouched in his trench, writing a letter home. He had not long before received one from the girl he left behind, Dorothy (Bobby) Ferens, announcing her engagement to an officer at the training establishment where Spender and she had met several months earlier.

'Bobby I gather has jilted me pretty roughly for another Battle Drill instructor,' he wrote on the 16th to his parents. 'Of course all of this was pretty bad for me, especially as I received and read her letter literally under and in fire.' Spender joked that the fury ignited by this rejection would now be directed at 'the Hun'. Putting a brave face once again on the hell of Cork Wood, he told them, 'I am extremely happy and as fighting is to be, I must say I like it. I have killed more Huns than anyone in my company and certainly more than any other officer. Don't I love myself!'

The hour of his departure from this blasted djebel was, however, drawing closer. On 17 March the 2nd Battalion, although pinned down by artillery fire, did not receive a direct attack. Rather, the weight of it fell on the 5th Sherwood Foresters to their north and French troops to the south.

Throughout the 17th the pitch of these attacks built, with shelling, Stuka strikes and infantry infiltrating Allied positions. At 6.30 p.m. the Foresters reported that 'it would not be possible to hold present positions much longer' and fifteen minutes later, the headquarters of 1st Parachute Brigade recorded, 'Foresters went off the air.'

The 2nd Parachute Battalion was one of the few bastions of the Allied defence holding firm, but with men streaming back on both flanks and German troops appearing on the plain behind them, attacking the Royal Artillery gun lines, it was apparent that the time to leave was approaching. In the event, it was not until just after 8 a.m. the following day that Frost was given the order to withdraw his men from the blasted hilltop that they had held for ten days.

For those grateful to be moving out, the relief was to be short-lived. Frost had determined that the brigade, heading down in company groups to the valley floor, should walk along the stream that flowed there: the Oued el Glia. The idea of taking this route, the men cursing it as they plunged knee-deep into the freezing water, was that the river's high banks would give them cover. And soon enough, the enemy observers, gaining the heights they had not long vacated, began to register shell and mortar fire on the column of men they could see moving to the south-west along the river.

'Johnny Frost on the other hand walked along the bank calling encouragement and urging us on like the cox of a university boat crew,' noted one of the soaked officers. 'Just how he survived the shellfire only the angels know and even they must remain mystified.'

Each man, sloshing forward, shrapnel flying past, just tried to keep putting one foot in front of the other. Private Lewis struggled to hold his trousers up, his braces having broken on the way down to the river, fuming at the situation he now found himself in.

Others got through the ordeal with humour, their withdrawal that morning living on in battalion folklore as the march 'up shit creek'. Lieutenant Timothy, walking beside Lieutenant Dicky Spender, found that he really did have a verse for every occasion. After another artillery round roared in but failed to go off, Spender remarked drily, 'thud, in the mud, another dud, thank Gud'.

At least a quarter of the shells proved likewise ineffectual, leading to a theory among the paratroopers that the ammunition, made by slave labour, had been deliberately sabotaged. They felt losses could have been much higher otherwise. Even so, that day's withdrawal had a price: two killed, eleven wounded and five missing. The ten days on that infernal djebel had cost the 2nd Battalion more than 150 casualties.

It was after nightfall when they reached their new positions. The brigade had taken up a defensive stance on a group of low hills that they dubbed 'The Pimples'. It was hoped that they would not have to fight for this new position, rather that the paratroopers might get a week or two out of the line, and this hope was granted them.

The first phase of this battle had been very costly to both sides, with reinforcements required to maintain its pitch as casualties mounted. The attacks on 1st Parachute Brigade had cost the Axis forces more than 800 prisoners as well as the killed and wounded. And for what? The sense strategically was that their local attacks could only buy time before the numbers of the Allied armies would eventually overwhelm them.

On the Eastern Front, meanwhile, the Germans had suffered their shattering defeat at Stalingrad. They were hardly in a position to send even more troops to North Africa. Yet the Sedjenane valley had been contested with extreme violence and all the skill that the elite troops on either side could bring to the fight. It had been draining for all involved and it was not over.

For the soldiers, a mobile bath unit provided healing hot showers and freshly laundered battledress. Dozens of them reported sick, with many suffering from trench foot, a consequence of weeks spent in damp dugouts without removing their boots.

Spirits were restored somewhat on 22 March when lorries were drummed up to take them to Tabarka, not far away on the coast, where there was enough spring warmth for them to bathe in the sea and feel the sun on their wracked bodies.

Meanwhile, Frost set to work writing to the next of kin of those who had fallen in defence of a barren hilltop in Tunisia. He found it a wretched and solitary business.

In an attempt to raise morale and create a more normal atmosphere, he set up a field officers' mess at a disused iron mine on the valley floor. Chairs were found or knocked up from loose timber, a kitchen established, newspapers even appeared and for the first time in many weeks there was a kind of decent daily regime. Whisky and gin were consumed in copious quantities and the nightly mess banter included many discussions about 'The Book'.

It had been the habit during the fights of the previous two months for officers to discuss who would die in the next battle, suffer a wound or come through unscathed, jotting these predictions in a notebook. Taking a sip of Scotch, they would discuss their imminent fate with equanimity, one recording, 'men do strange things when under constant stress'. Hearing this apparently light-hearted discussion of imminent doom, Frost was unamused. He ordered them to stop the practice, suspecting that before long its predictions would be put to the test again. He was right.

10. Red Devils

The 2nd Battalion's peaceful interlude was indeed short-lived. Just three days after their sea-bathing excursion, Lieutenant Colonel Frost found himself attending an Orders Group at the brigade headquarters, where instructions were issued for a series of attacks by 1st Parachute Brigade and its heterodox cast of supporting elements, including a battalion of Moroccan Goumiers.

The previous days had been a grim time for Geoffrey Pine-Coffin and his 3rd Battalion. While the 2nd was out of the line, Alastair Pearson's 1st Battalion had been given the task of retaking the 'Pimple' features, and then Pine-Coffin's that of holding them. The exposed hillsides were so rocky that digging in was impossible, and on 22 March 1943 Pine-Coffin's soldiers had been forced off a hill the troops had nicknamed the 'Bowler Hat' by German attacks.

Despite this local setback, their boss, Flavell, was now under orders from above to mount a large-scale attack in an attempt to regain the Sedjenane valley so that its road and railway might be restored to Allied control and a push made along the feature to Tamera. Supplications that the brigade was too exhausted to undertake such a major assault cut no mustard with the generals. Rather, they felt, the paratroopers' fighting qualities that had been so firmly established during the previous weeks made them the best people for the job.

In a letter to his parents, Richard Spender had written of the recent fighting, 'The general feeling behind the line is, I hear, that we've done a sort of Historic Thing.' He joked that he would rather not be part of history, given the privations involved.

To his brother, a fellow officer, he gave a more brutal account of the battle just passed and the one they now knew lay ahead: 'This place is absolute hell. Everybody gets knocked off 'mid scenes of

99

utter wet cold misery and still up we come for another bloodbath. Could you get me transferred out?' Spender joked, suggesting as posts that might be suitable: cook, parachute instructor, camouflage officer (theory only), Press representative or brigadier.

The 1st and 3rd Battalions had received some reinforcements in mid-March, but Frost's unit had not been so fortunate and its effective strength, as it contemplated this tough new mission, was around only 300 men. Frost had harboured some hopes that they might be returned to a parachuting role after their period out of the line, and was disappointed when the order came to move up to assault positions on 26 March.

While relieving the 3rd Battalion on the way, Frost's mood had been soured further by what he considered to be an inadequate handover by its boss, Geoffrey Pine-Coffin. The Scot and the Devonian had never had the best of relationships, and Frost considered that Pine-Coffin's inability to tell him which enemy units lay to his front showed a lack of professionalism. For his part, Pine-Coffin was exhausted and felt the frequent practice of assigning his companies to Frost's or Pearson's command during the previous weeks had left him little opportunity to show what he or his battalion could do.

Both men had stayed on good terms with Alastair Pearson, who had emerged in Tunisia as the outstanding commander in the brigade. He had picked up the Distinguished Service Order in February, and would be recommended for a repeat award, or bar to his DSO, just weeks later for his leadership in the Sedjenane valley battles.

Pearson was a few years younger than the other two and he was not a regular army officer. His ability to inspire the wide variety of men who came under his command in a national service army earned him the admiration of many, including his two fellow battalion commanders. 'He was one of those "amateur" soldiers who found their true quality on the battlefield,' one of Pine-Coffin's officers who'd been attached to the 1st Battalion wrote admiringly of Pearson. 'He was clear in his perception of any problem facing him and was never cluttered by traditional teaching although he

did not ignore it; moreover he appeared to be completely uncon-
cerned for his personal safety.'

Although both Frost and Pine-Coffin also showed great bravery, they could not quite match Pearson's blend of tactical grip and
informality with subordinates. And if Pearson was by acclamation
the star, they could vie for second place. Who knew, after all,
when one or other of them might perish?

As the brigade moved back onto the offensive, this complex blend
of comradeship and rivalry played out at lower levels also. Two of
Frost's lieutenants in B Company contended for promotion to a
vacant captaincy and wanted the honour of leading the battalion's
assault up one of the djebels that now lay to their front, so decided
to resolve it by the toss of a coin. The 'honour' went to Lieutenant
Victor Dover, who was not long arrived.

The plan they had to carry out on that night of 27 March
involved pushing across the Oued el Glia stream ('Shit Creek' to
the men who had walked up it several days before) and up onto an
enemy-held hill. The following day they would attack a second
upland position, called Sidi Mohammed, clearing the Germans
from it, then withstand the inevitable counter-attack.

Their advance, scheduled for 10 p.m., started an hour late. It
was a moonless night, and to prevent soldiers becoming disorientated Frost's command party would lay a white tape as it moved
uphill to mark the battalion's axis of advance. As they finally
moved off, a great barrage of covering artillery fire began, the 25-
pounders from divisional batteries firing over their heads as they
walked up. C Company was in the centre, leading, with A to its
left and B to its right.

It didn't take long for the platoon to walk into a minefield,
injuring Dover and six others. It was not going to be an easy night.
For Lou Lewis, the screeching of so many shells going overhead
was overwhelming. He glanced over his shoulder to see the gun
line off behind them, 'twinkling' as the artillery pieces spewed
their projectiles forward.

Finding himself on flatter ground, and among some enemy

trenches, Frost got C Company to clear them, sending several prisoners back down the hill. It was so dark that he feared people becoming disorientated, so he gathered in the other two companies. The objective had been achieved, or so he thought.

Counter-attacks by German troops started almost straight away, flares going up and streams of tracer racing over their heads in the darkness. But at first light things became a good deal more serious. Frost 'realized with growing horror' that what he had thought was the top of the hill was in fact a shelf some way below it, and that their enemy would now be able to fire down at them from the summit. Frost sent men to the left in an attempt to find an alternative to a frontal assault on the enemy machine guns above, but the defenders soon tried to settle the issue their own way.

From around 8 a.m. the Germans started to develop a counter-attack spearheaded by Witzig's paratrooper sappers. Groups of Fallschirmjäger began working their way downhill through the oak groves, engaging the British wherever they could see them. Casualties were ticking up in the 2nd Battalion.

By 10.30 the situation was 'becoming critical'. Frost sent word to the few officers still standing: the men should fix bayonets and charge the enemy on a signal from his hunting horn. He found that the mere order to ready the cold steel 'struck a wonderful note', raising the weary spirits of his troops.

It didn't prove necessary to go in with bayonets; instead Dicky Spender, the battalion poet who had just been made up to captain, led one attack in. It was to be his final act of bravery, for, closing on the machine gun with three other paratroopers, Spender was killed by a burst of fire. Elsewhere, 'A Company rose to their feet and firing from the hip with Brens, Stens, rifles, and even a Boys anti-tank rifle, added such a weight to the mortar and shell fire that even the tough Witzig parachute engineers could not face it.'

Forward observers meanwhile brought artillery fire down, at times just a hundred metres from Frost's forward positions, the shell impacts deafening them, sending the concussion from each blast right through their bodies. In some places, though, shells dropped short, flaying British troops with shrapnel.

With the situation critical and losses mounting, Flavell sent a company of 3rd Battalion up to reinforce the 2nd as they sought to expel Witzig's men from the cork trees. As these new men came up, they misread the confused melee in the woods, opening fire on B Company. The similarity of dress between the two nations' paratroopers, both wearing smocks and rounded helmets, counted against them in these critical moments.

Throwing himself to the ground, Lewis felt bullets kicking up the earth inches from his head. There were calls of 'Wahoo Mohammed' that morning – a parachute brigade battle cry – as the men sought to raise their spirits and identify themselves in the woods. But this did not stop the firing from the 3rd Battalion.

Then one of Lewis's NCOs took his life in his hands. Realizing that nothing less would convince those shooting that they were making an awful mistake, he stepped out from behind the cover of a tree, showing himself clearly while calling out to the new men to cease fire. This act of extraordinary sangfroid, something no enemy would do, 'saved the day', thought Lewis as the 3rd Battalion at last stopped firing.

Lewis and the other survivors in his platoon then moved up the slope in an attempt to drive the Germans back, but soon they were under withering fire, sending him onto his stomach again, trying to use the narrow stem of a tree to protect his head from the incoming bullets. Much as he might have willed himself smaller, Lewis felt a 'hammer blow', as one of the rounds struck his leg. The shock of it knocked him slightly out of line with the tree and, moments later, he took another bullet, in the arm, 'and I thought if I stay here I'll never get out alive'. One of his mates from jump training came forward to help, but Lewis told him to stay back for his own safety.

Lewis managed to roll away from the tree, and carried on rolling painfully across the hard ground until he was in a less exposed position. There, a medic crouched over him, pouring disinfectant sulphanilamide powder on the wounds and clamping on dressings. Men could not be spared to stretcher away the many casualties the assault force had taken, so those who could walk were pointed in the direction of their regimental aid post (RAP), back down the hill, and sent on their way.

Limping towards safety, Lewis realized his whole leg was red with blood, and so much of it had flowed that his foot squelched in its boot, but 'I didn't give a damn, I was out of it.'

Many of those coming off the hill that day encountered the regimental medical officer, Captain Ronald 'Flash' Gordon. This gruff Scot had a bedside manner well suited to the airborne forces. Another member of Lewis's company, Private David Brooks, also shot in the leg, was asked by Gordon for the syrette of morphine each of them carried. It soon became apparent it was for someone else.

'Aren't you going to give me that?' asked Brooks.

'You don't bloody need it, laddie,' Gordon replied, 'you're not bad enough'. He then told Brooks to walk down to the RAP.

'I can't get down there,' Brooks protested, eyeing the steep slope.

'You bloody well can, because nobody else is going to take you.'

Yet another soldier had approached the MO with one of his hands hanging by some threads of flesh. 'Look at this sir!' said the soldier, expecting help. Gordon produced a pair of scissors and snipped it off unceremoniously, telling the casualty, 'Sorry, I'm afraid you'll have to lose that, lad.'

Lewis made his way to the next waypoint for wounded men, the main dressing station, where medics were using an Arab hut as a triage point. Already faint and thirsty through loss of blood, he was given a cup of sweet tea 'that tasted like nectar'. From this point the wounded were loaded into ambulances and packed off for surgery at a field hospital.

As he made his way down the casualty evacuation chain, Lewis heard the crushing news that Fred Selman, the friend whose mother had prepared their farewell tea in Wiltshire early the previous autumn, had been killed by a British shell that had dropped short onto B Company's positions. And later, once he was coming round from surgery, he realized that the other mate who'd enjoyed that memorable day out, the South African Chalky White, was lying next to him, a critical case, having taken a serious abdominal wound by enemy mortar fire.

Lewis was one of scores of 2nd Battalion men who were treated in the army medical system that month. Some were patched up in field hospitals or in places set aside for the 'battle stress' cases relatively near to the front line before being sent back. Others, including Lewis, with serious bullet or shrapnel wounds got sent back hundreds of miles to the main hospital outside Algiers. There, Lewis found big venereal-disease wards, where there were 'as many [troops] with VD as there were, shall we say, legally!'

Bill Bloys, an A Company soldier from Essex who had been shot during the Cork Wood fighting, ended up in the same hospital outside the Algerian capital. Soon after evacuation, one of the nurses treating him in a field hospital told Bloys, 'You are the filthiest person I've ever seen.' His smock and trousers were stained with the red soil of the Sedjenane valley, he had a heavy growth of stubble and dried blood caked his kit.

While Bloys was in this forward hospital he had been treated by a German medical orderly, a prisoner of war who helped look after the wounded soldiers of both sides. This man, who spoke good English, told Bloys, 'We call you lot the Red Devils.' It wasn't about the beret, but the mark of the Tunisian soil and their wild spirit in battle.

Back in the hills above the road to Tamera the depleted 2nd Battalion fought on. On the evening of 28 March, Frost had combined all of the fighting remnants into a single company. Two companies from the 3rd Battalion had been attached to him also, another example of the practice that irked Pine-Coffin.

Early the following day, Frost sent a patrol out under Slapsey Brayley to see whether any enemy soldiers remained on top of the Sidi Mohammed feature. Brayley was by this point an acting captain, and the only one of A Company's officers still in the line. As he moved up to reconnoitre, other elements fanned out through the cork groves, mopping up enemy soldiers, taking the odd stragglers here and there.

The day was not without casualties caused by dropping mortar rounds or odd bursts of fire from those still contesting the position. But the furious violence unleashed by Witzig's men the previous day had abated. They'd had enough. Brayley soon reported back that the top of the hill was free of the enemy, so Frost moved up to secure his objective.

During the three days of fighting, the 2nd Battalion had suffered sixteen killed and sixty-three wounded. When the attached elements from the 3rd and elsewhere were added in, the toll was considerably higher. Frost's battalion itself could count only ten officers and 160 other ranks fighting fit at the end of this battle. They didn't know how many of the enemy they had claimed, but fifty-eight German prisoners had been taken, some of them reporting that Witzig had personally led the attack on the 28th. One of Frost's men joked that he should make Witzig second in command of their battalion.

Although the German doctrinal imperative to counter-attack was very strong, the broken amalgam of units opposite 1st Parachute Brigade was no longer capable of it. The vicious struggle over the barren hills of the Sedjenane valley, a contest to delay the inevitable for Axis forces in Tunisia, had closed. But those who had survived the battles of March 1943 were deeply marked by them.

The casualty-handling system worked in two directions, and, just after the fighting had ended, Allan Johnstone, Brayley's platoon sergeant, returned to A Company after treatment for a shrapnel wound to the jaw suffered in Cork Wood nearly three weeks earlier. Johnstone, who had himself been hospitalized with 'battle stress' in January, noted, 'the war seemed to have receded and everyone was slightly crazy'.

Johnstone had heard Maxie Forsyth speaking ill of Dick Ashford, the major who had been killed in February. Ashford's heroism on the Oudna raid and retreat meant that he was widely esteemed in the company, but that seemed to count for very little with the sergeant major, something Johnstone put down to 'the tensions and resentments that develop within a unit under active service conditions'.

Alan Moorehead, a war correspondent who visited 1st Parachute Brigade at this time, was taken aback by what he found. Having been struck by the stench of death from the unburied bodies in the oak groves around their position, he turned his eye to the soldiers themselves.

'In their whole approach to death these young men had completely altered,' he wrote. 'These men were soaked in war. They were grown old to war in a few weeks and all the normal uses of peace and the ambitions of peace were entirely drained out of them.' Alluding to the savagery of what had passed, he noted that the paratroopers 'were feared by the Italians – and by the Germans – as the most terrible animals'.

In this last formulation, Moorehead may have been influenced by some printed German orders found on a prisoner during the Cork Wood fight and shared among the 2nd Battalion officers: 'The British Parachutists are the toughest and hardest fighting troops in Tunisia today. They are Devils. If you should meet them, go carefully.'

Inevitably, as preparations were made for the relief of the brigade by American troops, there was anger at the grievous cost suffered by their battalions in a battle to which standard infantry units, with their greater numbers and more powerful support elements, would have been better suited.

Some focused their ire on Edwin Flavell, their brigadier, a First World War soldier who had presided over the squandering of a precious resource: the army's airborne volunteers of 1940–41. 'He took out with him a magnificent brigade and he frittered it away,' one paratrooper officer considered. 'He didn't have really any idea of how to operate airborne troops.'

Of course, those working with Flavell in brigade headquarters would have argued the point, putting the emphasis on the relentless demands made by divisional and corps commanders. In the last days of March, the exhausted paratroopers were ordered into action with further mopping up in the hills. 'We hardly know what to think,' one of Flavell's staff wrote at the time. 'It is like a crucifixion of the brigade,' he added, noting that 1st Parachute

Brigade had taken 800 prisoners in March and the other two, 'unconscionably slow', brigades in their division just seven.

An atmosphere of recrimination extended to the ranks and focused on leaders closer to home too. There was enormous grief for mates lost or broken. The survivors in 2nd Battalion knew that, through a combination of the Oudna fiasco and later fighting, those among them who had set sail from Scotland in November were now in the minority.

Private Lewis, recovering in hospital from his wounds, felt Frost bore his share of blame. There were rumours that the withdrawal from the Djebel Diss feature had happened in daylight because Frost was too drunk to be roused during the night. This charge was unfounded, but its currency among the soldiers showed that they were aware of Frost's weakness for whisky.

For the 1st Parachute Brigade's two most celebrated Scots, alcohol undoubtedly served to alleviate the stress of their many weeks in the line and sending so many fine men to their deaths. One paratrooper major who arrived in Algeria that spring noted, 'if anyone was more regularly drunk than Alastair Pearson, it was John Frost'.

When the brigade was moved out of the line in April, heading by stages back to Boufarik, less than fifty kilometres south-west of Algiers, everyone was given the opportunity to lose themselves in alcohol with a seventy-two-hour pass. The excesses can be imagined: men who had survived against the odds, cut loose in an orgy of drink and fornication. Frost noted, 'some elements made life extremely difficult for the military police'.

In Stratford-upon-Avon, Lieutenant Spender's parents had received the War Office telegram that so many dreaded: 'Deeply regret to inform you of report received from North Africa that Captain R. W. O. Spender Army Air Corps was killed in action on 28 March 1943. The Army Council desire to offer you their sincere sympathy.'

A little later, his father's last letter was returned to sender. Written on the morning that his son was killed, it signed off, 'Take care of yourself and God Bless you, lots of love from your affectionate Daddy.' The unopened message, had 'addressee is reported deceased' written on the envelope. This family's tragedy mirrored hundreds of others whose paratrooper sons had set out from Britain the previous November.

It was already becoming clear to those running the parachute brigade that its withdrawal to Algiers marked the end of its campaign in North Africa and the beginning of preparation for the next. One of the Parachute Regiment's early historians (and later commander of the 9th Battalion), Terence Otway, estimated that the 1st Parachute Brigade had taken 3,500 prisoners and caused 5,000 enemy casualties during the months between arriving in November 1942 and winding up operations five months later. During this odyssey they had suffered 1,700 casualties of their own. Otway argued that the weather, distances and terrain had all been fearsome. 'Add these factors to a tenacious, brave and well-trained enemy . . . and some measure of the great tasks which the brigade accomplished can be realized.'

At the time, the men who returned from Tunisia thanked the Lord for their survival, and those who led them wondered whether the next great move of the war would at last allow them to employ parachuting on a grand scale, and to prove the concept of airborne forces. What few of them had realized was that, while many had considered their campaign in Tunisia a profligate misuse of such a specialized corps, it had in fact established their reputation with their enemies as hard-fighting elite troops. One of the pioneers summed up the importance of the North African episode succinctly: 'that is where the Parachute Regiment made its name'.

As the 1st Parachute Brigade returned from the front to Algiers in April 1943, it was clear that it would have to be rebuilt, and that many other units needed to arrive, familiarize themselves with the Mediterranean and train with the mostly green aircrews. All this was being done with one aim in mind: to provide a large airborne element for the next stage of the war: the invasion of Sicily, codenamed Operation Husky.

Around that time, General Harold Alexander, commanding the entire British army group in North Africa, wrote to Brigadier

Flavell. Whether word had spread from prisoners and men they came into contact with is unclear, but by this point the Axis view of the paratroopers had become firmly fixed. 'They', the general wrote, 'have proved their mastery over the enemy who have a wholesome respect for this famous brigade, which is best described in their own words for them – The Red Devils.'

11.   Arrivals and Departures

A few weeks after his evacuation from the front, Private Lewis made his way to the Hotel Aletti in Algiers. It was a stylish building, an art-deco pile with a casino and fine dining. The Aletti was a place of assignations, where officers, businessmen and courtesans plied the lobby.

As he stepped into this other world, the wounds that had taken Lewis out of the fight were far less painful, but he remained on the books of the military hospital and did not yet consider himself fully fighting fit. The young soldier went to the bar and ordered a glass of muscat, then looked about for a place to sit.

Lewis was in uniform, with his airborne flash and red beret. By this time the Army Air Corps badge was being replaced by the distinctive new insignia of the Parachute Regiment. He took in the busy scene, savouring the sights, smells and tastes of survival. The chilled white wine seemed sublime, and he reflected, 'I will never ever complain, having got this far and survived, complain about anything ever in my life again.'

The mood was upbeat, the weather pleasantly warm without being oppressive, and the conflict in North Africa had come to an end. On 13 May 1943 Axis forces surrendered in Tunis, more than a quarter of a million of their men having been taken prisoner. The Red Army was achieving great success also. There was a sense of Allied momentum.

Lewis's reverie was disturbed by a captain who had appeared at his shoulder. Telling the private to remain seated, the man asked, 'You're one of those Red Devils we've been hearing about aren't you?' Lewis had learned on the grapevine that a team of photographers was being formed to accompany the airborne division into its next fight. Lewis had left word at the unit's office that he could be found at the Aletti Bar, and the captain had come to find him.

As the conversation progressed, a few things became clear: first, that the Army Film and Photographic Unit, or AFPU, had plenty of good photographers, but none of them wanted to do parachute training; second, that Lewis's boyhood dream of becoming a graphic artist might find fulfilment through photography; and third, if he played his cards right, this captain could take him directly from the hospital strength to that of the AFPU without him returning to B Company. Given the small number of surviving early volunteers in the battalion, Lewis had a feeling that if he went back to his battalion they would never let him go.

So, the decisions were taken quite smartly. Lewis would be very glad to join if they would have him, and the captain was delighted to find someone to fulfil his bosses' directives that the AFPU literally needed to be able to jump into action. And it got better for Lewis: he was swiftly promoted to sergeant, with the pay increase that implied, and would be taught how to operate a cine camera. The camerawork appealed to his creative instincts.

The AFPU team was one small element of the airborne force that was beginning to concentrate in North Africa. Having been the sole British representatives during those months of hard fighting, 1st Parachute Brigade would now witness the arrival of two similar formations, an airlanding brigade (the troops who would fly into the assault by glider), forming together the 1st Airborne Division, and an entire US airborne division, the 82nd. In addition to these tens of thousands of hand-picked troops, hundreds of additional aeroplanes and gliders had begun to collect on airfields from Algiers to Tunis as part of the preparation for Operation Husky.

The leadership of the 1st Parachute Brigade was to be entrusted to new hands. Flavell was out, to be replaced by Brigadier Gerald Lathbury, eight years his junior and an early volunteer for airborne forces as well as founding CO of the 3rd Battalion. The vicissitudes of an officer career in the British Army at this time were such that there were numerous people in the chain of command who could engineer the rapid sacking of someone who was failing or showing insufficient deference to their orders or superiors.

This, in turn, was the fate of Lieutenant Colonel Geoffrey Pine-Coffin, who was removed from command of 3rd Parachute Battalion on 31 May, a few weeks after Lathbury's arrival. Writing to his family, Pine-Coffin put his fall down to 'my row with the brigadier'. The exact nature of this dispute was known only to the two men, but Pine-Coffin's annoyance at playing Cinderella to the other two battalions was clear, and like many others in the brigade he was exhausted after months of hard fighting.

Lathbury had inspected the battalions in his brigade early in May, soon after his arrival. As former commander of the 3rd, he regarded it with a certain degree of *amour propre*. He may also have felt that Pine-Coffin's 'humane' regime needed to give way to a more disciplinarian approach. Pine-Coffin in any case was out of the war, but not for long. There were still plenty of people in airborne forces who respected his abilities, feeling they would be needed as battalion after battalion was added to the Parachute Regiment in 1943. He would return to the story a few months later.

Major General Boy Browning had appeared in Algiers also, where he was to undertake the role of airborne forces adviser to Lieutenant General Eisenhower in the coming battle across the Mediterranean. Browning therefore had the ability to cast a close eye over a good part of his empire, as units gathered in North Africa.

Browning's success in raising troops and convincing the British military hierarchy that they must play a major role in the next 'big party' was bearing fruit at last. So many soldiers were needed for this great expansion that the system used to raise the first few battalions, by summoning volunteers from among the most intrepid adventurers and 'soldiers of fortune' in the army, had to give way to the conversion of existing battalions to the parachute or airlanding role. Those who did the jump training, becoming parachutists, formed additional battalions of the Parachute Regiment with its new cap badge from mid-1943 onwards, whereas the men destined to go into action by glider wore a red beret but with their original infantry badge (artillery or other supporting arm) and the unit retaining its name.

Thus the 2nd Parachute Brigade, which had started forming prior to the 1st's departure for Algeria in the autumn of 1942, but by June 1943 had joined them there, comprised the 4th Battalion (one of the original volunteer units), the 5th (converted from the Queen's Own Cameron Highlanders) and the 6th (a revamped territorial battalion of the Royal Welch Fusiliers). A further brigade, the 4th, combined a volunteer unit gathered in India two years earlier (by this point called the 156 Parachute Battalion), a further one of volunteers raised in the Middle East army (11th Parachute Battalion) and one converted from a unit of the Sussex Regiment (the 10th).

Two points were readily apparent to the veterans of 1st Parachute Brigade as this host gathered in May and June 1943. The first was that Browning, not for the first time, had excelled himself in producing more troops than the joint airlift capabilities of the RAF and US Army Air Forces would ever be able to drop in a single wave on Sicily. The second was that this unorthodox assortment of newly trained battalions would, inevitably, be suspect in the eyes of the men who had come through the Sedjenane valley battles. The newcomers lacked that hard combat experience and (the 4th and 156 Battalions aside) were not felt to be part of that precious cohort of early volunteers to the airborne tribe.

On 10 May, the 2nd Battalion moved from the balmy, garden-like atmosphere of Boufarik to a dusty camp south of a place called Mascara, hundreds of kilometres south-west. There, other elements of the 1st Airborne Division, as well as many squadrons of transport aircraft, were being concentrated and beginning the hard training needed to prepare them for Operation Husky. The men's mood was not improved when they discovered the 'liberation parade' in Mascara was to be led by the pipe band of the 5th Parachute Battalion, fresh from Salisbury Plain.

Watching the new arrivals, the old sweats of the 2nd Battalion 'were generally fiercely resentful of the smart appearance of 2nd Brigade'. Those who had just come out all had the new Parachute Regiment badge on their berets, whereas those who'd been at the sharp end, as is so often the way in armies, seemed to be the last to receive it.

Towards the end of May the battalion started trials with a new method of dropping its men into battle: with weapons like rifles and Bren guns attached to them and personal kitbags with other equipment likewise. Until that point, while Stens and pistols were carried while jumping, larger weapons, ammunition and much other kit went into containers attached to their own parachutes. Now the long weapons would be put into a padded bag strapped to the jumper – and the kitbag lowered on a length of rope once each man's parachute had opened. In this way the battalion hoped, particularly at night, to land each man immediately ready to fight instead of groping about in the dark looking for a container.

Mascara was the place where hundreds of new recruits were produced for the 2nd Battalion and other elements of the brigade ground down by the late campaign. Most of these soldiers, 250 in the case of the 2nd Battalion, were drafts from the infantry in air-landing units, who were teased by the survivors of Tunisia as 'Four Jumpers', because they had been given their parachute wings after that number of drops before leaving England, rather than the customary seven or eight.

Sergeant Allan Johnstone had to merge the new men into 2 Platoon: 'We had an uneasy mixture of a few battle-weary veterans and a lot of fresh, mostly very young reinforcements, whom we were told had to be licked into shape.' Frost, his CO, wrote, 'really hard, prolonged training was now the order of the day. We . . . concentrated on moving across country by day and by night, and in ensuring that everyone had as much practice as they possibly could at using their weapons.'

During breaks from training, the men headed into the bars of Mascara. For many of them, these hours outside the immediate limits of military discipline, and with alcohol flowing freely, were times for venting the emotions built up in Tunisia.

Sergeant Frank Lyoness, the Irishman who had taken down German machine gunners with an anti-tank rifle, would pick fights with anyone not in A Company, the 2nd Battalion or, if necessary, the 1st Parachute Brigade. Maxie Forsyth, who had been appointed by Frost to the lofty post of acting regimental sergeant major, was another one whose anger at recent events made him a dangerous drinking companion.

Maxie Forsyth suffered a 'fall from grace', after a night's drinking in Mostaganem, a coastal town where groups were taken for sea bathing during breaks in training. Going up to the cliffs overlooking the port in an inebriated rage, he set off the smoke pots intended to screen ships there in the event of an enemy air attack. This caused Frost to demote Forsyth from the RSM job, but worse was to come.

A Company was, by June, under the command of Major Richard Lonsdale as the brigade began a series of drops it called Exercise Cactus. These were jumps by entire battalions that were meant to prepare the men for their mission in Sicily. So they were done at night, with the troops forming up on the ground, marching to an objective and staging a mock attack.

Lonsdale had been an early volunteer for airborne training, which he had done in India as part of the battalion raised there. He was a regular army officer with pre-service on the North-West Frontier. Forsyth, who had marked the tenth anniversary of his enlistment in May, ought to have had much in common with Lonsdale, but, returning to A Company in querulous mood after being removed from the RSM post, soon took against him.

As the men went aloft in Dakotas one night, Forsyth looked down the darkened cabin to see Lonsdale taking long swigs from a hip flask. After they had completed the exercise, Forsyth confronted his OC. 'I said, "Look, sir, in this battalion we drink, we're heavy drinkers, but not when we're jumping. In the plane, no drink."' Lonsdale told him to mind his own business. Forsyth had seen a few officers lose their nerve in Tunisia and decided that his new company commander drank because he was afraid. A fuse had been lit.

The Cactus exercises were a time for binding new recruits into companies, but also practice for those who had not yet dropped into action. The engagements of November 1942 had been operations by single battalions, using forty to fifty planes. Browning wanted to use the entire 1st Airborne Division, and while he soon found himself in a tussle with the Americans over the availability of aircraft, plans were advanced to drop the whole 1st Parachute Brigade against a key target in Sicily. That would involve more than 1,800 troops and 116 aircraft. Adding support elements such as anti-tank guns would mean that gliders would also be part of the operation.

One of the units that hadn't dropped into action before was the brigade's signal squadron, and it was there, in June 1943, that Lance Corporal Arthur Maybury was serving. An east London boy who joined the regiment early and had served with Lou Lewis and Chalky White in B Company of the 2nd Battalion, Maybury had been transferred into the signal unit just before 1st Parachute Brigade sailed for Algeria.

Maybury had already managed to turn a profit on his service in airborne forces, selling stories aimed at younger readers to Hutchinson & Co., which published them under the pseudonym 'Pegasus'. The first of these, *Thrills with the Paratroops*, appeared that summer, mixing in tales of spies and saboteurs with the exploits of a parachute squad under training. Following his initial success, Maybury started to wonder whether he might be able to get an account of his real-life experiences past the censor.

Although the signallers had taken casualties during the Tunisian fighting, most served with brigade headquarters a few miles back from the front line, so it was generally a safer place to be. That had preserved Maybury, who decided, sitting under an olive tree between exercises, 'to offset the intolerable boredom of inactivity in rest areas . . . with the distraction of flies, mosquitoes, windblown dust and the inescapable sun', to write a book about those early volunteers. 'Tragically few of the originals are left now,' he noted, scribbling in pencil on scraps of paper he had been able to glean that he wanted to record their exploits, 'because in my opinion they cannot be praised too much'.

Maybury had a certain apprehension about jumping again, having broken his leg doing it in December 1941, but he willed himself on. He wasn't alone in his misgivings, and two signallers who refused to jump on Exercise Cactus were referred for later court-martialling. The attitude to 'jibbers' or those 'lacking moral fibre' (LMF) in the brigade was on the one hand one of understanding, in the sense that almost all would confess to being afraid sometimes before jumps, and on the other of expediency in that it was felt they should be punished and returned to their original units as quickly as possible, out of sight and out of mind.

The exact role the signallers would play in the forthcoming operation was known only to their officers at this point, but the training gave them a few clues. In addition to the radios needed for communication within the unit, known as 22 Sets, they would also have larger ones for speaking to the higher command and Royal Navy ships offshore (65 and 66 Sets, respectively). These were big wireless units that broke down into several components and, too heavy to be carried backpack-style, had to be landed with special handcarts so that the signallers could move them into position. They were delicate devices, with their valve technology, and did not react well to the impact of parachute landing, as veterans of Bruneval could attest. But the signallers took spare sets and declared themselves happy after the Cactus exercises that they would get enough of them working to establish effective communications.

During the last days of June, the many elements of the airborne armada wound up their training, moving several hundred kilometres east to the northern Tunisian coast, to a point much closer to their intended targets. The Allies were in the last days of preparing for a deployment of these forces on a scale quite unlike anything they had done before. Hundreds of transport aircraft were gathered in preparation, collecting on half a dozen dusty airstrips established around the towns of Sousse and Kairouan. The majority of these were American, but the RAF's 38 Wing also brought dozens of Albemarle and Stirling bombers out for the operation.

Operation Husky would involve the landing of large seaborne forces who would then head inland, their passage eased by the insertion of airborne troops who could seize key bridges, or way-lay enemy troops sent to counteract the sea landings. It would be a dry run for the invasion of Italy, and to an extent for the great enterprise that all commanders knew awaited them – the invasion of France. The war had reached that moment anticipated by the British chiefs of staff in their arguments of the previous year, when the taking of the strategic initiative would mean invasions, complete with airborne forces, developments that would end the arguments about whether big formations of parachute or glider troops were necessary.

However, just as the RAF chiefs conceded this point, another group equally immune to Boy Browning's mixture of charm and upper-class patronage came to the fore: the Americans. They were providing the great majority of the aircraft needed for Husky and did not intend to take second place to the British, even if Browning had Eisenhower's ear at headquarters.

'A running argument developed with General Browning as to how many planes were going to be allocated between my division and the British 1st Airborne Division,' wrote Major General Matthew Ridgway, commander of the 82nd Airborne, who thought Browning 'was in a position to exert undue influence'. This fraught relationship with the Americans, often over the allocation of planes, would define the second phase of Browning's command, just as that with the RAF had shaped the first.

The compromise plan involved flying the large available force across the Med in a phased airborne assault over four nights. Furthermore, as was apparent to many of those who'd been on the training exercises in June and early July, it also meant pressing into service many aircrews fresh from Stateside who really had little idea about what would be required of them.

Ridgway's first assault element, 3,400 troops carried by 266 C-47s, would be dropped on the night of 9/10 July just behind the beachhead on Sicily's south-west coast. That same night, the British 1st Airlanding Brigade would be used in a glider-borne operation in the south-east, a little over 2,000 men in 144 gliders, to capture a key bridge. The seaborne forces would then arrive.

The following night a further regimental combat team (or brigade, in British usage) of the 82nd would go in, along with the British 2nd Parachute Brigade, which had been given the objective of a bridge near Augusta. On the fourth night it would be the turn of the 1st Parachute Brigade to take the bridge at Primosole, a key point on the 8th Army's route of advance towards the city of Catania.

These were the plans known to senior commanders for some weeks and finally briefed by Lieutenant Colonel Johnny Frost on 7 July to the men of the 2nd Battalion in their bivouac just outside Kairouan. On the eve of such a big operation there were inevitably nerves and those in A Company had not been helped by the sudden disappearance of their sergeant major, Maxie Forsyth.

During the seventy-two hours off that their men were given after the conclusion of their pre-operational training, the drink had flowed, events had transpired and Frost had finally had to give Forsyth the choice of a court martial or a reduction to the rank of sergeant and return to unit. This would mean banishment from the Parachute Regiment to his original outfit, the Argyll and Sutherland Highlanders.

The animosity between Forsyth and his OC, Major Lonsdale, had built to the point that the Scotsman felt obliged to impart some home truths. After much drinking, Forsyth told the major, 'his backbone was the same colour as his shirt: yellow'. There is no record of whether the two men came to blows. Offered a court martial or RTU, Forsyth chose the latter, because he believed the officers involved in a military trial would close ranks around Lonsdale. So ended the airborne career of a Bruneval veteran, recipient of the Military Medal and man who, as acting RSM, Frost had chosen as a partner in the running of the battalion.

The first night's operation went ahead, the Dakotas circled over the Tunisian countryside as formations built up, then headed off north towards Malta, turning there to get on course for Sicily. Among the British spectators to this display of airpower, thoughts naturally focused on the soldiers of the airlanding brigade, most of them crammed into US-supplied Hadrian gliders, smaller and rather inferior to Horsas (there hadn't been time to deploy many of them to North Africa) and whose pilots, with the minimum of training on Hadrians, would soon be trying to land them on a six-pence in the undulating Sicilian countryside.

On 10 July, with the naval landings getting underway, Frost and the other high-ups in the 1st Parachute Brigade started to hear disturbing reports of what had happened to the glider troops, who not only had suffered buffeting by strong winds but also had been shot at by Royal Navy warships. In the first of what was to be a series of tragedies resulting from poor coordination between airborne forces and Allied fleets, those afloat heard the aircraft and thought they were enemy bombers. Encountering the ensuing clouds of flak, most of the pilots towing the gliders had released them too early.

When the reckoning was finally done it would emerge that, of 144 gliders, just twelve had landed on or near their targets. Half had ditched in the sea, where, trussed up with so much equipment that they were barely able to move, let alone save themselves, more than 250 men had drowned in these death traps. Those who managed to break out of their ditched craft clung to the wreckage, praying for daylight and rescue by Allied ships. Among them was Major General George Hopkinson, commander of the 1st Airborne Division and an ardent advocate of the glider assault.

For the men waiting in the bivouacs around Kairouan these ghastly truths were not fully apparent on the 10th, but they were starting to assemble the scraps of information coming through.

Johnny Frost once more asked himself whether smaller wouldn't have been better, a company group of 120 men instead of an entire brigade 'that no longer existed as a fighting formation and could take no further part in the campaign . . . it was a severe blow to the division'. Hearing scraps of dreadful news dribbling in, many of those lower down the pecking order repeated their oft-spoken 'rather them than us' sentiment about going to war by glider.

The drop of 2nd Parachute Brigade planned for that evening

was abandoned because the advance of sea-landed troops meant its objectives were being gained by other means. A second combat team of the 82nd Airborne Division was, however, carried aloft that evening, producing another disaster.

As they flew through the night towards their beachhead, the fleet of 144 C-47s carrying this wave was once again mistaken by those down below for enemy bombers. Anti-aircraft gunners opened up from sea and land, filling the sky with flak, hitting plane after plane. In all, twenty-three US transport aircraft were shot down that night, resulting in the loss of more than 300 paratroopers and aircrew. Some aircraft veered off course, dropping the soldiers way off target, others headed back to Tunisia. Only about one quarter of the American paratroopers landed on or near their designated drop zones.

After two successive nights of debacle, the mood among those in Tunisia waiting to go into action can be imagined. On 11 July, prayer services were held in the 2nd Parachute Battalion, an unusual occurrence in a unit known for its irreligious nature.

Sergeant Allan Johnstone heard the stories coming through about the glider troops' fate. He was harbouring all sorts of doubts about what would happen, even if they got through to their objectives, saying, 'I was uneasy about the raw youngsters who were the majority in the platoon.' The sergeant knew that the more experienced men were meant to steady these green soldiers, but had his worries about them also. Like his friend Maxie Forsyth, many of those who had survived the Tunisian battles had been deeply marked by them: 'I doubt if many men who have experienced it go easily and willingly into battle.'

Setting off for their departure airfields on the morning of 12 July, this natural apprehension was exacerbated by the fate of those sent into action on the preceding nights. Everything about their emplaning seemed well organized – numbered lorries pulled up at the right airfields behind aircraft with the same numbers. (The staff officers had done their jobs, at least.) But after hours spent sitting about by the aircraft, puffing on cigarettes and drinking endless cups of tea, the mission was called off.

On the 13th, they set out again for the airfields. The brigade's three infantry battalions, each numbering around 550 men, matched with American C-47 squadrons. Some gliders with anti-tank guns, stores and some of those unable to parachute would be towed by the RAF's 38 Wing. Brigade headquarters, with its signallers and defence platoon, would parachute from eleven Albemarle bombers, each of which could take a stick of ten.

This was how Arthur Maybury would go to war, and he admitted freely to the apprehension: 'Although I have worn the wings for twenty months it is my first experience and I do not know whether to be pleased or sorry.' He had, after all, been making money by writing tales of paratrooper heroics, and now the time was upon him to demonstrate those qualities himself. Getting to the planes in the late morning, Maybury surveyed the others in his stick – mainly signallers he knew well but with a couple of gunners who were part of teams that would bring in artillery support.

They milled about the aircraft, trying to stay out of the sun, their pockets stuffed with cigarettes, eating the chocolate they'd been given with spoons because it soon became a runny mess in the Tunisian midday sun. The pilot of their bomber was teased with 'a lot of chaff and hoary paratroop wisecracks such as, has he ever flown before, shouldn't this wire be tighter, are the engines screwed in and does he have Gremlin-trouble?'

Then, after hours of waiting, a jeep drove up bearing an RAF officer, who announced, 'It's on!' The pilot was whisked away for briefing while, for his passengers, 'ten hearts sink to ten pairs of boots'.

Kit was readied, all manner of it strapped to them, including a Sten gun, eight magazines of ammo, rations, a haversack and a satchel that Maybury hung around his neck containing cipher pads, signal instructions, pencils and rubbers. The lance corporal was there as a cipher clerk – once they got the big 65 Wireless Set up and running he would have to encode and decode communications to and from the troops who would come up from the beach to relieve them. It had been impressed upon him that, if the enemy got hold of the cipher pads, secret Allied communications would be broken wide open; it would be a catastrophe.

When the order was finally given to climb into the Albemarle, the sun was already slipping down and the heat of the day was beginning to ebb. But the struggle to lever themselves up so heavily laden into the fuselage hatch left the men bathed in sweat, and once they were inside it was 'oven-like'. It was only when the engines had fired up and the bomber started to taxi that any kind of draught relieved their discomfort.

Maybury was lost in reflection as the mission got underway at last. 'Most of us are thinking the thoughts that pass through every man's mind when he knows he might be dead in an hour or two.' With the engine noise building for take-off and the aircraft starting off down the bumpy airstrip, Maybury imagined his widowed mother, to whom he was everything, sitting at home, and he reflected that it was 'a good thing she doesn't know what I'm doing at this very minute'.

They were airborne: Albemarles, Stirlings and Dakotas by the dozen roared up into the twilight. Frost and the 2nd were aloft, the other two battalions, signallers, sappers, gunners, the whole brigade, more than 1,800 strong. Even Lou Lewis was up in another Dakota, wearing sergeant's stripes, ready to photograph this unprecedented moment. After all the years of planning, talking and training, it was the first time that Britain would parachute an entire brigade into battle.

12. Under the Volcano

At around 10 p.m. on 13 July 1943, the first red lights blinked on in the C-47s approaching the Sicilian coast. The paratroopers stood, hooked up the static lines that would open their parachutes and waddled into their jumping positions. Putting a kit bag and weapon on each man would make good sense once they touched down, but, in the confines of the fuselage, it just made them feel particularly ungainly and overburdened. The planes carrying Lieutenant Colonel Johnny Frost with his headquarters team and the lead element of his battalion, A Company, had flown over the Royal Navy fleet, and at 10.15 the green light came on in Frost's plane. Others were not so fortunate.

The passage of the first wave of Dakotas had alerted the fleet to what many a nervous gunner thought was an air attack. It didn't seem that any lesson had been learned from the 82nd Airborne's tragedy of two nights earlier. Rather, the presence of some genuine Axis air intruders that evening had made many on board the vessels jumpy.

They opened up with everything from 2-pounder pom-poms to 4-inch guns, sending up streams of flak into the night sky. Those aircraft that ran this gauntlet then flew into the Axis searchlights, 37mm and 20mm flak, and machine guns. Nothing was going to be easy about Operation Marston, their codename for the action that night.

For one of the officers in 1st Parachute Brigade headquarters who was riding the flak in an Albemarle, the sensation grew increasingly frightening: 'heavy AA shells bursting all around us and it felt as if devils were trying to beat their way in'. Some of these blasts showered the aircraft with shrapnel, making a noise like stones bouncing off it. In others, the shards of metal penetrated the plane.

Sergeant Lou Lewis watched streams of yellow and red tracer coming up towards them, initially appearing like a snaking stream of pyrotechnics, but accelerating dramatically as they neared the aircraft, a series of bangs marking the penetration of the cocoon around them. The cabin door flew open and one of the American crew cried out, 'Goddamit the pilot's dying!' Stripping off the wounded man's clothing, they found a single shrapnel gash on his back and patched him up. Out of the window, Lewis could see another aircraft drop out of their formation, engine blazing, falling inexorably towards the dark sea below.

Many of the young aircrews, mindful of the disasters already experienced on previous nights, took violent evasive action, becoming quite disorientated and unsure where to drop their passengers, who meanwhile would end up in a heap on the floor, or in some cases even tumble out of the doors owing to the planes' wild gyrations. Other flyers made the decision to turn about and head back to Tunisia. Sergeant Lewis's pilot was one of them.

Elsewhere, Lieutenant Colonel Alastair Pearson of the 1st Battalion, finding the pilot of his C-47 refusing to fly on, drew a gun on him. Shouting above the noise of the engines and flak, Pearson told the American that he would be shot and a qualified pilot among the British passengers would take over if he didn't press on. That clinched the argument and Pearson's stick jumped over the drop zone.

For Lance Corporal Arthur Maybury, the relief of exiting the claustrophobic Albemarle was followed moments later by the realization that his stick was under intense machine-gun and 20mm-cannon fire. As they dangled beneath their parachutes, 'we swing like helpless fairground targets in the air . . . the white hot stream of tracer bullets is coming from behind me and passing directly below'. Having jumped eighth, Maybury looked up to see if the last two members of the stick would exit the plane. After some delay, they did. The aircraft was badly damaged and later, unable to reach Tunisia, made an emergency landing in Malta.

When the tally was eventually made, of the 116 planes that

carried 1st Parachute Brigade into the sky that night twenty-six returned to Tunisia without dropping, seventeen dropped only some of the men on board, eleven were shot down and six dropped their men over the sea. Of the unfortunates in that last category, one staff officer wrote, 'nothing has been heard since of any members of these sticks'.

For those who ended up back in Tunisia during the early hours, Sergeant Lewis joked that it was like unconsummated sex: 'An enormous amount of anticipation with no release at the end.' Just one-third of the aircraft carrying the brigade dropped troops on or close to the designated drop zones. Hundreds of other men were scattered about the Sicilian countryside.

Frost was initially unaware of this as he surveyed the scene on the ground. He had wrenched his knee, but was determined to carry on, peering into the darkness, trying to rally as many men as he could. Occasionally, flares put up by the Italians guarding the area helped light up the features. His drop zone was beside a canal that fed the River Simeto, and it was the bridge over this water course that was their objective.

All those who groped about trying to find their troops that night had studied the area of the Primosole bridge, both on aerial photographs and on a model built for briefing purposes. The 1st Battalion was meant to drop at either end of that bridge, the 3rd north of it and the 2nd to the south. Although the Simeto flood plain made it relatively flat, there was a ridge that ran parallel to the coast, dipping down to the river's southern bank. Atop this ridge was a series of hillocks dubbed Johnny 1, 2 and 3. Frost's men had the task of securing these, dominating the southern end of the bridge.

Around 11 p.m. Frost linked up with Major Lonsdale, who had mustered about fifty members of A Company and decided to wait for the others to come in. The cacophony of anti-aircraft fire continued, and the men already down had to watch the spectacle of enemy flak engaging the following gliders carrying anti-tank guns and stores as they flew in, causing several to crash. Moving off the drop zone, one officer heard, 'the ghostly sound of rushing wind, as a glider swooped over our heads to crash land on the road near the bridge'.

Two hours on, and, although some more men had walked in, the total of 112 under Frost's direct command was still less than a quarter of what he expected. The confusion, however, was about to get worse because the enemy, realizing the importance of the bridge and Catania, the city a few kilometres to the north, had started flying in elements of a Fallschirmjäger Division at the same time. Indeed, one element of the force, Fallschirm-Maschinengewehr-Bataillon 1 (the 1st Paratrooper Machine-Gun Battalion), had dropped onto the ridgeline that formed Frost's objective while he was trying to gather his men just below.

The early hours of 14 July therefore witnessed the bizarre and dangerous spectacle of two enemy bodies of paratroopers trying to locate fellow members of their units, as well as weapons canisters, over much the same ground, in darkness. Some of Frost's men found German containers, others heard whispered conversations among enemy troops moving nearby. In one or two places the clatter of Stens announced a contact at short range.

For Maybury and four fellow members of his stick, the moments following landing were profoundly disorientating. They had been dropped off target, initially believing it might be by a factor of several miles. Unsure of their whereabouts, unable to find the container containing their radio equipment and facing the possibility of imminent capture, Maybury made the decision to destroy the secret cipher sheets and signal instructions in his satchel. While he did so, ripping the papers into tiny pieces and burying them, the others in the group decided to head off without him.

He disposed of the papers and watched a plane getting shot down as the parachutists were jumping from it before, finally, the guns fell quiet. Hours earlier in Tunisia he had felt like 'a winged thorn for the flabby side of Mussolini, now I am a small apprehensive man feeling very lonely indeed'. His predicament illustrated two salient truths about being a parachutist: the first had been impressed upon them during their training, which was that after landing the airborne soldier has no 'front' or 'rear': enemy attack can be expected from any direction. The second was that, while Maybury had been relatively safe during the Tunisian fighting, miles back from the front, every member of the brigade was in the same boat after a jump like this one, even those in what were considered supporting roles.

Heading eastwards, towards the sea and, he hoped, some distinctive landmark, Maybury saw many discarded parachutes and other items of kit. Then, after hearing the fire of a sub-machine gun, he approached a group of around fifteen men. He couldn't fight them singly. It was time to join a friendly party or surrender if they turned out to be enemy. The lance corporal called out the password challenge. A voice came back, 'Who is it, mate?'

Once he recovered from the absurdity of this, Maybury joined the others plodding along. As luck would have it, they were members of his old battalion, the 2nd, and they were far closer to the intended drop zone than Maybury had feared.

Meanwhile, a couple of kilometres to the north-west, Frost had decided, after bumping into Brigadier Lathbury in the darkness, to take a few dozen men that he had assembled up onto the ridge to capture the hillock called Johnny 1. Unknown to him, another officer was also leading a party of strays up onto the feature, deciding to do so on his own initiative. On the way, both parties encountered scattered groups of Italian soldiers, who surrendered without resistance.

With even fewer members of the 1st and 3rd Battalions present in the right place, Lathbury needed to do something to take the bridge itself. He and his brigade major were there, a couple of hundred metres south of the span, as was the signal squadron boss, Captain George Rowlands, and one of their medical officers. As for soldiers, four signallers, some men from the HQ defence platoon and some sappers were gathered together.

Lathbury said to Rowlands, 'If we organize the people and arms that are here we might as well take the bridge by ourselves. What do you think, George?'

'I see no reason at all, sir, why we shouldn't,' replied the signals officer. Having failed to find any working radios or many of the people required to operate them, 'it was clear that brigade HQ could not function as any kind of communications centre as there were no sets or communications of any kind', Captain Rowlands wrote in his account of the operation.

Britain's first deployment of an entire parachute brigade in battle, far from being a textbook operation, was turning into an affair where the brigadier was having to play the role of a junior officer. The question of fulfilling their mission now devolved onto the random group of men who were assembled in vaguely the right place.

All sorts got involved in taking the bridge that night, from signallers to medics and the padre. Lathbury's party took the south end and members of the 1st Battalion the north. Some combat engineers appeared also, and once they were present removed the demolition charges set on the bridge by the enemy. This was dangerous and vitally important work.

In many places the Italian defenders obligingly gave up; indeed, they were soon coming in by the dozens to makeshift PoW 'cages'. But their Axis allies were preparing a more resolute response.

With the first glimmer of dawn a German reconnaissance flight flew low over the area. This confirmed news brought by a Fallschirmjäger staff officer, Hauptmann Franz Stangenberg, who had been up to Primosole during the early hours. He began gathering a *Kampfgruppe*, or ad hoc combat team, of around 200 men at Catania airfield, mostly signallers from divisional headquarters, ready to retake the bridge that morning.

While Stangenberg organized himself, the sun had appeared over the glistening Mediterranean and paratroopers, British and German, who had scaled the ridge south of the Simeto began to glimpse one another's positions. The German paratrooper machine-gun battalion had occupied the eastern (or seaward) side of the feature, and with the rising sun on their backs, started to send bursts of fire towards the Tommies they could glimpse attempting to dig in ahead of them.

Many rounds started to find their mark, for the ground was too rocky for proper trenches to be dug and the German MG34s, many mounted on tripods, successfully outranged the Brens at Frost's disposal. He soon realized that, bereft of the battalion's heavy support weapons — 3-inch mortars and Vickers machine guns that, like so much else, had got lost during the chaotic night — it would be very hard to answer this enemy fire effectively. To make matters worse, the Germans started to summon mortar support and, at around 8.30, four Messerschmitts made a low pass, strafing the bridge.

Maybury looked across the Simeto plain from his vantage point on Johnny 1. Everywhere below there were signs of the previous night's horror, 'blackened buildings still smoking . . . discarded parachutes in the fields . . . broken gliders . . . burnt out aircraft lie on the slopes and down by the bridge'. Ahead of them, dominating the Catania plain, was Mount Etna, a looming volcanic presence, its crater smoking.

Frost had about 140 men on top of his side of Johnny 1, and still hoped for reinforcements. If half of A Company had turned up, he wondered, where were the rest, members of the same sticks in many cases, who had not appeared on the hilltop?

One party under Sergeant Allan Johnstone, consisting of around a dozen paratroopers, had been directed by Frost during the night to climb the ridge. Moving on, they had glimpsed Germans and decided to stay put. Finding a hollow in the long grass, they laid up until dawn. Johnstone debated whether to push on with Sergeant George Fisher, one of his section commanders and a fellow survivor of Oudna and the Sedjenane battles.

Fisher felt that discretion was the better part of valour. 'Well, it's your decision, Johnno, but Monty's there,' he said, gesturing towards the beachhead. In other words: stay put and wait for relief.

The battle, however, was more dynamic than that, and, as the sun rose higher, men from the enemy machine-gun battalion started to push forward. One Fallschirmjäger toting a sub-machine gun found Johnstone's group and called for back-up to take them prisoner. The sergeant apologized to the others as they were led away to captivity.

It was at about 9 a.m. that Rowlands's signallers salvaged a success from their wretched night's work. A single functioning 66 Wireless Set, a type of radio that worked on the same frequencies as the Royal Navy standing offshore, had been assembled and powered up. An artillery forward observer made contact with HMS *Uganda*, a cruiser, and within minutes three of its 6-inch shells were ripping through the sky, heading for suspected German positions.

Uganda's gunfire support proved a leveller for the 2nd Battalion men atop the ridge, suppressing the Spandaus in a way they had been unable to. Great thumping barrages came down onto the German positions, raising clouds of dust and assaulting their ears. Even so, throughout the morning some machine-gun and sniper fire continued, causing a slow but steady stream of casualties.

Those who could contribute little to this fight (for example, men toting pistols or Stens that could not hope to reach the enemy positions) were sent on their way south, with orders to link up with Montgomery's advancing 8th Army forces if they could. These included Maybury and a small party of others who trekked south off the ridge.

By midday, Hauptmann Stangenberg's column from Catania airfield was close to the northern end of the bridge, taking the small groups of 1st and 3rd battalion men under fire. The Fallschirmjäger machine gunners south of the Simeto had started to feed prisoners back, wading the river to the north side. That included Sergeant Johnstone and his group from A Company.

It wasn't the first time the 2 Platoon sergeant had encountered the enemy at close quarters, of course; there had been many occasions in Tunisia when the boot was on the other foot. Passed on to the Wehrmacht in Catania, this group was among scores of prisoners that the Germans took around the Primosole bridge and managed to evacuate back to mainland Italy. Johnstone took it philosophically, noting, 'neither our captors nor the present Wehrmacht guards had frisked us as clean of valuables as I had seen our fellows do to prisoners in Tunisia'.

To the south, meanwhile, Arthur Maybury and another man

also fell captive, though fortunately for them it was into the hands of Italians, who seemed reluctant about the whole thing. They were taken to the local HQ, where an apologetic English-speaking Bersaglieri sergeant told them, 'Just now you are our prisoners, soon we shall be yours.' And so it was to prove.

At the bridge, the German counter-attack had gathered force, and by late afternoon the British paratroopers abandoned positions on the north side of it, falling back across under a spattering of Spandau and mortar fire. It was a matter of hanging on then, just south of the span, with neither side in possession of the whole.

That evening, leading elements of 4th Armoured Brigade linked up with the paratroopers, sending a company of infantry up to reinforce Frost on the ridge. Unfortunately for the newly arrived troops, the Germans also reinforced during the night, with a smartly timed airborne operation, dropping a battalion of assault pioneers on the north side of the Simeto.

An attack on the bridge at 6 a.m. on the 15th by troops of the Durham Light Infantry turned into a costly failure. Many men were mown down by Spandaus just fifty metres in front of the forward German positions. Following this upset, there was a brief conference on the Johnny 1 hilltop between Brigadier Lathbury and the commander of 4th Armoured Brigade, who proposed to renew the assault immediately. Lieutenant Colonel Alastair Pearson, standing nearby, remarked, 'Well if you want to lose another bloody battalion, that's the right way to do it.' Such was Pearson's persona and reputation that Lathbury 'persuaded all to listen to Alastair's advice'.

The next attack went in during the early hours of 16 July and was successful. Pearson was awarded the DSO, his third in seven months. The 1st Parachute Brigade's battle ended at this point, and the men were taken down to the seaport at Syracuse for transport back to North Africa.

While some added to their reputation at the Primosole bridge, others lost theirs. Captain Slapsey Brayley, by this point second in command of A Company, was one of those whose absence had puzzled Frost on the 14th, as they fought to hold on to the Johnny I position. Once the battle was over, Brayley appeared with half a dozen men.

'Hello, and where have you been?' the CO asked.

'Things seemed to be rather boisterous between where we were and where you were,' replied the Welsh officer known for belting his soldiers, 'so I decided to wait until things quietened down.' Months earlier, after Oudna, Frost had recommended Brayley for the Military Cross, so he was doubly annoyed by that officer's failure in Sicily.

Brayley's calculation, however, had not been so different from that of his former platoon sergeant Allan Johnstone, who had also decided to lie low that night. Who knew how many others did the same? But whereas Johnstone and those with him had become German prisoners, Brayley, with his knack for coming through, or just plain luck, had not. Frost saw to it that Brayley was dismissed from the battalion forthwith.

At the time of its withdrawal, 2nd Battalion's casualty list amounted to twenty-five men killed and 138 missing. In broad terms, the battalion's strength divided into thirds: those killed or captured, those who'd never jumped and those who fought and remained able to do so another day.

Some of the missing would appear during the coming weeks, having hidden out in the Sicilian countryside. Arthur Maybury and the man he'd been captured with were freed by 8th Army troops on the 16th, having the pleasure of fulfilling the Bersagliere's prophecy and marching into captivity the entire Italian company that had taken them before making their way down to Syracuse.

The verdict of the soldiers who'd taken part in Operation Marston was a bitter one. Frost regarded it as 'another humiliating disaster for airborne forces and almost enough to destroy even the most ardent believer's faith'. A 1st Battalion man summed it up as 'another fiasco'.

'It was a catastrophe,' Captain Rowlands, the signal squadron commander, wrote in his orderly book soon afterwards. 'Nothing could have been worse than the last operation and it must never, from a parachuting point of view I mean, be as bad again.' Both the dropping and signals aspects, he felt, could only get better, starting from this base.

There were positives, of course, the most important being that the 1st Parachute Brigade prevented the destruction of the bridge. The scattering of the brigade over such a wide area, though unintentional, had compounded Axis uncertainties about the scale and the objectives of the operation. The official report emphasized these outcomes: 'The objective was secured and chaos was caused in the enemy's lines.' It highlighted the failure of poorly trained aircrews to deliver the brigade on target.

Those who had been at a greater distance from the Primosole bridge, particularly officers who felt that future offensive plans would require airborne operations at scale, took a philosophical view of it all. General Eisenhower said Operation Husky 'had given us a peep into [airborne forces'] great possibilities'. Montgomery insisted that the taking of the bridge over the Simeto had saved 8th Army seven days in its advance. It had been a bitter experience, but as those from Captain Rowlands to Eisenhower avowed, it would be one where the lessons learned would be applied in future operations.

Down at the docks in Syracuse, men returning from Operation Marston walked up the front ramp and into the hold of a tank landing ship. They flopped down inside this cool, man-made metal cavern, rooting about in their kit to extract what was needed to get a brew of char on. Ignoring the insistence of the matelots that smoking wasn't allowed there, they fired up little stoves, boiled their tea, lit cigarettes and started swapping experiences.

Maybury revelled in this 'patter', as each man tried to tell his story in as deadpan a way as possible, all eager to encapsulate the hair-raising events of recent days. He even jotted down some of what was said, correctly thinking it would make great material for his book:

'A damn great chunk of metal made a hole the size of my head in the side of the plane.'

'If that plane made it back to base, I'll eat my helmet.'

'No, I wasn't fired at on the way down – what do you want for two bob [two shillings, or 10p] a day?'

'When I found a container after searching for an hour, it was a German one! Did I scarper!'

'We found poor old George dead on the DZ . . . we took his grenades, a good thing we did because we needed them later.'

And so it went on for hours, such was the relief of their survival and being out of the battle. Maybury joined in once the conversation ebbed enough for him to get a word in edgeways. He had made his first combat jump and his mother would see him once he got back to Blighty. But he had received a visceral lesson in the arbitrary fate of an airborne operation. He never again saw four of the men who had been in his stick and left him behind in the darkness while tearing up his cipher pads. They had simply disappeared into the vortex of war.

13.   The Volunteer Spirit

That summer of 1943 in southern England the constellation of camps across Salisbury Plain was a hive of airborne forces activity. From Bulford to Tilshead, Netheravon to Syrencot, men marched here and there, staff cars brought new inspections and convoys wove back and forth. The camps occupied by the 1st Parachute Brigade when it first came down south in the spring of 1942 had long since been taken over by new tenants.

A machine had been created to take soldiers, send them off to Hardwick and Ringway, then, assuming they passed, integrate them into battalions or squadrons and ready them for war. This mechanism was now performing at a higher rate: whereas the jump courses at first might have numbered sixty men, eighteen months later they were pushing more than two hundred through at a time, and, whereas in the spring of 1942 Boy Browning had been fighting to convince the RAF that a single division might be used in battle, one year later, with that original formation committed in the Mediterranean, another one, 6th Airborne Division, was being formed and Browning's aspirations were shifting a level up the military hierarchy to the formation of a corps.

Command of the new division was given to Major General Richard Gale. Outsize in stature (he stood 6' 3"), ego and reputation (he had formed the 1st Parachute Brigade before handing it on to Flavell in 1942), Gale – of course, nicknamed 'Windy' – hit the soldiers training on Salisbury Plain that summer with storm force.

Moving around, inspecting the troops, he routinely started his speeches to them by saying, 'My name is Richard Nelson Gale. I have been a soldier for twenty-eight years and I am a master of my profession.' One reporter observing these performances summed up the man: 'Tall, spare and ramrod straight with ruddy face, bristling moustache and bushy eyebrows Gale looked a "Poona

Colonel" every inch but this first impression was misleading.' That writer wasn't the only one to assume the general was some sort of Colonel Blimp who had spent too long in the Indian sun.

Many soldiers listening to Gale formed an instant prejudice against the general, one other ranker calling him 'very pompous, an absolute caricature of what a divisional general must have been like in the First World War'. However, that soldier and the wider family of units came to revise these first impressions, for their general was a perfect specimen of the army's 1940s 'hard trainer' archetype: he would start with huge demands and cutting observations, taking his formation on a journey through months of hard graft to the sunlit uplands of operational competence and fulsome praise.

Although Gale had been one of those working hand in glove with Browning from the outset, he established a quite different ethos within those units he commanded. While Browning was personally immaculate and a stickler for turnout, Gale wore an eccentric medley of clothing, including cavalry jodhpurs, silk scarves and sometimes a leather flyer's jacket. His preoccupation was more with performance than appearance, and the key to that in his view was leadership.

At the time that the early stream of volunteers came for parachute training, Gale had personally selected all the battalion and company commanders for the 1st Parachute Brigade. One veteran summarized Gale's philosophy: 'The most important characteristic which an airborne soldier would expect and look for in his officers was initiative.' He wanted men who, finding themselves on a drop zone at 1 a.m. with half their soldiers missing, and with no heavy weapons or communications, would push on and execute their mission without waiting for guidance from above. Gale had selected dozens of officers according to these criteria, but it should be noted that Frost, Pearson and Pine-Coffin, as well as brigadiers such as Gerald Lathbury and James Hill, all bore Gale's stamp of approval.

His ambitions for the new division, as well as making good the losses already suffered, required ever greater numbers of soldiers, but, even in an army of three million, there was a limited supply of volunteers. The breathless newspaper coverage of 1941 and 1942 had given way to a more sober understanding of the dangers involved in airborne operations, and, with the overall progress of the war looking positive on the Eastern Front and in the Mediterranean, many of those who had been longing for action could assume that they would get it soon in their own units with the opening of the 'Second Front', or the invasion of France.

For Jack Grayburn, who had appeared in Bulford in late June 1943, three years of soldiering without seeing action in the 2nd Battalion of the Oxfordshire and Buckinghamshire Light Infantry (also referred to by its old army line number, the 43rd, or just as the 'Ox and Bucks') had frustrated him to such a degree that, having witnessed a display by the 3rd Parachute Brigade in April that year, he had made up his mind to volunteer.

Joining the 7th Parachute Battalion, Grayburn found, instead of the action he craved, that there would be a wait of many weeks for a parachuting course, during which time he was given the task of drilling new arrivals. 'I find the prospects of a party here are just about the same as they were with the 43rd, which is almost too shattering,' he wrote.

This disappointment was compounded by the diffident reactions of many brother officers in the regiment he had just left and by those of people outside the army also. 'Owing to my volunteering I have come into quite a deal of unpleasantness,' Grayburn recorded, feeling it came from 'people who cannot understand my wanting to serve my country to the fullest of my ability'.

By this point married and with a three-month-old baby boy, the twenty-five-year-old Grayburn was sacrificing time with his family, as well as his pay as an acting captain, since the airborne forces had required him to transfer at the lower rank of lieutenant. But the hunger for 'a scrap', or 'party', burnt within him.

He was a club-level rugger player, keen boxer and before the war had taken up skiing also. Grayburn thus had a yearning to test his own limits as well as exhibiting a sense of patriotism and a keenness

to master soldiering if that was what a nation at war required him
to do:

> I may be a sentimental fool and may have signed my own death
> warrant, if I do [die] I will have done it in the firm deep conviction
> that I have done the right thing. It is a curious system which makes
> an officer like myself have to be subjected to the severest criticism
> from his best friends and drop his rank and four shillings a day,
> because he is going forward to volunteer.

The unit that this keen officer had joined was the 7th Parachute
Battalion, one of those converted from a normal infantry battalion
to the parachuting role. This measure was needed to make up the
numbers, for the War Office had recognized that sending out calls
for volunteers as they had in 1941 would no longer yield the quan-
tity needed. So in 1942 and 1943 several unsuspecting battalions were
paraded, heard a pep talk from a representative of airborne forces,
were informed about parachute pay of an extra two shillings a day
and were then told by their CO, 'Those not wishing to volunteer
take three paces forward.'

The onus was therefore on those who rejected parachute training to break ranks. 'I had been serving with most of the company
for five years,' one sergeant put it, 'and I suppose that what I volunteered to do was to continue serving with my friends.' In this
way the airborne forces preserved the idea, in theory at least, that
they were a *corps d'élite* joined by men of their free will, while taking established companies or battalions with their own leaders off
the shelf and making the most of the local regimental identities
involved.

The formation of the 6th Airborne Division thus saw the conversion of a battalion of the Royal Warwickshire Regiment into
the 8th Parachute Battalion; one of the Essex Regiment into the
9th; one of the Green Howards, a Yorkshire outfit, into the 12th;
and one of the South Lancashire Regiment into the 13th. The 7th,
which was brigaded with those last two, was previously a part of
the Somerset Light Infantry.

With its light infantry connection, the 7th was able to exploit both the professionalism, historical record and vim of that part of the army (exemplified by men like Grayburn, who was first posted there) and a regional affiliation, drawing recruits from the West Country and Channel Islands. Often referred to as the 7th Light Infantry (or LI) Parachute Battalion, it had been formed before those others and was already building its reputation within the new division. It and the 1st Canadian battalion, attached that summer, were considered its best elements.

The 6th Airborne Division would also need an airlanding brigade of three main elements (which retained their original identities as the Devonshire Regiment, the Ox and Bucks and the Royal Ulster Rifles) as well as the full supporting cast of artillery, engineers, signals and Royal Army Medical Corps units. On Salisbury Plain that business of converting roles was going on apace during the summer of 1943, with all of the orders, moves, courses and postings that attended it.

Inevitably, perhaps, some old sweats of the 1st Parachute Brigade looked askance at this headlong expansion and the means used to bring it about. One member of the 1st Battalion felt that converting whole units was 'bound to lead to some lowering of standards'. Even in Bulford that summer there was a recognition that the wild adventurers of 1941 were a different sort of soldier. 'There is just about as much muddle here as there is anywhere else,' Grayburn confided to his journal in July 1943. 'The standard is not nearly as high as it is alleged to be,' which he contrasted with 'the quality of the troops who went forward in the pioneer days'.

What that impatient lieutenant could not appreciate was the degree to which the survivors of Tunisia and Sicily had been changed by their experiences, or that much could still be done to exploit the spirit of those in the new battalions. The 'Mad Jock' of Tunisia and Sicily fame, Lieutenant Colonel Alastair Pearson, returning to England after Sicily, exhausted and suffering from malaria, would soon be put to work galvanizing the 8th Battalion. Contrasting its men with those of the 1st Battalion of 1941, he noted that 70 per cent of the early volunteers had been in action before as opposed to 1 per cent in the 8th Battalion.

James Hill, one of the brigade commanders in the 6th Airborne Division, hit upon the idea of banning anyone over the age of thirty-two from his units. This weeded out a good many of the old soldiers in those converted battalions, part of a process as they went through airborne training that saw the numbers of 'volunteers' fall from 60–70 per cent of the previous unit strength to around half that, or about one third of their original number. These, in turn, were topped up by new individual volunteers, who generally were sent to battalions first raised in their part of the country.

One of those men arriving at the 7th Battalion that summer noted that 'the average age was very young and we were very enthusiastic'. There were so many new arrivals that some of the units had an average age of just twenty. In this sense they were markedly less cynical or 'browned off' than many of the veterans.

Just as Pearson was posted to the 8th, so the commander of the new division would find a use for Lieutenant Colonel Geoffrey Pine-Coffin. Following his dismissal as CO of the 3rd Battalion by Brigadier Lathbury in May, Pine-Coffin had returned home from North Africa on a troopship, arriving early in June. After leave he was put to work on the airborne recruiting drive; being a decorated veteran of Tunisia, he was a good man to give pep talks.

That summer Pine-Coffin had a chance for a reunion with his son Peter and to take care of personal affairs more generally. The widower was also able to see girlfriends, family lore suggesting there were a number. Major General Gale knew and respected Pine-Coffin, and later that summer installed him as second in command of the 7th Battalion for reasons that would become apparent a few months later.

The insertion of Pearson and Pine-Coffin was part of a pattern in which Gale eventually disposed of all five of the COs of those battalions that had converted to the parachute role. As well as installing those with a sound grasp of airborne operations in command, this may also have served to keep his two parachute brigade commanders, upon whom Gale made great demands, on their toes. If they became casualties or failed on the battlefield, Pearson or Pine-Coffin could be elevated in their place.

If the trawl for additional soldiers was delivering results slowly but steadily with the infantry, it proved much harder for the supporting arms. Indeed, one of Pine-Coffin's targets in his recruiting efforts was signallers. Other specialists were needed too.

It was the divisional commander's hope to field first-rate medical support for the battalions that proved particularly difficult, because not enough men would volunteer. The response to this challenge was remarkable in its ingenuity. Credit for it was given to Colonel Malcolm MacEwan, who became the director of medical services in the division after serving in North Africa with Pearson and Pine-Coffin. MacEwan had been a fighter pilot in the First World War and had been awarded so many medals, among them the Distinguished Service Order (twice), Distinguished Flying Cross and OBE, that the troops nicknamed him 'Technicolor' because of the array of ribbons on his tunic.

MacEwan had a brainwave: he went to speak to groups of conscientious objectors. In an attempt to avoid the bitter social divisions that imprisonment and even execution of such men had led to during the First World War, a system was put in place that allowed them to serve in non-combat roles. Men who refused to take up arms were able to attend tribunals to make their case. These three-member panels would then pass one of three alternative judgments: a rejection of the petitioner's claim; a complete exemption from call-up; or service in the Non-Combatant Corps.

Thousands sent on in that last way had been used as navvies in the Pioneer Corps, and later to support Royal Engineer bomb-disposal units. However, by mid-1943 there were fewer explosive devices to tackle, boredom was setting in and many were interested in the airborne option. Their response was heartening. Having established that they would not carry arms, and that they would treat British, German and French civilian casualties equally, many agreed, one arguing, 'in many ways this was a group decision to accept this opportunity'.

Although bound by terms like 'non-combatant', 'conscientious objector' or, more colloquially, 'conchie', these men from diverse backgrounds fell into two broad categories. There were those from religious sects such as the Quakers, Plymouth Brethren or Mormons and then there were secular pacifists, many of whom were members of the Peace Pledge Union or PPU. Among those non-religious volunteers for the Parachute Field Ambulance (PFA) units forming at Bulford were a medieval historian, a senior typesetter and a garage mechanic. Established in 1934, the PPU peaked at 140,000 members in 1940, so airborne pacifists, much like those from the 'combatant' army, were a rather select bunch.

MacEwan succeeded in recruiting 190 'conchies' for the 6th Airborne Division's Royal Army Medical Corps (RAMC) units, about one-third of their total strength. Of these, 142 would pass parachute training, the remainder joining the 'chairborne warriors' who rode a glider into action. During their early service, for the most part they detected little hostility from regular soldiers or the wider public, one saying of their treatment, 'I was very struck by the fairness of the whole thing, that people in a war could refuse to take up arms.'

However, on arrival at Bulford, they noticed that, in the Naafi, 'we were cold shouldered, which is the nearest you would get to actual hostility'. Initially, the combatant members forming the majority of the two jump-trained RAMC units that they joined (the 224th and 225th Parachute Field Ambulances) were 'definitely rather suspicious of us and we found ourselves really rather unpopular for the first time', a pacifist objector noted a little mischievously, adding, 'They were rather proud of being paratroops, of parachute training, and to find a load of Bible punchers among them filled them with some misgiving because they thought they were very tough indeed.'

The strange alchemy of airborne training was such that after enduring fifty-mile marches and hurling themselves out of aeroplanes, combatant RAMC men began to realize that there was a hardness the conchies had in common with them, and that in any case they would share the same destiny.

Sergeants and corporals who melded these men into their medical sections (the non-combatants were not allowed to be promoted above the rank of private) understood that they were less trouble than a great many others, being often highly educated and keener on debating politics or theology than getting drunk or smashing up commercial premises. One puzzled sergeant, surveying his conchies in their Nissen hut at the end of a hard day's training, remarked, 'The trouble with you fellas is that you're always reading.'

David Clark, a newly qualified doctor posted to the 225th Parachute Field Ambulance as a captain formed an initial impression of the unit as 'a collection of malcontents from all over the army, all brave, some excellent soldiers, but many chronic misfits'. Over that summer he saw them transformed by training, but the singular quality of the conchies, as men who had stood up for their beliefs, was that they were, 'willing to be led, but refused to be driven'.

One of those who trained at Bulford that summer was George Skelly, a member of the Christian Brethren sect from Cumberland. Although Skelly worked the land, so might therefore have been allowed complete exemption from war service by the tribunal he attended in Carlisle, he chose a non-combatant role. Like many of those arriving on Salisbury Plain that summer, his pathway there had been via a couple of years of tedium in the Pioneer Corps followed by bomb disposal.

Skelly was assigned to 225th Parachute Field Ambulance, which paired with 5th Parachute Brigade. It assigned teams of medics to each battalion within that brigade, as well as providing a single field surgical team at its centre. The sections consisted of a doctor (with the rank of captain), an NCO and up to twenty orderlies or stretcher bearers, a mix of conchies and combatant soldiers. The 225th did their parachute jumps at Ringway that July. An instructor noted that Skelly was 'hard working, very good standard'.

What Jack Grayburn thought about being behind the conchies in the queue for jump training is not recorded, but upon Skelly's return from Ringway his section was attached to the 7th Parachute Battalion, and so it was with them that he did much of his field training, effectively becoming part of the unit. That this parachute battalion contained men as different in temperament and motivation as Grayburn and Skelly is testimony to the diversity of the national service army in general, and its airborne forces in particular.

Grayburn had, however, late in July, bumped into an old acquaintance who worked on the staff at Airborne HQ. Telling the officer of his keenness to escape camp life and get scrapping, that major 'arranged for me to leave this country early in September and go out to Africa to join whichever Brigade has got the next operational role'. Such were the power of connections and the vagaries of the officer-posting system.

After some wrangling with his boss at the 7th Battalion, evidently not best pleased at losing such a promising young officer, and passing his jump course in August, Grayburn was by September on a ship bound for Algiers, where he and some other drafts from the light infantry were destined to join Johnny Frost's storied 2nd Parachute Battalion. 'Never before', wrote the lieutenant, 'have I felt so terrifically elated about anything.'

14. Mustn't Miss the Bloodbath

For Johnny Frost and the rest of his 2nd Battalion, the weeks after Sicily passed in a listless and rather unsatisfactory way. There were some people to be moved on, generally those who had been shown up in the recent operation, but also promotions and a shuffling of captains and majors needed to replace losses. Inevitably, there would also be drafts of fresh men needed to replace the casualties suffered in Sicily.

Frost whiled away the time with a battlefield tour of their Tunisian campaign, taking officers and NCOs to revisit those hilltop scenes of slaughter, studying their positions from the enemy's perspective and generally asking themselves what they could have done better, or just differently. He also became involved in many a whisky-lubricated late-night discussion with the 1st Airborne Division's senior officers about how better to prosecute their next operation. Many of the debates centred around the correct place of the glider in future plans – a point of natural contention between the 'jumpers' and those, including their divisional commander, Major General George Hopkinson, who had taken the airlanding route.

These were lonely times for Frost, who felt the loss of some of the long-serving officers in the battalion and, of course, the return to Britain of the man in whom he could confide because they were both at the same level of command, Alastair Pearson. But what everyone knew was that Sicily had just been a stepping stone to an inevitable operation on the Italian mainland, and that the question was open about what part the division should play in it.

The Americans were to prove more forward leaning in this regard, at one point planning to drop the 82nd Airborne Division near Rome in a move to coincide with the surrender of its government to the Allies. Although the Italian government did capitulate on 8 September 1943, the Rome operation was scrubbed. However, once Allied landings began on 9 September, and heavy German resistance was encountered, the 'All American' division did parachute a regimental combat team into action in order to assist the breakout from the Salerno beachhead. Although these operations happened, mercifully, without a repetition of the friendly fire disasters in Sicily, the British were not ready to resume airborne assaults, feeling that further progress had to be made with the training of pilots.

The 1st Airborne Division was therefore involved in a seaborne landing to secure the southern Italian port of Taranto. It passed off largely without incident, apart from losses suffered by the 2nd Parachute Brigade when one of its transports detonated a mine in the harbour there. This setback cost hundreds of lives, compounding the 2nd Brigade's sense of being unlucky after their operation in Sicily was cancelled. Its 6th Parachute Battalion was particularly hard hit at Taranto. The war that developed in Italy, in which German forces skilfully fought a rearguard action on the country's narrow, congested coastal plains ought to have been highly suitable for landing operations – by air and sea – to bypass the enemy defence lines.

Although there were many plans to insert airborne and commando forces to do just this, such operations proved easier to conceive in theory than to pull off in practice. As the autumn wore on, there would be a growing realization that landing ships, aircraft and fighting troops were being drawn back from the Mediterranean to Britain to prepare for the 'big show': the invasion of France.

Jack Grayburn's mood soured on arriving in Algeria to discover the division had sailed for Italy. After a wretched night out in Algiers ('the wine was lousy, the company worse') he and his travelling companions set out for 1st Parachute Brigade's rear headquarters in Sousse. It was from there, after a series of disappointments and false alarms when he thought there might be no vacancy for him, then finally learned he was to be sent to the 2nd Battalion, that he left by plane for Italy on 12 October.

At the end of his long day's journey, Grayburn walked into the mess and bumped into Lieutenant Colonel Frost. Having already read much about his new CO, the lieutenant was somewhat star-struck, writing that Frost was, 'full of life and energy, cannot stand being idle and always thinking out some mad scheme for having a crack at the Boche'.

The question for Grayburn, of course, was whether such plans would bear fruit any time soon. Not long after his arrival the battalion went to the Adriatic port of Barletta to practise for a seaborne assault further up the coast. It was a time for landing-craft drills, practice on the ranges and a preparation for action that they were far from certain would come.

Grayburn and his two officer travelling companions were all sent to A Company. The more senior of these light infantry officers, Major Digby Tatham-Warter, was to command the company, with Grayburn and Andrew McDermont as subalterns. Grayburn was given 2 Platoon, the same one that had failed to salute Boy Browning one year earlier and which had got through a succession of platoon commanders and sergeants since then. Indeed, the average time in post for A Company's officers during that year had been three to four months, a turnover created by death, wounding, capture and promotion.

Taking the soldiers through their paces each day, Grayburn noticed a marked difference with the unblooded types he had led in the Ox and Bucks or, briefly, in the 7th Parachute Battalion. Drills and practice, he felt, were, for the veterans of his company, 'perhaps rather an inefficient remedy to boredom. There is only one type of training in their eyes and that is actual battle.' That was an expression of his own hunger for combat, as well as the ennui that the veteran soldiers affected on 'schemes' or training exercises.

Grayburn felt, as he mulled over the chances of action each evening with his brother officers in their makeshift Italian mess, that 'the ideal thing as far as I'm concerned would be for us to do a job now and then go home and prepare for the "European bloodbath" which is scheduled to take place next spring'. And while the average person late in 1943, even the average army officer, might have regarded the 'bloodbath' as something they'd rather give a wide berth to, among the younger officers in the Parachute Regiment, used with gallows humour no doubt, it meant the great battle they didn't intend to miss.

As for Grayburn's hope of an Italian job before the battalion headed back to Britain, it was not to be. Frost's constant quest for operations produced but a single airborne mission in Italy, under which Captain John Timothy and some NCOs were parachuted into various places in the south in the hope of rounding up parties of British prisoners of war who had escaped from captivity following the country's capitulation. It miscarried for a number of reasons, including the Royal Navy's failure to pick the men up from a coastal rendezvous.

On 15 November, Frost paraded his battalion at 10 a.m. in camp at Barletta. The intense activity of the previous weeks, practising for amphibious operations, had come to an end with many wondering whether the plan had ever been serious or simply a feint to worry the Germans into shifting their forces in anticipation of a possible landing. Frost had another message for the hundreds of soldiers assembled that chilly morning: they were going home. 'You could have heard a pin drop,' one of the A Company veterans recorded.

The colonel complimented the battalion on their discipline and work ethic during the months since Sicily and confessed his relief that they had not disgraced themselves in the bars and brothels of Tunisia after that operation. 'Finally,' recorded one officer, 'he said there was one thing he was not satisfied with and that was their too prolific use of the National Adjective.' Since they would be getting Christmas leave with their families, the CO asked that they moderate their effing and blinding in good time before going home.

Walking away from this parade, Lieutenant Grayburn marvelled at their CO's old-fashioned sensibilities. 'He is an amazing man is Johnny Frost,' Grayburn wrote. 'He allows his officers to brawl all over the mess, he gets very drunk himself, but if anyone should dare [sing] a dirty song, he will personally see that that individual is slung out of the Mess.'

Grayburn was mulling other things over, too, particularly that his plans to get into battle, with all the effort they entailed, from volunteering for airborne forces and completing his jump training to his tedious voyages by sea and across North Africa, had come to naught. Given the cost to him in burnt bridges with former regimental colleagues, as well as anxiety on the part of his family, he felt a chump. He reasoned that 'my first piece of action is going to be the European bloodbath, the [Ox and Bucks] will be in that anyway and I might just as well have stayed with them'.

Four days after Frost's speech, the 2nd Battalion embarked on a troopship. They sailed first to Algiers and changed ships before arriving back to a misty Mersey on 9 December. Their division left the 2nd Parachute Brigade behind in the Mediterranean as a theatre reserve force, while the 1st and 4th Parachute and 1st Airlanding Brigades came home for Christmas.

There had been orders, in the interest of security, to strip the soldiers of all airborne insignia before they disembarked: they were to masquerade as members of the Pioneer Corps. Similar precautions against any lurking enemy agents had been taken with other divisions returning from the Middle East. But as their transport cruised up the Mersey and alongside the quay, any observer would have understood that they were more than that; an army band on the quayside struck up, before giving way to a welcome speech by a representative of the War Office. The paratroopers lining the decks hooted derisively during this speech. They didn't want lip service, they just wanted to get home.

Once disembarked, the men were marched to trains, receiving applause and cheers from groups of Liverpudlians as they passed. 'One or two women who must've lost their sons in the Middle East were overcome and the troops were duly sympathetic,' Grayburn noted. Before boarding the waiting trains, each man was handed gifts funded by the mayor of Liverpool: a bar of chocolate, a pack of twenty cigarettes, a bundle of newspapers and a cup of tea. Their destination that day was Grantham in Lincolnshire, where billets had been prepared for them.

The fortnight's disembarkation leave was spent with family. Frost, still a single man, was able to get to his parents. One soldier from A Company who went home to Hornchurch in Essex found himself 'paraded around the shops' in uniform by his mother, in the hope that having a returned paratrooper might get them some cuts of meat on top of the ration. Not far away, in Wanstead, Lance Corporal Arthur Maybury celebrated Christmas with his mother.

Grayburn fell ill with hepatitis soon after returning and, after a spell in hospital, made his way to Roughwood Farm in Chalfont St Giles, where eventually he was reunited with his wife and son. It was a time for peace and reflection before the uncertainty and danger that lay ahead.

There was little rest for the 7th Parachute Battalion and its fellow units in Major General Gale's 6th Airborne Division that winter. Jumping from balloons and aircraft recommenced early in the New Year, and on 21 January the general put the 7th through unannounced drills to test their readiness. Gale repeated this formula around the division, constantly assessing, observing, driving and planning. While many in the 1st Division might still have hoped to lead the way to France, Gale knew with growing certainty that this vital task would be given to the 6th.

The general's intuition, based upon titbits gleaned from colleagues, as well as hints from above, was that airborne forces would secure the flanks of the great landings being worked up under the codename Operation Overlord that would begin the invasion of France by the Allies. On 17 February, during a long meeting with the now promoted Lieutenant General Browning, Gale was given the precise details of his role in this great drama. His troops were to seize two key bridges over the River Orne, on the eastern end of the Allied invasion force's front line, while denying others across the River Dives to the enemy and destroying a heavy gun battery that could be used to shell the beaches. In

29. General 'Windy' Gale in full flow, giving 6th Airborne Division a pep talk prior to D-Day.

30. Men of the 22nd Independent Parachute Company, Pathfinders for the main Normandy drop, synchronize their watches prior to taking off from RAF Harwell in Oxfordshire.

31. Members of the 225th Parachute Field Ambulance, crammed into a Stirling bomber on their way to Normandy, among them scores of conscientious objectors who, unarmed, acted as medics, orderlies and stretcher bearers.

32. This scene at RAF Tarrant Rushton gives a sense of the organization involved in landing 6th Airborne Division, each glider (mostly the heavy Hamilcars) being connected by rope to its Stirling tug, ready to depart in sequence.

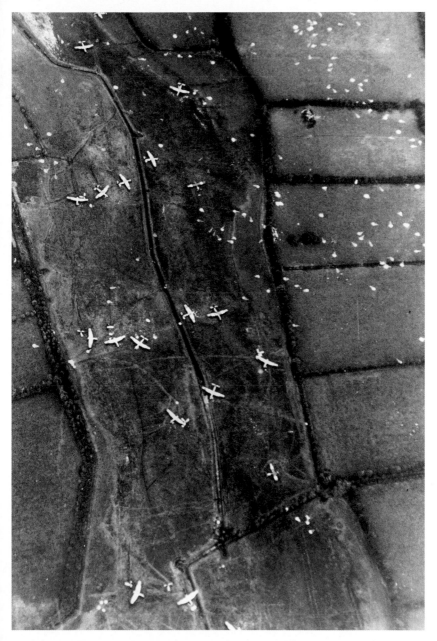

33. Drop Zone N became Landing Zone N as scores of gliders landed there on 6 June 1944, there being 355 of them dispatched in support of 6th Airborne Division, mostly carrying heavy equipment and stores.

34. Critical to the success of Operation Tonga, was the landing of a *coup de main* party on the night of 5/6 June adjacent to the bridges over the Orne and the nearby canal. Four of the six assigned Horsas landed close to their targets, deploying assault troops.

35. Having landed on the evening of 6 June, the passengers on a Horsa dubbed 'Charlie's Aunt' wasted no time unloading the jeep and cargo trailer on board.

36. Troops crossing the canal bridge at Bénouville. Once taken by airborne forces, it became an important asset for moving men and equipment within the Allied bridgehead.

37. Another jeep-and-trailer combination speeds into action, this heavily laden vehicle belonging to 6th Airborne Division's Royal Army Service Corps company, which delivered supplies.

38. A pair from the 6th Airborne Division's provost (or military police) company guarding a junction near Ranville in the airborne bridgehead.

39. Men of No. 4 Commando linking up with paratroops from the 7th Battalion in Bénouville on 6 June 1944.

40. Panzer IVs of the 21st Panzer Division were used to launch a number of counter-attacks against 6th Airborne Division, but generous provision of anti-tank weapons and artillery support meant they made little progress.

41. Men of 6th Airlanding Brigade, mostly from the Ox and Bucks bridge-storming party, pictured a few days after the Normandy landings in nearby Bénouville. The man on the left has a captured sub-machine gun.

42. Many of the fallen were initially interred in Normandy graveyards, in this case three men of the 7th Parachute Battalion and a member of the Royal Engineers.

this way, the airborne forces would protect the eastern (British) flank of Overlord.

As Browning, who had inserted himself into this equation as Airborne Corps commander, briefed the plan, this task was to be carried out by a parachute brigade and some glider-borne anti-tank batteries. Gale later wrote that he 'resisted this as forcibly as I could'. This formation, around 2,000 troops, would be grossly inadequate for the task as things stood. The issue, once more, was the shortage of airlift. Although Browning tried to secure more planes from Supreme Allied Headquarters, the Americans had big plans for airborne operations at the other end of the beachhead, the Cotentin Peninsula in Normandy, and, since they provided the lion's share of the Dakotas, could to a degree call the shots.

While Gale and Browning had to push back, the fact that the issue was resolved within five days suggests that generals Eisenhower and Montgomery were quick to grasp Gale's point. But, even though more aircraft would be found, as on Sicily, there would not be sufficient for the Americans and British to do everything they wanted in one lift. A second night's airlift would be necessary to reinforce the first. For Gale, this was an excellent outcome, allowing him to drop his two parachute brigades (the 3rd under James Hill and the 5th led by Brigadier Nigel Poett) on the first night of the operation and to bring in most of his 6th Airlanding Brigade less than twenty-four hours later.

Having got what he wanted, Gale swiftly started making practical preparations. A couple of days after the larger drop plan had been agreed, the CO of the 7th Parachute Battalion was packed off and Geoffrey Pine-Coffin put in his place.

The 7th had impressed Gale and he was giving the battalion an experienced CO to exercise the first of the division's primary tasks: the seizure of two bridges near Caen by one element, the 7th Battalion, of the 5th Parachute Brigade. The other two, the 12th and 13th, would effectively watch the 7th's back while they did it. The other 'primary' mission, to take the battery at Merville, would be given to the 9th Battalion, which, along with the other elements of the 3rd Parachute Brigade (Pearson's 8th Battalion and the Canadians), would hold the southern and eastern parts of the area, up to the Dives.

Gale's method for taking the two bridges involved a fail-safe approach. Having studied German operations at Eben-Emael and the seizure of the Corinth Canal bridge during the invasion of Greece, he assigned a reinforced company of airlanded troops (180 men) to descend by six Horsa gliders right onto these objectives. If the gliders never appeared – a reasonable assumption post-Sicily – or resistance proved too much for those men, Pine-Coffin's battalion of paratroopers would rapidly appear on the scene. The 7th would be equipped with collapsible assault boats so that, if things went from bad to worse and the Germans managed to set off demolition charges on those spans, they could cross the Orne and the canal running parallel to it, securing both bridgeheads ready for the arrival of Royal Engineer squadrons with heavy equipment the next day.

While Gale's parachute battalions were younger and less jaundiced by experience than those that had just returned from the Med, the incessant and demanding training left many of their soldiers exhausted. Dennis Woodgate, a teenager from Orpington in Kent, joined C Company of the 7th Parachute Battalion in the summer of 1943. His request for leave just before Christmas in order to attend his brother Francis's wedding was declined by the company commander, 'so you can guess what I called him when I got outside', Dennis wrote to the groom, a sergeant in the RAF. 'I have only just come in off a scheme,' Dennis added, using a common term for an exercise, 'and the time is round about half past ten at night. I will be doing a night jump on Monday and that's what we have been doing tonight.'

A few weeks later, the paratrooper wrote to his brother again: 'I been out on a scheme for 3 days and 2 nights and we was out all day Friday and I can tell you I'm just about browned off with them all.' Although the high-ups had not yet been briefed on the divisional plan in detail, there were unmistakable signs, even to those at Private Woodgate's level, that the big show would happen before long. 'I have not told Mum about this but it seems as though it won't be so long before I'm over the drink because we signed my overseas paper the other day,' Dennis confided in his brother, adding, 'but keep it quiet from Mum.'

Bob Tanner, a private who appeared in the battalion in March, had second thoughts on more than one occasion about the wisdom of volunteering for parachuting. The training was so hard and there was no let-up once he reached the battalion, so when it came to their NCOs, 'I could have shot the bastards.' But Tanner could also see that their leaders were people of great dedication and quality.

Lieutenant Colonel Pine-Coffin, his ultimate boss, struck Tanner with his humanity and professionalism: 'he never gave you the impression he was above you. He knew what you had to do . . . He never degraded you. Any officer who he thought wasn't going to come up to scratch, he got rid of them, he didn't want them.' At thirty-five, Pine-Coffin was almost old enough to be the father of Woodgate or Tanner, and, as 'Wooden Box' guided his men through their final weeks of training, he showed them the consideration that a man might have reserved for his own family had the war not intervened.

That May, the colonel relished having gone from leading the Cinderella unit of one brigade – the 3rd Battalion during the Tunisian fighting – to the chosen men of another, having the most vital task of the British airborne plan for Normandy. Although he could sense the soldiers' tiredness, he didn't let up, because, while Major General Gale might have been confident of the role the battalion would be playing, Pine-Coffin felt that during the exercises in March and April, 'brigades and battalions were being weighed up against each other and it was a trying time for commanders lest some error of judgement on their part or some case of slackness by any of their subordinates should prejudice their chances of their commands when the selection of the real jobs was being made'.

He instituted a period of zero tolerance for errors, a 'Ginger Week', during which 'no infringement of the smallest regulation was allowed to pass'. But the punishment was not jail or abuse, rather the teasing of those concerned, Pine-Coffin arguing, 'The whole week was a period of considerable amusement and was appreciated even by those unlucky enough to find themselves gingered.'

To what extent Pine-Coffin used the idea of jeopardy as a tactic to motivate his soldiers, that if they fell behind in standards they might not get a plum assignment, and to what extent he actually believed that relegation to a secondary task was possible can only be guessed at. But it ranks as another example of the hierarchy, from Gale down to Brigadier Poett and in turn to Lieutenant Colonel Pine-Coffin, using the mask of command with subordinates in order to instil uncertainty and maintain their motivation to perform. Certainly, a change of CO was possible even weeks before the operation, as the 9th Parachute Battalion discovered after its boss talked a little too freely in public about its mission.

By 13 May, if the 7th Battalion's CO had still really harboured any doubts about the unit's role, they must surely have vanished, for on that day they began exercises in Exeter, assaulting bridges that were of similar construction to those in Normandy and practising their emergency plan: river crossing using collapsible boats. By this point it was most unlikely that there would have been time to have trained another battalion in this way.

Time after time over four days, the men practised crossings the easy way, over bridges, and the hard, by paddling. Each attempt was marked by fusillades of blanks and the crump of thunderflashes. Walking up and down the bank of the Exe in his German jackboots, drawing on his pipe, Pine-Coffin must have taken great satisfaction in it all.

On 1 June, at the cinema in Tilshead Camp, any lingering uncertainty among the troops over their task was finally extinguished, as Pine-Coffin briefed the battalion on its role in Operation Tonga, the airborne part of Britain's wider Overlord mission. The unit was by this point entering isolation, unable to communicate with those outside, hemmed by barbed wire into encampments secured by military police. They then moved to Fairford in Gloucestershire, the aerodrome where they would embark for France. A twenty-four-hour delay caused by bad weather did little to calm anyone's nerves, but by the afternoon of 5 June it was clear they were going in.

The hours before loading up were a time of great tension. Their divisional and brigade commanders came by to gee the soldiers up, but all knew that there was great apprehension. Across the south coast scores of transport ships were setting out, while, at airfields inland, transport aircraft by the hundred were going through their final checks.

At Broadwell airfield in Oxfordshire, hundreds of members of the 13th Parachute Battalion, laden with kit and faces blackened, knelt in prayer. The padre blessed them, then their flag. Once embarked in their Stirlings, they sang 'Onward, Christian Soldiers'.

Meanwhile, at Fairford, there were also hymns and prayers for the 7th Battalion. 'As we were singing "Abide With Me" the first aero engines started up and within five minutes you couldn't hear yourself think,' one officer recalled. Their padre had read to them from Joshua, concluding, 'the Lord thy God is with thee wherever thou goest'. It struck Private George Skelly, the conchie stretcher bearer who was now part of their unit, as particularly apt. He was about to go into action unarmed and, despite his deep faith, 'wasn't feeling too brave'.

Stirlings and Dakotas took to the sky one after another, climbing into the darkness. Each one then circled, joining the squadrons gathering in numbers until the order was given for the entire formation to move south, over the inky waters of the Channel. Their fate was sealed: they would soon jump into the most terrible fight for survival, a bloodbath indeed.

15.   Twenty-four Hours in Normandy

Just after midnight, in the first minutes of 6 June 1944, the gliders belonging to the *coup de main* force cast off from bombers that had hauled them over to France. Diving from around 2,000 metres altitude they dropped at almost 200kph, descending in minutes to a height where even in darkness they could see the silvery reflection of the River Orne and the Caen Canal, running almost parallel to the west of it. These twin lines provided an excellent navigational marker for the hand-picked pilots who had spent months practising for this operation: the liberation of France.

Their mission was to land each Horsa a matter of metres away from the two key bridges near Caen. Each 'landing zone' was so small, being surrounded with all manner of obstacles from trees to anti-landing poles to the bridges and waterways themselves, that the Horsas had been fitted with special braking parachutes to bring them into these tight spaces at a tolerable velocity. The first one, speeding in at around 140kph, hit the ground, bounced, deployed its chute, then came crashing back to earth with a grinding noise, showering sparks and eventually slowing to a halt.

Inside, Major John 'Scarface' Howard, commanding the storming force (D Company of the 2nd Ox and Bucks with an extra two platoons, some Royal Engineers and medics attached, about 180 men in all), regained his senses after a moment's stunned apprehension. Emerging from the damaged glider, Howard realized that the pilot had put them down just fifty metres from the canal bridge, the Horsa's nose having broken through the barbed-wire defences in precisely the way, joking at a pre-operational briefing, he had suggested to the man at the controls that he might like to do it. 'It was the most exhilarating moment of my life,' thought Howard, who could hardly believe what was happening. 'There was no firing at all, in other words we had been a complete surprise.'

Another Horsa dropping down with similar pinpoint accuracy came crunching to a halt. After the sensory overload of their descent and landing, there was a moment of complete silence. The sergeant pilot then turned to look into the cabin behind him, announcing to the platoon commander, 'You are in the right place, Sir.'

There was no time to be lost. The Ox and Bucks quickly ran across the bridges, dealing with a couple of Germans who spotted them. It was not bloodless, a machine-gun nest had to be taken out, but it was very fast. Four of the six gliders allotted to the task had arrived within minutes, the other two coming down a few kilometres to the north. After the Sicilian airlanding catastrophe, it was a stunning success.

Just as those gliders began dropping, a small party of pathfinder parachutists, accompanied by half a dozen members of the 7th Battalion, landed on Drop Zone N, the centre of which was a kilometre or two from the Orne. It was to be the main landing zone for the 5th Parachute Brigade, and these men had been equipped with a Eureka transponder – the system being designed to give incoming aircraft a precise navigational fix on the drop zone. They were also carrying a green lamp that could be used to rally the 7th, assuming they were in the right place.

Enough had happened, even in that half hour after midnight, with so many aircraft overhead, for the German flak batteries to be pumping out shells as the main formations carrying the 5th Brigade approached the coast. Inside their Stirlings, Lieutenant Colonel Pine-Coffin's men readied themselves. Many had overcome their nerves and, as the flashes of bursting flak illuminated their planes, just wanted to get out as soon as possible.

Private Tanner had been turning over in his mind: 'Will I be hit? Will I lose a leg, lose an arm, be blinded?' All of their training exercises had emphasized that speed was of the essence that night, if you were hit you'd be left where you dropped, 'it's your hard luck . . . but you're not concerned about it, you can't afford to be . . . it's bye-bye, forget about them'.

Picking up the wounded would be the job of the RAMC

attached to the battalion, Captain John Wagstaff, and orderlies like George Skelly. As they flew into the flak, Skelly noticed that one of his roommates, 'like so many, he had no time for God', was singing the hymn 'Rock of Ages', 'with tears rolling down his cheeks'.

Pine-Coffin's aircraft, meanwhile, was approaching Drop Zone N at 12.50 a.m. When the green light blinked on, he launched himself out of the door and into that dangerous night. He watched the anti-aircraft and machine-gun fire as he came down, trying to pick out details in the darkness that would help him get his bearings.

For so many hanging in their harnesses over Normandy this was a moment of truth. But Pine-Coffin was under particular pressure. The division's most important objectives had been confided to him, and, as soon as he got to the bridges, Major Howard's *coup de main* party would come under his command. This night was the culmination of so much for Pine-Coffin, from Dunkirk to Ringway and then North Africa, so many risks run, so many brushes with death.

Landing with a painful thump, the colonel felt for a moment quite alone and disorientated. After doffing his parachute harness, he looked this way and that. He was gripped by uncertainty. 'It was a most desperate feeling', being near the rendezvous point but not knowing which direction to move in. He worried about Howard's men, 'everything could be so easily lost if the battalion did not arrive in time'.

Pine-Coffin soon found the pathfinder with the green lamp. He was nervous, so conscious of the time, yet he'd only found a handful of men and wasn't completely sure where he was. How many minutes had elapsed since he had landed – forty, fifty? Then, quite by chance, an airdropped flare illuminated a church spire, which he realized instantly was at Ranville, to the south-west of Drop Zone N and just a couple of hundred metres from the Orne.

By this point there were men dropping in three different zones and, following the pilots' evasive manoeuvres when hit by flak, at many places other than those planned. Broadly, though, the other elements of the 5th Parachute Brigade (the 12th and 13th Battalions) were also aiming for Drop Zone N, while the 3rd Brigade was split between one to the north-east, from which the 9th Battalion would hit the Merville battery and the Canadians secure the Dives River line, and another drop zone to the south, where Lieutenant Colonel Pearson's 8th Battalion would safeguard the south side of the divisional area.

Each man, once happy that his canopy had opened, was meant to pull a cord that would allow the kitbag he was carrying to drop below, hanging about twenty feet down on a length of rope. There were many mishaps. A good few of the ropes just snapped under the weight of the falling kitbag, the now unattached paratroopers watching their gear disappear into the darkness below. Some others found they couldn't detach the bags, landing with anything up to 90lb of additional weight still on them, with injuries often resulting.

Meanwhile, at his rendezvous point near Ranville, Pine-Coffin continued to employ the green lamp along with frequent calls by the battalion bugler in an attempt to rally his men. As the minutes passed, and still only a quarter or so of his fighting companies had turned up, he was starting to get anxious again. He was reluctant to move on the objective at anything less than half strength, but the timetable was such that, at around 2.15 a.m., Pine-Coffin decided he had no choice but to carry on.

At the bridges, the enemy had started to push back. Responding to early reports of the landing, some troops with armour moved up on the Caen, or western, side of the canal. A German vehicle, making its way gingerly forward, was soon in the sights of a light-infantry sergeant wielding a PIAT (Projector, Infantry, Anti Tank), a man-portable anti-tank grenade launcher. It used a powerful spring to loft a bomb up to fifty metres. 'We heard a "ping", we could almost see in our minds the bomb floating through the air,' Major Howard recalled, 'and thank God the first bomb to hit the leading tank was a direct hit.' The armoured vehicle (a halftrack, not a tank, in fact) was soon burning fiercely, its ammunition cooking off inside.

A few hundred metres east, in addition to his worries about the missing men, Pine-Coffin was also becoming aware that his heavy support weapons (Vickers machine guns and 3-inch mortars) had also gone astray. Radio communications were largely non-existent too, although some men from A Company moving up towards the Orne had a working radio, successfully picking up the code words 'Ham and Jam' from the Ox and Bucks operator at the bridges, confirmations that the glider troops had taken their objective. No sooner had word of this spread than men started to ditch the heavy kitbags containing inflatable dinghies.

Some parties of the 7th made it to the bridges, where the sounds of gunfire could be heard, before their CO. However, he led the biggest single group across at around 2.30 a.m.

Coming from the east, they first encountered the Ox and Bucks on the Pont Tournant, or swing bridge, over the River Orne, 'Howard's men were naturally in very high spirits and much friendly banter and chaff took place as the battalion hurried past them.' Pine-Coffin's boss, Brigadier Poett, was near the bridge, somewhat embarrassingly for the 7th Battalion's CO, given the precious time lost while he orientated himself and gathered his men at the rendezvous. Poett told the colonel to hurry, 'as if he thought we had been dawdling up to then', noted Pine-Coffin, rather nettled. His men pushed on a few hundred metres west to the canal bridge, which was of the type that could be raised to allow the passage of ships, in this case elevated with the aid of a great counterweight at one end.

Moving past the light infantry on the western end of that span, the paratroopers were entering enemy territory. As planned, A Company, or the seventy or so members of it who had assembled, turned left – south, more or less – after crossing the canal and moved to the outskirts of a village called Bénouville. B Company turned right, heading north along the canal bank a couple of hundred metres to another settlement, Le Port. C Company was held back as a reserve.

Howard's company was at this point also under Pine-Coffin's command, and about half an hour after the paratroopers from the 7th Battalion crossed the canal bridge, he pulled back the soldiers from the Ox and Bucks also into reserve.

While these defensive positions were being taken up, there were still hundreds of parachutists from this battalion, and several times as many if the whole force parachuting in were included, who were in the wrong place. One of the staff officers trying to find his way felt that 'the greatest danger was from our own troops, all of whom were a bit trigger happy'. Many of these men had miles to walk, some found themselves in areas close to the River Dives that had been flooded precisely to make the Allies' lives difficult.

With all this blundering about in the dark by small groups of men, dozens were inevitably taken prisoner. They had dropped among enemy units, though it had been hoped through careful study of aerial reconnaissance photographs not to deposit the parachutists right under the muzzles of German Spandaus. In the area where the 7th Battalion was feeling its way into defensive positions were soldiers both of Grenadier-Regiment 736, part of a second-line formation used for guarding the coast, and Panzergrenadier-Regiment 192, a rather more formidable and mobile fighting force belonging to the 21st Panzer Division, the main armoured reserve in that part of Normandy. The 8th Company of that panzer grenadier regiment, mounted in armoured halftracks, would form the main striking force against Pine-Coffin's men.

Several Marder armoured vehicles from Panzerjäger-Kompanie 716, the armoured anti-tank company of the local Wehrmacht division, were also brought into action. The Marder mounted a powerful gun on the hull of a converted light tank, and these vehicles, coming into the fight, would provide an armoured punch for counter-attacks towards the bridge.

On the eastern side of the Orne there was another panzer grenadier regiment that would soon be used against the southern flank of 6th Airborne Division. Wehrmacht territorial defence units there also included a couple of battalions of Russian and Turkic troops, captured Red Army men who'd thrown in their lot with the Nazis. These contingents wore German uniforms, with distinctive sleeve patches. For the most part they were less interested in fighting than their Wehrmacht masters and gave themselves up quickly.

One of the first tasks of the 13th Parachute Battalion was to dismantle a forest of posts, nicknamed 'Rommel's asparagus' by the defenders and designed to impede glider landings, in the area of Drop Zone N. This had to be done swiftly because seventeen gliders with heavy equipment were going to start landing there at 3.20 a.m. These brought in anti-tank guns, ammunition and other stores. The key thing for Major General Gale (who himself arrived by glider at 4.30) was to get some anti-tank guns into position before daybreak, when he felt it inevitable that some kind of armoured counter-attack would be launched.

Once on the ground, the general set about galvanizing his troops for this expected event. A reporter who had also come in by glider with the HQ heard the Norman darkness pierced by his distinctive, booming voice: 'Don't you dare to argue with me – Richard Gale! Get on I say, get on.'

Happily for the 6th Airborne Division, during the early hours most of 21st Panzer Division was paralysed owing to the absence of its commander and an order not to move into action without approval from higher headquarters. However, different rules applied in the coastal defence sector, where the 8th Company of panzer grenadiers from the 192nd Regiment, being under command of the local defence force, was moving in its halftracks against the paratroopers in Bénouville at about 4 a.m. In both that village and Le Port to the north there were numerous orchards and walled or hedged farmsteads. Add to that the continuing darkness and the result was a series of engagements at frighteningly close range.

Sometimes the first the British knew about the presence of the Germans in the next farm or field was when stick grenades came over a wall and landed at their feet. Some men were able to throw them back, but others took the shrapnel. In several places, including the Café Gondrée, right by the canal bridge, men were able to enter houses for protection and so they could use the upstairs windows as firing points. There were also some abandoned German trenches near the bridges that allowed some soldiers to get into cover.

Lieutenant David Hunter, a twenty-one-year-old Scot, took those of his platoon who'd turned up to explore southwards in Bénouville, towards the chateau of that name. But, hearing German words nearby, he asked one of his corporals to look through a hedge to see if he could spot the speakers. Shots rang out and Hunter realized, 'Oh God! I'd sent the brave wee man to his death.' The first glimmers of light were beginning to appear, as his men spotted a group of Germans crossing a field 200 metres away. Hunter sought a fire position to take them on from a nearby house, but the French owner barred them, shouting that he was afraid for his children.

Before Hunter could come up with a better way to fight this advancing enemy, grenades came over from a nearby orchard. The young lieutenant had been wounded by shrapnel in the ear, ordering his men to 'get the hell out of here!' They moved back into the main part of Bénouville, unable to occupy the positions they'd been previously assigned, falling in with the company commander, who was also wounded.

As the morning wore on, the panzer grenadiers brought halftracks (and possibly Marders) into the southern part of the village. One A Company man, twenty-year-old Private John McGee, 'started to walk up the middle of the road towards the tanks, firing the Bren gun from his hip'. This apparently suicidal tactic caused the crews to close their hatches and another paratrooper took advantage of their momentary disorientation to race up to within a few yards of the armoured vehicles, throwing Gammon bombs to disable two of them.

Two stricken vehicles (once again, the report that they were 'tanks' was inaccurate) were abandoned by their crews and the enemy push into the south of Bénouville stymied. The A Company men may well have mistaken a Marder for a tank, though their suggestions that they fought off a Panther proved ill-founded.

Dawn was to bring startling evidence of the great invasion getting underway. The booming of heavy naval guns shattered the early morning stillness. 'The vibration of air and sound', Lieutenant

Richard Todd, Pine-Coffin's assistant adjutant noted, 'was far beyond anything I could have imagined . . . the sights and sounds were literally breath-taking.'

The concussion assaulted the eardrums, and an A Company man said that when the big naval shells came over, 'it felt like they were tearing the skies apart'. This violation of the senses announced something more than wanton destruction, it reminded the paratroopers that their relief, by the seaborne forces, was a good deal closer. A little later, their feelings were stirred again when some RAF fighters passed low over the bridges, performing victory rolls as a form of tribute.

However, the brightening sky allowed enemy forward observers to bring in mortar fire and snipers to begin taking pot shots, which became a particular problem for B Company. Suffering from a lack of effective radio communications as they were, soldiers had to be sent as runners with scribbled or oral messages from one commander to another. Each time, they took their lives in their hands, bullets pinging off the sides of buildings or the road as they passed.

B Company's runner, Private Sid Cornell, was one of those who made his name that day. Cornell, who at thirty was old for the ranks, had a characteristic then unusual in Britain's national service army: he was black. He was known to many in the unit by the nickname 'Darky'. One of Cornell's officers later commented that they had been 'innocent . . . of the stupid nuances of racial prejudice'.

Cornell, though, knew when there was ill intent behind the words: stocky, skilled at boxing and 'hard as nails', he'd leathered a few who'd pushed their luck. Some soldiers used a more respectful nickname, Grandpa, because the presence of a thirty-year-old private soldier in that battalion was extremely unusual. His maturity, coupled with his toughness, meant that he soon distinguished himself on the battlefield. At one point, the B Company commander and Cornell went off to stalk a sniper, just the two of them. They found their man and dispatched him quickly.

Another action followed when some paratroopers noticed that

the church tower in Le Port was being used as a sniping post. Several men entered the building, heading for its staircase, but their footsteps prompted those above to send stick grenades clattering down the stone steps. The problem was eventually dealt with by firing a PIAT at the church tower.

The defensive positions on the western canal bank came under a series of attacks that morning from the panzer grenadiers. There was the push from the south into Bénouville and a number of probing attacks by company-strength groups (fifty to a hundred men at this point) from the north and north-west into Le Port.

A push from that last direction had succeeded around breakfast time in edging through very close to the canal itself, leaving A Company cut off to the south of it. This push also resulted in the 7th's makeshift aid post being overrun. The officer commanding the 7th's anti-tank platoon was cut down by one of the armoured vehicles as he tried to stalk it with a PIAT. The arrival of enemy troops in the northern part of Bénouville was doubly serious because nobody was sure of the fate of those inside the regimental aid post, and those wounded from this point on, particularly in A Company, found it hard to get help.

The infiltration of many panzer grenadiers into the buildings of Bénouville and Le Port led to further face-to-face encounters. Private John Butler, in the same platoon as Dennis Woodgate and, like him, just twenty years old on D-Day, was kneeling in a defensive position in Le Port when 'suddenly a big Jerry came into view with his rifle pointing towards me'. Butler emptied the half magazine left in his Sten gun into the German, 'but to my horror the man didn't fall down as I expected and just stood looking at me, I was in absolute terror.'

Staggering towards Butler with a bayonet fixed to his rifle, 'the man came at me, collapsing on top of me, and his bayonet pierced my left thigh . . . I pushed his body off me and realized he was dead.' Butler felt ashamed that he had been so frightened, choosing to conceal for the time being the wound to his leg.

At around 10 a.m. two figures were seen crossing the Pont Tournant, heading on towards the canal bridge. Striding along, sporting desert pink jodhpurs, a cravat and a para smock, was their divisional commander. Gale had the commander of 6th Airlanding Brigade with him and was followed up by Colonel Malcolm MacEwan, who came to investigate the casualty-handling situation. 'It was a remarkable morale booster,' said one of the men, 'albeit rather foolhardy under the circumstances', with all the sniping going on.

As they neared the canal bridge, Gale spotted two small gunboats coming up the waterway and called out a warning to Pine-Coffin at his makeshift HQ, just over the bridge. The leading craft, having engaged the 7th Battalion's command post, was hit by Bren gun and PIAT fire in response and was soon foundering. The other boat turned about quickly and headed north, towards the port of Ouistreham. Two prisoners were taken from the lead boat while Gale and Pine-Coffin conferred.

The excitement on the canal having passed, the checking of watches resumed. Under the plan, a Special Service Brigade of commandos led by Lord Simon 'Shimi' Lovat, should have been reaching the bridge by this point. In the fog of war, nobody was entirely surprised that this hadn't happened, but enemy action was slowly wearing down Pine-Coffin's force. Unbeknown to the CO, because they were cut off, all of A Company's officers had become casualties. Their commander carried on giving orders from a trench, following a serious thigh wound, and Lieutenant Hunter managed to keep his men fighting despite the shrapnel he'd received from a grenade in the early hours.

Pine-Coffin was particularly worried that the gap formed by the isolation of A Company would expand into the area of his command post at the western end of the canal bridge. This would not only isolate B Company in Le Port but also put the use of the bridge itself into doubt. Fearing the 7th Battalion could be overrun, Gale had before his departure ordered about fifteen men from Howard's Ox and Bucks company to cross the bridge, reinforcing the positions on the western bank.

Some of these men had found a position in cover and were rooting about their kit for some food when 'a stream of bullets ripped through the tree inches above our heads, showering us with twigs and leaves'.

Evidently spotting this action so close to his HQ, Pine-Coffin came gingerly across at the crouch with Lieutenant Todd, each man having armed himself with a Sten and grenades. Eyeing the splintered tree, Pine-Coffin said, 'That is not too healthy old boy, he's firing a shade too close for comfort, we'd better deal with him, eh?' The two men loped off and a few moments later the light infantrymen heard sub-machine-gun fire.

Evidently the Spandau had been silenced. Pine-Coffin and Todd reappeared, 'with broad smiles on their faces, looked towards us, and the Colonel said, "Well lads, that's fixed them up" . . . two grand officers who gave the impression of having not a care in the world'.

The close-quarter battle, Pine-Coffin wrote, 'did not present much of a problem as the prospect of meeting the enemy face to face was relished by the battalion . . . no one had any doubts about their ability to deal with the Germans'. He could easily have been writing about himself here, since several of his men, quite understandably, found this fighting extremely difficult. True to the stoical, understated character that officers of his generation displayed, Pine-Coffin would not, when giving later accounts of the action, mention his mission with Lieutenant Todd and their swift dispatch of a machine-gun team.

It was around noon when those at the 7th's command post first heard the sound of distant bagpipes. Pine-Coffin and Lovat had agreed that the green berets would give this signal as they approached the red. For a time, the colonel held back his bugler from giving the pre-arranged response, being concerned that the area around the bridge was still subject to too much enemy fire.

Lovat, however, was becoming impatient, and around ninety minutes later his scouts probed their way through the orchards just south of Le Port and close to his HQ, where Pine-Coffin had been most concerned about enemy infiltration. These new arrivals soon joined in the task of trying to mop up the Germans in the area.

One of the commandos surveyed the scene: 'All movement was made at the double or crawling . . . both Jerry and Airborne dead and wounded lay sprawled in the road and in trenches. The whole area was pitted with shell and mortar holes and the air reeked of smoke and cordite.'

Caught between the bridges and forces advancing out of the beachhead, many German units had started to draw back to the south. This opened up possibilities of civilian movement here and there, seized first by French refugees, who appeared at the canal bridge throughout the late morning. These locals, sometimes individuals, sometimes families, made their way along the roads despite shouted warnings from the paratroopers. The reduction in enemy troop numbers also made passable some of the roads leading inland from the coast to those sufficiently brave or oblivious of danger to try it.

So it was that a convoy of Royal Engineer lorries carrying bridging equipment (a fail-safe plan in case the Germans had blown the Orne crossings) appeared at the northern end of Le Port, to the surprise and amusement of the paratroopers defending it. A similar arrival, of a Royal Army Service Corps resupply convoy, also beat the tanks and combat elements of 3rd Infantry Division to the canal bridge that afternoon. The airborne men got the lorry drivers into cover as soon as they could.

Although Lovat's men had initially helped the paratroopers, they were needed further east. At around 3 p.m., once gathered as a unit, they marched across the bridge with Lovat and their piper at their head. 'The finest sight of the lot was Lord Lovat and the Commandos coming through', Bob Tanner would recall, 'with their green berets, not a helmet on. They were coming through as if they were on a parade ground, you wouldn't think there was a war on.'

'A curious period of many hours followed the passage of the commandos,' Pine-Coffin wrote. 'As the afternoon wore on and still no signs of a relieving battalion the question of holding on for another night had to be considered carefully.' He wondered, not unreasonably, since a couple of convoys of rear-echelon types in lorries had already come through, what was holding up a fighting division.

The concerns about holding on reflected the sense that German sharpshooters and mortars were still causing casualties. They hadn't been much above half strength when they occupied the positions, and by this point in many places 'platoons' with a notional strength of thirty men had only a handful left. Many still holding the line had wounds with blood-caked dressings and were faint through hunger. Although they had compo rations when they jumped in – the usual items such as a beef block, oatcakes, chocolate and boiled sweets – most men had polished these off. One or two French householders had given them alcohol, the momentary pleasure of downing champagne or Calvados giving way to an even deeper fatigue.

It was 6 p.m. before leading elements of the 3rd Infantry Division appeared, and a couple of hours after that before the 2nd Battalion of the Royal Warwickshire Regiment started taking over the 7th Airborne Battalion's positions. Armoured scout cars were used to extract the survivors of A Company from Bénouville. So grateful were they for this relief that one commented he didn't mind lying on boxes of high explosive in the open-topped vehicle that took him to safety. Only twelve of the seventy or so members of A Company who'd gone to Bénouville eighteen hours earlier came out unharmed.

At 9 p.m., with the paratroopers moving to a rest area, an aerial spectacle began with the 6th Airlanding Brigade's Horsas swooping down into the drop zone they had used in the early hours of that morning. The pilots lined up individually, each coming in at a different angle and in a few cases colliding once they were on the deck. But they just kept landing, scores of gliders, one after the other, bringing 2,000 more troops to the fight.

Pine-Coffin stood by the bridge as his men filed back across at close to 1 a.m. on 7 June, pretty much exactly twenty-four hours after landing. 'They came through tired, dirty and hungry and many of them wounded as well, but all of them with their heads held high.' His brigadier, Nigel Poett, also appeared, thanking the soldiers as they passed. Whatever the early skittishness between the two men when the outcome had still been in doubt,

Pine-Coffin knew that his battalion had held fast despite multiple counter-attacks, and that his mission had been a complete success.

The initial reckoning, scribbled in the 7th Parachute Battalion's War Diary, was that eighteen men had died and thirty-six had been wounded. But this was quite wrong: the record would show that the death toll on 6 June was sixty-eight. That included, for example, the occupants of two downed Stirlings that the CO did not know about that evening. This would prove to be the heaviest single day's loss of any Parachute Regiment unit during the Second World War.

That the 7th Battalion and, of course, the D Company Ox and Bucks *coup de main* party had achieved a remarkable success was understood straight away. It was a vindication of years of planning, sacrifice and argument in the corridors of power.

Elsewhere that day, beyond the view of the 7th Battalion soldiers at the Caen Canal, there had been intense fighting too. The 9th Battalion under Lieutenant Colonel Otway had overcome a series of awful setbacks to take the Merville battery. Hundreds of its troops had been scattered, key heavy equipment had been lost and three gliders that were meant to land atop the objective had missed the target. Even so, their CO had pressed on with the attack, carrying the position with just 150 soldiers.

Alas, the heavy guns that were thought to occupy the casemates of this position were not there; rather, some lighter weapons had been put in place. Having succeeded in their mission, preventing the battery from opening up on the landing beaches, Otway's unit was so weak it had to relinquish its positions the following day, requiring the battery to be retaken.

The other units within their brigade had succeeded in dropping onto the five bridges over the River Dives and occupying key positions to secure that line.

It had always been expected that the 6th Airborne Division would face an armoured counter-attack on D-Day, and indeed it materialized, but not at the strength that had been feared. Some piecemeal attacks were made by troops in the area on the morning of 6 June, but these resulted in the rapid loss of three German assault guns and the falling back of accompanying infantry. The armour in this case was knocked out by a couple of the sixteen 6-pounder anti-tank guns brought in by glider during the early hours.

A *Kampfgruppe*, or battle group, of the 125th Panzer-Grenadier Regiment was organized during the day by its commander, Major Hans von Luck. His aim, using a company of fourteen Panzer IV tanks (in full, Panzerkampfwagen IV), a battalion of his mechanized infantry, the divisional reconnaissance battalion and some assault guns was to drive on the east bank of the Orne to Ranville, ideally taking the bridge over that river by nightfall. The delay caused by confusion in command, naval gunfire and air attack, however, meant that he didn't begin his push northwards until 5 p.m. that day. This made little headway, and members of the 21st Panzer Division were awestruck when they saw the arrival of the 6th Airlanding Brigade that evening, 'the lack of suitable means to defend against the incoming flight was shattering and had significant psychological effects'.

In just under twenty-four hours, the airborne bridgehead of two parachute brigades had been transformed into one of four through the arrival of Lovat's commandos and the 6th Airborne Division's glider troops. No wonder the enemy found it hard to deal with.

Von Luck, who had been aware during the day of arguments in the high command about whether to commit the division to immediate counter-attack or hold it back in the expectation of further landings elsewhere, was one of those demoralized. By late on 6 June, he wrote, 'It was clear to the last man that the invasion had succeeded, that it could now only be a matter of days or weeks before the Allies would have landed sufficient forces to be able to mount an attack on Paris.'

As exhausted British paratroopers went to get their heads down in the early hours of 7 June, there was still much fighting ahead, and many stories to be exchanged about some of the unlikely heroes who had emerged and about who had been where on that extraordinary day.

16.   The Quality of Mercy

The second night in the bridgehead was a time to eat and sleep a little, as well as to make sense of what had just occurred, to hear how friends had been lost and names made. Many of the men who'd gone astray on the first night drifted in, arriving in small groups, having been directed in by other elements of the division. It also meant getting some elements of the 7th Parachute Battalion organized, such as those with Vickers medium machine guns (or MMGs) and mortars. These were vital to their firepower but had been unavailable during 6 June because the containers holding the weapons had been lost in the dark. Indeed, it was well into the next day before Pine-Coffin's people were able to arm those two support platoons.

In their bivouacs, men swapped experiences of what had just passed. A good deal of it concerned the medics attached to the 7th Parachute Battalion.

Even before light on 6 June, it had established a regimental aid post or RAP in Bénouville. The officer commanding the RAMC section with them, Captain John Wagstaff, had converted two houses on opposite sides of the main street into places where the wounded would get initial treatment, for example to staunch bleeding, before being sent back down the casualty-evacuation chain.

When German troops pushed around Bénouville to cut off A Company, they had appeared in the street outside the RAP. Wagstaff and some others had hidden. The captain watched from an upstairs window as 'two Germans came into the courtyard, inspected our equipment and spoke to the owner of the house'.

They left, then, joined by an armoured vehicle, worked their way a short distance up the road where the other part of the RAP was. There, gunfire broke out in which a couple of RAMC medics and the battalion padre, George Parry, and possibly some wounded were killed. The Germans generally respected the red cross in Normandy, so what had happened? Had they deliberately opened up on the wounded and their helpers, or had those inside fired first?

Leonard Mosley, a reporter attached to 5th Parachute Brigade, later wrote it up under the headline, 'Airborne Padre Was Brutally Murdered'. The *Daily Record* article included a claim that 'the Nazi troops, who seemed to be in a completely frenzied condition, thereupon set upon the wounded, shooting and bayoneting them'. Revd Parry, wrote Mosley, had tried to place himself between the enemy soldiers and wounded, 'and in the struggle that followed bayonets or knives were used by the Nazis, and Padre Parry was cut down'.

Evidently the RAP had been overrun, and some of those inside killed, but it was the type of event that would spark all manner of rumour among soldiers fighting nearby. Even those a hundred metres away could not have known for sure what happened inside that building or its courtyard.

There were, however, two survivors from the overrun aid post: Bill Roper, who was a conscientious objector, and another RAMC man, Stan Carrington. They avoided Revd Parry's fate, hid, and, when relieving troops from the beachhead appeared in the street outside, made their way to safety, where, as might be expected among Tommies after such a trauma, 'we enjoyed a cup of tea'.

Roper's account, recorded later, was that, as the Germans had appeared at their part of the RAP, 'we dropped what we were doing, ran into an outhouse and got into a large wine barrel (empty) lying on its side. The Padre was killed as he made a dash for cover.' The implication was that Parry and the two RAMC corporals had been shot, but even much later there was uncertainty about the circumstances. However, neither Wagstaff nor other survivors from the medical section ever substantiated the newspaper's claim that Parry had been bayoneted or stabbed while trying to save patients.

In the midst of this close-range fight on D-Day there were no clear answers to what had happened, but Wagstaff decided to move the RAP and its surviving members from Bénouville to the Café Gondrée, closer to the canal bridge. During the days that followed some other members of 225th Parachute Field Ambulance came down to help him treat the dozens of wounded who came through.

One soldier who gained some attention was the conscientious objector George Skelly, who had walked into the night with A Company in the early hours of 6 June. Private Skelly had, later that morning, embarked on a highly dangerous mission to help the wounded in his company, which had been cut off. Creeping through the outskirts of Bénouville he had found some casualties, quickly setting about packing gunshot wounds with dressings and sprinkling sulphanilamide powder on them. Quite soon, the contents of his medic's bag were exhausted, Skelly recalling, 'I felt helpless and lost.'

Making his way to the captain, who had taken over command of the company from its wounded OC, Skelly asked permission to make his way back to the RAP for help. The officer agreed, sending the medic on his way with a 'best of luck'. It would take him the best part of three hours to complete the short journey, much of it crawling on his belly. Several times he had to stop, because 'I was fired on by a machine gun and by snipers.'

At one point, being a man of such strong religious convictions, Skelly, lying on his front, read a psalm from his pocket Bible. He trusted in its words, 'Be merciful unto me, O God, be merciful unto me: for my soul trusteth in thee.' When he finally reached the Café Gondrée, the private reported to Captain Wagstaff, who 'told us that A Company were still holding out and had heavy casualties. They required more dressings and stretcher bearers to evacuate the wounded.'

Since Skelly was the only unwounded stretcher bearer available for the job, they could hardly send him back on his own. But later a couple of light armoured vehicles belonging to the Royal Engineers that had arrived on the scene were decked out with Red

Cross flags and sent south to Bénouville. The injured company commander was among those brought out, noting, 'no German fired on those vehicles when they were evacuating wounded'.

Skelly's officers were so impressed with his running the gauntlet from Bénouville that they recommended him for the Military Medal. Pine-Coffin endorsed this, setting his face against the principle observed up to that point of the war that conscientious objectors shouldn't get decorations. His backers prevailed and Skelly's citation was later approved.

Another conchie from the 225th was similarly recognized for an action on the morning of D-Day. He had been in a group of stretcher bearers sent out to clear casualties left the previous night on Drop Zone N. German snipers had tried to pick them off as they went about this task, killing two and wounding four among the stretcher parties. Since they were unarmed, wearing Red Cross insignia and obviously clearing the wounded, this infuriated many British paratroopers.

On both sides in Normandy there were daily dilemmas about the rules of war, or the morality of killing. When they'd been training in England, General Gale had told them, 'I don't want any bloody nonsense about taking prisoners. You are there to kill Germans!' This chimed with what the paratroopers had been told about leaving their own wounded behind on the first night of the operation: prisoners and wounded were a distraction, they would slow you down on the way to the bridges, or whatever else your objective was.

The Germans fighting around those Norman villages had got the message, which was similar to the doctrine of their own airborne forces. Questioning two prisoners a few days later, a staff officer reported their view that, 'we'd been told that the British Paratroops, anyone they capture, they kill'. Yet their survival, and that of hundreds of others who'd surrendered during the first few days, demonstrated that there was no such blanket order. But in the first day or two, men undoubtedly died because the rules of the game were momentarily fluid, and some took literally the exhortations Gale had given them in England.

Captain David Tibbs, the 225th's doctor attached to the 13th Parachute Battalion, commandeered a rickety farm vehicle on the first night to carry casualties. He encountered some paratroopers who had shot a pair of enemy soldiers on a motorcycle combination, and they asked Tibbs if he could take one of the wounded men. Unsure of his vehicle's ability to make it up the gradient ahead with another casualty on board, Tibbs said no.

Moments after he set off, he heard a gunshot. The paratroopers had killed the wounded German. The doctor went back and told them, 'I was going to collect him on the way back and didn't want to have any extra cargo on the way up. I should have explained that to you. My fault.'

Encounters with the enemy that night left much to the decisions made by frightened young men, most of whom were in action for the first time. Another conchie sent out with a stretcher party on the first night found himself captured by a German patrol that was trying to move out of the airborne division's landing zone under cover of darkness. After a while they set the paratrooper and his casualty free because moving a wounded man on a stretcher was slowing them down too much.

During the early hours after landing, the commander of 225th Parachute Field Ambulance established its central operating base, known as the main dressing station, or MDS, at the Château de Guernon-Ranville, just south-west of their drop zone and a short distance south-east of the Orne bridges. It was here that the casualties from Wagstaff's RAP and those of other units within 5th Parachute Brigade were brought to be stabilized prior to being evacuated from Normandy. At the MDS they could carry out emergency surgery and blood transfusions as well as patching people up. This ability to conduct operations within the MDS was something that Gale in particular had insisted upon, knowing that it might be days before his wounded could be evacuated to proper hospitals. D-Day was to prove so bloody for the 6th Airborne Division that they were all but overwhelmed.

One medic at the MDS noted, 'we admitted 500 casualties in the first twenty-four hours and by the morning of D+2 we were so cluttered up with the wounded, in the cowsheds and everywhere, one did not know where to put the next one . . . my own department, Resuscitation, resembled a slaughterhouse.'

On 7 June, a German advance came close to this dressing station. A panicked driver ran into the barn where Tibbs was treating casualties, saying the Germans were just yards away. A wounded Glaswegian sergeant levered himself up and picked up his Sten, calling out, 'Stop yer blathering, ye fucker, or ye'll be the first to go!' Tibbs continued his account, 'The driver disappeared hurriedly and there was a general movement amongst the wounded as they struggled to arm themselves.'

One of those Tibbs spoke to in these moments of panic, a seriously hurt Catholic padre, urged Tibbs: 'David, remove my gun. If the Germans find my pistol, they'll shoot me.' Noting the fashion for many medics (the combatant ones, that is) and padres to carry pistols, Tibbs realized how dangerous it was and how little guidance they received in England on either the wisdom of this or the laws of war more generally. 'In the quiet that followed,' the doctor wrote later, 'I reflected that it was wrong for the wounded to be armed, especially under a Red Cross flag, so I told my orderlies to collect and hide all weapons.'

It's possible that those killed in the 7th's Regimental Aid Post at Bénouville died because of such factors – a confusion about who was carrying weapons while under protection of the Red Cross. As the fighting wore on it became commonplace for British RAPs to contain German casualties, or indeed captured medical orderlies, and vice versa. The understanding that shooting up an aid post might well kill your own people as well as the enemy's became widespread. And the non-combatant medics inside those ad hoc medical posts did think quite differently from the typical airborne soldier, one arguing, 'I didn't feel the slightest bit of hostility towards German soldiers, they were as much victims of this situation as British casualties or French civilians.'

Something else changed after 7 June, too: the terrible pressures on the MDS were eased when large-scale evacuations over the beaches began. The wounded were taken by ambulance across the

Orne bridges, then north to the seaside, being ferried out to hospital vessels and then onwards to England. This system took some days to establish.

Skelly and his non-combatant brethren continued to run their daily risks on the front line. Bill Roper, one of those who'd survived the events at the Bénouville RAP, later summed up their mission: 'We felt it was a great privilege to serve these men, having parachuted with them in training and then in action . . . We felt we were able to serve God and our fellow men in this way.'

The combatant members of parachute battalions came to respect and revere their attached conchies. They ran the same risks unarmed, often showed real guts and might save their lives, after all. As the Wehrmacht launched counter-attacks on the airborne bridgehead, the medics' skills would be put to the test repeatedly.

17. Normandy's Killing Fields

By 7 June, with the initial shock of the Allied landings over, frustrated German commanders had at last received the order to make a more serious attempt to counter-attack the 6th Airborne Division. The armoured assault feared by Major General Gale was finally about to materialize. Between the 7th and 13th of that month this became the period of decisive trials for them.

On the morning of 7 June a group of tanks from the 22nd Panzer Regiment's 4th Company, numbering fourteen tanks on D-Day, backed up by mechanized infantry, started to push north near the village of Escoville. This unit, part of von Luck's *Kampfgruppe*, were engaged in probing attacks to find a way to unlock the airborne division's defences.

The tanks were Panzer IVs, the Wehrmacht's workhorse and a very capable vehicle. But they had to crawl forward, often at a walking pace, since they knew the enemy was ahead and could surmise he would have anti-tank weapons. Frequent British artillery strikes meant the tanks' crews often closed down, shutting the vehicles' hatches for better protection, though this also reduced their situational awareness.

Each shuffle or tactical bound of this movement involved driving between one bit of cover, for example buildings or a hedgerow, across open ground to another. While one tank advanced, others would cover it, the gunners peering through their sights, scanning places that might conceal an enemy gun or tank.

Their experience of that morning is revealed in a divisional history by Werner Kortenhaus (who served in that company). The serial number of each tank of the 4th Company began with a 4, and, cresting a ridge that overlooked the 6th Airborne Division's landing grounds, 'Panzer 431 was hit. The loader was killed immediately.' If the enemy was close enough, panzer grenadiers could machine gun anti-tank gun crews, but British artillery shells forced the infantry to go to ground. They were blocked.

The company commander took the decision to pull back a few kilometres to the west, but the still-advancing Panzer 433 had lost contact. A communications problem, or something worse? He ordered Panzer 435 forward to investigate: 'It was immediately knocked out by two anti-tank rounds.' Then Panzer 432 was struck on its main gun, putting it out of action. Three of his tanks had been lost and 433's fate was unknown. The commander decided to consolidate his position and forget any further advance.

These probing actions had come up against the Royal Ulster Rifles (part of the glider brigade flown in the previous night) and the 12th Parachute Battalion. They had sufficient 6-pounder anti-tank guns with them to see off the threat.

What von Luck's hapless subordinate was discovering was a lesson that would become all too evident to Allied commanders, that the countryside of rural Normandy, studded with villages and woods and criss-crossed by hedges, gave formidable advantages of concealment to the defender. At the broader level this made it impossible for Allied forces to advance at the speed dictated by General Montgomery's plan, with its initial aim of reaching the city of Caen by the end of D-Day. But at the tactical level it also made it very tricky for the Germans to counter-attack in order to mop up the airborne bridgehead.

There were further probing attacks on the 8th, followed by another set-piece move against Escoville and Hérouvillette, a kilometre to the north, on the 9th. Once again a well-organized defence, in which the British troops lining the hedgerows could use their anti-tank guns while having the backing of the 3rd Infantry Division's artillery, over to the west of the Orne, and naval gunfire from cruisers just off the coast, proved decisive. The Germans lost four tanks in less than an hour, including Panzer 400, the 4th Company commander's vehicle, he being seriously wounded. Their accompanying panzer grenadiers had suffered forty killed. 'The losses were bitter,' a member of the 4th Company wrote. 'The failure came as a shock, nobody had expected the enemy to be so strong.'

Their battlegroup commander, Major von Luck, blanched at the firepower available to the Allies: 'At any movement, even of an individual vehicle, the enemy reacted with concentrated fire from the navy or attacks by fighter-bombers.'

Inevitably perhaps, the German defenders felt these materiel advantages gave the Allies a decisive edge, but much of what was going on in the hedgerows was about the actions of platoons or companies, small groups of British soldiers whose steadiness was essential to the defence of the bridgehead and who were at great risk also from artillery, even on occasion their own. The German high command had by 9 June ordered reinforcements in, including the 346 Infanterie-Division. It had been occupying positions to the east of the Allied bridgehead, and was now to move west in order to engage the British airborne division.

During the days following 6 June the airborne bridgehead came under pressure from north and south, and in places its depleted battalions yielded ground. Probing attacks from the south during 7–9 June had managed to check the British and push northwards into the Bois de Bavent. Gale worried that this could allow the attackers to drive a wedge between his two parachute brigades.

On the northern flank, German attacks initially reclaimed the Merville battery. Then, during the night of 9/10 June, elements of the newly arrived 346th Division managed to infiltrate northwards, sending one regiment southwards towards Bréville while the other, Grenadier-Regiment 858, moved south-west towards Ranville. By the early morning of 10 June leading elements of the 858th Grenadier Regiment had penetrated as far as some woods just north-east of Drop Zone N, little more than three kilometres from the Orne Pont Tournant.

At first light on 10 June, the drop zone revealed itself as a chaotic scene with dozens of Horsas still scattered about the cornfields. The arrival of the enemy this close to the 5th Parachute Brigade headquarters, the Orne bridges, their MDS and so many other vital points could have turned into a major crisis for the 6th Airborne Division.

For, in truth, as the German attackers in Bénouville had discovered four days earlier, once they were very close, the British forward observers became reluctant to call in large artillery barrages for fear of hitting their own troops. Instead, it evolved into an extraordinary opportunity to write off a German regiment, and for those like Pine-Coffin, who had buried so many comrades, to take revenge on a grand scale.

Sometime after 8 a.m., hundreds of German troops began to advance onto Drop Zone N in a south-westerly direction from a wood line. As they did so, they were being watched by a couple of companies of the 13th Parachute Battalion, the Vickers machine-gun platoon of the 7th Battalion as well as some of its snipers and a host of other curious British observers crouching in the hedgerows. The 13th covered the southern edge of that open ground, being close to Ranville itself. The soldiers from the 7th lined the western side of the drop zone. This allowed the British battalions to rake their enemy with fire from two sides.

A war correspondent was among the paratroopers, noting, 'the German infantrymen came on at a run', initially dropping down among the gliders as if that would give them any cover. Then they got up and moved forward again, 'gaining in confidence from the stillness'.

Pine-Coffin joined his men watching this spectacle. He ordered the machine guns and his nearby 3-inch mortars to make ready. The CO of the 13th Battalion had likewise told his men not to fire until his order and they had all manner of weaponry, including several captured MG42 machine guns, pointed at the advancing grenadiers.

'I wouldn't have believed it if I hadn't seen it,' said a brigade staff officer. 'Shoulder to shoulder they came across the ground.' When the Germans were only a hundred metres from the southern hedgerow lined by most of the 13th Battalion men, the British opened fire. Dozens of Brens and Enfields were joined in this murderous volley by the captured MG42s, now turned on their former owners by the paratroopers, spewing out hundreds of rounds in moments. The 7th Battalion was further away, but it had the weapons for it, and Pine-Coffin gave his men the nod.

'The 13th opened up with fire, then the 7th with machine guns and mortars. It was absolute carnage, which sickened me,' the watching staff officer remembered, 'seeing all these men mown down in numbers and coming on, still coming on.'

'You suddenly saw Germans, grimacing, wildly clutching their bodies, throwing up their hands and then falling by their dozens into the corn,' wrote the watching journalist. One or two brave officers, even in the midst of this, tried to get their men up, to fight through the ambush.

The range from the 7th Battalion men was further, 'but this was very suitable for both MMGs and mortars and they took a heavy toll', Pine-Coffin opined, adding that his snipers 'O'Sullivan and Woolcot had a real field day too'.

With this storm of bullets and mortar rounds cutting down men and corn alike, the will of the 858th Regiment could not last long. 'Some of the Germans stood up and put their hands in the air,' according to a lance corporal of the 13th Battalion, 'but it was too late to stop firing, they were all mown down.' A few dozen of those caught in this terrible maelstrom did manage to flee down into Le Mariquet woods (on the southern side of the DZ, to the west of the 13th's positions). But the losses were grievous.

One of the British eyewitnesses estimated that there were 400 enemy bodies left behind in that field. So many, indeed, that French farmers were hired to help in the task of collecting and burying them.

The paratroopers were not finished. At 3 o'clock that afternoon a couple of companies of the 7th Battalion were formed up to assault the woods, to where dozens of Germans had fled. Pine-Coffin was promised tank support for this operation and in the end eight Shermans of the 13th/18th Royal Hussars were committed. Like von Luck's panzer troops, they were to discover the ample opportunities for concealment in the Norman undergrowth that gave defenders so many advantages. Five of the Shermans were knocked out, Pine-Coffin judging, 'the tanks were stationary for anything up to twenty minutes and paid the penalty for doing so'. But they added to the toll of German troops killed that day, and the paratroopers from the 7th cleared the woods, accounting for another forty enemy killed and a hundred prisoners.

A German account of these events described the fate of the 858th Grenadiers as 'one of those tragedies that the war produced', estimating the loss that day at 'several hundred men'. The official casualty return for the 858th Regiment suggested that British estimates of 400 lives lost may not have been too far off the mark.

The following day Captain David Tibbs, the RAMC doctor, was sent out with stretcher parties to see if they could find any survivors in the cornfields. In several places he could see paths through the crops left by wounded men crawling away: 'You would walk along such a trail for perhaps two hundred feet or more and at the end find a dead German.'

Moving into Le Mariquet woods, Tibbs discovered more corpses frozen in the bizarre attitudes of death, but also something else that offended his sensibilities: 'I found that several of our men were already there, stripping the dead of wrist watches or other valuables.'

For Pine-Coffin, hardened by combat, a man with umpteen scores to settle, it had been an excellent chance to get the mortars and Vickers machine guns into action, a 'field day'. To Tibbs the enemy had been 'absolutely slaughtered', and in the woods they had been 'shelled mercilessly'.

Their general, who was already uneasy about the Germans infiltrating via the Bois de Bavent, must have regarded the outcome of the Battle of Ranville as very fortunate, because it had sapped the energy of a fresh division just at the time that he could most benefit from its weakening. Gale regarded dominating the woods and village to the north as the pivotal moment of the division's fight in Normandy, for 'unless we could clear Bréville our chances of retaining the bridgehead would be slender indeed'.

In order to fight this battle, Gale drew liberally on the support of I Corps, under whose command the airborne formation had come. They could provide him with enormous amounts of artillery support as well as infantry to bolster the position as his own battalions were so depleted by casualties.

So, on 11 June, Gale ordered a reinforcement battalion from the Black Watch to mount an attack on Bréville. Despite large-scale artillery support they suffered heavily from the enemy's Spandaus and mortars and fell back. Gale decided to try again the following night, committing the 12th Parachute Battalion as well. Because they could muster only around 300 men, a company from one of the airlanded battalions and a squadron of Sherman tanks were added to the force. They would also have the support of four field and one medium regiments of Royal Artillery, a total of 112 artillery pieces.

The Royal Artillery had emerged as one of the British Army's major qualitative edges in Normandy – able to deliver terrifying quantities of fire at short notice, ably placed on target by skilled forward observers who accompanied units. On the night of 12 June they had planned a short, sharp fire mission of ten to fifteen minutes with shells fused to airburst. Going off at height, typically around thirty feet, they would rake the enemy, including those cowering in trenches, with shrapnel.

Moving off to the attack at 10 p.m., the paratroopers could hear the rumble of the batteries west of the Orne starting their fire mission. But as the shells screeched overhead it soon became apparent that something was terribly wrong. Dozens of paratroopers were felled by the shrapnel whizzing crazily about their heads. Among others, this bombardment killed their CO and seriously wounded the brigadier of 6th Airlanding Brigade as well as Lord Lovat, who was there as an observer.

Although momentarily without unwounded officers, the 12th Battalion pressed on. Its former CO, there in another role, Colonel Reginald Parker, placed himself at the head of the troops. Seeing devastation in the burning village, with many British soldiers lying wounded in the rubble, he ordered the forward observer to bring in another stonk on the part of Bréville still in enemy hands. This, and the tanks moving forward, lacing any possible enemy positions with machine-gun fire, helped to secure the victory.

The local inhabitants were caught up in this nightmare. Next to the burning church, Parker observed 'in the ruddy glow of the flames, a party of screaming women and children rushing in a frenzy towards Ranville'. Bréville had been gained, but at a heavy cost. The 12th Parachute Battalion had three officers and twenty-eight other ranks killed and more than a hundred men wounded. It was barely 150 strong at the end of the action. To Major General Gale, 'it was that turning point' in his battle to eliminate the enemy presence in the centre of his area.

The following day, Pine-Coffin's 7th Parachute Battalion, which had moved into the village of Hérouvillette a couple of kilometres west of the Bois de Bavent in a supporting role, was also subjected to 'friendly fire', though with mercifully less serious results. A flight of four RAF Typhoons dived on the village, spewing down rockets from the racks under their wings.

These aircraft had become the scourge of German convoys moving towards the front, but on this occasion had confused Hérouvillette for the neighbouring, enemy-held village. The screeching of the incoming rockets struck fear into those on the receiving end, not unlike the Stukas of the Blitzkrieg years. Pine-Coffin testified they were 'most alarming weapons when you are at the wrong end of them'. While the battalion hunkered down in hard cover, there was one casualty, Private Skelly, the stretcher bearer who had distinguished himself on D-Day.

Skelly had taken shrapnel wounds in his legs and left arm. For a time, as he was evacuated to the RAP and then to the MDS, his comrades in the Parachute Field Ambulance doubted whether they could save his left foot. He was moved back to England and eventually to the Royal Infirmary in Liverpool, not so far from his family in Cumbria. There Skelly made a full recovery, a fact he put down at least in part to the prayers from Christian Brothers in the area.

The position of the 6th Airborne Division was by mid-June as follows: it had successfully secured a bridgehead approximately five kilometres by eight; in doing so it had taken heavy casualties, but withdrawing the division to Britain to rebuild it was not an option since their higher commanders were constantly short of well-trained infantry. Gale would later write, 'I was convinced that no commander will readily release troops that are deployed in battle.'

So, anticipating that 6th Airborne might be in Normandy for months, the staff set up divisional rest areas where soldiers could visit a mobile bath unit, read the papers and even take in a show put on by the Entertainments National Service Association (ENSA) or see a film. Some caught George Formby, singing with his ukulele, others one of the latest American pictures, projected onto a sheet tacked to a farmer's wall. As Montgomery's 21st Army Group launched a series of large-scale offensives aimed at capturing Caen and breaking out of the Normandy beachhead, the paratroopers were left in a supporting role. That city, lying at the hub of rail and road connections, was to become totemic in the hard fight to break out of the Normandy beachhead.

The German troops opposed to them, including the heavily battered 346th Division, were in a similar position, holding on but unable to generate any offensive action while battles raged to the west of them. They did, however, use mortars and multi-barrel rocket launchers to punish those in the bridgehead on a regular basis. The Nebelwerfer (or 'smoke launcher') was a towed rocket launcher with six barrels for 150mm projectiles. It was cheap to make and, if loaded with high explosive instead of smoke rounds, could plaster an area with a great weight of fire in a short period of time. Allied troops soon nicknamed them 'Moaning Minnies' because of the distinctive noise made by the rocket motors as they raced into the sky.

One officer of the 7th Parachute Battalion described hearing a launch: 'Six reports and the characteristic blood-chilling moan rising in intensity seemed to fill the sky and beat every sense out of me but the one for self-preservation . . . when they landed, I was incapable of rational thought.' Even the most sanguine observer would have understood that the odds of surviving for long in these conditions were not good, particularly as an officer, given the need to lead by example.

Within a couple of weeks of D-Day, none of the 7th Battalion's nine rifle platoon commanders who had parachuted in were still in post, all having become casualties. Even among COs, who were meant to take a more detached view of the action from a little further back, Johnson of the 12th had been killed and Otway of the 9th evacuated as a casualty. In terms of total strength, the airborne division's parachute battalions had each been ground down to between 200 and 300 men, about half of the strength they had arrived with.

Pine-Coffin and his fellow COs realized that this new situation of static warfare and frequent bombardment would wear down his people if he did not try to dominate the enemy-held ground to their front. It would be done through patrolling, sniping and generally unbalancing the Germans. 'The gaining of patrol ascendancy was an interesting game and was tackled systematically and with enthusiasm by all concerned,' he wrote.

Intelligence was plotted from aerial photographs, prisoners and previous patrols in order to pinpoint enemy positions. He could strike them by a variety of means, from fighting patrols to snipers or by calling in artillery barrages. Given the effects on his own troops of such weapons, he was always on the lookout for enemy mortars or Moaning Minnies, hoping to knock them out.

On 18 June, while the battalion was in the line in a village called Le Mesnil on the edge of the Bois de Bavent, he sent a large-scale raid by B Company to sort out a German mortar position in a group of farm buildings.

Very little went to plan during the mission, led by the acting company OC, Captain Bob Keene. Moving forward towards the buildings they dubbed thereafter 'Bob's Farm', they were surprised to find an enemy platoon formed up and about to mount its own action. Keene quickly changed his plan, moved to attack them, and there was a firefight. Pushing through to the farmyard, having taken casualties among his men, Keene discovered his mission had been a futile one: 'We reached the so-called mortar pits and, to our dismay, they were not pits at all but large craters caused by Typhoons who had beaten the place up with their rockets.'

Extracting his men after this disappointment, Keene discovered his company sergeant major had been killed while manning a Bren gun, having lost a duel with a Spandau. Although Keene and his boss, Pine-Coffin, professed themselves happy with the mission, arguing it had cost 'the Boche' six prisoners and thirty killed, it had also worn down B Company once more. Two men had been killed on the mission and sixteen wounded, among the latter three officers that the battalion could scarcely afford to lose. The D-Day jumpers were being taken out daily.

Private Dennis Woodgate, in 9 Platoon of C Company, twenty years old by this point, had also survived D-Day's fighting at the canal bridge, which was renamed Pegasus Bridge by the division. He had managed to write a first letter home to his parents in Orpington on 14 June. They received it on 21 June, his mother swiftly passing on Dennis's news to his brother in the RAF: 'So far he is OK thank God. He said tell Dad plenty of wine and beers in France.'

Letters home were subject to censorship, usually by one of their company officers, so Dennis was circumspect. On the other hand, he knew that the course of the battle in broad terms could be reported. Writing to the paratrooper's brother, Woodgate's mother Mary paraphrased what she'd learned from his letter of 14 June 'when they left England they landed safe and captured a bridge but it was a bloody fight. I only hope he comes back safe.' But by the time she wrote those words her son Dennis was already dead.

On 20 June the men of the battalion, still occupying positions in Le Mesnil, were enjoying what for them was a quiet day. It was a place from which they could patrol the Bois de Bavent, keeping the enemy on his toes. But the enemy had his own ideas about that, and when opportunity allowed would send a shower of mortar or Nebelwerfer shells at positions spotted by their own soldiers. At around 5.30 p.m. a salvo came into the British position, one round of which dropped right into the trench occupied by Private Woodgate and another man, killing both instantly.

★

The apparently random nature of deaths like this convinced a great many who had endured the first few weeks of fighting that they would never survive Normandy. Private John Butler, the soldier who'd been bayoneted by a dying German soldier on D-Day and was serving in the same platoon as Woodgate, had gone through a succession of further horrors. Since 19 June he had narrowly missed being killed by an incoming mortar round, stonked by British artillery dropping short, picked out for attention by an enemy sniper, then hit again by German mortar fire.

On the last occasion, in July, the incoming rounds had seriously wounded two machine gunners in a neighbouring trench. Butler saw one man had lost his lower leg, and he struggled to get a tourniquet on. 'I was too late as the first shell had done the damage and he had been bleeding freely for about 3 minutes.' The man died in front of him.

The following day, the battalion's medical officer diagnosed Butler as having battle exhaustion, 'or what the lads call bomb happy'. He was sent to a rest camp for four days. In truth, this 'rest camp' was not particularly restful, because it was close to the Orne bridges, which were frequently targeted for air and artillery strikes.

Soon after Butler returned from his four days out of the line, on 10 July, he was tasked with other members of C Company to take part in a second raid on Bob's Farm. Butler found himself equipped with an MG42, providing covering fire during a raid by B Company. He heard the sound of incoming Moaning Minnie shells, but there was nothing he could do, the blast from one blowing him out of his trench and several feet across the ground.

Dazed, and realizing that his hand was bleeding, Butler tried to get back into his trench, only to see it had been caved in by the explosion. He found an empty foxhole and jumped in, just as another salvo of rockets hit their position, shaking every man to his core. Some of his mates were calling on him to help, there were more wounded. Butler would not budge: 'I felt so dizzy and scared, that at first I flatly refused to go and dived into my trench again.' He called it an attack of jitters.

Then something in him broke. Even though shells were still falling, 'I felt that I couldn't sit in a trench a moment longer, and although the barrage was still as intense I just had to get out and run.' He made it back to the RAP, where the medical officer declared him to be a battle-exhaustion casualty. Butler was evacuated down the line to the beachhead and did not return to action. Those weeks in Normandy had broken him.

As in Tunisia, when units became ground down they had to find replacements. Numbers were helped a little by the periodic return to the line of lightly wounded men treated in the bridgehead; sometimes they couldn't be fussy where the rest came from. In June the 7th Parachute Battalion had been sent three officers and a hundred other ranks. These were troops from the normal infantry-replacement system rather than trained paratroopers, standard national servicemen too, not volunteers. Like Frost in North Africa, Pine-Coffin found himself wondering whether this might herald a change of role, noting 'some despondency in the ranks. It seemed possible that our parachuting days were over.'

The wider story, as the 6th Airborne Division had fought to secure its part of the Allied bridgehead, was of a methodical if somewhat slow and costly progress by the troops to their west. Little by little the Allies had managed to push forward. During the second week of July, British and Canadian troops had finally fought their way into Caen, a bitter street battle all too audible to those a few kilometres away on the eastern side of the Orne.

On 18 July Montgomery had launched Operation Goodwood, deploying three armoured divisions onto the same side of the river as the airborne division. After observing the spectacle of hundreds of RAF bombers pounding the Bourguébus ridge to their south, the paratroopers watched the clouds of dust as the massed armour pushed in that direction towards their objectives. Goodwood did not attain all of its objectives, and cost the British hundreds of tanks, but, in the sector occupied by the 6th Airborne Division, it changed things quite dramatically. The enemy to the south of places like Longueval and Hérouvillette had been pushed way back. Major General Gale's airborne division would still be toe-to-toe with the Germans to the south-east and on the line of the River Dives, but it was a reduced frontage and they would be subject to the fire of fewer mortars and rocket launchers.

As the Allies consolidated gains during early August, Gale evidently thought there was a risk of morale and standards falling in his division. Casualties still occurred, though at a much reduced rate compared to June, and, given that the breakout battle was being fought by motorized and armoured forces, there were many who questioned why paratroopers still had to be there at all. So, they were subjected to numerous inspections, and the officers to pep talks by Windy Gale, the 7th Battalion War Diary noting, 'the gist of all these conferences was a "gingering up" in the Div to stamp out slackness'.

There was to be one more trial before the 6th Airborne could extricate itself from Normandy, and that came soon afterwards. By this point in August, the collapse of the German army in northern France was underway. The Americans off to the west had launched a breakout operation in late July, which had succeeded in enveloping to the south much of the enemy deployment. On 12 August the Allies started closing this 'Falaise Pocket' at its eastern end, pummelling dozens of German divisions while trying to prevent the withdrawal, of formed units at least, back towards the Belgian border. In this emerging battle the 6th Airborne Division was given a mission; to assist the breakout by moving south, via the town of Troarn, before heading eastwards in pursuit of that retreating enemy.

After several weeks of living under threat in the bridgehead, tramping through the same villages over and over again, the campaign had suddenly become mobile. The division was in pursuit of a retreating enemy, even though it had almost no motor transport in its own organization. The Germans had chosen to conduct a rearguard action east of the Dives, where the ground starts to rise from the river plain, giving their machine gunners and forward observers a vantage point. It was here that Major General Gale planned a phased operation, with one brigade taking bridges over a canal running north–south on the flood plain and the other following through to take a village called Putot-en-Auge on the slightly higher ground.

During the night of 18/19 August the canal crossings were forced, and by the early hours the 5th Parachute Brigade was getting close to the village. Picking their way through the fields, the 7th Parachute Battalion found a 20mm flak gun and detained some other parties of Germans who had been sent on a dawn patrol. Lieutenant Colonel Pine-Coffin had deployed one of his companies to his left flank, lining a hedge in case the enemy should approach across an open field to its north. He was trying to work out how to tackle the defences of the village to his front, where a couple of machine guns had already sent some salvos in their direction, when there were reports of movements in the field off to his left.

Dozens of eyes scanned the men who approached through the morning mist. Pine-Coffin felt they might be members of the 13th Battalion. They shouldn't be there, but he had been long enough about the business of war to know it was common enough at night for people to be where you weren't expecting them, and the last thing he wanted to do was open fire on friends.

As the men trudging along in the field, several dozen of them, drew closer, he realized some were Germans. Prisoners? But they were armed. They were all Germans. He ordered a platoon of men to skirt silently back along the hedge so that they could get Bren-gun fire onto the flank of this advancing company. Soon they were less than a hundred metres from his men in the hedgerow.

'It was a dream target, almost too good to believe but at the same time seemed too much like murder to be seized at once.' Pine-Coffin had been hardened by war, no doubt, but he had his limits. Some chivalry remained within him; perhaps he'd just seen too much slaughter in Normandy. His flanking party was commanded by a lieutenant who spoke German, and once in place he called out to them to surrender.

The advancing troops stopped stock still and then there was consternation. Some asked others what they should do; a couple, fearing what might happen, dropped down onto the field. Then 'one of the Germans did a very stupid thing', wrote Pine-Coffin. Dropping prone, he brought his Spandau into action, firing into the hedge occupied by Pine-Coffin's men. 'Many of [the Germans] were killed in the first few seconds' by the paratroopers' return fire, although the encounter did not turn into an annihilation, like the Ranville action of 10 June had. 'The firing was kept to a minimum,' Pine-Coffin noted. About half of the German soldiers, fifty men, were immediately taken prisoner. A similar number lay in the field, dead or wounded. Half a dozen escaped back into the mist.

That morning, the 12th Parachute Battalion cleared Putot and the 13th pressed on beyond, both battalions suffering more heavily from casualties than the 7th, with its supporting role. The brigade pressed on to the next defended river barrier, where a few days later it fought another tough action at Pont l'Évêque.

The French campaign was, however, coming to an end for them. Word came to make ready to return home. A rapid pursuit of the enemy across France into Belgium by armoured troops was taking place, called the 'Great Swan' by the armoured boys, who had used the phrase 'swanning around' during their campaigns in North Africa, and the continuation of the campaign would now be up to them and divisions of motorized infantry. Major General Gale's troops began to retrace their steps, all the way back to the Orne bridges, the beachhead and home.

Many bitter lessons had been learned when the division's six parachute battalions (five British and one Canadian) had jumped in with a total of around 3,300 men. Their losses amounted to 40 officers and 495 other ranks killed, 85 officers and 1,470 other ranks wounded, and 20 officers and 620 other ranks missing. The total, 2,730, underlines the very high risk of those who jumped becoming casualties or being captured, even allowing for reinforcements to that baseline 3,300 during the campaign.

After the pain suffered in relative obscurity in Tunisia, and the costly catastrophe of Sicily, they had boosted the reputation of airborne forces and the Parachute Regiment to a remarkable degree. Indeed, the action by the Ox and Bucks glider troops and

7th Parachute Battalion to take and protect the Orne bridges might justly be called the most successful by the Red Devils of the war up until then.

The achievements by this young division were being keenly watched in Lincolnshire. There the veterans of the 1st Airborne Division strained at the leash, waiting for the signal to get into action. It would not be long in coming.

18.   A Touch of Frost

While the 6th Airborne Division was engaged in its Normandy fight, the 1st Airborne Division was rebuilt in England. This involved a now-familiar process of receiving fresh drafts, then restarting the business of airborne training, with all its route marches, days on the firing range and night drops over rural England. Many of the division's units had not fully recovered their strength, or had some men in their ranks who had still not completed their jump training.

The first half of 1944 had not been a particularly easy time for the veterans of North Africa and Italy. To understand why, it is necessary to backtrack to the months before D-Day. Men in the 2nd Parachute Battalion, and their brigade more widely, knew that they had garnered a considerable reputation in the army. Indeed, many of those who wanted to follow in the footsteps of Lieutenant Jack Grayburn, who had joined the battalion in Italy, heard the 1st Parachute Brigade revered in training establishments or the messes of Bulford as the pioneers, the true crème de la crème.

Even in March or April 1944, many members of that brigade were convinced that they would be playing a leading role in the invasion of France. On 14 March, they'd been visited by General Montgomery, who, as everyone in the forces knew, had come home from the Mediterranean to open the Second Front. Lieutenant Grayburn had never seen the great man before and thoroughly enjoyed his talk, but noted of the men, 'for all their comments, I don't think the troops were impressed'.

Quite a few of the Red Devils had heard a Monty pep talk before, including in Tunisia, when he had told them to go and kill Italians. Employing his usual theatrics, the general had sported a red beret as he gave an impromptu speech from the back of his vehicle just before the Sicily drop. One sergeant, resenting the use of what for them was hard-won headgear, had muttered, 'I bet he couldn't jump off that jeep.'

Monty was just spinning them along in any case. The decision had been taken months before to commit Major General Richard Gale's 6th Airborne Division as the Normandy spearhead. The 1st Parachute Brigade, returning from the Mediterranean, had hardly endeared itself to the rest of the military. Many of its troops exhibited a lawless and condescending attitude that irritated others in the army. To one general inspecting them early in 1944, those veterans 'thought they knew it all'.

Alas for the airborne soldiers, the man who expressed that caustic opinion was Major General Robert 'Roy' Urquhart, who had been appointed in command of the 1st Airborne Division at the start of the year, taking over from Brigadier Ernest Down. Down's predecessor, George Hopkinson, had been killed in Italy, and, unlike those two men, Urquhart had no previous connection with the airborne family. Rather, the big Scot, 6' 2" no less, was an officer who had emerged from the hard school of Monty's 8th Army, where social ties counted for little and those who failed to deliver were quickly sacked. Urquhart had impressed his master by his handling of an infantry brigade in Italy, and thus captured what many in the army would have thought of as a plum assignment.

Johnny Frost, with customary pith, judged that his fellow Caledonian 'was not a man to court popularity', though Urquhart, who quickly saw that the division was in need of intensive training, merited respect if not affection, in Frost's view. In the spring of 1944 then, the new boss and his paratroopers sized each other up, the soldiers despising him as an outsider and he concluding that they really weren't as good as they thought they were.

One of the first things Urquhart did was to post new COs to the 1st and 3rd Parachute Battalions. In the case of the 1st, which as the original volunteer battalion held some who had been serving in it for three years, this went spectacularly wrong. Urquhart believed that these units needed to be 'gripped' – have the rough edges abraded away while being schooled in the modern army system.

So in February 1944 Lieutenant Colonel Kenneth Darling, a regular army officer from a well-to-do family who had attended Eton and Sandhurst before commanding a Territorial battalion of the Royal Fusiliers, was chosen. Arriving in the 1st Parachute Battalion (and not knowing the real plan, owing to the secrecy surrounding Overlord), he believed he might soon be leading them to France, writing to his parents, 'it is an inspiring thought that I should have been selected for command of this battalion which inevitably must play a leading and decisive role in the great operations which will take place in the near future'. Breathlessly, he told them that the previous CO had won the Distinguished Service Order three times.

Darling was a man on a mission. 'He had to go and clean up the mess,' the battalion's DSO-laden former CO Lieutenant Colonel Alastair Pearson later opined, 'and he went in like a terrier after that.' That characterization derived from Darling's short stature and intense manner. There were many things about the battalion that offended his sensibilities, from their devil-may-care insouciance to their irreligious nature. He wrote home that he had instituted church parade after a four-month gap without one, 'a pretty funny state of affairs!!'

Addressing his men on 3 April, the new CO left them with no doubt that he expected better. His speech to the battalion was noted as 'a "straight from the shoulder" talk on what he wants done and how, concerning training and discipline'.

The 1st Parachute Battalion was not unique in facing a crisis of sorts on return from the Mediterranean theatre. Many of those who had fought hard overseas felt they had 'done their bit', a view reinforced by family who shuddered at the thought of their going back into battle. These tensions among returnees produced a high rate of absence without leave, for example in the 50th Infantry Division, and a mutiny in one battalion of the 7th Armoured Division.

So it may be imagined how the veteran paratroopers took to the regime imposed by their new CO and a new regimental sergeant major appointed at the same time. 'They believed in a lot of discipline and blacking boots and polishing buttons,' one survivor of the North African battles believed. This battle of wills built rapidly in the battalion during April until, on the 11th of that month, on an evening that they were due to go for a drop, 200 men refused to draw their parachutes or leave their quarters.

Some characterized this as a 'mutiny', others suggested it was a 'strike', but there was no doubting the seriousness of the challenge to the chain of command. Indeed, at one point it was suggested that the 2nd Battalion was stood by to put their comrades in the 1st under close arrest. Hearing about the situation, a brigadier from the local headquarters appeared, and had the men paraded in front of Grimsthorpe Castle, the Lincolnshire stately home where many were billeted.

Addressing the red berets before this elegant Vanbrugh house, he asked them to nominate a spokesman for their grievances. Nobody wanted the label of ringleader, but after a suitably awkward period of silence the men started to call out their grievances, summed up by one as 'too much spit and polish'.

A promise was given that these complaints would be heard and acted upon, following which the men agreed to take part in the planned drop during the early hours of the 12th. A period of anxious consultations ensued, company commanders spoke to their men on 13 April. Two days later Major General Richard Gale appeared, holding meetings with long-serving members of the battalion. The choice of Gale, outside the 1st Battalion's chain of command (it was Urquhart who was their divisional commander, after all, and Gale had to take time away from intensive preparations for Overlord), spoke to his authority in the airborne forces as the founding commander of the 1st Parachute Brigade.

After Gale's visit, things moved swiftly; Darling was removed on 19 April and posted elsewhere. In his place David Dobie, a highly respected company commander in the 3rd Battalion during the bitter Tunisian battles, was put in charge. There were many other changes, drawing on talent elsewhere, with Major John

Timothy, for example, given one of Dobie's companies. A 2nd Battalion veteran of Bruneval, Timothy had led the raid in Cork Wood that captured two German machine guns.

Darling, while observing the rules of censorship, wrote to his parents to explain the awkwardness of his undoing after a disastrous two months in command, 'I have a perfectly clear conscience on the subject, and it is very nice the way many officers say how rotten they think the whole show was.' He would later say of the 1st Battalion, 'they thought they knew all the answers, which they certainly did not'.

While it did not result in any of the same theatrics, the 3rd Battalion also was perceived to have a 'discipline problem' at this time. Lieutenant Colonel Pine-Coffin had been sacked in May 1943, and his successor as CO was replaced before the 3rd went into battle later in 1944.

Johnny Frost's 2nd Battalion, under his practised eye, must have seemed like a rock of stability by comparison. But even his unit that summer contained a mixture of very different types of soldier: the survivors of North Africa, including many NCOs; recent drafts of untested private soldiers; and a clutch of officers desperate to get into action, of whom Lieutenant Jack Grayburn was the perfect example.

When the scales finally fell from the eyes of those who had wrongly assumed they would be going to Normandy, Frost read the mood, noting that it was 'a great blow to some'. One of Grayburn's brother subalterns in A Company wrote in his diary that 'the men were so jealous of the newly formed 6th Division that they daren't go home and tell their people that the 1st Bde, the cream of the elite, was still at Grantham'.

Their response was to train hard and play hard. Hearing the news of their comrades' successes at the Orne bridges, 'the only thing to do was to go and get tight at the Angel or Red Lion . . . I don't believe that a complete Div[ision] of troops were ever so browned off.' Many of the misadventures of the 2nd Battalion's men that July and August involved alcohol. Even majors got into trouble, Victor Dover, in command of C Company, having been given fourteen extra duties (a sanction more often awarded to second lieutenants still in their teens) when police stopped him with women in his army car.

Doug Crawley (the officer who'd walked back to friendly lines while temporarily blinded after the Oudna drop) was by this point a major in command of B Company. He had a particular way of dealing with disciplinary issues. Two men who admitted stealing speed-limit signs a few miles from camp in a drunken prank were paraded in full kit, then told they had an hour to return the signs and get back to camp or face fourteen days' detention. They succeeded. Crawley, as one of his soldiers put it, was 'capable of maintaining discipline with an element of training, no black marks on the record of those concerned'.

Major Digby Tatham-Warter, meanwhile, had A Company. Frost compared him to the English Civil War Royalist commander Prince Rupert: a charmer with a devil-may-care attitude. One of the long-serving corporals in his company commented, 'we were a new battalion', owing to the many replacements. While this was an exaggeration, it was true that neither Tatham-Warter nor any of his platoon commanders had parachuted into combat before.

Jack Grayburn was perhaps the keenest of all. If he had bemoaned his luck as 'almost too shattering' in the summer of 1943, when he realized that his transfer to airborne forces would not take him swiftly into action, it can be imagined how frustrated he was a year later, his fifth in the wartime army without experiencing battle. His attempt to find action had, in fact, gone completely awry, one of his many missteps being his pulling strings to get transferred out of the 7th Battalion in 1943, thus depriving him of a daring role on D-Day.

He was sufficiently energetic not to have given in to despair. Instead, he had channelled his energies into his platoon and raising money for the Airborne Security Fund. Grayburn had organized a boxing benefit night and a wild afternoon at the Stoll Theatre in London, where he and some of the soldiers had ended up cavorting on stage with the cast of a comedy revue before filling their berets with donations.

As for 2 Platoon, his military responsibility, it contained only a handful of the men who had come through the Oudna experience with Slapsey Brayley as their boss. Sicily had seen almost half the platoon captured and some others killed. Among the survivors at Grantham was Sergeant Frank Lyoness, who remained a hardened and dedicated soldier in command of one of the platoon's sections.

There's no doubt Grayburn drove them that summer. One of the platoon concluded, 'after a couple of months with him, I decided that he would get me killed because he wanted to win the Military Cross'. That private managed to move from 2 Platoon to company headquarters.

Was Grayburn a 'medal hunter'? Certainly, there were such men in the regiment, seeking distinction in battle. A fellow subaltern felt that Grayburn's motivation was 'a consuming hatred of Germans'. However, Grayburn confessed neither to such an emotion nor to a desire to win the Military Cross in his journal, even if it did testify to his yearning from the outset of war to experience battle.

Two others who had previously got away from the 2nd Battalion were also training in Lincolnshire that summer, destined to go back into action with their old outfit. Sergeant Mike Lewis, the East End boy who was transferred to the Army Film and Photographic Unit after being wounded in the Sedjenane valley fighting, was by this time with No. 5 AFPU, the team attached to the headquarters of 1st Airborne Division.

Lewis had mastered the DeVry film camera, a cumbersome block of a machine that shot 35mm film for the newsreels. It was planned that a team of photographers would drop into action with the division as well as some news reporters and a military censor. While Lewis was an old hand at jumping, several of the others had to get themselves trained that summer.

Lewis's old B Company friend from the summer of 1942, Arthur Maybury, had come through North Africa and Sicily in the brigade signal squadron. That summer Maybury put the finishing touches to the book he'd always intended to write as a tribute to the originals who volunteered for airborne service in 1941–42, but what he probably could not have suspected was that he was destined to return to action alongside his old battalion that summer.

In May 1944, Maybury had transferred from the signals to 89 Field Security Section or 89 FSS, part of the Intelligence Corps. With his facility for languages, lively mind and journalist's ability to write quickly under pressure, he was a good find for this outfit. This small corps divided its work into two elements; intelligence sections that gathered information about the enemy in order to keep British commanders well informed, and security ones like 89 FSS that sought to protect 1st Airborne Division from enemy attempts to infiltrate it or steal its secrets.

At the time that Maybury joined the section of around a dozen members they were billeted in a pub in Harlaxton, a village not far from Grantham. Military intelligence people customarily kept themselves to themselves, and the security precautions they observed created an air of mystery about their work.

Maybury used his down time during the first half of 1944 productively to earn money through his sideline, writing about the paratroops under the pseudonym Pegasus. He completed his non-fiction book *Parachutist* and submitted it for publication. He also wrote another of his books of adventure stories for young readers for Hutchinson: *More Thrills with the Paratroops*.

Spies and saboteurs loomed large in these fictional works, and evidently the idea of field security work appealed to him. Maybury's ability to profit from his military service, gathering characters and recording situations he encountered in the army, was unusual, to say the least.

In the summer of 1944, though, 89 FSS was just one of the many elements within Major General Urquhart's division whose work was hampered by uncertainty and frequent changes of plan about where they would be employed. After all, the intelligence pictures in France, Belgium and the Netherlands were quite different from each other. In each area the geography, enemy strength and friendly (in terms of resistance groups) or hostile (collaborators) nature of the local community varied accordingly, and their work that summer involved repeated efforts to understand the environment of one possible drop zone only to see it ditched for another.

For Lieutenant General Frederick 'Boy' Browning the late summer of 1944 was a period of bewildering activity and planning. A conference with the American generals setting up the First Allied Airborne Army one day could be followed by a flight to his HQ at Moor Park in Hertfordshire the next and consultations at the War Office in London the day after.

Having seen the 6th Airborne Division hurled successfully into action, Browning was simultaneously trying to establish his headquarters as one fit to command a corps (i.e. a group of divisions numbering upwards of 20,000 troops) while searching for a suitable operation for the use of such a mass of airborne forces. Little wonder that one of his American antagonists at the time called Browning 'an empire builder'.

The relationship with US colleagues, never easy for the Englishman, became increasingly vexed. The Americans held the dominant position in terms of transport aircraft and had far more troops available for operations, not least because they had swiftly extracted their airborne divisions from Normandy after D-Day, whereas Gale's 6th remained stuck in. The US had formed its own XVIII Airborne Corps HQ, able to lead operations by the 17th, 82nd and 101st Airborne Divisions. If there was scope for a big operation of this kind, didn't they have all the tools themselves?

This jockeying for position between military bureaucracies had led to the formation of an airborne army, no less: a formation that might normally be expected to direct 50–100,000 troops in the field. The notion that there would ever be the transport aircraft to get two airborne corps into action simultaneously, one British, the other American, was fanciful in the extreme. But the new HQ was a sort of statement of ambition, showing the desire of both the US and UK militaries to exploit the airborne arm to the full, if necessary by launching major operations in quick succession, during what remained of the war.

A search for the next suitable target for airborne assault after

Normandy had begun very soon after D-Day, with generals' staffs looking at notions of landing in western France, or of seizing Boulogne, taking bridges, and/or cutting off the retreat of German troops in north-east France or even Belgium. Each time, events moved faster on the ground than the apostles of airborne warfare could manage to put their ideas into practice.

By late August, with the enemy in retreat from northern France, an ambitious plan, Operation Linnet, was hatched to pave the way for the advance of XXX Corps towards Brussels. This was planning on a big scale, involving 1st Airborne Division, the US 82nd and 101st and the 1st Polish Parachute Brigade. Troops were moved to airfields, the great fleets of Dakotas, gliders and their tugs began to gather. The ground forces would be grouped under the command of Browning's I Airborne Corps HQ. But bad weather and the changing picture on the battlefield put paid to it, and by 2 September Linnet was cancelled.

The strains, not least of trying to mount an operation quickly enough to make a difference, then led to a flare-up between Browning and his American superior Lieutenant General Lewis Brereton, commanding the First Allied Airborne Army. While the troops were still at the airfields Brereton proposed a different set of objectives in the Aachen–Maastricht area of the Netherlands, Operation Linnet II. Browning objected that there was not enough time to prepare and brief the plan. Brereton disagreed, at which point Browning threatened resignation.

It did not occur to the British general until too late that, faced with his rejection of Linnet II, Brereton might simply use the US XVIII Corps HQ to run it instead. Late in the day, Browning withdrew his resignation. Although the operation was later cancelled, this series of events at the high level early in September, known only to a few at the time, did serve to define the balance of power between Browning and Brereton, undermining the former's ability to object strongly thereafter.

With the cancellation of Linnet II, units returned to their bases, trying to see the humorous side of the situation but feeling the tension nevertheless. Major General Urquhart was disturbed by this run of cancelled drops, noting that 'there were already signs of that dangerous mixture of boredom and cynicism creeping into our daily lives'.

This was exacerbated when yet another operation, Comet, came down the chain of command on 7 September. This one was Montgomery's idea, based on a feeling that the Germans had been bundled out of Normandy, then Belgium, in such a demoralized fashion that, if the momentum could be maintained, a series of bridges could be captured by airborne forces that would pave the way for Allied armies to reach all the way to the Rhine at Arnhem.

It was intended that the three bridges concerned would be taken by a force of four brigades dropped more or less simultaneously: three from the 1st Airborne Division plus the Poles. An airfield would be secured and another division assigned to Browning, the 52nd Lowland, would be flown in. To Browning, writing home to his wife Daphne du Maurier, Operation Comet promised him action 'at long last'.

As its details were briefed down the chain of command, the reaction was less enthusiastic. The plan involved glider *coup de main* parties on the bridges at Grave, Nijmegen and Arnhem, to be swiftly reinforced by paratroopers, as in Normandy. Hearing it spelt out at a briefing, one officer whispered to his neighbour leading one of the bridge parties, 'a wooden cross or a Victoria Cross'.

When Johnny Frost explained the plan to his officers he did so in a way designed to appeal to their hunger for action and banish all doubt: 'the Brig. has promised me this, that the 2nd Battalion will without any doubt be put in the best position for taking part in the bloodiest part of any battle we may have and believe me, it will be some blood bath'. Given the issues with the 1st and 3rd Battalions during previous months, and Frost's firm grip on his own battalion, it was logical that Brigadier Lathbury should give them the key role in seizing the Arnhem bridge.

That was a big structure, though, spanning a broad river in a large town. Would 1st Parachute Brigade really have the numbers to hold out against any sort of determined opposition? Hearing the Comet plan, one of Frost's subalterns wrote in his diary, 'it did seem like rather a complicated method of committing suicide'.

When Comet was in its turn cancelled late on 9 September, many were relieved to head back to camp. Those who could obtain passes went out to get drunk.

A day or two later, Lieutenant Colonel Johnny Frost was walking through camp and noticed Bill Bloys reading a newspaper, the *Daily Sketch*. Bloys was a veteran of the Tunisian campaign who had been transferred from A Company to HQ Company to be part of Frost's small protection detail.

'How's the war going?' asked the colonel.

Bloys relayed the latest news from the Eastern and Western fronts: the enemy seemed to be falling back on all sides.

'There won't be any Germans for us to kill, time we get there!' said Frost ruefully.

By 12 September Browning was briefing yet another operation at his headquarters at Moor Park. It was, by the count of later historians, the sixteenth proposal considered that summer to get 1st Airborne Division back into the war. By the 2nd Battalion's count, of operations they'd actually made preparations for it was the sixth.

The new plan, Operation Market, also involved an airborne assault on the three Dutch bridges, but on a much grander scale than Comet. The US 82nd and 101st Airborne Divisions would be involved too, with the British and Poles focused on just one target: Arnhem. In Phase 2, code-named Operation Garden, the British XXX Corps would force its way along the route to that town, crossing the bridges taken by the Americans on the way.

This grand design, Market Garden, owed its theory to Montgomery, and pretty much everything about its execution to the decisions made by Lieutenant General Brereton and the air commanders at his headquarters. The allocated force was too large for one lift, and would have to come in by daylight, across three days. Since the flyers would be more nervous of German air defences, this meant abandoning the glider *coup de main* parties and landing troops further away from their targets, in particular from Arnhem.

While the plan envisaged relief by XXX Corps in forty-eight hours, they would have more than eighty kilometres to cover against opposition. Browning's chief staff officer, Brigadier Gordon Walch, noted a conversation between his boss and Montgomery: 'General Boy said he thought it was possible, but that perhaps they might be going a bridge too far with the air lift available. His opinion was understood and appreciated.'

Because of his rescinded resignation of earlier that month, Browning was hardly in a position to push his point. There were doubts among his people about going by day, dropping so far from Arnhem bridge and staggering their build-up of forces over three days. But Monty wanted it and the Americans were leaning in hard.

Very few of those at Urquhart's briefing on 12 September, however, chose to say anything when he invited questions. 'Not one brigadier or unit commander spoke,' the Polish brigade commander noted, astounded by the absence of comment. 'I looked round but most of them sat nonchalantly with legs crossed . . . and waiting for the conference to end.'

One of Lathbury's staff at 1st Parachute Brigade felt that 'we were all infected with this feeling of impatience, intense impatience. It wasn't just the 15 or 16 that had preceded this, I'd been doing this since 1941 . . . years of being buggered about.'

As brigades and battalions broke the plan down into its constituent parts, there were discussions about the distance of the main drop zone from Arnhem and the fact that inserting the division over three days would mean one brigade would have to guard the drop zone, awaiting the reinforcements, reducing the force heading to the bridges to just one brigade, the 1st Parachute, which was little better than the Comet plan. There were also intelligence reports about German armour regrouping in the area. None of this made much difference to the protagonists. The division had plenty of anti-tank guns and PIATs, and, as for that distance to the bridge, they would cover it.

Their mood was such that, in the pungent words of one staff man, 'I think really, if we'd been asked to drop in the middle of Berlin and to hang on until the Russians came, I think we'd have been perfectly happy to go.'

What about those at the unit level, though? Late at night on Friday 15 September a group of officers returned to the mess from a two-day bender in Nottingham, where the pubs at least had beer for those doing war work in the factories. The following afternoon, a hungover Lieutenant Robin Vlasto, one of Grayburn's fellow platoon commanders in A Company, went to have it all explained at a briefing.

'We couldn't take it seriously at first,' he noted. 'This was Flap No 6, as registered on the board in the orderly room, and all hope of the 1st Division being given a chance before the armistice was signed had been given up long ago.' Their OC, Major Tatham-Warter, radiated confidence about the mission, and it was, after all, the scrap that his fellow former light infantryman Jack Grayburn had longed for.

Vlasto jotted the key details of what had to be done in his notebook. Lieutenant Colonel Frost told them the success of the operation, would depend – and he noted these in capitals – on SURPRISE, SPEED and GRIM DETERMINATION. His company was heading for the main Rhine bridge, which would have the codename Waterloo. They did not expect there to be any up-to-date tanks about, though possibly a few old training types.

Among the experienced hands, preparing their kit the night before the jump, there were different attitudes. Sergeant Mike Lewis would be jumping with his old comrades in the 2nd Battalion, filming their descent. He'd survived disasters, from Oudna to Sicily, so felt, 'one couldn't help but be pessimistic'. A veteran in the 1st Battalion noted the enthusiasm of the officers who hadn't been in action before but felt those looking forward to it among the other ranks were 'not so many, pro rata, as the officers'.

The following morning, Sunday 17 September, they managed breakfast before leaving camp. Grayburn went for two poached eggs, some haddock, rounds of toast and marmalade, washing it all down with coffee. They mounted up in lorries for transport to Saltby aerodrome near Grantham after that, the Naafi staff waving them off, commenting, 'They'll be back in an hour's time, with another weekend's leave!'

As they waited by their aircraft, Frost did the rounds, geeing up each stick with some words of encouragement. Did the mask of command hide doubts beneath that smiling countenance? Apparently not: 'I certainly did not anticipate much difficulty as far as our task was concerned.' It was a beautiful sunny morning, which certainly lifted the mood of many.

As they waited by the planes, many smoked or made last-minute equipment checks. Some munched on the egg-and-bacon rolls given out by the Naafi wagon. Sergeant Lewis was fretting about getting a tracking shot along the long lines of Dakotas, trying to get a jeep to drive him along.

He found Major Crawley, a friendly face among all the khaki and weaponry. The B Company boss and Lewis had been together through the withdrawal from Oudna late in 1942. Levelling his DeVry camera, Lewis filmed Crawley and a group of NCOs looking over their stick lists, then donning their parachutes.

It was a bright Sunday morning, their aircrews, RAF lads, were confident. But among the veterans of previous drops, there could hardly have been any complacency. Frost's personal record, making his fourth operational jump, was highly unusual. Just nineteen of the almost 500 men loading up with the 2nd Battalion that morning were, like him, veterans of Bruneval.

There were some others, like Corporal Arthur Maybury, who had got their wings among the early pioneers but had jumped operationally only once before. In his case, Sicily had been an unforgettable baptism in the confusion and fear of parachuting alone at night into a battle. This morning, though, he would be among friends, for he too was destined to enter battle with his old battalion. As part of the field security team, he had a secret mission to discharge in Arnhem. Lives, quite literally, would depend upon it.

A great many of them, like Lieutenant Grayburn, urging 2 Platoon towards their planes, had never done this before. He was about to see the action he'd been waiting five long years for. His wife Marcelle and small son John would have him back soon enough.

At 10.30 a.m. they started emplaning, and less than an hour later the first Dakota was lifting off the Saltby runway, heading for the Netherlands. Formations built in the sky; people going to church saw the great masses of planes, waving unseen to those above. Even the most unmilitary civilian understood that these hundreds of planes passing overhead meant thousands of men were heading into danger.

Inside his Dakota, Frost read the *Sunday Times* and took an occasional smoke. Looking around the cabin, he could get the measure of the others easily enough, seeing the 'transparent insincerity of their smiles and furious last minute puffing at their cigarettes'. He had spoken during the preceding year of the 'bloodbath', the great slaughter that would accompany the war's last stage. And now, flying over the North Sea, he was leading his men right into it.

19.   The Bridge

Mike Lewis barely had a moment to think about his own kit as he landed on Dutch soil. His mission was to film thousands of parachutes blossoming in the sky, streams of men stepping out of Dakotas, floating down to earth. It was around 2 p.m. as their feet touched down. Lewis was pleased to have taken some film as he descended. But, of course, you never knew until it had been processed. It was precisely the type of grand spectacle that his bosses wanted recorded, a dramatic illustration of Allied power, and the unstoppable nature of their war against Hitler. These were images that they knew audiences in the picture house back home would want to see.

Early reports had started coming from German HQs as the vast aerial armada passed overhead, warning of a sky black with aircraft. General Kurt Student, architect of Germany's airborne forces, was another witness, stepping out of the headquarters where he commanded an army in the Netherlands to soak up the sights and sounds. 'It was a spectacle that impressed me deeply,' he wrote. 'I did not think of the danger of the situation but reflected with regret [upon] the memory of my own airborne operations.' When the general's chief of staff appeared, Student exclaimed, 'Oh how I wish I had had such powerful means at my disposal!' And indeed Student's reflection underscored the degree to which the vision of Allied commanders had been married to the enormous productive capacity of the factories that had churned out wave after wave of droning planes.

It was a demonstration of enormous power. Nearly 1,500 Allied transport aircraft and 320 gliders landed around 20,000 airborne soldiers in the space of an hour and a half. Sergeant Lewis recorded the hive of activity on Drop Zone X, open heathland several kilometres to the west of Arnhem.

Yellow smoke billowed at the 2nd Battalion rallying point, and soon enough the familiar tones of Lieutenant Colonel Frost's hunting horn could be heard above the throb of Dakotas still passing overhead. Paratroopers everywhere, struggling out of their harnesses, assembling Stens or unsheathing Enfields, looking about, searching for familiar faces, then setting off this way and that, a great jumble of people sorting itself into respective units gathering at their rendezvous points.

Those who'd dropped on operations before realized that daylight was an enormous help when finding your mates and weapons containers. And nobody was shooting at them either. One 2nd Battalion corporal felt exultant, saying it was 'just like an exercise in England, unbelievable'. There were smiles and waves from a few Dutch gathered there, some of whom swiftly gathered parachutes into the baskets on their bicycles.

A few men were hurt on landing, among them Sergeant Frank Lyoness, that veteran fighter in A Company who was one of Grayburn's section commanders in 2 Platoon. He was carted off to the nearby Queen Elizabeth Hospital, but the rest of A Company massed swiftly, fully aware of the honour that had been bestowed upon them of leading the whole brigade into town and capturing the main bridge there.

As they moved off, there was a crackle of fire, a party of Germans in a couple of lorries had driven straight into the path of 3 Platoon at the head of their company. A good number of Germans had been killed and several captured. Nearby 3rd Battalion hit a staff car, the bloodied body of a senior officer tipped out of one of its doors. The 2nd Battalion resumed its advance, heading eastwards along a route pre-marked by their staff officers.

Lieutenant Vlasto, the 1 Platoon commander, taking over the lead, wrote in his diary, 'This is all quite fantastic, to be walking along the main Arnhem road without anyone to hamper us at all.' Jack Grayburn with his 2 Platoon was there as well, acknowledging the greetings of the Dutch, wondering what lay ahead.

It was a hot afternoon and the men, laden with kit, soon worked up a sweat. Locals came out with fruit and water, even beer and wine. There were hugs and kisses too, and thanks for liberating them. Many of the troops enjoyed the spectacle, feeling it was 'a victory parade, the civilians are quite delirious with joy'.

Their boss, Johnny Frost, appeared among the A Company soldiers, telling them to keep moving. One of the experienced corporals there was glad for the intervention: 'With due respect, he was right; we had taken far too long, put it down to inexperience as most of the lads had never seen action before.'

They made their way through woods and suburban houses towards the town of Oosterbeek, stopping occasionally to deal with sniper fire before being driven on again by their NCOs and officers. B Company was following behind A, while Major Dover's C Company branched off south across the open polder towards a railway bridge that formed the first of three spans across the Rhine that they were looking to secure.

Near Oosterbeek-Laag railway station, things started to get trickier for Frost's main column. They'd been walking for hours, and it was nearing 6 p.m. The leading element, A Company, passed through a viaduct and spotted two German armoured cars. The vehicles opened fire and two of Lieutenant Vlasto's men fell, which 'brings me down to earth with a jolt'. There was sporadic fire. Some of the A Company men, trying to keep the pace up, slipped into back gardens to outflank this resistance.

At the station a German NCO and a party of about a dozen men from a nearby SS training school had joined the fight and were using a Spandau to good effect. Following on behind the leading British element, soldiers from one of B Company's platoons were caught by the viaduct, having five men killed in a few minutes, including twin brothers Tommy and Claude Gronnert. Their mates responded with Bren-gun fire and used one of their light mortars to put down smoke.

Meanwhile, A Company was trying to maintain momentum, and C Company was about to receive a very unwelcome surprise. Approaching the railway bridge, some of the paratroopers tried to rush it, but Major Dover could see two enemy soldiers running across and, moments later, it became clear what they'd done. There was a huge blast, which destroyed the centre of the railway bridge, knocking down the foremost of Dover's soldiers. The Germans had just denied Frost one of the crossings.

At Oosterbeek-Laag, meanwhile, Brigadier Lathbury had turned up, telling Frost not to get held up. It was an unwelcome intervention because the 2nd Battalion CO hardly needed reminding. Eventually, the SS party at the station, their flanks having been turned, fell back, and relieved members of B Company continued their advance. As they moved forward, soldiers glimpsed the great arching structure of the main road bridge through the houses: 'We thought, we're nearly there.'

By this point it was early evening and the light was beginning to falter. Moving through the western suburbs of Arnhem was the 2nd Battalion, but also a curious mixture of others belonging to units with other tasks: there were sappers who intended to secure the bridges; signallers as well as staff from Lathbury's brigade headquarters, whom he had urged forward; military police; and a few members of the 89 Field Security Section, including Arthur Maybury.

Even that small group, just a dozen men, had become split up. Their boss, Captain John Killick, went to root about in a nearby hotel that one of the German generals was using as his command post. Killick was hoping to find German secrets left behind in that hastily abandoned place. Maybury, meanwhile, had tagged along with members of B Company, his old mob from 1942, walking towards the centre of town. In his pocket the corporal had a highly secret piece of paper compiled with intelligence from Dutch resistance groups in Arnhem. It bore the names of Dutch Nazis, collaborators, who would be detained once Maybury and the military police had established a position in Arnhem centre.

While these different parties of British soldiers moved gingerly into town, more Germans were arriving too. The landings had caused momentary shock in their command, but different groups had begun to head towards the British, some intent on resisting them, others still quite ignorant of the real situation.

Making his way back from the railway bridge to one of the east–west routes running into town, Major Victor Dover briefly chatted to a staff officer from brigade, who had already concluded that Operation Market was 'a grand military cock up'. Heading east, Dover's men spotted a large group of Germans, about eighty of them, deploying, almost casually at a street junction, apparently unaware of the danger they were in. He moved swiftly to the attack, blasting them with Brengun fire, light mortars and then PIAT bombs. The projectiles from these anti-tank launchers, as had already been found in Normandy, could be very effective against people. Five PIAT rounds were fired with grim effect: 'bodies were flung in all directions'.

Between 7.30 and 9 p.m., the first elements of Frost's force arrived at the remaining two crossings: A Company men at the easternmost, an impressive structure that carried the main road link over the Rhine, and some Royal Engineers (followed later by B Company) at a makeshift pontoon crossing a short distance to its west. The main bridge had been blown during the German invasion of 1940, so the pontoons had gone in as a temporary measure while it was repaired. The big, arched, span, an imposing structure with pillboxes at each end, had, in fact, been reopened only a few weeks earlier. It was so large that the roads leading to it were on high embankments, allowing the traffic on riverside roads to flow underneath the access points on and off the bridge.

Arriving at the pontoon bridge late that evening, Major Crawley's men saw something that a sapper reconnaissance party had already discovered. The centre section of the bridge had been removed for use elsewhere. That made sense, taking into account the reopening of the main crossing point and the fact that the floats hindered navigation on the river. All the same, it was an unwelcome revelation to Crawley because it changed the 2nd Battalion's calculus considerably. Everything depended on seizing the two ends of the main bridge, but the option of attacking its southern defences with a force sent over the pontoons had now disappeared.

At the main bridge, elements of A Company had been knocking on doors, gaining access to houses that could be used to dominate the bridge. From 9.30 onwards there were a series of attempts by platoons from this company to deal with the defences on the bridge. During the first, men from 3 Platoon had got onto the bridge and explored very close to the pillboxes at its northern end before being spotted and fired upon, then pulling back.

Around 10.30 Frost arrived and the hunting horn was used to gather members of A Company together on the river bank beneath the bridge in order to form a plan. The CO, noted one of the lieutenants, 'seems extremely happy'. He gave orders for defensive positions to be taken up around the northern end.

Not long after this a second attempt, this time to rush the defences, was made by Jack Grayburn and his men from 2 Platoon. They were hit with a hail of rounds from Spandaus and 20mm cannon, having to fall back with eight casualties, including the lieutenant himself, hit by shell splinters in his right shoulder. Seeing the strength of this resistance, Major Tatham-Warter, the company commander, sent Lieutenant Vlasto, with his 1 Platoon and some sappers, under the bridge to attack from its other side. Mounting the stairway that led from the river embankment up to the span, and only metres from the pillboxes, they then executed an attack using a flamethrower, among other weapons. Although the aim had been to flame the pillboxes, this jet of fire set alight a nearby hut that was being used to store ammunition.

'All hell seemed to be let loose after that,' Frost later recorded. 'Amid the noise of machine-gun fire, a succession of explosions, the crackling of ammunition and the thump of a cannon, came screams of agony and fear.' This conflagration blocked the bridge for hours to both sides. Instead, they traded machine-gun fire across the river, tracer darting this way and that until the early hours.

By the end of the day, Frost was established at the north end of bridge with A Company as well as elements of engineers and brigade headquarters people (staff officers, signallers and the defence platoon). Late on, some Royal Army Service Corps men arrived with a captured truck they'd filled with ammunition at Drop Zone X, driving it to the town centre just before parties of German troops moved into position, dividing the British force. The trap had effectively snapped shut behind the 2nd Battalion.

It had already become apparent to those leading the 1st and 3rd Battalions that it was going to be near impossible to follow Frost into the town. Finding his men under heavy fire in the Oosterbeek area, Major John Timothy, leading one of 1st Battalion's companies, noted, 'We were hit straight away, I lost two officers in about ten minutes.'

A group from the 3rd Battalion, less than a company, did manage to explore its way along the railway line into Arnhem that night, but the rest of their unit had been stopped dead. Frustrated with the impasse, both Brigadier Lathbury and his boss, Major General Urquhart, appeared at the front, trying to drive their paratroopers through by sheer force of personality.

But the 1st and 3rd Battalions would suffer heavily the following morning trying to break through. And both Lathbury and Urquhart vanished as far as their HQs were concerned, the two men having taken refuge in a house surrounded by enemy troops. This setback was to cost the landing force dear.

Major Crawley, meanwhile, had decided to spend the night occupying some houses close to the northern end of the pontoon bridge. Some of the others who'd gathered there and were not part of his company decided to push on. Among them were Maybury and Craftsman John Watkinson. Moving along the Rijnkade (the thoroughfare along the north embankment of the Rhine), the party was hit by a burst of gunfire. Both Maybury, who had taken several bullets to the abdomen, and Watkinson were down. Hammering on the doors of the *huishoudschool* (domestic science school) building on that street, their comrades got them taken inside where Wilhelmina Schouten, a teacher there, helped to dress their wounds.

In a story that was to be repeated many times across Arnhem during this fight, the Dutch improvised their own medical care for wounded airborne soldiers. A doctor was sent for, and, despite the risks of navigating streets full of trigger-happy soldiers, duly arrived.

This man, a fifty-year-old general practitioner named Jan Zwolle, then struggled during the early hours, with the limited medical equipment at his disposal, to save the lives of Maybury and Watkinson, using school furniture as his operating table. But while Watkinson survived, Maybury, the self-styled 'Pegasus' who chronicled the early exploits of the Parachute Regiment, did not. He was buried in the back garden of a nearby house.

While treating the mortally wounded corporal, Dr Zwolle took possession of the list of Nazi collaborators that Maybury had been carrying. Whether Maybury entrusted it to him or he simply found it is unclear, but as the battle in Arnhem intensified its possession would be his downfall.

The opposition that built that evening consisted mainly of SS troops gathered together in a *Kampfgruppe* under Heinz Brinkmann, the commander of SS-Panzer-Aufklärungs-Abteilung 10 (the 10th SS Armoured Reconnaissance Battalion), part of the Panzer Division 'Frundsberg' that had been re-equipping nearby. He had a small number of armoured vehicles and some infantry from SS-Panzergrenadier-Regiment 20 with whom to contest the northern bridgehead. The orders coming from corps headquarters were clear, the bridge had to be reopened as soon as possible, in order to allow troops to get south to Nijmegen, where the American landings constituted a critical risk.

With first light on Monday the 18th, Frost felt a little more confident. He had been heartened by the arrival of several dozen men of C Company, the 3rd Battalion, who had managed to infiltrate the town. And sending word to Major Crawley, he managed to bring most of that company in towards his position on the northern end of the bridge.

There were four 6-pounder anti-tank guns at his disposal and a brigade command post had been established (albeit minus its brigadier, Lathbury, who had momentarily disappeared) next to his own battalion one, and his soldiers were in resolute spirits. A good supply of ammunition had arrived in the night, and Frost had about 340 troops in his surrounded enclave.

On the other hand, there had also been some portents of serious trouble. The Germans were already sufficiently strong in the centre of Arnhem that they began to isolate and overwhelm elements of the 2nd Battalion. And, of course, Frost's men had not 'taken' the bridge, even if their possession of its northern end would allow them to deny its use to the enemy.

Major Dover and most of C Company had spent the night in a group of buildings several hundred metres to the north-west of Frost, but the enemy was tightening its hold on the area. While inspecting his positions at dawn, Dover had been hit, by either a bullet or a piece of shrapnel that had gone through his backside from one flank to the other. Patching him up, one of the C Company wags told his major that the wound could get him discharged: 'You'll be no bloody good in the Army but the Navy will have you . . . !'

The major was still able to walk, just about, and, receiving a message from B Company, decided that he too should move his men towards Frost's position, via the riverside route. They quit the buildings where they'd spent the night, setting off along the streets at pace, trying to get southwards towards the Rhine. But they soon became aware both of enemy troops moving on parallel routes with armoured half-tracks and frequent difficulties with enemy machine guns at street corners and junctions.

At this point they dived into several houses, there being about twenty-five men with Dover, while others tried to head west, back towards the drop zone. But it did not take long for the intensity of enemy fire and his own limited ammunition to convince Dover that they were engaged in a futile struggle. 'Only those who have had to make such a decision to surrender can fully appreciate the depths of despair which accompany it,' he later wrote about the decision to come out under a white flag.

Crawley's B Company meanwhile had set off to move the short distance along the Rhine embankment to the main position. With machine guns on so many road junctions, and able to engage them from the southern side of the river, it meant running the gauntlet.

One of the platoon commanders 'hit on the idea that we would lob a couple of phosphorus bombs, smoke, into the middle of the road and then make a bolt for it *en masse*'. And so they moved with smoke and fire towards the rest of the battalion. But in this shift, one of Crawley's platoons, acting as rearguard, became isolated and took shelter in a house.

So it was that, just a few hours into daylight on 18 September, Frost had effectively lost more than a company of his small force. C Company, with its few remaining Bruneval veterans, was effectively written off, though some men hid out a while longer, and Crawley had left behind one of his platoons also. Once isolated in small groups, the paratroopers' ability to care for their wounded, redistribute ammunition or communicate with their mates all diminished rapidly.

That morning would also witness one of the most dramatic actions of the entire battle, when SS-Hauptsturmführer (captain) Viktor Gräbner pushed across the bridge with much of SS-Panzer-Aufklärungs-Abteilung 9 (the 9th Armoured Reconnaissance Battalion), belonging to the other division forming the nearby SS-Panzer corps, the 'Hohenstaufen'. His column of vehicles was first spotted at around 9.30 a.m. moving towards the southern ramp onto the bridge.

Because of the camber of the bridge's access roads, the German armour was initially hidden to the British defenders as it trundled up the ramp. Gräbner's column was a mixture of vehicle types, with some armoured cars at the front, followed by halftracks (of the SdKfz 250 and 251 types). Curiously, Gräbner himself was riding in a captured British armoured car, a Humber that was presumably a trophy taken during the division's hard fighting in Normandy that summer.

The British, once they saw vehicles on the bridge itself, were determined to let the column get to the place where they could hit it hardest, which was on the elevated section of roadway north of the bridge end, but before it joined the down ramp that brought traffic to street level. As the lead vehicles motored along, anti-tank guns were adjusted, PIATs readied and fresh magazines inserted into Bren guns in upstairs windows from which soldiers overlooked that elevated road section.

The first four armoured cars drove undamaged across mines the British had laid, through some anti-tank fire, and sped down the off-ramp into the town centre. It took until the fifth vehicle for the 6-pounders to find their sweet spot, the 57mm shell hitting home and bringing it to a halt. A paratrooper in an upstairs window watched as the others ran into each other and his mates started pouring fire down.

'All hell broke loose,' one of the SS halftrack's occupants recalled. 'All around my vehicle there were explosions, and noise, and I was right in the middle of this chaos.' Some of the SS drivers tried to back up, but there were already other burnt-out vehicles and objects jamming the roadway, so they tried going forward again.

The confusion was compounded by a strike on Gräbner's armoured car. He was probably killed soon after the action began, though his body was never found. In many cases the stricken vehicles blazed with a crazy intensity as the fuel and ammunition inside was consumed. The occupants were charred beyond recognition. Soldiers seeking to escape this inferno were cut down by Bren gunners and snipers.

It continued for two hours, quietening down occasionally, then flaring up at any sign of movement. British forward observers plastered the area with shells and mortar bombs for good measure. At least ten vehicles were knocked out and dozens of lives taken. Many of the paratroopers relished it. Frost summed up their mood as 'our most enjoyable battle'. The soldiers, exulting in this early victory, revived the brigade's old North African war cry, bellowing 'Wahoo Mohammed' from the rooftops. It was a call that rang out many times in those days, as both a mark of brotherhood and a taunt to the enemy.

With Frost's men well established around the northern bridgehead, and growing numbers of enemy soldiers pushing against them, the streets had become extremely dangerous. Surveying the roadway to the bridge itself, one paratrooper commented, 'anybody who seems to move up there, they're getting hit'. Frost knew the only chance of securing the entire span was to attack from the south, but unable to locate the missing centre section of the pontoon bridge, or any other boats of a size to replace them, he realized that it would be impossible to capture the entire bridge: it was a matter of holding on.

During that Monday afternoon his signallers finally managed to get through to stations from XXX Corps, advancing up from the south. This lifted spirits, evidently, though they did not learn the precise position of the relief force. In fact, the 82nd Airborne Division had taken the bridge at Grave (the first of the three major crossings needed for the success of Operation Garden) swiftly. The battle advance of the ground column towards Nijmegen, the second great obstacle and target of the 101st Airborne, however, was going less well.

Hopes of XXX Corps covering the eighty-odd kilometres to Arnhem in the forty-eight hours originally intended were slipping away. For much of the route, dubbed 'Hell's Highway', armour was forced to stay on an elevated roadway because of the softness of the surrounding ground, making it easy for the enemy to pick them off. Even if their advance had been considerably faster, however, the issues facing Frost's defenders were mounting.

By the afternoon, the eastern side of the bridge was coming under pressure. More German units were arriving – all manner of reinforcements from second-line fortress units to convalescents and training-school detachments. It was in the eastern area where a new *Kampfgruppe* under Major Hans-Peter Knaust was formed. He had brought eight tanks from a training base in Bielefeld, across the German border, where they had been used for driver training. It was in the afternoon of 18 September when a couple of them, Panzer III tanks, with supporting infantry and mortar fire, had advanced along the riverside road and were getting close to the bridge. There were fierce close-range exchanges with the Brigade Defence Platoon until the tanks were knocked out, one by a 6-pounder shell, the other at close range by a paratrooper firing a PIAT. With these vehicles burning, the attack fizzled out. The

Mark III tanks were almost obsolete by this stage of the war, hence their prior role in Bielefeld, but more formidable armour was on the way.

This battle, with its resulting losses, required some rearrangement on the part of the defenders. Some troops from A Company were pushed across to the eastern side of the bridge, their places on the western side of it being taken by B Company. Soon enough, however, some of their men too were drawn into a seesaw fight over some buildings on that eastern side.

Opposition to the defenders was increasing rapidly. Faced with determined men in buildings, the Germans began to employ the street-fighting tactics learned on the Eastern Front. Where bullets were inadequate, they would blast and burn the occupants out of buildings. Firing from across the river with 37mm flak guns, they used tracer shells to ignite roofs. And that afternoon, after the failed tank attack on the embankment, they brought up a 150mm infantry gun, a stubby cannon designed to hurl a big high-explosive projectile over short distances.

'I was about to open up when there was a tremendous explosion above us', recalled one of the B Company Bren gunners who'd come across to the eastern side of the bridge. 'The field gun had opened fire, and when the shell hit, so much rubble and dust showered down on us it was difficult to see for a while.' He tried picking off the gun crew, who weren't far away, and soon enough they fell back.

However, the attackers were able to get a line of fire on the grand building north of the bridge being used by Frost as brigade headquarters. Whether it was the same gun or a different one, its 150mm rounds took a heavy toll: Frost wrote that 'each hit seemed to pulverize the masonry and the appalling crash of these missiles against our walls scared the daylights out of headquarters'.

Frost had taken command of the overall force in the area (including the various supporting arms, brigade HQ and 3rd Battalion men) so left the running of the 2nd Battalion to his second in command, Major David Wallis. However, his period in charge was to last only a matter of hours, for that evening, while returning from reconnoitring his positions, and having forgotten his password, Wallis was shot and killed by a jumpy paratrooper.

Monday's battle for the eastern side of the bridge had been directed by Major Digby Tatham-Warter. He and the two fellow light-infantry lieutenants (Grayburn and Andrew 'Mac' McDermont) who had joined the 2nd Battalion together in Italy in 1943, became key players during the drama of the following hours. With each move across the open areas around the bridge becoming so danger-ous owing to flying bullets or falling shells, Tatham-Warter took to walking across with an open umbrella.

One of the platoon commanders, seeing the major setting out from the shelter of a building, asked, 'Where are you going?'

'I thought I would see some of the chaps over there,' Tatham-Warter replied.

'That won't do you much good,' the lieutenant nodded at the brolly.

The major, feigning surprise, replied, 'Oh my goodness, what if it rains?' then set off.

Whether such theatrics were simple eccentricity, a man crack-ing under pressure, or intended as a morale booster, as much for himself as for the men, Tatham-Warter and his umbrella became a familiar sight, running the gauntlet of Arnhem's streets. He later suggested that he had carried it because he could not remember passwords and did not want to suffer the same fate as Major Wallis. Given his familiarity with this key sector, Frost decided to give him acting command of the 2nd Battalion after that officer was killed.

By the evening of Monday the 18th, Frost's men had taken more than a hundred prisoners. Caring for them further stretched the medical supplies, food and water at their disposal, but the captives were housed in one of the basements, where the CO and his intel-ligence officer went down to see them, hoping to glean more about enemy plans.

They found an SS NCO, presumably a survivor of Gräbner's column, a few of whom had been brought in that evening. Frost was a little unsettled at finding a man from an SS-Panzer division fighting in the area at all, and the prisoner played up to him, announcing proudly, 'we are just the first instalment'. It wasn't unusual for defiant captives to insist they would win, but learning about the presence of these battle-hardened armoured units in the area, when he'd been expecting second-line troops, left Frost confessing, 'I was stunned.'

Their situation, it was clear to him, was becoming precarious in the extreme. Frost tried to get around his positions, telling the soldiers that XXX Corps was on its way and the rest of the division was trying to fight its way through from Oosterbeek, but privately he had begun to harbour serious doubts. The ammunition brought up late the first night had been distributed and they would not be getting more. There was a steady stream of casualties, with no means of evacuating them, and the German positions blocking any link-up with the other two battalions in their brigade were becoming stronger.

Frost did not know the detail, with communications being so poor, but throughout Monday paratroopers and glider troops had tried in vain to fight their way through, being pushed back to Arnhem's western outskirts. The company under his old Bruneval comrade, Major John Timothy, was down to just six men fighting fit.

On Tuesday 19 September, the Germans kept up the pressure. New units arrived, with platoons and companies fed into the battle piecemeal. On the Rijnkade, the river embankment, the east to west attacks of the previous day were renewed by Knaust's *Kampfgruppe*, with more Panzer III and IV tanks, SS-Panzer grenadiers and an 88mm gun being brought to the fight. The 88 was used to shell the houses around the north-eastern end of the bridge that had been in contention throughout Monday, causing further British casualties.

The attackers, though, came on gingerly, afraid of the desperate men who still clung to the wrecked buildings. 'They were fantastic marksmen,' one of the SS grenadiers noted, 'and we were the ones who had to move, to attack. When they shot, they almost always hit their target.'

In places, though, the incendiary ammunition being fired in did its work well. An office building belonging to the town's electricity and tram company, which had been held throughout Monday by Mac McDermont and men of his 3 Platoon, was a particular target. It was set on fire and the paratroopers were forced to retreat westwards. The loss of this place, on a corner only metres from the bridge overpass, with arcs of fire in several directions, was a particular setback for the defenders.

A little later, Major Tatham-Warter, anxious to recover this important spot, ordered McDermont to retake the building. With grenades and Stens, they went in. As McDermont cleared the ground floor and headed onto the stairs, one of the German defenders felled him with a burst of sub-machine-gun fire. The building was retaken, though only briefly.

McDermont's great friend Jack Grayburn had been moving among his troops, inspiring them, despite the pain from a wound received during his abortive attempt to rush the bridge on the 17th. As a result, Grayburn's right arm was in a sling. But he remained apparently unfazed by the mounting toll around them, another officer commenting, 'I have never seen anyone so nonchalantly brave.'

In other houses a few dozen defenders still held the eastern flank of Frost's position. Pummelled by artillery and tank fire, they husbanded the few rounds they still had while tending their mates who were hit. The evacuation of casualties had become impossible in many places, the streets being raked with fire, and there were reports of stretcher bearers being gunned down. German soldiers made the same accusation against the paratroopers. It was becoming a merciless fight.

The intensity of battle was too much for some men. According to one officer, 'One sergeant did go quite berserk', after a tank round hit one of the British-occupied houses: 'An old campaigner, his nerve just went.' Others decided it just wasn't worth it.

Private Bob Peatling, an A Company signaller, had been part of the group that had gone out with Major Wallis the previous night when he'd been killed. Peatling had taken refuge in a police station with half a dozen military policemen who'd made it into Arnhem during Sunday evening. Their sergeant decided it was time to give up. When he led his soldiers out of the door, 'they shot him straight away'. The other men were taken, but Peatling held back, having 'made my mind up that they weren't going to take me prisoner'. He found a place to hide in the police station's attic.

At last light, the defenders became aware of a new challenge. Two Tiger tanks, part of a company brought up from a nearby garrison in Germany, approached the bridgehead from the north, moving slowly down towards the river, firing their machine guns along the streets. They were right among the buildings still being occupied by the paratroopers when one of the defenders managed to get a hit with a PIAT. It wasn't easy to kill a Tiger tank with a single strike from one of these bombs, the vehicle weighing in at over fifty tonnes and with thick armour. Even so, realizing the danger, the Tiger crews pulled back for the time being as darkness fell.

Surveying the situation that evening, Frost and Tatham-Warter conferred.

'I would like to know if this is worse or not so bad as the other things you've been in?' asked the major.

'Difficult to say,' Frost replied, with admirable sangfroid. 'In some ways it is worse, and in some ways not.'

However, he knew well that, by that evening, the stock of PIAT bombs was pretty much exhausted and ammunition more generally was very low. Worse, the number of casualties was approaching 200, over half of the force that Frost had gathered early on at the bridgehead. Later, and more candidly, he told Major Gough, the reconnaissance squadron commander, 'Well, Freddie, I'm afraid it's not been a very healthy party and it doesn't look like getting any healthier as time goes by.'

It was that evening that Frost was given an offer of surrender by the enemy, sent in with one of his captured soldiers under a flag of truce. The soldier decided to remain with Frost. That was answer enough.

★

Early the following morning, Wednesday the 20th, the signallers finally managed to connect Frost with Major General Urquhart at his divisional headquarters just outside the town. The 2nd Battalion's ability to resist was almost exhausted, but this was the first time that the two men had spoken since Frost's arrival at the bridge.

Urquhart, who had been out of contact for two days, having sought refuge from an enemy patrol, briefed Frost on the hard fight being experienced by the rest of the division, and the slim prospect of XXX Corps relieving them quickly. Frost realized that his time was almost over, worrying that the wounded could all be burnt to death if the buildings they were sheltering in were consumed by the fires that now raged across the town.

Arnhem's centre had become a scene of devastation, those dwellings that had escaped the flames being raked with machine-gun bullets and plunging mortar fire. Chatting in the back garden with Major Doug Crawley at around dawn, Frost was hurled into the air, landing face down with great pain in his legs. Realizing that a shell or grenade had hit them, he looked across to Crawley and saw that he too was wounded. A piece of shrapnel lodged near Frost's left ankle caused him enormous pain as he tried to direct the defence.

Tanks had once again appeared in the streets, a Tiger approaching close to the houses around the elevated approach to the road bridge where many of the surviving soldiers had gathered. The two dozen or so survivors of A Company were there under the command of Captain Antony Frank and Lieutenant Jack Grayburn. Even making it from the relative shelter under the roadway to the brigade command post required them to run right in front of the Tiger.

Frank had come to the view that further defence was pointless and they should make their way west, towards the rest of the division. The Tiger, which had been lacing the street with machine-gun fire, then opened up with its 88mm gun at the road over the paratroopers' heads, bringing a shower of masonry down onto them. It was now or never; Captain Frank and half a dozen others rushed across the road.

Grayburn, with his right arm in a sling, was 'firing a pistol with his left hand', a gesture of pure, futile anger towards this armoured behemoth. He turned to Private Steve Morgan and said, 'It's time to go, lad.' As Grayburn ran across the road, he was cut down by machine-gun fire from the tank.

Morgan had raced across too, and now, crouching, tried to reach out to him. 'Leave me, leave me,' called Grayburn, who knew he was finished and wanted the others to save themselves. As those who had made it across prepared to move west, an officer, probably Frank, called out to Grayburn, 'Goodbye, dear boy.' Grayburn did not die immediately, but later at a dressing station.

Elsewhere, many others had reached the same conclusion as Major Freddie Gough, who told one of the soldiers at HQ, 'It's going to be every man for himself here.' Some looked for possible escape routes through the Germans, others for hiding places.

Lieutenant John Patrick 'Pat' Barnett, who'd been left on the street by a couple of others after being shot in the head, heard them saying they'd come back with help. That wasn't a promise he put too much faith in, reflecting as he lay there, '*If* I'm still here and *if* you can still get back.' In fact, it was a German stretcher party who found him first and took him for treatment. One more in the bag.

By twilight, the main headquarters buildings had been set on fire by phosphorus shells and, deciding that the wounded would otherwise soon perish, Frost 'then ordered all opposition from the brigade HQ to cease and the wounded to be surrendered'. A party of 120 under Major Hibbert was to move off in the hope of continuing resistance or escaping, but, for Frost and a great many others, it was over.

British and German troops who, moments earlier, had been trying to kill one another, then set to work removing the wounded from the basements.

Frost and Crawley found themselves lying together on their stretchers out in the street.

'Well, Doug,' said the colonel, 'I'm afraid we haven't got away with it this time.'

'No, sir,' Crawley replied, 'but we gave 'em a damn good run for their money.'

20.   The Cauldron

Although the mopping up of Lieutenant Colonel Johnny Frost's bridge party was almost complete, a second desperate battle still raged a few kilometres to the west, where the bulk of 1st Airborne Division occupied a pocket between its original Drop Zone X and the western suburbs of Arnhem.

Late on the afternoon of 17 September, Sergeant Mike Lewis and another cameraman from No. 5 AFPU, Sergeant Dennis Smith, had tried to follow the 2nd Battalion to the bridge in order to film its capture. Moving into woods near the Oosterbeek suburb, they had come across an airborne jeep with two dead soldiers in it. Without standing on ceremony, for time was of the essence, they had pulled the two corpses from the vehicle in the hope of being able to speed into town.

However, Lewis's journey east had come to a halt a short time later when, with the sounds of gunfire ahead, paratroopers had told them they'd be mad to go any further. Like much of the 1st Parachute Brigade, Lewis had therefore failed to reach the objective on Day 1, and the chances of getting through sank very quickly.

At the time that Frost had gone into captivity, late on 20 September, Sergeant Lewis was well ensconced with a Dutch family in their home on the western outskirts of Oosterbeek, a few hundred metres from the Hartenstein Hotel, where divisional headquarters had been set up and the rest of the press party had located itself.

Lewis had enjoyed dinner with his Dutch hosts on the 17th, but they had all quickly realized that, as fighting intensified, they would have to stay in the cellar, which is where he remained for much of the next forty-eight hours, with limited film stock and only the vaguest idea of what was happening in the wider battle.

The original plan envisaged the 1st Airborne Division's glider brigade holding the drop zone for its second big contingent, the 4th Parachute Brigade, to arrive on 18 September before the combined force secured Arnhem. This second large airdrop had indeed happened on the 18th, though later than originally intended, but in many respects the British part of Operation Market was already in serious trouble by then.

German battlegroups were squeezing the drop zone from the west, and by 19 September steadily driving back those who were trying to get into the centre of Arnhem. So, the newly arrived men quickly took heavy casualties, the 156 Parachute Battalion, for example, being down to ninety fighting men by the end of the 19th. Some equipment for the Polish Parachute Brigade, unable to be dropped at its originally planned zone south of the Arnhem bridge, had been brought in by glider that evening, the unit suffering losses from an entire division of Luftwaffe flak troops that had moved into the area that afternoon.

On the 20th, Sergeant Lewis left the cellar of his refuge and was shocked to see the amount of damage that had been wrought upon the neighbourhood. Lewis by this time had located his colleagues and more film stock at the Hotel Hartenstein. It was a journey of a few hundred metres through the woods to get there, but dangerous all the same. When he arrived, he realized the place was already subject to enemy sniper fire and raced in.

Sergeant Lewis found Major General Urquhart, who, having reappeared the previous day, had ordered his troops to stop trying to break into Arnhem. On the 20th he instructed them to shorten their defensive perimeter: they were under attack on all sides, had suffered heavy casualties and there was no longer any need to secure the main drop zone. This cockpit of violence, slowly shrinking under Nazi pressure, became known as the Cauldron.

Lewis found Urquhart sitting on the floor in a corridor, the rooms being too dangerous because of sniper fire, and suggested to the general that he and a staff officer might like to look at a map on a sheltered part of the garden terrace so that he had something to film. 'I mocked that up,' the sergeant photographer would admit later, having given with his pictures some sense of authority or grip to a man he believed was barely in control of events.

Lewis was able to talk to the war correspondents at the hotel, keen to glean information. His No. 5 AFPU colleagues and he had concluded that it was generally too dangerous to go outside for photography. In a letter he wrote that day, Sergeant Smith was candid about their plight: 'We are completely surrounded and our perimeter is becoming smaller every hour, now it is a matter of fighting for our lives. If our land forces don't make contact with us soon then we've had it.'

Urquhart had that morning got a message through to Lieutenant General Boy Browning, who had flown his I Airborne Corps headquarters in by glider on the afternoon of 17 September. They were in the area to the south under the control of the 82nd Airborne Division. 'Fighting intense and opposition extremely strong,' Urquhart told his superior; 'position not too strong.'

German units pressing in on the Cauldron included all manner of combatants mobilized across the Netherlands and north-west Germany. They came, generally in small sub-units, from naval and air-force units, special police squads or Dutch collaborators, training schools and convalescent units. But at the heart of the operation to crush the Oosterbeek pocket were three SS *Kampfgruppen*, with six or seven battalion-strength sub-units – a force of perhaps 5,000–7,000 men. This was not much bigger than the force Urquhart commanded, at least on the 18/19th, and it fought largely with mortars, machine guns, anti-aircraft guns and a few armoured vehicles.

The key quantum that was missing for 1st Airborne Division, but which conferred great advantages on their German attackers, was artillery: field guns, mortars and Nebelwerfers, with what was, compared with the few 75mm guns and 3-inch mortars at Urquhart's disposal, a plentiful supply of ammunition.

Crushing firepower of the kind used previously to support the airborne landings, breaking up successive German attacks in Normandy and even at one point saving Johnny Frost's position in Sicily, was not available. Naval gunfire was impossible at Arnhem, so far from the sea, and even the XXX Corps forces, still out of artillery range, trying to fight their way to the Rhine, would be limited in the amount of fire they could lay down, given their need to support their own operations and keep open the corridor they were carving through enemy forces. Soldiers inside the Cauldron were angered that, in the absence of such support, there were so few ground-attack missions mounted by the Allied air forces.

This situation left Browning and Urquhart as generals exercising very little power. Radio communications were often atrocious, so they had only a vague picture of the battle, they had very little firepower to call on and Urquhart could do little more than manage the slaughter of his people in the Cauldron. Little wonder that Browning, trying to spur the Americans and XXX Corps to more rapid action, became so frustrated that he hurled an inkwell at the wall of his makeshift HQ.

What the pilots of air transport forces did do, day after day, was fly resupply missions into the Cauldron. Lewis managed to film one of these drops as it came in, the Dakotas, holding steady under fire, dropping supply containers and wicker panniers. He filmed with his DeVry as a couple of airborne soldiers unpacked 6-pounder anti-tank rounds. As enemy air defences thickened, these daylight resupply drops required a particular type of heroism from the aircrews, as dozens of planes were shot down.

Thursday 21 September was to prove a particularly grim day for the flyers. Skilfully exploiting early warning from units along the flight path, the Luftwaffe scrambled fighters to intercept the lumbering transports. Of the Allied planes bringing in supplies that day, twenty-one were shot down and sixty-one damaged. Out of ten aircraft belonging to one RAF squadron, only three returned to Fairford that evening.

By 11 a.m. on 21 September the SS corps running operations in Arnhem reported that the bridge fight was effectively over and that Colonel Frost had been captured. Troops cleared the wreckage of Gräbner's column and the bridge was once more back in use.

At the police station a couple of hundred metres away, Private Bob Peatling was still hiding in the attic. For him, becoming a prisoner would involve too much shame. 'My thought was how could I write to my father, a First World War Middlesex man, from a prisoner-of-war camp? I'm not doing that.' So instead he drank the water from the toilet cistern, cooked what scraps of food he could find and waited, hoping that someone in the Dutch resistance might find him.

Colonel Johnny Frost was one of many wounded men taken for treatment. He was an object of curiosity to many of the German officers knowing of his reputation. 'The SS men were very polite and complimentary about the battle we had fought,' he wrote, 'but the bitterness I felt was unassuaged.'

Chalky White – the South African sergeant who had gone through parachute training with Mike Lewis and been badly wounded in Cork Wood – received an even more convivial reception from one of the SS commanders, who told him, 'I'm going to give you a brandy, you fought well.'

Major John Timothy, the veteran of Bruneval and North Africa prior to taking command of a 1st Battalion company during Operation Market, found that his interrogator was particularly well briefed. He knew many details about Bruneval, leading Timothy to conclude that some of the men captured on that raid had talked.

Those burnt and blasted out of buildings in the town centre were collected in one of the churches, a police station, or simply in the open spaces around the bridge. The unwounded were then marched in parties, eventually ending up at a railway depot, from where they would be processed prior to being taken to German prison camps. Bill Bloys was only mildly embarrassed to be relieved at this stage of wads of Dutch guilders that he had liberated from a Dutch bank, hiding the fortune in the big rear pockets of his para smock.

Private James Sims, one of the B Company paratroopers, marching down the Rhine embankment with his dirty, tired comrades, heard calls of encouragement from the panzer crews they passed – 'Well fought, Tommy' and the like. He marvelled at it, given the bitterness of the close-range battle they had just been through: 'They seemed to regard war in much the same way as the British regarded football.'

Not everything, though, unfolded in such a sportsmanlike manner. At the Queen Elizabeth Hospital, where hundreds of casualties had been taken, an SS man murdered a British Army doctor, walking up to him and shooting him in the head. And when two paratrooper officers leapt from a lorry carrying prisoners, the SS guards opened fire on them as they escaped, then turned their guns on the men who had stayed put in the lorries, killing six of them. One of the officers, Major Tony Hibbert, made good his escape.

The situation at the hospital during these days was sufficiently fluid to allow many of the wounded who had been taken there to be spirited away and hidden by Dutch helpers. These included Lieutenant Colonel Dobie of the 1st Battalion, Brigadier Lathbury, the 1st Parachute Brigade commander, and, after the fall of the bridge, Major Digby Tatham-Warter, who had been commanding the rump of 2nd Battalion men in the town centre. They, Hibbert and more than 130 others would eventually be gathered together by the resistance in order to make their way back to Allied lines.

Alive to what was going on at the hospital, the Germans started to remove its patients. Sergeant Ernest Ballinger from the 2nd Battalion noted in his diary that he was taken from there to Apeldoorn on 23 September for onward transfer to the Stalag XIB prison camp.

For the Dutch who had helped the British, the consequences could be hideous. Dr Jan Zwolle, the doctor who had tried to save Arthur Maybury's life, was later stopped at a checkpoint and discovered to be carrying the corporal's list of suspected local collaborators. On 19 September he and four other men accused of 'terrorism' and helping the invaders were summarily executed in a house in the town centre. They were among forty locals killed by the Germans in such acts of vengeance. In the days that followed, the Nazis would evict the entire Arnhem civilian population.

As the battle developed on 21 September, with German troops switched from the conquered bridgehead to the west, in order to drive back the British from Arnhem's western fringes towards Oosterbeek, a new nightmare began for the civilians on that axis. More heavy armour and flamethrowers had been brought into the fight. As Sergeant Lewis commented, 'They were burning us out, house by house.' The troops contested each building above ground, while the residents cowered in the cellars below.

This grim fight pitted some of the best forces involved against each other in this battle. The remnants of 1st, 3rd and 11th Parachute Battalions and the 2nd South Staffordshire airlanding troops who had been trying to force their way into Arnhem now had to fight the rearguard action being led by Major Richard Lonsdale of the 11th – the man who, fifteen months earlier in Tunisia, Sergeant Major Maxie Forsyth had accused of cowardice and who had been returned to his unit for his trouble. In this fighting, Lonsdale's men earned two Victoria Crosses and he a Distinguished Service Order.

SS-Hauptsturmführer Hans Möller led the assault pioneers of 9th SS-Panzer Division against them. His impression of their drive westwards was that 'the Red Devils still fought back and battled for every room and every house, for every piece of ground or garden, no matter how small it was, like cornered tigers'.

In this close-quarters battle, the paratroopers took every chance they could to turn the tables. At one point a Sturmgeschütz III tracked assault gun was hit by a British anti-tank round, its half-trained crew bailing out in shock. German officers looked on in growing alarm as paratroopers leapt into the vehicle, started its engine and attempted to turn it round, slewing the gun in their direction. Luckily for them, the Tommies could not work out how to fire the main gun, but did send bursts of machine-gun fire down the street towards them.

The German advance, however, was proving inexorable, slowly compressing the Cauldron. Even so, it was decided to go ahead that afternoon with the drop of the main part of the 1st Polish Parachute Brigade. The Poles suffered heavy casualties as they came down, which mounted as attempts were made to get them northwards, over the river, into the Oosterbeek Cauldron, a futile waste of their gallantry since attention was about to shift to moving people in the opposite direction – evacuating the remnants from that besieged pocket north of the Rhine.

Nevertheless, on the evening of the 21st, leading elements of the 43rd Infantry Division, XXX Corps' spearhead, had got sufficiently close to the river to begin firing in support of Urquhart's men. Forward observers called in their targets and Sergeant Lewis, hearing the shells ripping the air overhead, called it, 'the most gorgeous sound I'd ever heard'.

These developments caused the Germans to redouble their efforts. On the morning of 22 September the colonel commanding the main battlegroup of the 9th SS, the Hohenstaufen Division, was ordered to 'annihilate them as soon as possible'. The surviving British occupied a space around 900 metres long on the bank of the Rhine, stretching about two kilometres to the north.

Urquhart's units had been ground down to a point close to that annihilation that their enemy desired. In the notionally 'freshest' of his British units, 4th Parachute Brigade, there were sixty-five officers and men left in 156 Parachute Battalion, just thirty in the 10th and hardly more than a hundred in the 11th. Food and ammunition were low.

Mike Lewis, meanwhile, had taken the risk of another visit to the Hartenstein Hotel, where the newsmen sat about wondering how much longer it could all go on. With precious little movie film left, Lewis decided to take some photographs and, gathering a handful of soldiers together, captured four battle-weary paratroopers walking towards him through a wrecked outbuilding of the Hartenstein Hotel. One or two of the onlookers hooted their derision, but the twenty-six-year-old Londoner had captured what has arguably become the most enduring image of the battle.

Among the hungry men at the hotel there was bitter humour about the many supply drops that had fallen into the hands of the enemy and the useless things, like a canister of berets, that had actually got through to them. Picking up a copy of a newspaper, parachuted in at such great risk to the aircrews, Lewis read head-lines of victorious Allied advances into the Nazi Siegfried Line defences. 'No one could speak at that,' he recalled. 'I mean, here we are having seven different kinds of shit knocked out of us and according to this newspaper it was the other way around.' Among the small cadre in the Cauldron who had experienced the Oudna drop or Sicily, the verdict on Arnhem was already 'another cock up'.

To the south of them the debate among senior commanders would shift between 23 and 24 September from trying to get troops of the 43rd Division across the Rhine to reinforce Urqu-hart, to accepting that putting more troops, even a few thousand of them, into the Cauldron was pointless. It would simply be the cause of further heavy casualties, given their likely inability to stop the SS battlegroups overwhelming them. XXX Corps was at the limit of its reach, and the long corridor it had opened up, more than seventy kilometres up to the Rhine, was under pressure in various places. They could not risk more troops being cut off by the Germans, therefore much of the artillery, tank and air support they mustered had to be devoted to preventing that, rather than to crossing the Rhine in strength.

The fate of the 1st Airborne Division was effectively settled on the evening of 24 September when Urquhart signalled Browning, 'all ranks now exhausted . . . even slight enemy offensive action may cause complete disintegration'. The Germans had that day committed a small number of King Tiger tanks to the battle. That was not in itself decisive, but sending in these huge vehicles did underline their determination to finish off the British, and raised the very real possibility of the Cauldron being overrun.

Next day, Urquhart and the general commanding 43rd Division put together a plan to get the 1st Airborne Division's survivors out that evening. An operation was quickly organized to bring them across in assault boats, and, after darkness fell, the remaining mem-bers of Urquhart's force began their withdrawal to the river bank. White tapes were strung through the trees to guide the men, who, once they neared the bank itself, became aware of machine guns firing arcs of tracer into the sky from the south side. These marked their left and right, the safe place to get across.

As the soldiers lined up awaiting the boats, many were panicked, Lewis noticing, 'suddenly there were an awful lot of wounded around, jumping the queue and I knew what was going on'. But he remained stoic, judging that the swift, dark waters of the Rhine might claim him if he tried to swim and that he needed to get his footage and kit out.

Quite a few others didn't want to wait. They waded into the waters, determined to swim for it. Some were carried off by the current, never to be seen again; others, particularly those who stripped off so they were unencumbered by clothing or kit, made it across. Lewis's boat eventually came and he climbed in. Sharing it was Alan Wood, a *Daily Express* correspondent, and a few other types from divisional HQ.

By dawn, the evacuation was complete. Urquhart's division took some 11,500 men to war: 3,900 returned; 5,960 became prisoners, of whom more than half, around 3,000, were also wounded; 1,485 were killed in action.

German losses were rather harder to calculate, both because of the hotchpotch of units used and because many elements, such as the SS-Panzer divisions, were engaged in multiple places during the fighting, not just in Arnhem. One respected analysis suggests they took around 2,500 casualties in the Arnhem battle; at normal ratios between a quarter and a third of this figure would have been fatalities. It may be surmised, then, that their total was considerably less than the British one.

When those who'd crossed were mustered on the south side of the river, the 2nd Parachute Battalion would number just sixteen. The quartermaster sergeant calling the muster was overcome with emotion. Having been in the centre of Arnhem, the great majority of the battalion, like its CO Johnny Frost, had fallen into enemy hands.

As the Arnhem battle wound down, hundreds of its soldiers were being processed into prisoner-of-war camps, supervised by the Red Cross. They would be allowed to write home, while dwelling on everything that had gone wrong and their exasperation. For Frost captivity 'was shaming, like being a malefactor, being no longer free'.

A handful of his men did avoid this fate, escaping by way of the hospital or hiding out in other circumstances. These included a B Company private who'd been rowed across the river by Dutch helpers and an A Company platoon sergeant who hid for weeks in a well-stocked cellar before making it back. Bob Peatling was moved from the police station where he'd hidden and passed along a Dutch resistance chain, living for months behind enemy lines.

Major Digby Tatham-Warter became one of 139 men to return to Allied lines in October under Operation Pegasus, a skilfully executed collaboration between the Dutch resistance, Britain's MI9 escape organization, the evaders themselves and the US forces who guided them in to Allied lines.

A significant proportion of these escapees belonged to two units, the 10th Parachute Battalion and 133rd Parachute Field Ambulance, having been hidden by Dutch householders after landing outside their drop zone. Gathering parties of fugitives together, the resistance added shot-down Allied aircrew as well as other waifs and strays. Just two members of the 2nd Battalion (Tatham-Warter and Captain Frank) made it back this way.

As for Lewis and two fellow No. 5 AFPU photographers, they were on a plane back to England within days. Their images provided some of the most telling testimony of a battle that truly caught the public imagination.

The words of Alan Wood, the reporter who shared a boat across the Rhine with Lewis, dramatized their ordeal to the wider world that had not been present: 'If in the coming years a man says, "I fought at Arnhem", take off your hat and buy him a drink.'

21. Lessons Learned

The aftershocks of Arnhem spread rapidly through the airborne family. Lieutenant Colonel Geoffrey Pine-Coffin knew very quickly how grievous the human loss had been. He had, after all, served in the 2nd Parachute Battalion in 1942 and commanded the 3rd until near the end of its campaign in North Africa; many of those lost were his friends.

On the morning after the evacuation across the Rhine, he weighed up the strange workings of fate. Had Brigadier Lathbury, whereabouts unknown at that moment, done him a favour when he sacked him as CO of the 3rd Battalion in May 1943? Yes, Pine-Coffin wrote, it 'was probably a good thing in the end. There is something about an ill wind I think which would apply there.'

Although he did not yet know all the details about who had gone into prison camps and who would remain forever in the Dutch soil, Pine-Coffin was moved by these events to write a series of instructions for his son Peter's guardian, 'in the event of my getting bumped off'. The boy, seven years old, at this point had been sent to Sherborne prep school and, presumably in consideration of his tender years, deceased mother and absent father, was living with the headmaster's family.

A bank account had been set up for the guardian to use, and while Pine-Coffin was a paragon of imperial values in terms of the distant parenting of children, he wanted nothing spared for his boy: 'He is really the only expense I have and I don't mind what I spend on him.' Since he had acting lieutenant colonel's pay, the daily parachute allowance and rarely ate or lodged at his own expense, he was flush.

Arnhem, though, had reinforced what he already knew only too well from his experience in an elite infantry regiment, that total war consumed lives on a monstrous scale, and the fate of individuals was arbitrary: 'I shall be glad when the war is over and one can settle down without wondering how long I will have before the next excitement.'

And, indeed, one of the few things he could be pretty sure about was that there would be more 'excitement'. The 1st Airborne Division had been smashed at Arnhem, and would take many months to rebuild – if, indeed, the War Office decided that was even worth doing, given that the final defeat of Nazi Germany seemed a matter of mere months away. So, all eyes were on the 6th Airborne Division, which had returned from Normandy in August and was receiving the fresh drafts of volunteers needed to prepare it for further action. For those involved in leading airborne formations there was a determination that the lessons be learned from Market Garden.

The litany of failures discussed by the airborne men included the decision to fly the division in over multiple days, with all the knock-on problems that produced, from the need to protect drop zones to the enemy being ready to maul those subsequent arrivals as they came in; that the drop and landing zones had been too far from Arnhem's bridge; that intelligence had been inadequate; that Lieutenant General Brian Horrocks and his XXX Corps had lacked urgency; and, following on from that, that the command arrangements had been too unwieldy.

Major General Richard Gale, as the 6th Division's boss, had a particular interest in this last topic. He would later write that Boy Browning 'was in no position to exercise command in the field'. His I Airborne Corps HQ was a weak organization, barely practised, without good enough communications to manage a battle or the 'corps troops' (artillery, engineers and so on) to give emphasis to his orders. Johnny Frost was, if anything, even more damning than Gale, opining, 'the very presence of the Airborne Corps HQ was nothing but a nuisance'.

In a situation where the air organization dropped the three divisions in and another HQ (Browning's) was then meant to take control of the ground battle, until a third (XXX Corps) moved up through the captured bridges, there was all manner of scope for confusion. Critically, Gale noted, 'it is the command structure that fixes responsibility'. Would not Horrocks have made greater efforts to save 1st Airborne Division if it had been under his own command? Gale thought so, contrasting the situation with his own in Normandy, where his division had been under the corps landing nearby on the beaches, bringing with it all the heavy firepower that could come in by sea, to Arnhem, where plans to resupply by air, even to land another division by this means, were exposed as fanciful.

All these detailed points dodged the essential truth about Market Garden, which was that the whole concept of landing troops so far from those who could support them (principally by artillery) involved taking reckless risks. It ignored the enemy's ability to bring in forces from across the Netherlands or northern Germany during the first two days after the landing and their ability to improvise an effective response quickly.

In truth, 1st Airborne Division was in serious trouble from a few hours after it landed, when it failed to take the bridge and the link between Frost's 2nd Battalion and the rest of his brigade was severed. On this point, the 1st Parachute Brigade commander himself reflected, 'my plan was designed for and could only have succeeded against weak opposition. It was a gamble to get to the bridge quickly.'

Browning sought to shuffle off responsibility, for example writing to his wife on 24 September, as the decision to give up at Arnhem was being made, that it was, 'not now my battle but a matter for XXX Corps'. He also deployed a line that was to become a familiar one in the coming weeks, that, 'apart from the latter, the thing has been a great success, but the whole thing is overshadowed by the tragedy in the north'.

This version of events, that the 82nd and 101st Airborne had done a fine job and ground forces performed prodigies linking up with them, was echoed in the verdict of higher command. 'The whole corps, British and American, has done magnificently,' Montgomery wrote to Browning. The army group commander later declared Operation Market Garden '90% successful'.

The implication was that Market Garden's inspiration, of advancing rapidly more than eighty kilometres to the Rhine in order to cut off large German forces and shorten the war, had been worth a try. And while nobody publicly suggested it, the loss of several thousand men in such a daring venture would have been considered trivial by Hitler or Joseph Stalin. That was effectively the calculation that underlay Monty's approach.

However, the operation's failure had caused disquiet in Britain, and the army had tried and tested means of cauterizing such wounds. Those responsible would be quietly shuffled off, and officers in the know would read the *Gazette*, looking for the decorations received – or not – to weigh up the verdict on an operation.

Browning himself evidently blamed Horrocks and Urquhart. The latter, when he had appeared at Browning's HQ during the early hours of 26 September, was given a cursory interview by Boy. Urquhart was given no opportunity to detail his ordeal or give his own explanations, later describing it as a 'totally inadequate meeting'.

If Browning was happy to push Urquhart out into the cold, he was well aware that Montgomery and General Eisenhower, who by this point was running the whole of the Allied effort, would need their own scapegoats. Browning tried to shift the issue to one of intelligence failure, writing in early October, 'everyone, from the Supreme Commander downwards, has been caught out and surprised by the way the German has recovered now that he is right back and fighting on his own doorstep'.

But if the experience of British airborne forces should have taught him anything – from the response to their landings in Tunisia late in 1942 to the retaking of the Primosole bridge by a German captain with a couple of hundred rear-area troops the following year – it was that their enemy had a formidable ability to improvise responses to unforeseen events. These earlier episodes had also featured rear-area or non-combatant units mixed in with more capable ones. Market Garden had failed because it required an optimism bordering on the delusional to believe that risking men so far behind enemy lines was a good idea.

That storied veteran Lieutenant Colonel Alastair Pearson probably spoke for many in the airborne fraternity when he blamed Montgomery, noting, 'he was well warned'. And indeed, Browning's suggestion to the field marshal that 'perhaps they might be going a bridge too far' would define the whole episode for many. However, the politics of high command were such that Montgomery could not be removed for this failure and Browning could. By late November he was packed off to the Far East as chief of staff to his old mentor Admiral Louis Mountbatten. Gale was given the command of I Airborne Corps, and Major General Eric Bols, a sharp officer who'd risen through commands under Montgomery's aegis, took the 6th Airborne Division.

As Browning left for hotter climes, those managing the airborne arm had limited means at their disposal. The Americans, by contrast, had three airborne divisions and were developing their XVIII Corps headquarters in order to be ready for the last great show of the war, which, as the generals understood after the failure of Market Garden, remained the crossing of the Rhine.

The British were to use what they had in ways that would foreshadow the future use of airborne forces as highly trained reserves that could be deployed rapidly, even if that didn't involve the drama of a parachute assault. In addition to the 6th Airborne Division, Britain deployed the 2nd Independent Parachute Brigade in Italy.

The 2nd Brigade had been involved in much hard fighting in that theatre throughout late 1943 and most of 1944. It did not, however, deploy by parachute at all during those battles. In August, it did take part in a set-piece jump, during Operation Dragoon, the Allied invasion of southern France. This was the only jump made by the 2nd at brigade strength during the war and it encountered little resistance.

Then, in October, the 2nd Brigade was rapidly switched to Greece, where the Germans were retreating at speed. After a drop by a small contingent of the 4th Parachute Battalion to take an airfield, the bulk were flown in by that airhead.

43. The sky full of aircraft and parachutes above the Dutch countryside on 17 September 1944, as Operation Market Garden got underway. This remarkable image was captured by a reconnaissance Spitfire.

44. Men of the 1st Battalion, the Border Regiment, one of the airlanded battalions that arrived to the west of Arnhem on the first day of the operation.

45. Sergeant Mike Lewis captured film of Dutch locals greeting their liberators. This still shows members of 21st Independent Parachute Company (including the sergeant, who jumped with his arm in plaster) and one 3rd Battalion man.

46. A party of German prisoners captured soon after the landings being escorted near the Wolfheze asylum, about ten kilometres north-west of Arnhem.

47. An aerial view showing the elevated roadway leading off the main bridge at Arnhem with the burnt-out remnants of the SS column that was ambushed there on the morning of 18 September 1944.

48. A German photographer in Arnhem snapped these captured British paratroopers being led away. Their maroon-red berets are evidently worn with pride.

49. A 3-inch mortar team in action during the Cauldron battle on 21 September 1944. Mike Lewis's AFPU colleague Sergeant Dennis Smith captured many dramatic images of this fight.

50. Another image from Sergeant Smith, men of the 1st Parachute Battalion trying to fight their way into Arnhem on 17 September. They did not succeed, so the 2nd Battalion remained isolated.

51. Many of those pressed into action during the Cauldron battle were not infantrymen by training: here two glider pilots hunt for a sniper in Oosterbeek on 21 September.

52. Major General Robert 'Roy' Urquhart outside his HQ at the Hartenstein Hotel. Although Sergeant Lewis, who filmed him, and Sergeant Smith, who took this image, tried to make him look like a man in charge, poor communications and a period spent hiding from the Germans at the outset meant his role was limited.

53. Allied forces did eventually liberate Arnhem, but not until April 1945 when this image of an unknown paratrooper's grave was taken near the bridge defended by the 2nd Battalion.

54. Shortly after being appointed Colonel Commandant of the Parachute Regiment, Field Marshal Montgomery, sporting a maroon-red beret, visited its troops in the Ardennes to confer awards. Among them, right behind the man with a Sten gun, is Sergeant Sid Cornell.

55. The Ardennes battles of December 1944 and January 1945 were bitterly cold as well as costly for the 13th Battalion. This image of an airborne sniper team in action shows the snow suits adopted at this time.

56. An airborne view of the Operation Varsity Rhine-crossing operation gives some idea of the smoke that obscured many landing and drop zones. Some came from burning buildings, but the Allies also deployed smoke generators to cover the river assault itself.

57. This somewhat staged-looking shot features a 6-pounder anti-tank gun flown in to Hamminkeln during Operation Varsity. This weapon, carried in a Horsa, was vital to airborne operations from Sicily onwards.

58. Lieutenant Colonel Pine-Coffin (right) pictured during a roadside rest on 30 April 1945. The facial wound he suffered the previous month is still fresh.

59. Men of the 6th Airborne Division marching across northern Germany in April 1945, the handcarts and backpacks giving an idea of the heavy burdens endured during this long, victorious journey.

During the months that followed, Greece descended into civil war and it fell to the paratroopers to foil an attempt by left-wing partisans to seize power. The British were drawn into vicious street fighting, taking and losing life on a significant scale. Once withdrawn from Greece, the brigade was assigned to the 6th Airborne Division, deploying to meet a growing emergency in Palestine.

This pattern of operations showed both that the 2nd Parachute Brigade had remained a force in being despite, or perhaps because of, not being involved in a grand airborne operation, and that it had proved extremely useful as a theatre reserve, putting highly trained men where they were urgently needed. The regimental motto Utrinque Paratus, Ready for Anything, was a fitting rubric for the wide variety of missions it carried out. During the course of a year it had operated in Italy, France, Greece and the Holy Land, setting the pattern for the post-war employment of paratroopers as a reserve that was indeed 'ready for anything'.

So, when Hitler had launched a great offensive in the Ardennes late in 1944, largely undetected by Allied intelligence, perhaps it should have come as no surprise when the generals looked to airborne forces for help. Word reached Pine-Coffin, the other 6th Airborne Division battalion commanders and staff officers in December 1944 that their hopes for Christmas leave were dashed and they needed to be ready for immediate deployment. The enemy made rapid headway initially, creating a deep salient or bulge which gave the battle its eventual name. With US forward troops being overrun, reinforcements were sent in, with two US airborne divisions soon in the thick of the fight.

The 6th Airborne Division was warned for action on 22 December. 'Immediately the rumour mongering began,' one subaltern later wrote. 'It was Warsaw. The Siegfried Line. An airborne corridor to Berlin.' But moving by lorry down to the south coast on Christmas Day, they were soon disabused of these fanciful notions. Their division was to be thrown into the line in Belgium to contain any further German advance.

They travelled across the usual Channel ferry routes before being driven up to the border country. The 7th Parachute Battalion had undergone many changes since dropping into Normandy six months earlier. None of its four company commanders and only one of those leading its nine rifle platoons had taken part in that drop. That said, Pine-Coffin's second in command, Major Nigel Taylor, had led A Company into Bénouville and had since recovered from his wounds, and there were about half a dozen others who had survived France or transfer to serve on.

Those in the ranks who'd come through Normandy, such as Bob Tanner in B Company, had in many cases put up stripes. Sid Cornell, the intrepid B Company runner who had shone during the campaign, had been made a sergeant and awarded the Distinguished Conduct Medal. It was said among the men that Pine-Coffin had tried to push the case for awarding Cornell the Victoria Cross: 'our revered colonel . . . incurred, to the detriment of his own career, the wrath of the military hierarchy by trying to fight them for the award'. They believed senior officers had downgraded the award to that of the DCM.

Among the foot soldiers sent in as emergency replacements, some chose to stay, which required them to go on jump courses. To complete the state of flux, dozens of new eighteen- and nineteen-year-olds just through the Ringway system had been folded into the unit. Pine-Coffin himself was the constant in the battalion.

By the time his brigade, the 5th Parachute, had entered the line in the snowbound Ardennes, the German offensive was already running out of steam. Even so, the fighting was to remind them that their enemy retained an offensive spirit even in circumstances that most Allied soldiers would have considered hopeless. It would also demonstrate to those in the 7th Battalion the utterly arbitrary nature of a unit and its fortunes in one of the less well-remembered episodes of the war.

On 3 January, the division began an offensive, piercing the deepest part of the German salient into Belgium in order to push them back. It was extremely cold, and the men had been issued with white snow suits so they didn't stand out against the frozen landscape. The 7th and 13th Battalions were advancing south-eastwards on parallel axes. Pine-Coffin's people were heading towards a village called Wavreille; the 13th under their boss, Lieutenant Colonel Peter Luard, had fixed their sights on Bure, a commune a few kilometres to the south of it.

Both battalions moving forward had the benefits of operating alongside regular army troops, from tank support to forward observers who could call in great barrages of shells. The landscape made it essential, for, in this rolling country, ridges or other high points gave great visibility over large stretches of territory, and, as they knew all too well from Normandy, if you could be seen, you could probably be killed.

For the 7th, this battle proved cold and uncomfortable but casualties were mercifully low. Five tanks were knocked out as they sat on a ridge giving 'overwatch' support to the advancing paratroopers, but fortunately the enemy did not decide to contest Wavreille in a major way.

The 13th Battalion (originally converted from a Lancashire regiment), getting into position on a wooded ridge, could look down at Bure below the snowy fields. Unfortunately for them, the village being in a trough, the enemy could also observe them from the opposite side. As Luard's two leading companies prepared to set out across the fields, they were hit.

'Within minutes I'd lost a third of my men,' the major commanding A Company recorded. 'Mortar bombs rained down on our positions, closely followed by the scream of shells', remembered his signaller. 'This was followed by machine-gun fire and by the sound we knew it was an MG42.' They had all come to know that awful ripping noise.

With 400 metres to cover to reach Bure, they knew they had no choice but to charge into that fire or be murdered where they lay. They stepped forward, sinking often knee deep into snow, pushing on as more men went down, their blood splashed over the virgin whiteness.

The 13th Battalion's survivors managed to make it into the village, but a grim close-quarter battle was just starting. The German panzer grenadiers, who had occupied some of the houses, had at least one tank at their disposal, while anti-tank guns on higher ground picked off the Shermans escorting the paratroopers.

Next day the battle continued, one sergeant noting that 'the Germans were very close, were firing across the street and at some stages, some members of my company were in the downstairs of a house while Jerry was upstairs'. Often rooms were cleared with sub-machine guns and grenades, but at times the antagonists were in isolated positions so close that they didn't dare risk using their firearms.

A corporal, trapped in a house with four others on the third day of fighting, realized that an enemy soldier was about to come in and drew his paratrooper's fighting dagger: '[I] waited patiently for the German to stick his head through the door, as he did I stuck the knife under his chin and up through his brain. I hit him so hard that the tip of the dagger went through his skull.'

Throughout this sanguinary fight, the medics of 225th Parachute Field Ambulance dealt with numbers as high as anything they'd seen in Normandy. The crew of conscientious objectors had by this time been diminished somewhat by losses, but several from Normandy still served, as did the head of the section supporting the 13th, Captain David Tibbs. He was astounded when he learned that, in the middle of the battle, one of his combatant sergeants and the padre had driven their ambulance into the middle of Bure to rescue casualties.

Moving into view, the German tank that had caused them so much trouble rumbled up next to the British vehicle. 'To everyone's astonishment (including the German troops) the top hatch opened and the tank commander emerged, head and shoulders showing, a prime target for our men,' Tibbs wrote later. 'He called out in good English, "This time you can do it, but do not come back".' This tank, later struck by a shell from a Sherman Firefly, was abandoned by its crew, and after three intense, bloody days the action at Bure came to an end.

There were some superficial similarities between the 13th Battalion's fight in Bure and that of the 2nd in Arnhem. In three days in Bure, sixty-four of Luard's paratroopers were killed. More than twice this number were wounded. As well as suffering a similar toll to Frost's unit, they also experienced a house-to-house battle of great intensity.

Yet the battle for Bure remains an episode largely forgotten, despite its heavy toll. The fact that it did not follow a parachute jump, with all the daring associated with that, may well have been one of the reasons. For Pine-Coffin and the others in his battalion it was another reminder of the way the fate of so many lives within it could be decided within moments. Their unit's toll in the Ardennes campaign, twelve men killed, was mercifully light. In an age of machine guns and mortars, luck could count for an awful lot. The 13th Battalion's had run out for a variety of reasons when it came up against skilled defenders in Bure. Those in the 7th Battalion would just have to hope that theirs held out until the war was over.

With the enemy falling back from the wooded Belgian borderlands, the 6th Airborne Division was deployed to the River Maas, where it formed the Dutch–German border. There the two sides eyed one another suspiciously, exchanged occasional shots, but largely observed the rule, 'if you don't tickle us we won't tickle you'.

Late in February, the 6th Airborne Division returned to Salisbury Plain and the 7th Parachute Battalion to Bulford Camp. Their stay would not prove a long one, for the top brass was actively planning a grand airborne finale to the war in Europe. It would incorporate many of the lessons learned in Market Garden, not least a huge airlift to insert the landing forces as quickly as possible, rather than over days.

The whole operation was being run by the US XVIII Airborne Corps. It might have felt like no more than their turn following the use of the British corps HQ for Market Garden. Whether in airlift effort or airborne divisions (of which the US Army had three in north-west Europe, effectively twice the British numbers), the American numerical advantage was now considerable, and for that reason they would call the shots.

22. Varsity to VE Day

Up on the small hill south of the Rhine, the staff types were fussing. It was 24 March 1945, and a huge Allied operation to breach that watery defensive barrier had been underway since late the previous evening. Hundreds of thousands were involved, employing everything from enormous artillery barrages to clouds of smoke dispensed by riverside generators in order to mask the crossings. There were fleets of Buffalos too, tracked transporters so big you could drive a Bren carrier or jeep straight inside. And the audience on Xanten hill had a grandstand view.

There among the uniformed figures, pointing their binoculars this way and that, were General Alan Brooke, Chief of the Imperial General Staff, Field Marshal Bernard Montgomery, a host of senior staff men and the prime minister. Winston Churchill, puffing on a cigar, was keen to see the whole thing. He was in the mood, having donned service dress and yearning to see the great orchestra of war unleashed upon Germany.

'He was determined to take every risk he could possibly take and if possible endanger his life to the maximum,' General Brooke wrote wearily to his mother when the visit was over. For Churchill, the man who almost five years before had ordered the formation of a parachute force in the British Army, the pièce de résistance was about to be delivered.

The rumble could be heard out west, behind them, and then the first specks appeared in the murky sky. Churchill, who had been sitting on a grass bank, leapt up, calling out, 'they're coming!' He described the spectacle: 'In the course of half an hour, over 2,000 aircraft streamed overhead in their formations.'

Even this was an underestimate; something like 2,700 aircraft were involved, throbbing above, squadrons carrying the US airborne division arriving from France and the British one from the east of England in an almighty piece of aerial choreography and staff work. The British 6th Airborne Division was about to drop into action as part of Operation Varsity, which involved 7,220 troops and their equipment coming by air in 796 transport planes and 420 gliders.

Despite Churchill's understandable delight, this was an American show, planned to avoid previous pitfalls. The XVIII Airborne Corps commander had accepted that he would use only one of the two available US divisions, because he wanted the whole thing done in one huge wave rather than a series of drops. Further, it would be carried out in daylight, there would be no long approach marches (the troops were dropping a short stroll away from or actually on their objectives), targets were well within artillery range of the relieving troops, and the approaching air armada was timed to arrive *after* the ground troops had forced the river, so the paratroopers would not be left in the lurch.

Of the six soldiers introduced at the start of this book, five serving in the same battalion three years earlier, only one, Geoffrey Pine-Coffin, was now hooking up his static line and getting ready to drop. Another, Mike Lewis, would be filming the operation from the ground. Two, Maybury and Grayburn, had been killed in Arnhem, and another, Johnny Frost, languished in Colditz. Maxie Forsyth, meanwhile, still campaigned elsewhere with the Argyll and Sutherland Highlanders.

It was around 10.20 a.m. when Brigadier Nigel Poett's 5th Parachute Brigade, including (as it had in Normandy) Pine-Coffin's 7th Battalion along with the 12th and 13th, began jumping. It was following the 3rd Parachute Brigade, and by this point the defenders were putting up a lot of flak.

Having promised to drop 'low and slow', the American pilots opened their throttles, pulled back on their sticks and tried to rise above the streams of gunfire coming up towards them. This might have been an effective tactic against small arms, but the anti-aircraft guns, a whole family of them, from 20mm to 88mm, could still find the range nicely.

For those leaping out of the Dakotas, 1,000 feet of altitude was twice as much as they would have liked, 'the men were in the air for a long time' and all manner of people were trying to kill them. Corporal Bob Tanner of the 7th Battalion could feel the bullets whistling past his head as he hung under the canopy, then, crack!, one of them clipped his thumb as he held on to the parachute's webbing straps. Then further rounds severed two of the lines that connected him to it. Another member of Tanner's section looked down, mesmerized by the tracer, smoke and gun flashes, recording, 'we descended into hell'.

Many landed in woods, one private from the 7th horrified to see more than thirty paratroopers from another battalion hanging lifeless in the trees. Someone had shot them in this defenceless condition and their blood dripped down, 'it was like walking through a butcher's shop', said Private Gordon Elliott.

In other places men dropped onto fields, an easier landing but vulnerable to raking fire from Spandaus. There was the usual drop zone muddle of men trying to find their units. Lieutenant Colonel Kenneth Darling, by this point in command of the 12th Battalion following his earlier removal from the 1st, tetchily asked one lieutenant, ' "have you seen my battalion?" which I thought was a silly question since they were landing all around us'.

Dropping right onto their objectives meant very different fates for the paratroopers. One man, getting close to the ground, saw a German soldier unsling his Schmeisser sub-machine gun. Landing literally at his feet, the paratrooper assumed he was about to die, but instead the German helpfully collapsed his canopy, surrendered and then for good measure produced several comrades who wished to do likewise. Less fortunate landings involved getting blasted by Spandaus or even 20mm flak guns.

Accompanied by a couple of members of his headquarters team and a signaller, Lieutenant Colonel Pine-Coffin was trying to get on top of his battalion's situation. Most had been dropped on target, but A Company had gone adrift somewhere. Communications were customarily atrocious on airborne operations so they were trying something new: American walkie-talkies. They worked, though Pine-Coffin found carrying one an encumbrance. Although weighing only five pounds (2.3kg), it was another piece of kit to carry and the battery life was short.

Then, with a flash and an ear-splitting blast, an 88mm shell dropped close by, showering them with red-hot metal. The man next to Pine-Coffin was killed and a piece of shrapnel sliced off the end of the colonel's nose and cut open his right cheek. For a moment, he was dazed and unable to speak as his mouth filled with blood. A medic staunched the wound, taping up his face, and then Pine-Coffin was ready to go on. There was no question of handing over to his second in command.

The colonel, despite his pain and disfigurement, felt some admiration for the commander of the 88, carrying on with his mission despite the odds: 'He kept that gun firing and did an immense amount of damage.' The flak gun in question was located about 700 metres away in an area that should have been cleared by his missing A Company, but it was soon dealt with by others.

The British paratroopers had landed in a corridor between the River Issel and the Rhine, which at this point runs six or seven kilometres west of the smaller stream and the city of Wesel. They were meant to secure landing zones for the arrival of glider troops who would take three bridges over the Issel. In this way the landings would hasten the collapse of the Rhine defence, by putting paratroopers behind the enemy defending the river itself as other Allied forces assaulted their front, at the same time preventing German reinforcements from crossing.

As the parachute battalions mopped up the drop zones, taking prisoners or dispatching those who fought on, gliders were casting off from their tugs around 1,000 metres above the Rhine. It wasn't easy for the pilots to get their bearings, for a pall of mist hung over the Rhineland. Some of this was from the 2nd Army's smoke-screen, but buildings across the battlefield were also alight. While the glider pilots strained to pick out landmarks, their aircraft stood out all too clearly to the flak crews on the ground who watched them wheeling, trying to line up for landing.

The paratroopers knew the gliders had released because it almost immediately 'caused a considerable diversion of enemy artillery fire and provided a most welcome relief for us'. Those looking up now saw the gliders descending through puffs of smoke from air-bursts: heavy fire that soon started taking a grievous toll.

Coming down in broad daylight was undoubtedly an ordeal for the glider pilots – and it should be noted that following Market Garden there was a shortfall of hundreds of them. There were insufficient volunteers for the Glider Pilot Regiment to make this good, so 200 RAF pilots had been drafted in for Varsity and would now have to run the gauntlet.

Captain David Tibbs, the RAMC doctor, saw that gliders were 'on fire in the air, crashing to the ground or being raked with fire as soon as they landed'. A direct hit from an 88 shell blew one Horsa apart while it was still hundreds of metres up, scattering its men and cargo across the landscape.

Another medic, riding in one of the Horsas, saw holes sud-denly appearing in the sides and heard the rattle of shrapnel on the fuselage. The men shouted to the two pilots to get it down as fast as possible. The flyers needed little encouragement, and soon had the Horsa in a dive so steep that the passengers wondered if they'd be able to pull out of it. A case of PIAT bombs slid down the cabin floor towards the cockpit and petrol was gushing out of the fuel tank of the jeep they carried as cargo.

Somehow, the pilots managed to get the nose up and make a hard landing. But, like so many others arriving on the landing zones, the passengers found that, far from letting up, the flak crews just found them an easier target on terra firma. The medic threw himself out and down, 'we simply had to glue ourselves to the ground'. It was in these circumstances, treating wounded glider crews, that a Canadian, Corporal Frederick Topham, won the VC.

Inside the troop-carrying Horsas, men of the 6th Airlanding Brigade knew they had to push on and capture the Issel bridges. One private shook the hand of his pilot for getting them down, then looked about, 'gliders were crash landing all around us. Two were destroyed within yards of our forming up position with a total loss of life.'

Despite the carnage, sufficient infantry were pulled together to move on the bridges. They didn't have far to go, and soon over-whelmed the opposition. The 6th Airborne Division and its US counterpart the 17th, which had similar objectives, had succeeded in their mission. It was a matter of just a few hours before the armoured and infantry brigades that had crossed the Rhine began moving through them.

The victory came at a cost, though. The 6th Airborne Division suffered 1,400 either killed, wounded or missing, of which the 7th Parachute Battalion's share was seventeen killed and fifty-three wounded. This pointed to the uneven price paid by the glider riders, who took 900 casualties. Just 88 of the 416 British gliders released over the target area made it down undamaged.

Notwithstanding this, General Gale judged the level of losses acceptable, and General Eisenhower declared Varsity 'the most successful airborne operation carried out to date'. Undoubtedly, they eased the passage of those crossing the Rhine, though the air-borne operation's modest goals (compared to Market Garden or even Overlord) played an important part in defining its success.

The Rhine Crossing mission ushered in a period of marching and fighting for the 6th Airborne Division. Its journey would take it in a north-easterly direction, across that part of Germany to the shores of the Baltic Sea as the Third Reich imploded. Caught between this western advance and the Red Army's approach from the east, Germany sank into turmoil. Some wanted to defend the Fatherland to the last extreme, others had had enough: they simply intended to give up as soon as possible, and preferably not to the Russians. But to British airborne soldiers approaching defended places, it was never clear whether those they faced fell into the first or second category. For this reason, with the end of the war in Europe evidently approaching fast, many preferred not to take risks. Their nervousness was expressed by one lance corporal in the 13th Battalion: 'The worry was that after all that had gone before one could still get hit, hurt, or killed during the last few phases of the war.'

A couple of nights after parachuting in, Corporal Bob Tanner went out on a patrol with eight others, including his officer Lieutenant Ron Hinman. They were investigating an enemy anti-aircraft position, upon which, after deliberations in the darkness, they delivered a swift attack. Lance Corporal Thomas Sanderson, a Bren gunner, offered the weapon's sling to another, saying he wouldn't need it any more, earning him a sergeant's rebuke of 'don't bloody talk like that, man'.

Taking the Germans under fire, Hinman's men swiftly assaulted the position, moving from one flak gun position to another. There was some resistance and it claimed the life of Sanderson, fulfilling his prophecy, but, overall, the patrol scored a significant success. Lieutenant Hinman and his seven surviving patrol members had taken eight 37mm anti-aircraft guns, three anti-tank guns and forty prisoners.

As the airborne division moved swiftly on, backed by the tanks and artillery that regular forces could provide, countless prisoners came in. The soldiers took the opportunity to relieve many of their valuables, and 'in a week or so we all had as many pistols, cameras and watches as we wanted'. Civilians, many of whom hung white flags out of their windows along the Allied route of advance, did their best to ingratiate themselves with the new powers that be.

While some of the captured Hitler Jugend (Hitler Youth) and SS remained insolent until the end, many ordinary folk were happy to give the paratroopers food. They, in turn, started handing their rations to the legions of displaced people who began to flow across northern Germany, many of them slave labourers from previously Nazi-occupied countries trying to return home. The French and Belgians were tramping west, Poles and Balts to the east.

The death throes of Hitler's Reich led many of the paratroopers to scathing observations. One officer in the 5th Parachute Brigade, Captain David Clark, wrote home to his mother, 'most of the Germans are servile in the extreme. I shall never again listen to anyone who speaks for the Germans being a proud race.'

For the thousands of airborne soldiers captured during the preceding years this state of flux created all manner of hardship and uncertainty. Many were forced to endure 'death marches' as camps in the path of the Red Army or western Allies were emptied. Some used this opportunity to make good an escape, but for most it was a matter of hanging on until they reached the next stopping place, confident in the knowledge that liberation could not now be long at hand.

A couple of weeks into their advance from the Rhine, on 7 April, Pine-Coffin's battalion received new orders. Their brigade had reached a point north-west of Hanover and was being urged to press ahead rapidly, Allied commanders already having realized that they were in a race with the Russians.

The 7th Battalion was urged to push on to Wunstorf airfield, from which the Luftwaffe was still flying missions, as the regime buckled. There followed a series of events that underlined the grave dangers that those soldiers, thinking increasingly of when they might return home, still faced.

Pine-Coffin was driving at the head of their battalion at about 2.30 that afternoon in a White armoured scout car when he noticed two men disappearing into a trench beside the road about fifty metres in front of them. He pulled up while B Company, in four troop-carrying lorries, moved up behind him on an airfield roadway.

His suspicions were validated moments later, when, after a bang, a Panzerfaust, or hand-launched anti-tank rocket, flew over his head. Worse was to come: the B Company truck column sailed into an ambush, Pine-Coffin hearing the zipping fire of Spandaus.

In one of the leading cabs, Hinman's driver was killed instantly. The lieutenant tumbled out of the door while, in the back, as Bob Tanner recalled, 'I've never seen lorries cleared so fast'. The soldiers were down on the hard tarmac with bullets slamming into vehicles and their bodies. Tanner heard the hiss of their lorry's punctured tyres. Then a 20mm flak gun joined in.

They knew that, lying in an open space like this, they would soon die; the only way was forward. There was a cry of 'Everyone with bayonets, fix 'em!' Lieutenant Hinman turned to the No. 2 on Tanner's Bren, Ken Clarke, and said, 'Nobby, let's get the bastards!'

No sooner was Clarke on his feet than 'I went over backwards with this sledgehammer blow to the chest. I had been hit by at least five bullets.' A Spandau had put a couple of rounds through his arm, one in his neck and the others in his chest.

Pine-Coffin hunkered down in his ditch, feeling frustrated: '[We] were much too far forward to control the battle and anyway were pretty securely pinned ourselves.' In the midst of this mayhem, with one rocket after another flying over his abandoned scout car, he marvelled at the incompetence of 'the Panzerfaust enthusiast; he was an extremely bad shot ... despite the range being only about thirty yards, he missed it continuously'. But eventually one of the rockets struck home, blowing up the scout car and its radios.

Watching B Company rush forward in exactly the way he would have ordered anyway, Pine-Coffin realized he would have to head back to get them more support. This, he grasped ruefully, 'had to be done on foot and was very unpleasant', running through machine-gun fire to the rear, in the opposite direction to his leading company. B Company had already put down smoke from its light mortars to cover this advance; Pine-Coffin, meanwhile, set about trying to get tanks and heavier fire support from the brigade commander.

As they ran forward towards the enemy Tanner was thinking, 'They're going to get me, they're going to get me.' Certainly, they got Lieutenant John Pape, leading 4 Platoon, a Canadian loan officer who'd joined them in Normandy, who was cut down.

Back at the lorries, bullets were still striking the fallen men hit in the initial ambush. Private Gordon Jamieson, a conscientious objector serving with the 7th as a medic, crawled towards Nobby Clarke in an attempt to save him. But Jamieson, whose brother Ernie was a conchie doing the same work nearby, was hit in the head and died moments later.

Leading sections of B Company had meanwhile reached two

houses, one of which they believed to be a source of fire. They went to work with Stens and grenades, Tanner saying that, of the two dozen or so occupants, 'none of them got out alive'.

The action continued for two hours in all, the airfield being overrun, complete with a large haul of aircraft, including twenty-three fighters and two bombers. A good few defenders were captured too, including two 'insolent' SS men who were frog-marched back by the B Company paratroopers. Hearing about the fate of their medic, Gordon Jamieson, 'the mood of the chaps was: kill 'em'.

At this point the dead man's brother Ernie intervened: 'He wouldn't allow us to touch them,' Tanner recalled. 'He wouldn't allow us to do anything to them. His argument was this was the price of war.'

This demonstration of religious principle had impressed all of the fighting men, so the prisoners were spared. The influence of conchies among the soldiers was high by this late stage of the war, for nobody could doubt their bravery enduring these risks unarmed. For their part, one of their number argued that the presence of these men of principle 'humanized the situation' and may have tempered extremes of violence. Certainly it did at Wunstorf that day, and perhaps more generally too.

With the general sense of urgency prevailing, Pine-Coffin pressed on with his battalion the few kilometres to the nearby town of Neustadt. Having had six men killed and several wounded, some changes were made as they went: a sergeant took command of Lieutenant Pape's platoon and Sid Cornell stepped up as the platoon sergeant or senior NCO of his.

It was already late at night on 7 April when they reached Neustadt, walking in their noisy army boots in single file down each side of the main road. They could hear voices, even apparently a party going on in one *Bierstube*. There was a pause. Their orders were to take the bridge there that crossed the River Leine. This had led some to expect a single crossing, whereas in fact there were two. They rushed the first, over a branch of the Leine, just after midnight without incident, one of them thinking, 'there's nothing to this'.

But they hadn't reached the second bridge yet, and, as they did, Cornell's platoon commander noted, 'All the men knew there was a risk that the bridge might blow up.' As a precaution, they went at the trot. 'We were running and jumping over obstacles and suddenly I realized that the obstacles were explosives and that the whole bridge was mined.' A dozen defenders lurked on the other side, firing a couple of desultory shots before running away.

Twenty or so men had reached the far side of the bridge before it went up. 'The place was sheer carnage,' one of those who'd made it recalled. 'The force of the explosion had thrown bodies up into the trees.' Sergeant Cornell's lieutenant couldn't see him: 'We looked around on a scene of utter destruction, small fires, bits of wood and corpses were burning.'

Not all the charges – 200kg bombs brought from the airfield – had gone off. A few remained on the town side of the bridge where the bulk of the battalion now wondered how they would help those across the Leine. 'You could hear the cries of the wounded,' said Tanner. 'We tried everything we could to try and get across these spans but couldn't do it.'

It took hours to rig up a makeshift route across the fallen arches, during which time the survivors on the far side were helped by a German woman who opened her house to the wounded. The actions of 7/8 April had cost the 7th Battalion twenty-seven killed, thirty-three wounded and six missing. Among those killed on the bridge was Sergeant Sid Cornell DCM, whose survival since D-Day, despite constantly being in the thick of it, had made him a totem within the battalion. He had also been known as 'grandfather' within the 7th, being thirty-one on the day he died.

In his report of these events, so near the end of the war, the CO emphasized his gratitude to the padre, to Captain John Wagstaff and to the RAMC soldiers (combatant and conchie, the distinction was irrelevant here) of his section. 'I find it impossible to express my appreciation in words,' Pine-Coffin wrote. 'All ranks of the [battalion] would wish to give the most credit for any success gained by the men to this modest but untiring band of officers and men.'

It was their evident humanity that had impressed him.

Sergeant Mike Lewis had not until this moment had the most fulfilling of campaigns. He wasn't sorry that he hadn't dropped on Varsity, but he'd arrived on the scene in time to take some footage of the wrecked gliders. He'd moved on from there, winding off shots on his DeVry movie camera of the 15th Scottish Division rumbling through Celle and other typical campaign footage. On 15 April, however, the British Army had discovered a site of unspeakable horror at Belsen. The word spread quickly on the AFPU grapevine, so he joined a couple of its other cameramen working there.

Peering through the barbed wire were thousands of emaciated people, 'eating us up with their eyes'. Lewis managed some phrases in Yiddish, which was the language used at home by his parents, mangling them with some German he'd picked up in his campaigns. The inmates in their lice-ridden blue and white striped uniforms looked at him even more intently. Lewis reported, 'One of them said in a voice of wonder, "You are Jewish? And you are free?"'

The scenes captured by AFPU cameramen were to make a deep impression among newsreel viewers in Britain and the wider world. Great piles of bodies, 10,000 unburied dead, had to be dealt with by the army. The smell was overpowering: 'the stench of death and the death of all human dignity and hope'. Lewis had done so much to fit in, to leave his Jewish identity behind, trying to forge a new one in the Parachute Regiment. Now this terrible revelation that 'all the stories I'd heard about the persecution of people from my mother and father, they were true'.

Former camp guards were dragooned into lifting emaciated corpses into mass burial pits. Their efforts were not enough, given the numbers. An army driver with a bulldozer was sent to push the dead in. Lewis could convey the visual horror of this, as he stood there filming, but not the sensory overload: 'The blade sometimes didn't catch the bodies cleanly and they split open and the smell was terrible.'

The sergeant would spend a fortnight documenting Belsen's hideous sights. But the survivors also needed urgent help to keep them alive and to control disease. Medics from the 225th Parachute Field Ambulance were among those drafted in to help.

The very people praised in such high words by Pine-Coffin that month found at Belsen a horror to challenge their compassion. 'Our general attitude to the Germans changed to their disadvantage,' one of the medics wrote home. 'No film or photos can depict properly the atmosphere of this place.' He felt the evil of Belsen prompted theft from German civilians as well as soldiers, and anger with them for claiming ignorance of the crimes committed in their midst.

Just a couple of kilometres from Belsen the final deliverance of victory in Europe would be marked by the signature on 4 May of a surrender by Hitler's successor as Führer, Admiral Karl Dönitz to Field Marshal Montgomery on Lüneburg Heath. However, the 6th Airborne Division had one more rush to make during the last days of the conflict.

Arriving in Wismar on the Baltic Sea coast at the beginning of May, the paratroopers had completed a march of nearly 500 kilometres, then come face to face with the Red Army. Despite the vodkas drunk and photographs with accordion-playing Red Army soldiers, an atmosphere of distrust was already prevalent. An understanding of the great crimes of retribution, including the widespread rape of German women, was already growing in the paratroopers' minds. In at least one case, members of the 7th Battalion intervened to stop Russian soldiers taking German women away.

In Wismar, then, the ending of the war in Europe was not greeted with the same wild abandon as, for example, that shown by men of the 7th Armoured Division who entered Hamburg at about the same time. There, salvos of flares had been fired into the night sky and heavy drinking at al fresco parties was the order of the day.

Japan remained undefeated, yet nobody was talking about sending tanks to fight them. An airborne division, on the other hand, was precisely the kind of formation that might get there fast enough to make a difference.

VE Day was thus treated by many of the Red Devils as the end of one war, but not necessarily as the guarantee of their personal survival or of preservation from horrors more generally. Summing up the latest campaign in a letter to his mother, a doctor in the 225th Parachute Field Ambulance wrote, 'I am sick of tales of rape of all sorts and kinds, of beatings and of starvings. Of murders and slaughter . . . I am depressed.'

Writing to the commander of the 6th Airborne Division, Eric Bols, Lieutenant General Gale observed that the defeat of Hitler and prospect of fighting the Japanese were affecting recruitment. Whereas up to 2,000 soldiers had previously volunteered each month, the number was down to 1,500 by March 1945.

In the event, the division would not be required to fight in the Far East. A Gurkha parachute battalion from the 44th Airborne Division dropped into action on 1 May 1945, as part of an operation to retake Rangoon. But this was to prove the only drop of its type in the war against Japan.

The Rhine Crossing campaign had allowed for a dramatic finale to the war of airborne forces in Europe. Far better for them that it should have done so than being remembered for Operation Market Garden, however strongly many may have judged that to have been a risk worth taking. As if to underline the compact between them and the man who had sent six of its battalions to their destruction at Arnhem, Field Marshal Montgomery agreed to become colonel of the Parachute Regiment.

Monty's decision showed just how far the whole venture had come since Churchill's vague directive of five years earlier. They had established themselves emphatically, embedding themselves within the army's fabric.

23. Every Man an Emperor

On a rainy summer's day in June 1945, Lieutenant Colonel Geoffrey Pine-Coffin went to Buckingham Palace. He was there to receive the Distinguished Service Order twice over. His first DSO had been earned in Normandy, and although he had donned the ribbon he had waited until this day to receive the actual medal. The second award or bar was for his leadership during Operation Varsity.

In a photo snapped outside the palace, Pine-Coffin is wearing a generously cut service dress uniform, or perhaps he had lost weight during the late campaign. His disfigurement, a hard scar across the right cheek, is very evident. Having been an absent father for so much of the war, Pine-Coffin is holding his son Peter's hand, the boy being dressed in school uniform for his big day up in Town. Also enjoying the occasion is a companion in a mink jacket, hat and mid-length dress, referred to by Peter in subsequent years simply as 'that woman'. Taking someone to Buckingham Palace ranked as quite a date, and, as a widower who had survived the war against the odds, Pine-Coffin cared little about family disapproval or societal prudery.

These were times when many of those being honoured for their deeds during the war beat the same path for investitures by the king. In December, Marcelle Grayburn, widow of Lieutenant Jack, was there to receive his posthumous award of the Victoria Cross. Earlier in 1945 Lieutenant Colonel Alastair 'Mad Jock' Pearson had been recognized with a fourth DSO award, a record achieved by only eight men in the Second World War.

The great majority who had fallen were unsung, of course. Corporal Arthur Maybury, whose remains were shuffled from a back garden to a temporary soldiers' grave before finally being laid to rest in a Commonwealth cemetery in Oosterbeek, was given no special awards or mentions, though his mother at least continued for a time to receive royalties from his books.

Sergeant Major Macleod Forsyth survived the war and also gained a rare distinction: he was one of a handful of British soldiers given a decoration by the Soviet Union as an act of Allied solidarity. In his case, the Order of the Red Star was awarded for his actions in the Battle of the River Sangro in Italy while fighting with the Argyll and Sutherland Highlanders.

Johnny Frost had returned from captivity and, like so many others, found it a lonely, unsettling experience 'I soon realized that nobody was going to be able to form a welcoming party for the rather battered prisoners arriving in dribs and drabs.' Like many men home from the wars, thoughts turned to marriage for Frost, who, after returning to the 2nd Battalion in Bulford later in 1945, met his future wife while she was driving a YMCA tea wagon.

Sergeant Mike Lewis had moved even more quickly. He had been dispatched with paratroopers from the 13th Battalion to Denmark in May 1945, just after VE Day, as part of a move to prevent a power vacuum there prior to the re-establishment of the government. He spotted his Danish bride to be, Lis Varnaae, singing in an Andrews Sisters tribute act at a club in Copenhagen.

For Lewis, like many in the 6th Airborne Division, the war was not actually over, because orders were soon issued to send them to the Far East. Having experienced North Africa, Arnhem and Varsity, Lewis really wasn't sure he could face going to another battleground. He was given an appointment with an army psychiatrist, who proved very sympathetic, recommending the sergeant for a posting to *Soldier* magazine instead.

As it happened, although the airborne division was indeed sent eastwards, it did not arrive in time to face the Japanese and was redeployed to Palestine, where growing trouble between Jewish settlers, Arabs and the British Mandate authorities foretold one of the enduring post-1945 conflicts.

By the late summer of 1945 the Parachute Regiment's war had ended. It had deployed fourteen battalions on operations in

Europe and the Mediterranean theatre, six of which had been wiped out during the Market Garden campaign. It had lost 188 officers and 2,004 other ranks killed in action. Total casualties (i.e. including the wounded and captured as well as the dead) for these theatres have been estimated at 16,000 – a sobering number, given that the total strength of the two airborne divisions and one independent brigade employed there in mid-1944 was around 28,500.

This book began with five of its main subjects serving in the 2nd Parachute Battalion (the sixth arrived later). Its dramatic raid on Bruneval at the start of 1942 marked the beginning of thirty-one months of campaigning, culminating in its Arnhem battle, during which time it had 200 men killed in action and lost nine during training accidents. The most remarkable casualty figure about this unit, though, was the number of its men who ended up as prisoners of war: more than 800. Its mishaps, from Oudna to Sicily and then Arnhem, make it seem like a revolving door, delivering highly motivated and trained soldiers into captivity. By way of comparison, one of the 7th Armoured Division's tank battalions, serving for five years in successive campaigns (including some major setbacks) from France in 1940 to the desert war, Italy, Normandy and Germany, had around ninety men taken prisoner.

The pioneers paid the price as the role of airborne forces evolved. Sergeant Major Forsyth would describe the Bruneval raid in which he took part as 'the best planned operation of the lot', but it was the type of raiding action in which a small number of highly trained individuals knew what they were doing. As the scale of their missions grew there was a sense among many of the 2nd Battalion's men that they made the sacrifices for the learning experiences of others, notably senior officers and air-transport pilots.

Certainly, the record of the 7th Parachute Battalion, which went into action for the first time on D-Day, is emblematic of the development of airborne forces during the war. It lost forty-eight men as prisoners during its year of campaigning, but the toughness of its fights, from the Orne to the Ardennes and the Rhine Crossing, were reflected in its losses of 214 men killed and several hundred wounded. Under Pine-Coffin, the 7th Battalion had the advantage of being used within reach of supporting artillery and close to relieving forces, unlike Johnny Frost's men.

Further, just as the operational use of parachute forces evolved, so did the ethos or culture of the regiment raised to carry out these missions. There emerged a distinct cleavage between the original six volunteer battalions (the 1st to 4th gathered in Britain, 151/156 in India and 11th in Egypt) and those later converted from other infantry units.

The volunteers of 1941–42 were experienced soldiers, bored by the inactivity that the strategic situation had relegated them to, hungering for action. At Bulford in the summer of 1942, Pine-Coffin had been thirty-three years old, Sergeant Forsyth thirty and Lance Corporal Maybury twenty-eight: they had been formed as soldiers in regiments of the line, and fear of a return to unit was one of the few things that kept many of their messmates in order. Many imagined Bruneval as precisely the type of night-time derring-do that they had signed up for.

Recall the cards given to the men on their qualification as parachutists, which began with the words, 'You are the elite of the British army.' This sense of being a corps d'elite, or the crème de la crème, persisted among the original units long after it had become apparent that small-scale commando raids like Bruneval were to prove the exception rather than the rule.

Even in May 1944, a photograph of officers of the 2nd Battalion shows how many of them clung on to the distinctions of their original units, emblems of their previous identity. Some of those with distinguished war records in the Parachute Regiment, like Major Doug Crawley, chose to return to their original regiments to command when it ended.

Only later did it become clear that the natural path for the type of men initially drawn to parachute training – experienced soldiers seeking the challenge of raiding operations in small units – would be to seek selection for the Special Air Service Regiment. But by 1945 it had become evident as far as the Parachute Regiment was concerned that, rather than being a special operations force, it had become a superior kind of regular infantry, deploying swiftly into battle at the battalion or brigade level and remaining in the line for months if necessary.

As the commanders of airborne forces were to discover, it was the second wave of parachute battalions formed that proved best suited to this role. Those in the units converted from line infantry duties were on average much younger, and were in any case soon joined by equally inexperienced officers and men who had not had time to discover any other strong identity in the army. Hence Brigadier James Hill, one of the first volunteers, who later went on to command a brigade of these newer units, argued that 'they proved magnificent material and easy to mould when in good hands'. The younger men in those units weren't just less 'bolshie', they were also more open to the idea that they were part of a new tribe in the army, with new ideals. It was a measure of the absence of cynicism within these units that they engaged enthusiastically in religious services, for example before D-Day, unlike the hard-bitten veterans of the 1st Parachute Brigade.

What the regiment clung to, as it pushed 2,000 soldiers a month into the arduous Hardwick Hall training mill in 1944, was that these men were volunteers. Some of those who agreed to join when their battalions converted in 1942 or 1943 hadn't really known what they were getting into and simply wanted to stay together. But the fact that remaining with their friends meant passing paratroop and jump training bound them and newcomers together, strengthening their ties and their sense that they were hand-picked troops.

'The very act of arriving on the battlefield by parachute inspires a sense of superiority,' Lieutenant Colonel Pine-Coffin wrote. 'Everyone feels twice the man he did before the jump.' Although leaping from the air would later become largely irrelevant to their soldiers' use in war, it remained the key rite of passage for those wishing to join the airborne tribe. The Parachute Regiment's training regime required soldiers to prove themselves that way; it was part of their basic conditioning, boosting the confidence of those who had come through it. Montgomery argued, 'they have "jumped" from the air and by doing so have conquered fear'.

This element, the confidence instilled by parachuting, remains a defining factor in the regiment today. It has become a given in its celebrated actions of recent decades, from the Falklands to the Balkans and Helmand Province in Afghanistan, that they did not involve parachute assault but that the training to conduct one was a contributory factor in their fighting effectiveness.

Back in 1944, Major General Roy Urquhart, an outsider who nevertheless took pride in the airborne units he commanded, reckoned the parachute troops had a small but significant margin over regular infantry. By special training, 'they managed to eliminate some of the weaker elements'. The fact of volunteering was particularly important for those with commissions, which Urquhart reckoned produced 'on the whole a higher calibre of officer in the parachute battalions'.

The notion that it was an organization that brought an edge to soldiering grew, and as the regiment matured it placed less emphasis on the soldiers' elite status. It could be counter-productive with other units and encourage a bad attitude among some soldiers. It was, though, part and parcel of the ethos that Boy Browning had attempted to inculcate when taking over the airborne troops. Their printed Airborne Division ethos cards gave the soldiers six bullet points where their behaviour had to meet their general's standards.

The middle four of these were eminently logical: the need to master their weapons, be calm, remain fit, or think quickly. The sixth revealed a particular sensibility on the part of their leader towards the lower orders: 'Do not chatter. It will endanger the lives of your comrades.' It was, however, Browning's first injunction that underscored his Guards mindset: 'You must be better disciplined and smarter in your turnout than any other troops.'

We have already seen how Browning's preoccupation with 'turnout' – the first ethos card bullet point – resulted in soldiers parading barefoot on Netheravon airfield while he inspected their feet and made sure the number of nails in their boots was the regulation eleven. It also saw him excoriated as a martinet and worse by many of the NCOs who were supposed to impose these standards. Even in the hellish cold and mud of Tunisia, stern instructions came down on saluting, headgear and recovering the blankets from dead men.

While the 1940s army could never have been free of petty officialdom, and the bolshie national service soldier revelled in his right to complain, Browning's obsessions set up constant tension, wasted a good deal of time and, in the view of some, exacerbated the disciplinary issues that plagued the early volunteer battalions.

Johnny Frost and others argued that discipline improved once they became more practised at handling their soldiers, the wiser officers finding ways to appeal to their professional pride or tax them with exercise rather than sending them to jail. In fact, matters were ameliorated by adopting principles of discipline well understood in the British Army since General Sir John Moore, the light infantry pioneer and trainer, had set them out more than a century earlier. It might be added also, though Frost did not seem to realize it, that the loss as casualties of so many of the early volunteers and their replacement with younger men may also have helped make the life of the military police a little easier.

Browning's status as a divisive figure has in more recent times been tied to his role as one of the architects of Operation Market Garden. The battle, and in particular the fate of the 1st Airborne Division in Arnhem, spawned one of the biggest controversies in the history of the British Army – which is a remarkable observation for an organization that has relished post-war recrimination throughout its existence. There have been dozens of books, many documentaries and countless newspaper articles on the operation in general, and in particular on whether it was an avoidable tragedy.

Evidently, there is a national weakness for military disasters and their re-litigation through subsequent history. If one seeks an empirical form to that, just contrast the number of books published on the largely successful Rhine Crossing airborne operation with that on the Arnhem catastrophe. Furthermore, the film *A Bridge Too Far*, based upon Cornelius Ryan's book of the same name, has arguably done more to define Browning's reputation than any amount of historical publishing.

In it, Dirk Bogarde plays Boy as cold and aloof, ignoring the intelligence of enemy armoured troops near Arnhem. While the film caused distress to Browning's widow, and spawned protestations that it hadn't done justice to his role in creating Britain's airborne arm, the portrayal was hardly surprising when taking into consideration the views of colleagues like General Richard Gale, or, indeed, Johnny Frost, that Browning should never have attempted to lead the operation in the field and may well have allowed his hunger to do so to warp his military judgement.

The verdict on Browning, then, is quite paradoxical. There can be no doubt that he exploited his influence in the army and the upper echelons of society to deliver the men and means of establishing both the Parachute Regiment and airborne forces more generally. He remained focused on this when Churchill, for entirely understandable reasons, given his national responsibilities, lost sight of the project between signing off on the creation of parachute units and their employment at Bruneval.

By assuming the role of midwife to the nation's aerial assault forces, Browning undoubtedly secured a prominent place in British Army history. He defined its symbols and did much to inform its early beliefs. It would be all too easy to forget that his project faced enormous resistance from the RAF, and that many of the other special units formed in the Second World War, not least the army commandos, failed to establish themselves in the same way and subsequently disappeared from the order of battle.

Yet Browning's period of leadership also marked something of a false start for those forces, in terms of both their ethos and their use on the battlefield. The emphasis on turnout and drill was reduced by his successors, and his campaigning for the use of ever larger airborne formations, unsustainable after 1945, in some ways contributed to the Arnhem debacle and made it hard to maintain the volunteer principle.

It was, of course, Frost who emerged as one of the heroes of *A Bridge Too Far*, sympathetically played by Anthony Hopkins as a paragon of British grit and sangfroid. This version of the man, in a line of stoic heroes from Trafalgar to Rorke's Drift, made Frost a celebrity late in life.

The contrast between Frost, presiding over costly mishaps from Oudna to Sicily and then Arnhem, and Pine-Coffin, whose operational drops from Bône to Normandy and the Rhine were all successful, is instructive. The seizure by glider troops of the Orne bridges, and the *holding* of them by his 7th Parachute Battalion, was arguably the greatest British airborne action of the war, yet Pine-Coffin sank into obscurity after 1945. It cannot be simply about suffering, since the 7th Battalion's losses were greater than the 2nd's at their bridge. Rather, the fame of the 2nd Battalion's stand derives from the fact that its men were seemingly abandoned and, perhaps, a national penchant for noble failure.

Like many of the heroes who emerged in the war, Frost was not comfortable with celebrity. He was also puzzled by some of the interest in the Arnhem epic and began to tire of constant questions about the operation and his personal role in it. 'I am a very busy farmer and have not the time to answer your questions,' he wrote in response to queries from yet another historian in 1977. 'All the points you mention have been covered by accounts which have appeared in various books since the end of the war and it is up to you to ferret them out.'

The interest in Arnhem from military historians may also in some measure have resulted from a sense that it was a fleeting moment. General Gale opined, 'I do not believe that anything like the scale of employment we witnessed in Europe is likely to arise again,' knowing as he did how hard it would be post-demobilization to marshal the necessary armadas of aircraft.

Gliders had proven very hard to use without sustaining significant casualties and, fortunately for those who might otherwise have had to ride in them, were swiftly superseded by helicopters for air assault. But for the British armed forces, whittled down after demobilization, there was also an understanding that really large airdrops could only be done by the Americans. Sparring with the RAF for diminished resources resumed as soon as the guns fell silent.

Within a couple of years of the war ending, an RAF paper noted: 'There has never been a really properly thought out appreciation of the airborne forces problem . . . if such an appreciation were made really honestly and objectively, the conclusion would be that airborne forces are not worth it in a major war.'

If there were some in light blue who had defaulted back to Bomber Harris's view of the airborne arm as a diversion of strategic effort, there were also some in the army who thought that these formations creamed off too many good soldiers and were rarely useful, spending much of the war sitting around.

This last point hardly stands up to scrutiny, for between Dunkirk and Normandy hundreds of thousands of soldiers did very little. Take one example: the 52nd Lowland Division, somewhat larger than an airborne one, was stood by for a variety of missions after June 1940, including as mountain troops or to be landed by aircraft, without seeing action at all until October 1944. In the meantime, parachute brigades had spent many months fighting hard and suffering casualties in front lines from Tunisia to Italy and Normandy.

As for the diversion of effort, there were 28,000 serving with airborne forces in Europe in mid-1944, 40,000 if India and the Far East are included, or around 1.5 per cent of the army's strength at the time. Given the numbers languishing in other functions that were rarely used late in the war, such as many of the air defence artillery units, that hardly seems an extravagance.

Germany, on the other hand, had to keep substantial forces in reserve in case of British landings by air or sea: for example, many of its divisions in Norway, the Low Countries or indeed France beyond Normandy following D-Day. This was in itself an effective use of Allied resources.

Those storied battalion commanders of 1st Parachute Brigade, Pearson, Frost and Pine-Coffin, three men with eight DSOs between them, failed to flourish in the peacetime army. Pearson left very quickly (though he remained involved with the Territorial Army), going back to his family's bakery before turning to farming.

As for Pine-Coffin, he spent a few years running recruit training for the Parachute Regiment, a fitting use for someone with such a paternalistic concern for his soldiers, retiring with the rank of colonel in 1958. He lived out his remaining days on an army pension at a hotel in Portsmouth, an establishment run by one of his lady friends.

Johnny Frost was the only one of the three to become a general, but even that was as a result of commanding a reserve division in the years leading up to his retirement in 1968. Certainly, he did not rise to the top, despite his renown.

Kenneth Darling, on the other hand, had what it took to reach the most senior rank in the peacetime army, despite having suffered revolts of two parachute battalions under his command (the 1st in April 1944 and the 13th while in the Far East in 1946). He ended his career as Commander-in-Chief of Allied Forces in Northern Europe.

Of those lower down the chain of command, one of the most remarkable characters was Desmond Brayley, 'Slapsey' to the men of A Company, 2nd Battalion, decorated in North Africa but sacked by Frost for lying low during the Sicily operation. Brayley became a wealthy industrialist and an enthusiastic backer of Prime Minister Harold Wilson.

Occasionally violent and often unstoppable, Brayley was given a knighthood, then a peerage by Wilson in 1973. After a brief spell as army minister Brayley resigned amid allegations of business irregularities, and was subsequently accused of buying his honours from the Labour leader with large donations of cash.

Macleod Forsyth survived until 2008 and took part in numerous 2nd Battalion reunions as well as making a pilgrimage to Bruneval in 1985. The circumstances of his removal from the Parachute Regiment, his many rows with officers and in particular the company commander whom he accused of cowardice, remained a source of regret and anguish throughout his life. When he sat down with an interviewer from the Imperial War Museum in 1999 to record his wartime experiences, Forsyth said of his return to the Argylls, 'believe me, it hurt'.

Mike Lewis became a professional cameraman after demobilization, working for many years for BBC News. In 1982 he and his Danish wife moved to Australia, where he died five years later. He never forgot his friends in basic training, particularly Fred Selman, who took Lewis to meet his mother in the autumn of 1942, before they left for North Africa. Until the end of his life Lewis would send flowers each year on 27 March to Florence Selman, to mark the anniversary of her son's death. Although he wrote to Florence and visited her in later years, Lewis could never bring himself to tell her that her son had been killed by friendly fire.

Mothers became central figures in the remembrance of those who had fallen. They joined in pilgrimages to the battlefields of Normandy and Arnhem, some even making it to North Africa. Jack Grayburn's took his loss with stoicism, feeling it was probably better that such an active, sporting man should have gone that way than survived the war with terrible wounds. 'We shall miss him terribly,' she wrote to one of Jack's schoolmasters at Sherborne, 'but I'm grateful that he has not come back to us with injuries that would mean a life of pain & inactivity. Better far that the loss & sorrow is ours, than that he should suffer so.'

For some there was not even the comfort of having a grave to visit, since a few lost before jumping or in gliders remained 'missing' in perpetuity. For others, pilgrimages could bring some meaning or understanding to their loss.

After the war, Edith Maybury went to Arnhem. She met the schoolteacher who had helped her son after he was mortally wounded. Having lost her husband in the First World War, and having no other children but Arthur, his loss had left her quite alone in the world. His body had been laid to rest in the Commonwealth War Cemetery by the time of her visit. For his headstone she chose a message of religious faith: 'All the glorious universe is life. There is no death, 'tis but a higher birth.'

She also gave the Arnhem museum copies of a couple of his

books published under his Pegasus pseudonym. There was pride in his achievements, evidently. Edith Maybury wanted people to know he may have been a fallen soldier, a corporal, a paratrooper, but he had achieved other things in his thirty years too.

This sacrifice had been motivated by many factors, from the desire not to let comrades and family down to proving themselves as soldiers, or the need to defeat a vicious national foe. The question of establishing a new regiment and ensuring its survival after 1945 was probably incidental to the great majority of those who served in it. Even so, the pioneers took pride in a kind of wartime celebrity and, once established, the symbols of badge, beret and Bellerophon exerted a powerful loyalty upon those who bore them.

The things that these marks of distinction were supposed to stand for evolved in the years after Boy Browning was posted away from airborne forces. And it did not take long, after the war, for new formulations to emerge. Indeed, the 'culture' or values that the regiment was supposed to represent were well summed up by Field Marshal Montgomery a couple of years later. In contributing a foreword, as colonel, to a history of the Parachute Regiment's war years, he coined some memorable phrases about its soldiers' striving for excellence. Instead of Browning's directive on 'turnout', the word 'smartness' is used in a way that encompasses intellectual energy or initiative as much as appearance. It was Montgomery who, as architect of the Market Garden gamble, owed the airborne family the greatest debt, and who proved key in distilling the experience of war and ethos that had emerged from it:

> They have the highest standards in all things, whether it be skill in battle or smartness in the execution of all peace time duties. They have shown themselves as tenacious and determined in defence as they are courageous in attack. They are in fact men apart – every man an Emperor.

Acknowledgements

The writing of this book would have been impossible without the support and understanding of a good many people. Principal among them were: Jon Baker of the Airborne Assault Museum, who went above and beyond the call of duty throughout this process; Neil Barber, whose histories of the Orne bridges events are classics; Nicolas Bucourt, who curates the excellent Bruneval Facebook pages; Daniel Crewe of Penguin, my editor and the person whose idea this book actually was; John Delaney of the Imperial War Museum; John Grayburn, for graciously sharing his father's journal; John Greenacre, an author cited herein, who helped me research the early power struggles over airborne forces; Mark Hickman of the online Pegasus Archive, a great source of unit war diaries and biographical information; Bob Hilton, former paratrooper and regimental history buff second to none, who fielded so many inquiries from me; Trevor Horwood for bringing his eagle eye to the production process; Robert Kershaw, author of the superb German-centric history of Market Garden, who kindly reviewed this manuscript; Helen Lewis, daughter of Mike and an expert on his story, the subject of her PhD and later book; Jonathan Lloyd, my agent for so many years, who still comes up trumps; Paul Nixon for help with family research; Richard Pearson of the King Edward VI School archive; Michael Pine-Coffin, who provided an almost inexhaustible supply of expertise about the 7th Battalion as well as allowing me access to his grandfather Geoffrey Pine-Coffin's papers; Alpana Sajip at Penguin; Stephen Walton, always helpful, at the Imperial War Museum archive at Duxford; and Caroline Wood our picture researcher. Any errors are my responsibility alone. Lastly, I must give my most heartfelt thanks to my beloved Hilary, who, after all these years, says, 'I know when I have lost you to a book', and through that combination of a big, supportive heart and hard-won experience waits for me to emerge from the other side.

Notes on Sources

Chapter 1: First Blood

half hoping the mission might be called off . . .: Frost makes this confession in his autobiography *A Drop Too Many* (Cassell, 1980).

'Lulu', 'Annie Laurie' and 'The Rose of Tralee': Flight Sergeant Cox, quoted by George Millar in *The Bruneval Raid: Stealing Hitler's Radar* (Cassell, 2002).

'The windowless fuselage of a bomber is oppressive, dark . . .': from *Parachutist* by 'Pegasus' (Jarrolds, 1944). The pseudonymous author was in fact Corporal Arthur Maybury, who features extensively in this book.

'to capture various parts of HENRY': the orders are reproduced in *Without Tradition: 2 PARA 1941–1945*, by Robert Peatling (Pen and Sword, 2004). Peatling, who served in the war with the 2nd Battalion and remained a key figure in its old comrades' network, compiled many fascinating accounts from veterans.

'I was able to recognize the ground . . .': Frost, *A Drop Too Many*.

'it had become essential . . .': ibid.

The contaner holding a radio needed to contact . . .: Captain John Timothy, a participant in the raid, Imperial War Museum (IWM) Audio 17182.

there was plenty of experience in the small group of men . . .: details of Charteris's party have been compiled over many years by French local historian Nicolas Bucourt and can be found on his Facebook page www.facebook.com/brunevalraid/.

a German patrol from the local defence force . . .: the identity of the defence force emerges from the local German commander's report, reproduced in Peatling, *Without Tradition*.

'going away from the camp and [they] were in a laughing mood': Private Dick Scott, quoted ibid.

'In a matter of minutes the apparatus was dismantled . . .': Captain Peter Young, IWM Docs 19990.

Running in a blind panic away from the attack . . .: the story of this German and his watch was told by Bruneval veteran Bob Dobson to Peatling for *Without Tradition*. The prisoner subsequently asked for his watch back, and McKenzie was told by his officers to return it. Having sent it for repairs, the Scottish sergeant found himself out of pocket.

another German soldier had died in a moment of black comedy: this macabre tale features in various places, including Maybury's book *Parachutist*. Bucourt got a first-hand version of it from Peter Venters, one of those who opened up on the German, whom he interviewed before his death.

One vital radio needed to contact the flotilla of landing craft . . .: Frost, *A Drop Too Many*, and Lieutenant John Timothy, IWM Audio 17182, recount the communications problems.

'The job was done': Timothy, IWM Audio 17182.

'With a sinking heart': Frost, *A Drop Too Many*.

'God bless the ruddy navy, sir!': ibid.

'Our evacuation plan went by the board': ibid.

'Christ! Lift this or we're prisoners!': Macleod Forsyth, IWM Audio 18780.

'sped off much too quickly before the ramp was closed . . .': Scott quoted in Peatling, *Without Tradition*.

Chapter 2: Lap of Honour

'Every vessel in port clanged their bells . . .': Captain Peter Young, IWM Docs 19990.

'These are black days!': Field Marshal Lord Alanbrooke, *War Diaries 1939–1945* (Weidenfeld and Nicolson, 2001).

the London Evening Standard splashed . . .: Nicolas Bucourt's Facebook page has a gallery of global press coverage of the raid.

'I expect the scientists wanted the radar': Forsyth, IWM Audio 18780.

Only a minority of the 2nd Battalion's 570 men . . .: numbers of men and officers from 2nd Battalion War Diary, National Archives (NA), WO 166/8553.

'We basked in the reflected glory': Sergeant Eddie Hancock, IWM Docs 21756.

'[we] could have had any amount of free beer': Sergeant John Allan Johnstone, IWM Docs 7159.

'German casualties are estimated at a minimum of 40 killed': after-action report reproduced in Peatling, *Without Tradition*.

'The operation of the British commandos . . .': ibid.

'there were Seaforths, Camerons, Black Watch . . .': Forsyth, IWM Audio 18780.

'one felt like something out of Madame Tussaud's . . .': Maybury, *Parachutist*.

'what you call Soldiers of Fortune . . .': Brigadier (Stanley) James Hill, IWM Audio 12347.

'It was really a mercenary battalion . . .': Alastair Stevenson Pearson, IWM Audio 21033.

men who failed to keep up with long route marches . . .: the rigours imposed on the 1st Battalion under Lieutenant Colonel Eric Down are described in Major Anthony Hibbert, IWM Audio 21040.

One soldier from the Essex Regiment who appeared there early in 1942 . . .: this was Bill Bloys, IWM Audio 17273.

'ex-clerks, insurance agents, salesmen . . .': Maybury, *Parachutist*.

two members of Forsyth's company who had fought in the Spanish Civil War . . .: Private Peter McCormack and Sergeant Thomas Maguire. The latter appears in the International Brigade database. Johnstone, IWM Docs 7159, an excellent unpublished memoir, refers obliquely to Maguire's Spanish service. On McCormack, information from Nicolas Bucourt.

the son of Yiddish-speaking immigrant parents . . .: Michael Lewis, IWM Audio 4833. His daughter Helen Lewis's excellent book *The Dead Still Cry Out: The Story of a Combat Cameraman* (Text Publishing, 2018), published in Australia, describes Michael's origins, his struggles with his family and experience of anti-Semitism.

'we were being blended . . .': Lewis, IWM Audio 4833.

The younger son of a landed Devon family . . .: much information about him has been gleaned from his grandson, Michael Pine-Coffin.

'Tall, lean and tough, with long-nosed . . .': the officer was Richard Todd, later a celebrated film actor, and the description comes from his autobiography *Caught in the Act* (Hutchinson, 1986).

'Even men of very high rank indeed': Maybury, *Parachutist*.

'the learner parachutists' smile . . .': Frost, *A Drop Too Many*.

In the 2nd Battalion's March return of twenty-four officers . . .: 2nd Battalion
War Diary, NA, WO 166/8553.

cockneys to A Company, northerners to B and Scots to C: Hancock, IWM
Docs 21756.

Some had exploited the trawl for men to get rid of undesirables . . .: this tendency
is mentioned by a few of the parachute pioneers, including Frost in
A Drop Too Many.

'the news almost exclusively with the all-services raid . . .': Jack Grayburn's private journal, family papers, kindly shared by his son, John Grayburn.

Chapter 3: Whitehall Warriors

On the ride up he was a little uneasy: this feeling and much else in this chapter from Frost's memoir *A Drop Too Many*.

'almost unbearably cocky': ibid.

Filing into the room came the service chiefs . . .: the attendees are listed in the
NA record of the meeting CAB 65/25.

'the bombing of German industry was an incomparably greater contribution . . .': from
Portal's memo of August 1942, which can be found in NA AIR 75-45.

the service's failure to acquire around a hundred civilian airliners: the fate of
these aircraft is discussed in John Greenacre's excellent *Churchill's
Spearhead: The Development of Britain's Airborne Forces During World
War II* (Pen and Sword, 2010).

'Are we not in danger of being fobbed off?': Churchill, quoted ibid.

'for raiding purposes and for assisting in minor operations': Portal's August
paper, NA, AIR 75-45.

'more aircraft, more aircraft, more aircraft': Frost, *A Drop Too Many*.

Chapter 4: Mad About the Boy

Major General Browning reached Langley's End . . .: this and many other
details of his life are from Richard Mead, *General 'Boy': The Life of
Lieutenant General Sir Frederick Browning* (Pen and Sword, 2010).

'month in, month out, he worked for this, but always against resistance': anonymous staff officer quoted in Browning's obituary in *Pegasus Journal*, Summer 1965.

'One was given a job to do and left to get on with it': from Gordon Walch's unpublished memoir, part of his papers, IWM Docs 9487.

'mannered arrogance': Brian Urquhart, *A Life in Peace and War* (Orion, 1987).

'I was dreading this visit . . .': Frost, *A Drop Too Many*.

That spring, Browning and his team had also hit upon . . .: Greenacre, *Churchill's Spearhead*, covers the myriad preparations of the airborne division.

'My first impression . . .': Maybury, *Parachutist*.

able to cover fifty miles during twenty-four hours . . .: Frost, *A Drop Too Many*.

walked in stages over two days eighty miles . . .: 2nd Battalion War Diary, NA, WO 166/8553.

'Hitler's Racial Myth': ibid.

'a solid welding together . . .': Frost, A Drop Too Many.

'If there was any happiness to be found . . .': Lewis, IWM Audio 4833.

leaving Geoffrey Pine-Coffin to become second in command . . .: 2nd Battalion War Diary, NA, WO 166/8553.

'On 16 April Churchill . . .': ibid.

'the desirability of employing airborne forces . . .': Mountbatten memo of 15 April 1942, quoted in Mead, *General 'Boy'*.

'we cannot go on with 10,000 men and only 32 aircraft at their disposal': ibid.

an argument had been made in relation to the Far East . . .: this case, energetically made by Julian Amery, Secretary of State for India, is recounted in Greenacre, *Churchill's Spearhead*.

'for the defeat of Germany it will sooner or later be necessary . . .': Brooke's memo is contained in NA, CAB 121-97.

'compel [the enemy] to defend a relatively vast area': ibid.

Portal's arguments were fed by Air Marshal Arthur 'Bomber' Harris: Harris's critique of Brooke can be found in NA, CAB 121-97.

One of the Bruneval raid lieutenants was sent across to act as liaison officer . . .: this was John Timothy, IWM Audio 17182.

the 3rd Battalion made the British airborne arm's first battalion-scale drop . . .: 1st Parachute Brigade War Diary, NA, WO 166/6677.

The United States was, by July 1942 . . .: Major Charles E. Fitzpatrick, *Joint Planning for Operation Torch* (US Army War College, 1991).

Lieutenant General Dwight Eisenhower, was keen to see how it was working out : 1st Parachute Brigade War Diary, NA, WO 166/6677.

Chapter 5: Thirsting for Action

'a fierce verbal onslaught . . .': this anecdote is drawn from Sergeant Hancock's unpublished memoir, IWM Docs 21756, a fascinating record of early Parachute Regiment days from the ranks.

'indignation reigned, expletives and comments abounded': ibid.

'Bullshit Browning' or 'Bastard Browning': Browning's biographer acknowledges these monikers in Mead, *General 'Boy'*.

'We'll do it for you, Eddie': Hancock, IWM Docs 21756.

'too much bullshit – we joined for action': Johnstone, IWM Docs 7159.

'as a result of his Guards background': Hancock, IWM Docs 21756.

'we were not training to beat the Germans in a drill competition': Maybury, *Parachutist.*

'our greatest problem in those early days . . .': Frost, *A Drop Too Many.*

'the men universally hated him': this is Bill Aldcroft quoted in Andy Johnston, *Churchill's Warriors: Personal Stories of British Airborne Troops in the Second World War* (Travelogue, 2017).

Mike Lewis and Fred Selman, tired at the falsification of the scores . . .: Lewis tells this anecdote in IWM Audio 4833.

'You are the elite of the British Army . . .': Airborne Ethos card, Airborne Assault Museum.

'I look very swell in my purple hat': General Napier Crookenden Papers, IWM Docs 6248.

'quite a few chaps didn't like wearing them': Bloys, IWM Audio 17273. Bill Bloys transferred to A Company and, since he survived countless battles, his testimony is of great interest.

Spender . . . had volunteered for the paratroops . . .: Richard Spender, letter to his parents, 12 February 1943. Spender's correspondence, hereafter referred to as the Spender Papers, was purchased in 2011 by his old school, King Edward VI School, Stratford-upon-Avon, and now reside in the archive there. I am most grateful to Richard Pearson, the school's archivist, for his help with this project.

Johnny Frost also proved a lagging convert to the maroon beret : Bloys, IWM Audio 17273.

Many others retained dress from parent regiments . . .: one has only to look at the photographs of regimental officers, for example those of the 2nd Battalion before Arnhem, to see this.

'we used to drink like fish': Forsyth, IWM Audio 18780.

'them yellow bastards': Johnstone, IWM Docs 7159.

'probably not unjustly': ibid.

'Respectable folk might have been excused . . .': Maybury, *Parachutist*.

'eleven studs in each sole . . .': Hancock, IWM Docs 21756.

They borrowed three bicycles and set out . . .: Lewis paints a vivid picture of this in his IWM Audio 4833 recording.

On 9 October 1942, a group of dignitaries gathered in the fields near Figheldean . . .: this unfortunate drop is described by a few participants, including Frost in *A Drop Too Many*, Maybury in *Parachutist* and Lewis in IWM Audio 4833.

'it was a Rolls Royce': Hancock, IWM Docs 21756.

'Pure luxury': Maybury, *Parachutist*.

Orders to deploy overseas had been received . . .: 1st Parachute Brigade War Diary, NA, WO 166/6677.

'desperately trying to shake their chutes loose': Lewis, IWM Audio 4833.

He shouted at the brigadier . . .: Edwin Flavell, whom we shall meet later.

'We all knew that the difficulties would soon be resolved . . .': Frost, *A Drop Too Many*.

'We were all thirsting for action . . .': ibid.

Chapter 6: Oudna

'a blazing city in the distance': Lewis, IWM Audio 4833.

'a romantic picture . . . ': Private Thomas Davies quoted in Niall Cherry, *Tunisian Tales* (Helion, 2011).

'I think it evil smelling and poverty stricken': Lieutenant Richard Spender, letter to his aunts dated 5 December 1942, Spender Papers. Spender arrived after the main party and was not therefore able to go on the Oudna operation.

'*the Arabs smell like sewage plants . . .*': Spender, letter to his brother dated 3 December 1942, Spender Papers. Spender appears to have been retelling mess gossip about the price of sex, as in another letter he suggested that he had remained true to a girl he'd left behind in England.

'*the aircraft were Dakotas straight from America . . .*': Pine-Coffin put together an informal, unpublished album of his experiences after the war, the contents shared with me by his grandson Michael Pine-Coffin.

During their twelve-day sea voyage . . .: Hancock, IWM Docs 21756, gives a good account of the trip.

two men from A Company had returned to the school blind drunk: these were Joe Goldsmith and a man named Stinson (by Johnstone, probably a pseudonym), the latter being knocked out by Brayley. The events of that evening are covered by the two excellent A Company memoirists, Hancock, IWM Docs 21756, and Johnstone, IWM Docs 7159.

The son of a Pontypridd café owner . . .: taken from Brayley's entry in the *Dictionary of National Biography*.

Some of the paratroopers admired Brayley for his courage . . .: Johnstone was later Brayley's platoon sergeant and clearly admired his brass neck; IWM Docs 7159.

'*He tended to solve disciplinary problems physically*': Hancock, IWM Docs 21756.

'*Operations made most difficult*': 1st Parachute Brigade War Diary, NA, WO 175/181.

'*we feared that we might never get our parachute operation*': Frost, *A Drop Too Many*.

'*settled with savagery*': ibid.

Frost was ashamed of this disorder . . .: Frost is quite open in his autobiography about his inability to understand the men's wild behaviour. He also says that Ashford was not easy to manage because of his 'socialistic tendencies'.

One lieutenant in the 2nd Battalion penned this vivid portrait . . .: this is Victor Dover, quoted from his book *The Silken Canopy* (Cassell, 1979).

each of them had drawn what the army called G1098 kit . . .: details from Bloys, IWM Audio 17273. Jon Baker of the Airborne Assault Museum has pointed out to me that the string vest was not actually part of the G1098 kit, but Bloys put it in his list.

they'd been given condoms too . . .: Hancock, IWM Docs 21756.

'We look more like a fucking travelling circus . . .': Dennis Rendell, quoted in Peatling, *Without Tradition*. In his IWM Audio 19055, Rendell quotes Berryman a little differently. A couple of other accounts allude to Berryman also, including Hancock, IWM Docs 21756.

perhaps inevitably nicknamed 'Maxie' by the Londoners: Johnstone, IWM Docs 7159, gives many insights on Forsyth.

'The Germans were dead on target': Hancock, IWM Docs 21756.

'come on the Cockney boys!': ibid.

'This made my position untenable': Frost's account of the mission is in the 2nd Battalion War Diary, NA, WO 166/8553, and is also reproduced in Peatling, *Without Tradition*. Details such as timings in this chapter are largely drawn from this.

They had some rifle-fired grenades too: the EY or No. 68 grenade launcher. Lewis described this battle in detail in IWM Audio 4833.

Then Private Wilkinson appeared . . .: Lewis does not seem to remember Wilkinson's name in his interview. It would appear, given that no such soldier appears on the Commonwealth War Graves Commission records for this time and place that 'Wilkinson' may have been a pseudonym given by Johnstone in his memoir, IWM Docs 7159.

'cleft wide open from neck to legs . . .': Lewis, IWM Audio 4833.

a pair of Messerschmitts reappeared: the number of planes and other interesting supplementary details are from Helmut Wilhelmsmeyer, a WW2 German paratroop officer, in his article on Oudna in *Pegasus Journal*, August 1986.

'I do not exaggerate . . .': Johnstone, IWM Docs 7159.

'was a tower of strength': Rendell, IWM Audio 19055.

About seventy men of A Company . . .: ibid.

a barn belonging to the Rebourg family: much detail about this encounter from Hans Teske, IWM Audio 19101.

Chapter 7: In the Enemy Camp

Hans Teske had kept his secret . . .: Teske, IWM Audio 19101.

Those who had gone through Hardwick Hall . . .: Maybury, *Parachutist*, is interesting about this.

escaping in Arab clothing . . .: detail from Teske, IWM Audio 19101.

Walter Koch, was the man organizing the hunt . . .: a most interesting German-centric account of the Depienne events was provided by former Fallschirmjäger officer Helmut Wilhelmsmeyer in an article in *Pegasus Journal*, August 1986. The April 1972 edition of the same journal has a good a report on Koch and the incident involving his rescue of the captured men from C Company.

Crete became a high-water mark for Hitler's airborne forces: there are a good many histories of the invasion, including Antony Beevor's *Crete 1941* (Penguin, 2005). Details such as the 600+ aircraft from US official history: https://history.army.mil/books/wwii/balkan/20_260_4.htm.

motorcycle-sidecar combinations from their reconnaissance company were carried . . .: Teske, IWM Audio 19101.

Koch had two battalions of his own regiment . . .: details of Koch's force from Wilhelmsmeyer in *Pegasus Journal*, August 1986.

Oberstleutnant Koch was aware of and opposed to such a policy . . .: Koch's opposition to the Commando Order was, some old comrades later claimed, a factor in his murder in hospital while recovering from an accident in 1943. The 2nd Battalion men learned of this from reunions with their old adversaries, such as that reported in *Pegasus Journal* in April 1972.

'British paratroopers will be treated as prisoners of war!': two veterans from C Company left accounts of this incident. Gavin Cadden uses this formulation, which was published in *Pegasus Journal* in October 1977. Lieutenant Buchanan also survived the war and gave accounts of it.

'You are the chosen ones of the German army': the 'Ten Commandments' appear in various places, including Maybury's *Parachutist*.

'we picked up one or two fast asleep': Teske, IWM Audio 19101.

'he quoted his wife and child as the reason': Hancock, IWM Docs 21756.

'*my adjutant . . . soon had the very depressed prisoners talking*': this quote is attributed to Hauptmann Wilhelm Knoche, a battalion commander in the 5th Regiment, by Wilhelmsmeyer in his *Pegasus Journal* article.

'*running commentary from the Arabs who told us exactly where the British were*': Teske, IWM Audio 19101.

Captain Jock Short, chatted amiably . . .: ibid. After the war Teske tracked down Short's widow to tell her more about his fate.

The canny Joe Goldsmith from 2 Platoon . . .: details given in a letter of 12 December 1999 from Goldsmith to Bob Hilton, who kindly shared it with me.

he had dispatched Lieutenant Euan 'Junior' Charteris . . .: Frost's official report in the 2nd Battalion War Diary, NA, WO 166/8553, and *A Drop Too Many* both mention this.

A lieutenant and several men had been killed . . .: this action is described by several of those who were there, including Frost, Teske and Rendell.

Chapter 8: Sauve Qui Peut

two men rode across the Tunisian hillsides . . .: Johnstone in his memoir, IWM Docs 7159, paints a vivid pen portrait of this.

'*We were quite vague about where we would find 1st Army*': ibid.

'*extreme fatigue*': Frost's report in the 2nd Battalion War Diary, NA, WO 166/8553.

'*there was no escape . . .*': Johnstone, IWM Docs 7159.

'*You should have heard the cheer that went up . . .*': letter home from Les Shurmer, quoted in Peatling, *Without Tradition*.

Around 140 men assembled . . .: figure in Shurmer's letter and Frost, *A Drop Too Many*.

'*My main reaction to having had the battalion cut to pieces . . .*': Frost, *A Drop Too Many*.

'*the most disgracefully mounted operation . . .*': this Frost quotation, harsher in tone even than his own book, is in Cherry, *Tunisian Tales*.

'*many of us chose that day to be particularly stupid*': Frost, *A Drop Too Many*.

Frost could hardly vent these feelings of guilt and anger within his own battalion: nevertheless, Victor Dover in *The Silken Canopy* described Frost as angry and introspective in the days after their return from Oudna.

a fellow Scot with whom he would sink too many whiskies to count: Major Anthony Hibbert, IWM Audio 21040, describes Frost and Pearson as heavy drinkers. Frost himself, quoted by Cherry in *Tunisian Tales*, describes Pearson as the only one who showed him any sympathy after Oudna.

Three weeks after the 2nd Battalion's return from Oudna, Frost and Geoffrey Pine-Coffin . . .': quite a few details here come from Browning's report of his trip to North Africa, reproduced in Cherry, *Tunisian Tales*.

With the RAF still trying to stymie the development of airborne forces back in Whitehall . . .: both Greenacre, *Churchill's Spearhead*, and Mead, *General 'Boy'*, attest to this.

Frost had come to the view, ever since Bruneval . . .: he states this a few times in *A Drop Too Many*.

'quite suicidal': this quote from Pine-Coffin's album of the campaign.

with court martial or sacking as his only options . . .: Frost tells the story of his interview with Brigadier 'Swifty' Howlett in an amusing way in *A Drop Too Many*, though, makes clear there was underlying menace. Bloys, IWM Audio 17273, says that Frost later told him that objections to the mission were met with the threat of court martial.

an officer, six NCOs and forty-five other ranks, arrived at the 2nd Battalion: 2nd Battalion War Diary, NA, WO 175/526.

'we took all the bluff and bullshit from older members': unpublished memoir of R. Priestly, IWM Docs 4214.

'get some hours in under shellfire before you talk to me': story related by Major John Timothy, IWM Audio 17182. Timothy spent most of his service with 2nd Battalion in B Company, but took part in Bruneval with C, and at this time had evidently been loaned to A.

they were able to perform this service without too many casualties . . .: between mid-December and their move north at the start of March, the 2nd Battalion had fourteen men killed in action, including three in a single incident where a borrowed Bren carrier struck a mine. Bill

Bloys, IWM Audio 17273, among others, speaks of this period as one where the soldiers gained confidence as a result of their patrolling.

'*I have lived in a sewer, a hayrick, a tent . . .*': Spender Papers, letter of 1 February 1943 to Mr Knight. The following comments about rain and the equating of paratroopers to other soldiers come in the same letter.

'*It is ten minutes to midnight*': Spender Papers, letter of 12 February 1943 to his parents. Bill Bloys served for a time in Spender's platoon before transferring to A Company and testified to his qualities as a soldier in IWM Audio 17273, as did Victor Dover, another subaltern who became a particular friend, in *The Silken Canopy*.

So it was that in the middle of the day on 3 March . . .: 1st Parachute Brigade War Diary NA, WO 175/181.

Chapter 9: Cork Wood

In the early hours of 8 March 1943, paratroopers of the 2nd Battalion . . .: this chapter is based on many accounts but the principal ones of interest in this first section are Macleod Forsyth, IWM Audio 18780, Allan Johnstone, IWM Docs 7159, and Bill Bloys, IWM Audio 17273.

'*We're over here, sorry we thought you were the Germans*': Forsyth quoted by Cherry, *Tunisian Tales*.

'*went absolutely bananas*': ibid.

'*He gave a thin tired smile and said . . .*': Johnstone, IWM Docs 7159.

A Company began to get an uncomfortable feeling: ibid.

'*being in the front trench of the battalion, it was rather worrying*': Bloys, IWM Audio 17273.

'*If you don't come back, can I have your pudding?*': ibid.

'*the early morning quietness was pierced by the vicious chatter of a Spandau*': Johnstone, IWM Docs 7159.

'*ran past Company HQ so fast he nearly burnt us*': Forsyth, IWM Audio 18780.

'*Come on boys, the bastards are more frightened of you than you are of them!*': Forsyth, IWM Audio 18780, explaining how he had been awarded the Military Medal, though curiously the citation for this award suggests it was given for his conduct during the Oudna episode.

'A flight of Stukas dived on A Company': Frost, *A Drop Too Many*.

'The Germans want you to surrender . . .': Bloys, IWM Audio 17273.

. . . Timothy led a section of eight men forward: Timothy's Military Cross citation said he captured the machine guns 'singlehandedly', but this is hyperbole. Bloys, IWM Audio 17273, gives a very clear account, naming those who took part in the attack.

'Go easy on them, they've fed me and given me water': Bloys, IWM Audio 17273.

'What a bloody mess': Forsyth, IWM Audio 18780.

'I'll get the bastard somehow': Bloys, IWM Audio 17273.

That afternoon Lyoness spotted a four-man Spandau team . . .: Bloys, IWM Audio 17273, gives the most detailed account of this engagement.

'We were like a fortress with those machine guns': Bloys, IWM Audio 17273. Frost also refers to the use of captured Spandaus in *A Drop Too Many*, suggesting every platoon in the battalion ended up with one.

The soldiers thrown against them came from the Fallschirm-Pionier Abteilung and Fallschirm-Regiment Barenthin . . .: the 1st Parachute Brigade War Diary, NA, WO 175/181, and its intelligence annexes are a good source for the opposition in this battle. In addition to the airborne units, 756 Infantry Regiment, a battalion of the 69th Panzer Grenadier Regiment, one of Bersaglieri and a couple of German 'march battalions' were involved at various points along the brigade frontage.

'to represent the seriousness of their situation . . .': ibid.

Early on the 11th a troop of four Churchill tanks . . .: ibid.

'particular attention will be paid to saluting both in and out of the line': 2nd Parachute Battalion War Diary, NA, WO 166/8553.

'Officers and men alike were "Bolshy" . . .': article by Major Alan Bush, 3rd Battalion, in *Pegasus Journal*, December 1992.

'was a stickler for Guards style discipline': Bill Aldcroft provides the anecdote about Lord and the inspection in Johnston, *Churchill's Warriors*. He actually confuses many details, conflating Lord's disciplinary issues with those that occurred in the 1st Battalion in April 1944, but it is clear that Lord was a divisive figure and that many in the brigade resented the application of peacetime discipline in these conditions.

'*The men considered themselves to be fighting soldiers . . .*': Bill Aldcroft, ibid.

'*We said, "We'll use a blanket . . ."*': Forsyth, IWM Audio 18780.

'*It felt then as if the world had never been anything else but mud . . .*': Lewis, IWM Audio 4833.

'*Bobby I gather has jilted me pretty roughly . . .*': Spender Papers, letter of 16 March 1943 to his parents. In his reply of 28 March, Spender's father told him to remember that he had never been engaged to Bobby and that, according to her, she had broken off their romantic relationship before he embarked for North Africa. Dicky, though, clearly still carried a torch for her, and they corresponded after his departure.

'*it would not be possible to hold present positions much longer*': 1st Parachute Brigade War Diary, NA, WO 166/6677.

'*Johnny Frost on the other hand walked along the bank . . .*': Dover, *The Silken Canopy*.

Private Lewis struggled to hold his trousers up . . .: Lewis, IWM Audio 4833.

Lieutenant Timothy, walking beside Lieutenant Dicky Spender . . .: Spender's verse appears in several accounts. Timothy gives this version in his IWM Audio 17182 interview, and indeed it corresponds to Spender's own writing of it in a letter of 24 March 1943 to his brother.

Frost set to work writing to the next of kin . . .: in his memoir *A Drop Too Many* Frost said he struggled to find the right words in these letters.

the nightly mess banter included many discussions about 'The Book': Dover, *The Silken Canopy*.

'*men do strange things when under constant stress*': ibid.

Chapter 10: Red Devils

The previous days had been a grim time for Geoffrey Pine-Coffin . . .: Cherry, *Tunisian Tales*, gives a good account of this, with an amusing quote from Pearson, telling Pine-Coffin that the 3rd Battalion's task of holding the 'Bowler Hat' feature will be far harder than the 1st's of taking it.

'*The general feeling behind the line . . .*': Spender Papers, letter to his parents of 16 March 1943.

'*This place is absolute hell*': Spender Papers, letter to his brother, 24 March 1943.

Frost had harboured some hopes that they might be returned to a parachuting role . . .: expressed in *A Drop Too Many*.

Frost considered that Pine-Coffin's inability to tell him which enemy units lay to his front . . .: Frost is critical of 3rd Battalion in *A Drop Too Many*, though not of Pine-Coffin by name. But it becomes evident when reading that book that this is because Frost cannot bring himself to name Pine-Coffin a single time in it, a notable omission, given the extensive cast of minor regimental officers who are named. It's hard to escape the conclusion that he has followed the adage of not saying anything if you can't say something nice.

felt the frequent practice of assigning his companies to Frost's or Pearson's command . . .: this emerges from an annotation Pine-Coffin made in a copy of *The Red Beret* that was shared with me by his family, concerning an operation in January 1943. He writes: 'Typical of the bad way in which the 3rd Battalion was so often employed. Companies were always taken away from it by order of brigade. In the whole campaign the [battalion] had only one battle when it fought as a [battalion]' (this being in the Argoub battle on 26 February).

'*He was one of those "amateur" soldiers . . .*': article by Alan Bush in *Pegasus Journal*, April 1993.

decided to resolve it by the toss of a coin: Dover's *Silken Canopy* is the source for this.

'*twinkling*': Lewis, IWM Audio 4833.

'*realized with growing horror*': Frost, *A Drop Too Many*.

'*becoming critical*': 2nd Battalion War Diary, NA, WO 166/8553.

'*struck a wonderful note*': Frost, *A Drop Too Many*.

'*A Company rose to their feet and firing from the hip . . .*': Johnstone, IWM Docs 7159. It should be noted that he was away from the battalion at the time, recovering from wounds, but this must have come from discussions later with messmates.

at times just a hundred metres from Frost's forward positions . . .: 2nd Battalion War Diary, NA, WO 166/8553.

misread the confused melee in the woods, opening fire on B Company: Lewis, IWM Audio 4833.

There were calls of 'Wahoo Mohammed' that morning . . .: the origin of the
    1st Parachute Brigade battle cry became the subject of debate after
    the war, for example Pine-Coffin writing about it in *Pegasus Journal*
    in January 1952. It would seem that it was a thing the soldiers did
    when copying the calls of local herdsmen who were trying to attract
    one another's attention. It started in the 3rd Battalion and spread to
    others, but was later heard in other places, from pubs in southern
    England to the streets of Arnhem.

'saved the day': this passage, unsurprisingly, relies heavily on Lewis, IWM
    Audio 4833.

'Aren't you going to give me that?': Corporal David Brooks, IWM Audio
    18265.

'Look at this sir!': the wounded soldier was Bob Fermor, according to
    Johnstone, IWM Docs 7159.

'You are the filthiest person I've ever seen': Bloys, IWM Audio 17273.

'We call you lot the Red Devils': ibid.

Frost had combined all of the fighting remnants into a single company: 2nd Bat-
    talion War Diary, NA, WO 166/8553.

joked that he should make Witzig second in command of their battalion: Timo-
    thy, IWM Audio 17182.

'the war seemed to have receded and everyone was slightly crazy': Johnstone,
    IWM Docs 7159.

Alan Moorehead, a war correspondent who visited . . .: these quotes from
    Moorehead's work are reproduced in Dover, *Silken Canopy*.

*'The British Parachutists are the toughest and hardest fighting troops in Tunisia
    today'*: this quotation from German orders was included in Dicky
    Spender's letter home of 16 March 1943. Given the use of the word
    'Devils', it might also suggest that the 'Red Devils' nickname
    emerged from the Sedjenane valley battles.

'He took out with him a magnificent brigade and he frittered it away': Hibbert,
    IWM Audio 21040.

'We hardly know what to think . . .': the 1st Parachute Brigade Signal Squad-
    ron War Diary, kept by Captain George Rowlands is a most interesting
    account of North Africa and Sicily, almost a journal: NA, WO 175/182.

Frost was too drunk to be roused during the night: Lewis, IWM Audio 4833,
    says that Frost's batman told him this.

This charge was unfounded . . .: the 1st Parachute Brigade War Diary makes clear that the withdrawal was triggered by a brigade order, and, owing to the phased nature of the operation, this was given at 8.10 a.m.

'if anyone was more regularly drunk than Alastair Pearson, it was John Frost': Hibbert, I WM Audio 21040. Frost himself was quite open about his consumption of alcohol, hence the tongue-in-cheek title of his memoir, *A Drop Too Many*. However, it is a different thing to suggest that this ever impaired his judgement in battle.

'Some elements made life extremely difficult . . .'. Frost, *A Drop Too Many*.

'Deeply regret to inform you . . .': this and quotation from his father's letter, Spender Papers.

the 1st Parachute Brigade had taken 3,500 prisoners and caused 5,000 enemy casualties . . .: Terence Otway, *Airborne Forces of the Second World War 1939–1945, Army* (Imperial War Museum, 1990).

'Add these factors to a tenacious and brave and well-trained enemy . . .': ibid.

'that is where the Parachute Regiment made its name': Colonel John Waddy, I WM Audio 21036.

'They', the general wrote, 'have proved their mastery . . .': the general's message is quoted in an article on the origin of the 'Red Devils' nickname on the Airborne Assault Museum website, paradata.org.uk.

Chapter 11: Arrivals and Departures

Private Lewis made his way to the Hotel Aletti . . .: this encounter is described by Lewis in his I WM Audio 4833 recording and in greater detail in his daughter Helen Lewis's *The Dead Still Cry Out*.

'I will never ever complain, having got this far . . .': Lewis, I WM Audio 4833.

'You're one of those Red Devils . . .': Helen Lewis, *The Dead Still Cry Out*.

'my row with the brigadier': Pine-Coffin's letter to Kathleen Lang (his cousin), 26 September 1944, shared by Michael Pine-Coffin.

'were generally fiercely resentful of the smart appearance of 2nd Brigade': Johnstone, I WM Docs 7159. He also refers to the 5th Battalion's role in the Mascara parade. I make no apology for relying repeatedly on this account for this period. It's quite excellent.

Now the long weapons would be put into a padded bag . . .: the adoption of this new method is referred to in the 2nd Battalion War Diary, NA, WO 166/8553, and Frost, *A Drop Too Many*. It has also been suggested that the 21st Independent Parachute Company adopted it first.

Most of these soldiers, 250 in the case of the 2nd Battalion: 2nd Battalion War Diary, NA, WO 166/8553.

'Four Jumpers': Bloys, IWM Audio 17273.

'We had an uneasy mixture of a few battle-weary veterans . . .': Johnstone, IWM Docs 7159.

'really hard prolonged training was now the order of the day . . .': Frost, *A Drop Too Many*.

would pick fights with anyone not in A Company . . .: Johnstone, IWM Docs 7159.

'fall from grace': ibid.

'I said, "Look, sir, in this battalion we drink . . ."': Forsyth, IWM Audio 18780. He never names Lonsdale, but this can be easily deduced from the details Forsyth gives.

That would involve more than 1,800 troops and 116 aircraft: these figures come from the weighty official *Report on the Operations Carried Out by 1st Airborne Division During the Invasion of Sicily (Operation Husky)*, which can be found in the Walch Papers, IWM Docs 9487.

Thrills with the Paratroops: this book was followed by *More Thrills with the Paratroops* and *Paratroops in Action*, all published by Hutchinson. The precise publication dates are unclear, but the first appears to have come out in mid-1943, the second at the end of 1944 and the third later still, presumably in 1945.

'to offset the intolerable boredom of inactivity in rest areas . . .': Maybury, *Parachutist*.

two signallers who refused to jump on Exercise Cactus . . .: 1st Parachute Brigade Signal Squadron War Diary, NA, WO 169/8838.

. . . declared themselves happy after the Cactus exercises . . .: 1st Parachute Brigade Signal Squadron War Diary, NA, WO 169/8838.

'A running argument developed with General Browning . . .': Matthew Ridgway, *Soldier: The Memoirs of Matthew B. Ridgway* (Harper & Brothers, 1956).

Ridgway's first assault element, 3,400 troops carried by 266 C-47s . . .: there are various histories of Operation Husky and the 82nd. For a general reader Rick Atkinson's *The Day of Battle: The War in Sicily and Italy,*

1943–1944 (Little, Brown, 2007) is very good, as is *82nd Airborne Division: 'All American'*, by Mike Verier (Ian Allan, 2001).

Frost had finally had to give Forsyth the choice of a court martial or a reduction to the rank of sergeant and return to unit: Forsyth, IWM Audio 18780.

'that no longer existed as a fighting formation and could take no further part in the campaign . . .': Frost, *A Drop Too Many*.

On 11 July, prayer services were held . . .: 2nd Battalion War Diary. On the 'irreligious nature' of the unit, see Hancock, IWM Docs 21756. Sergeant Hancock, a man of faith himself, says that church parades were abandoned soon after their arrival in North Africa because of the diversity of beliefs in the battalion. Frost also refers to the religious service before Sicily in *A Drop Too Many*, from which one can infer it was something of a rarity.

'I was uneasy about the raw youngsters who were the majority in the platoon': Johnstone, IWM Docs 7159.

'I doubt if many men who have experienced it go easily and willingly into battle': ibid. Johnstone's point about the veterans within the unit is fascinating and, given the behaviour of some who dropped on Sicily, who either hid or gave themselves up quickly, evidently well made.

'Although I have worn the wings for twenty months it is my first experience . . .': Maybury, *Parachutist*.

Maybury surveyed the others in his stick . . .: the Sicily drop is extensively written about in *Parachutist*. Maybury also gave a hand-written report of these events to his OC, which can be read in the Signal Squadron War Diary, NA, WO 169/8838. There are some differences between the two accounts, and, where these occur, I rely on the official account on points of fact.

Chapter 12: *Under the Volcano*

At around 10 p.m. on 13 July . . .: many details of timings etc. from 2nd Battalion War Diary, NA, WO 166/8553.

'heavy AA shells bursting all around us . . .': Rowlands in the Signal Squadron War Diary, NA, WO 169/8838. His account of Operation Marston is very valuable, being full of detail and a near contemporary record.

'*Goddamit the pilot's dying!*': Lewis, IWM Audio 4833.

Pearson told the American that he would be shot . . .: unsurprisingly this story appears in a few places, including Pearson's obituary in *Pegasus Journal*, June 1996.

'*we swing like helpless fairground targets in the air . . .*': Maybury, *Parachutist*.

When the tally was eventually made, of the 116 planes . . .: Walch Papers, IWM Docs 9487, *Report on the Operations Carried Out by 1st Airborne Division During the Invasion of Sicily (Operation Husky)*.

'*nothing has been heard since of any members of these sticks*': Rowlands in Signal Squadron War Diary, WO 169/8838.

'*An enormous amount of anticipation with no release at the end*': Lewis's memorable simile comes from his daughter Helen's *The Dead Still Cry Out*.

Around 11 p.m. Frost linked up with Major Lonsdale . . .: Frost, *A Drop Too Many*, as well as the battalion War Diary.

'*the ghostly sound of rushing wind . . .*': Lieutenant J. Helingoe quoted in Hilary St George Saunders, *The Red Beret: The Story of the Parachute Regiment 1940–1945* (Michael Joseph, 1950).

(the 1st Paratrooper Machine-Gun Battalion), had dropped onto the ridgeline . . .: there are extensive details of the German side of this battle in Helmut Wilhelmsmeyer's article in *Pegasus Journal*, December 1985.

'*a winged thorn for the flabby side of Mussolini . . .*': Maybury, *Parachutist*.

'*If we organize the people and arms. . .*': Rowlands in Signal Squadron War Diary, WO 169/8838.

Hauptmann Franz Stangenberg, who had been up to Primosole during the early hours: Wilhelmsmeyer, *Pegasus Journal*, December 1985.

'*blackened buildings still smoking . . .*': Maybury, *Parachutist*.

One party under Sergeant Allan Johnstone. . .: Johnstone, IWM Docs 7159.

'*Well, it's your decision, Johnno, but Monty's there*': ibid. I wonder about the character of Fisher, one of those accused of smashing up an Italian restaurant in Salisbury one year earlier and assaulting its owner, but a little more reluctant to get stuck in once actually on Sicilian soil.

A single functioning 66 Wireless Set . . . had been assembled and powered up: Rowlands in Signal Squadron War Diary, WO 169/8838.

'*neither our captors nor the present Wehrmacht guards . . .*': Johnstone, IWM Docs 7159.

'*Just now you are our prisoners, soon we shall be yours*': Maybury, *Parachutist*.

'*Well if you want to lose another bloody battalion . . .*': this version of Pearson's words comes from Julian James, *A Fierce Quality: The Fighting Life of Alastair Pearson* (Leo Cooper, 1989). Since he evidently had Pearson's cooperation, I use it. However, in *A Drop Too Many*, Frost quotes Pearson saying, 'I suppose you want to see another battalion written off too.'

'*Hello, and where have you been?*': Frost does not name Brayley, but it takes very little detective work to figure it out. Brayley, one may speculate, like a good few others who had served bravely through Oudna and Cork Wood, had endured enough by this point.

2nd Battalion's casualty list amounted to twenty-five men killed and 138 missing: 2nd Battalion War Diary, NA, WO 166/8553. Some of these missing returned, most remained prisoners.

'*another humiliating disaster for airborne forces . . .*': Frost, *A Drop Too Many*.

'*another fiasco*': Private Doug Russell, IWM Audio 29603.

'*It was a catastrophe . . .*': Rowlands, Signal Squadron War Diary, WO 169/8838.

'*The objective was secured and chaos was caused in the enemy's lines*': Walch Papers, IWM Docs 9487, *Report on Operation Husky*.

'*had given us a peep into [airborne forces'] great possibilities*': Greenacre, *Churchill's Spearhead*, quotes Eisenhower's and Monty's reactions.

Maybury revelled in this 'patter' . . .: and indeed the section recounting this episode in *Parachutist* goes on for many pages; I have simply selected highlights, because they give a good flavour of how these men spoke.

He never again saw four of the men who had been in his stick . . .: Maybury does not reveal this in *Parachutist*, which had undergone wartime censorship. Rather, it emerges from his written report attached to the Signal Squadron War Diary, WO 169/8838. My phrasing here is equivocal, for the men may have survived the war as prisoners.

Chapter 13: The Volunteer Spirit

Command of the new division was given to Major General Richard Gale: details drawn from Victor Dover, *The Sky Generals* (Cassell, 1981), General Sir Richard Gale, *Call to Arms: An Autobiography* (Hutchinson, 1968) and the Gale Papers, Airborne Assault Museum.

'*My name is Richard Nelson Gale . . .*': Dover, *The Sky Generals.*

'*Tall, spare and ramrod straight with ruddy face . . .*': Chester Wilmot, *The Struggle for Europe* (Greenwood Press, 1972).

'*very pompous, an absolute caricature . . .*': James Bramwell, IWM Audio 9542. Bramwell, a product of Charterhouse, Oxford and the Peace Pledge Union, was assigned as a medic to the 9th Battalion.

'*The most important characteristic which an airborne soldier . . .*': Dover, *The Silken Canopy.*

'*I find the prospects of a party here are just about the same . . .*': Grayburn's journal, shared with me by his son John.

'*Owing to my volunteering I have come into quite a deal of unpleasantness*': ibid.

He was a club-level rugger player, keen boxer . . .: a detailed biography of Grayburn was put together by Roger Cook for the benefit of Chiltern Rugby Club and can be found online at https://amershammuseum. org/wp-content/uploads/2013/11/Jack-Grayburn-VC.pdf.

'*I may be a sentimental fool and may have signed my own death warrant . . .*': Grayburn journal.

'*Those not wishing to volunteer take three paces forward*': the quote comes from the Lancashire Regiment's parade and is included in Andrew Woolhouse, *13 – Lucky for Some: The History of the 13th (Lancashire) Parachute Battalion* (Independently published, 2013).

'*I had been serving with most of the company for five years . . .*': Colour Sergeant Harry Watkins, quoted ibid.

It and the 1st Canadian battalion, attached that summer . . .: this view emerges from various accounts, including Gale, *Call to Arms*, and Hill, IWM Audio 12347.

'*bound to lead to some lowering of standards*': Robert Holmes, IWM Audio 9120.

70 per cent of the early volunteers . . .: Pearson, IWM Audio 21033.

James Hill, one of the brigade commanders . . .: Hill, IWM Audio 12347.

'*the average age was very young and we were very enthusiastic*': Bob Tanner, IWM Audio 11448.

Colonel Malcolm MacEwan, who became the director of medical services . . .: there is an excellent potted biography of MacEwan on the Airborne Assault Museum ParaData website, a rich resource for the study of these troops.

'*in many ways this was a group decision to accept this opportunity*': Vic Newcombe, IWM Audio 9400.

MacEwan succeeded in recruiting 190 'conchies' . . .: David Tibbs, *Parachute
   Doctor: The Memoirs of Captain David Tibbs*, ed. Neil Barber (Sabrestorm,
   2012), with much detail on his time in 225th PFA.

Of these, 142 would pass parachute training . . .: information from Airborne
   Assault Museum ParaData website.

'*I was very struck by the fairness of the whole thing* . . .': Newcombe, IWM
   Audio 9400.

'*we were cold shouldered* . . .': ibid.

'*definitely rather suspicious of us* . . .': Bramwell, IWM Audio 9542.

'*The trouble with you fellas is that you're always reading*': ibid.

'*a collection of malcontents from all over the army* . . .': Captain David
   H. Clark, whose privately published memoir *1945: My Crisis Year*, is
   in the IWM archive, IWM Docs 11674.

George Skelly, a member of the Christian Brethren sect from Cumbria . . .: an
   article on George and his brother John appears on the BBC People's
   War website, www.bbc.co.uk/history/ww2peopleswar/stories/43/
   a3697743.shtml.

'*hard working, very good standard*': parachute course notes are held by the
   Airborne Assault Museum.

'*arranged for me to leave this country* . . .': Grayburn journal.

Chapter 14: Mustn't Miss the Bloodbath

He also became involved in many a whisky-lubricated late-night discussion . . .:
   Frost, *A Drop Too Many*. He suggests some of the other paratroopers
   chided him for even entertaining glider enthusiast General Hopkinson's ideas.

'*the wine was lousy, the company worse*': Grayburn's journal.

'*full of life and energy, cannot stand being idle* . . .': ibid.

'*perhaps rather an inefficient remedy to boredom* . . .': ibid.

'*the ideal thing as far as I'm concerned* . . .': ibid. It will become clear later
   that Frost himself used the term 'bloodbath' too, so it's likely that it
   was used at the mess table and Grayburn picked it up there.

'*You could have heard a pin drop*': Priestly, IWM Docs 4214.

'*their too prolific use of the National Adjective*': lovely phrasing from Grayburn journal.

'*He is an amazing man is Johnny Frost*': ibid.

'*my first piece of action is going to be the European bloodbath . . .*': ibid.

'*One or two women who must've lost their sons . . .*': ibid.

'*paraded around the shops*': Bloys, IWM Audio 17273.

on 21 January the general put the 7th through unannounced drills . . .: 7th Parachute Battalion War Diary, NA, WO 171/1239.

'*resisted this as forcibly as I could*': Gale, *Call to Arms*.

'*so you can guess what I called him when I got outside . . .*': Woodgate Family
Papers, IWM Docs 25043.

'*I been out on a scheme for 3 days and 2 nights . . .*': ibid.

'*I could have shot the bastards*': Tanner, IWM Audio 11448.

'*brigades and battalions were being weighed up against each other . . .*': Pine-Coffin's
journal, written up just after the war as a potted history of these events
and shared with me by his grandson, Michael Pine-Coffin.

'*no infringement of the smallest regulation was allowed to pass . . .*': ibid.

exercises in Exeter, assaulting bridges . . .: this is covered by Pine-Coffin in
his journal and in the 7th Parachute Battalion War Diary, NA, WO
171/1239.

laden with kit and faces blackened, knelt in prayer: Captain Alfred Clark, 13th
Battalion, quoted in Woolhouse, *13 – Lucky for Some*.

'*As we were singing "Abide With Me" the first aero engines started up . . .*': Captain Harry Leach, IWM Audio 31554.

'*wasn't feeling too brave*': Skelly's church produced a pamphlet after the
war, 'A Paratrooper's Exploit', in which he told his story. Its exact
date is unclear. I am most grateful to Michael Pine-Coffin for sharing
it with me.

Chapter 15: Twenty-four Hours in Normandy

Just after midnight, in the first minutes of 6 June 1944 . . .: as a general history of
this action, Neil Barber's *The Pegasus and Orne Bridges: Their Capture,
Defence and Relief on D–Day* (Pen and Sword, 2009) cannot be bettered.

'*It was the most exhilarating moment of my life . . .*': Howard quoted ibid.

'*You are in the right place, Sir*': Roy Howard (glider pilot) quoted ibid.

'*Will I be hit? Will I lose a leg, lose an arm, be blinded?*': Tanner, IWM Audio 11448.

'*it's your hard luck . . . but you're not concerned about it, you can't afford to be . . .*': ibid.

'*like so many, he had no time for God*': Skelly, 'A Paratrooper's Exploit'.

'*It was a most desperate feeling*': Pine-Coffin's journal.

'*We heard a "ping" . . .*': Howard in Barber, *The Pegasus and Orne Bridges*. The claim of a destroyed 'tank' is not supported by the evidence, of either German deployments, casualty returns or post-battle photographs. Although the vehicle was actually a halftrack, the 'tank' claim was enthusiastically repeated in later years by the sergeant firing the PIAT, a man who also claimed to have fought at the Primosole, Orne and Arnhem bridges – claims equally without foundation.

he led the biggest single group across at around 2.30 a.m.: there are varying versions of what time these soldiers arrived, but in Chester Wilmot's Normandy notebook, Liddell Hart Archive 15/15/62, based on interviews with men from 7th Battalion and the Ox and Bucks in the couple of days after the operation, the journalist notes in a few places that they arrived around 2.30 and had taken up their positions on the western side of the bridges by 3 a.m.

'*Howard's men were naturally in very high spirits . . .*': Pine-Coffin journal.

'*the greatest danger was from our own troops, all of whom were a bit trigger happy*': Captain Ernest Lough, IWM Audio 12381.

seventeen gliders with heavy equipment were going to start landing there at 3.20 a.m.: from official report '6 Airborne Division, Report on Operations Carried Out in Normandy 6 Jun – 27 Aug 44', in the Walch Papers, IWM Docs 9487.

Major General Gale (who himself arrived by glider at 4.30) . . .: ibid.

'*Don't you dare to argue with me . . .*': Wilmot, Normandy notebook.

'*Oh God! I'd sent the brave wee man to his death*': account by Hunter shared with me by Michael Pine-Coffin.

'*get the hell out of here!*': ibid.

'*started to walk up the middle of the road towards the tanks, firing the Bren gun from his hip*': ibid. McGee's Military Medal citation suggests it was a Sten gun. Both accounts appear at fault in suggesting the brave paratrooper was up against 'tanks', but certainly there were halftracks and Marders in the area.

their suggestions that they fought off a Panther proved ill-founded: fascinatingly, Chester Wilmot, interviewing men of the 7th Battalion just after the battle, noted their claims of seeing off 'a Panther' tank in his notebook, but each time added a question mark in brackets. Perhaps some of those he spoke to were expressing their scepticism from the off. Certainly, no corroborating evidence has ever emerged of a Panther tank in action at this time and place.

'*The vibration of air and sound*': Todd quoted by Barber in *The Pegasus and Orne Bridges*. This is the same Richard Todd who, as a film star, played Major John Howard of the Ox and Bucks in the movie *The Longest Day*.

'*it felt like they were tearing the skies apart*': Phillip Crofts, ibid.

B Company's runner, Private Sid Cornell . . .: draws on the biographical sketches of Cornell on the ParaData and Pegasus Archive websites.

'*innocent . . . of the stupid nuances of racial prejudice*': Lieutenant R. Hinman, in an article written for the 7th (LI) Battalion Newsletter concerning a battlefield pilgrimage made by surviving veterans in 1985. The text was provided by Michael Pine-Coffin.

The officer commanding the 7th's anti-tank platoon . . .: this is alluded to by Pine-Coffin in his journal and explored in more detail by Barber in *The Pegasus and Orne Bridges*.

'*suddenly a big Jerry came into view with his rifle pointing towards me*': Butler's account, IWM Docs 17891.

'*It was a remarkable morale booster*': John Vaughan quoted by Barber in *The Pegasus and Orne Bridges*.

Pine-Coffin was particularly worried that the gap . . .: Pine-Coffin journal.

'*a stream of bullets ripped through the tree . . .*': this remarkable account, complete with quotes from Pine-Coffin, comes from an Ox and Bucks soldier, Dennis Edwards, and is quoted in Barber, *The Pegasus and Orne Bridges*.

'*That is not too healthy old boy . . .*': ibid.

'*did not present much of a problem . . .*': Pine-Coffin journal.

'*All movement was made at the double or crawling . . .*': Cliff Morris quoted in Barber, *The Pegasus and Orne Bridges*.

So it was that a convoy of Royal Engineer lorries . . .: this is mentioned by Pine-Coffin but in more detail by Richard Todd in recollections quoted in Barber, *The Pegasus and Orne Bridges*.

'*The finest sight of the lot was Lord Lovat . . .*': Tanner, IWM Audio 11448.

'*A curious period of many hours followed . . .*': Pine-Coffin journal.

'*They came through tired, dirty and hungry . . .*': ibid.

the record would show that the death toll on 6 June was sixty-eight: based on Commonwealth War Graves evidence and that gathered by the Pegasus Archive.

the heaviest single day's loss of any Parachute Regiment unit . . .: the Pegasus Archive gives the 9th Battalion's losses during the same twenty-four hours as forty-one men. The 2nd Battalion at Arnhem lost sixty-three men killed in action across the entire week.

the rapid loss of three German assault guns . . .: this incident is well described in Woolhouse's book on the 13th Battalion *13 – Lucky for Some*. The three lost vehicles were the German conversion of captured French Hotchkiss tanks to carry 75mm anti-tank guns. These vehicles were deployed by 21st Panzer Division.

A Kampfgruppe, or battle group, of the 125th Panzer Grenadier Regiment . . .: Werner Kortenhaus, *The Combat History of the 21st Panzer Division*, English version (Helion, 2014).

'*the lack of suitable means to defend against the incoming flight . . .*': ibid. Kortenhaus both served in this division during this battle and was its historian.

'*It was clear to the last man that the invasion had succeeded . . .*': von Luck quoted by Woolhouse, *13 – Lucky for Some*.

Chapter 16: The Quality of Mercy

'*two Germans came into the courtyard . . .*': Wagstaff is quoted in Barber, *The Pegasus and Orne Bridges*.

'Airborne Padre Was Brutally Murdered': article by Leonard Mosley in the
  Daily Record, 29 June 1944.

'we enjoyed a cup of tea': long after the war, Bill Roper corresponded
  with Michael Pine-Coffin, who kindly copied Roper's account
  for me.

'we dropped what we were doing, ran into an outhouse . . .': ibid.

'I felt helpless and lost': Skelly, 'A Paratrooper's Exploit'.

'I was fired on by a machine gun and by snipers': ibid.

'Be merciful unto me, O God . . .': Psalm 57:1, King James Version.

'told us that A Company . . .': Skelly, 'A Paratrooper's Exploit'.

'no German fired on those vehicles . . .': Major Nigel Taylor quoted in Barber, *The Pegasus and Orne Bridges*.

Another conchie from the 225th was similarly recognized . . .: he was Private
  Geoffrey Brown, citation reproduced by Woolhouse in *13 – Lucky for
  Some*. Bert Roe of 225th PFA also received the Military Medal, and
  P. Lenton, 224th PFA, was another non-combatant recipient of this
  decoration. That makes four that I have traced, though, amusingly,
  the comrades of each insisted in later years that their mate was the
  only MM recipient among conscientious objectors.

'I don't want any bloody nonsense about taking prisoners': this Gale quote
  comes from David Tibbs, *Parachute Doctor*. There are other refer-
  ences, for example Private Ray Batten, 13th Battalion, says, 'the
  crossroads were to be held at all costs and no prisoners to be taken',
  quoted by Woolhouse in *13 – Lucky for Some*.

'anyone they capture, they kill': Captain Ernest Lough, who was actually a
  7th Battalion officer serving on the 5th Parachute Brigade staff,
  IWM Audio 12381.

'I was going to collect him on the way back . . .': a remarkably honest account
  from Tibbs in *Parachute Doctor*.

Another conchie sent out with a stretcher party on the first night . . .: this was
  Vic Newcombe of 224th PFA, IWM Audio 9400.

'we admitted 500 casualties in the first twenty-four hours . . .': this account
  comes from a letter from a 225th PFA medic written to his mother
  in 1946, Claffey Papers, IWM Docs 22646.

'Stop yer blathering, ye fucker, or ye'll be the first to go!': Tibbs, *Parachute
  Doctor*.

'I didn't feel the slightest bit of hostility towards German soldiers . . .': Newcombe, IWM Audio 9400.

'We felt it was a great privilege to serve these men . . .': Roper, correspondence with Michael Pine-Coffin.

Chapter 17: Normandy's Killing Fields

On the morning of 7 June a group of tanks . . .: details from Kortenhaus, *Combat History of the 21st Panzer Division.*

'Panzer 431 was hit. The loader was killed immediately': ibid.

'The losses were bitter': ibid.

'At any movement, even of an individual vehicle . . .': quoted by Woolhouse in *13 – Lucky for Some.*

elements of the newly arrived 346th Division managed to infiltrate northwards . . .: ibid. Woolhouse reproduces the German orders for this operation, presumably taken from a captive or corpse.

'the German infantrymen came on at a run': this is Leonard Mosley again, quoted ibid.

'I wouldn't have believed it if I hadn't seen it . . .': Lough, IWM Audio 12381.

'The 13th opened up with fire, then the 7th . . .': ibid.

'You suddenly saw Germans, grimacing . . .': Mosley quoted by Woolhouse in *13 – Lucky for Some.*

'but this was very suitable for both MMGs and mortars . . .': Pine-Coffin journal.

'Some of the Germans stood up and put their hands in the air . . .': Lance Corporal George O'Connor, 13th Battalion, quoted by Woolhouse in *13 – Lucky for Some.*

there were 400 enemy bodies left behind . . .: Lough, IWM Audio 12381.

'the tanks were stationary for anything up to twenty minutes . . .': Pine-Coffin journal.

'one of those tragedies that the war produced': Kortenhaus, *Combat History of the 21st Panzer Division.*

The official casualty return for the 858th Regiment . . .: returns for the regiment say it suffered 64 killed, 205 wounded and 401 missing on 9/10 June, the 'missing' figure being particularly revealing. Its sister regiment the 857th was used in Bréville against 3rd Parachute Brigade. Casualty returns reproduced in Niklas Zetterling, *Normandy 1944: German Military Organization, Combat Power and Organizational Effectiveness* (J. J. Fedorowicz, 2000).

'You would walk along such a trail . . .': Tibbs, *Parachute Doctor.*

'I found that several of our men were already there . . .': ibid.

'unless we could clear Bréville . . .': Gale, *Call to Arms.*

So, on 11 June, Gale ordered . . .: much of the detail in this passage comes from Saunders, *The Red Beret*, which was based on detailed information from many in the Parachute Regiment.

'in the ruddy glow of the flames . . .': Parker quoted ibid.

'it was that turning point': Gale, *Call to Arms.*

'most alarming weapons . . .': Pine-Coffin journal.

There Skelly made a full recovery . . .: Skelly, 'A Paratrooper's Exploit'.

'I was convinced that no commander will readily release troops . . .': Gale, *Call to Arms.*

'Six reports and the characteristic blood-chilling moan rising in intensity . . .': Captain W. Parrish, quoted in Saunders, *The Red Beret.*

. . . none of the 7th Battalion's nine rifle platoon commanders . . .: Pine-Coffin journal.

'The gaining of patrol ascendancy . . .': ibid.

. . . led by the acting company OC, Captain Bob Keene: Keene's detailed account of this raid was attached to the battalion War Diary and is in Pine-Coffin's journal.

'We reached the so-called mortar pits . . .': ibid.

'So far he is OK thank God': Woodgate Family Papers, IWM Docs 25043.

'when they left England they landed safe . . .': ibid.

On 19 June he had narrowly missed being killed . . .: Butler, IWM Docs 17891.

'I was too late . . .': ibid.

'or what the lads call bomb happy': ibid.

'I felt so dizzy and scared . . .': ibid.

'some despondency in the ranks': Pine-Coffin journal.

'the gist of all these conferences . . .': 7th Parachute Battalion War Diary, NA, WO 171/1239.

It was here that Major General Gale planned a phased operation . . .: very well explained, including with aerial photographs, by Woolhouse in *13 – Lucky for Some*.

'It was a dream target . . .': Pine-Coffin journal.

Their losses amounted to 40 officers . . .: the casualty figures for the parachute battalions (as opposed to the whole brigades or the division, which would include supporting troops) were compiled by Saunders for *The Red Beret*.

Chapter 18: A Touch of Frost

revered in training establishments or the messes of Bulford as the pioneers . . .: this emerges from Grayburn's journal and Robin Vlasto, another fresh A Company subaltern, whose Arnhem diary is in the Cornelius Ryan Papers. Ryan left his papers to Ohio University and much of his working material for *A Bridge Too Far* can be accessed online via the Ohio University portal.

'for all their comments, I don't think the troops were impressed': Grayburn journal.

'I bet he couldn't jump off that jeep': anecdote in Victor Dover's *The Silken Canopy*.

'thought they knew it all': Major General Robert 'Roy' Urquhart, IWM Audio 21034.

'was not a man to court popularity': Frost, *A Drop Too Many*.

'it is an inspiring thought that I should have been selected . . .': Darling's letters are in his papers, IWM Docs 13223.

'He had to go and clean up the mess . . .': Pearson, IWM Audio 21033. Pearson is a little coy about who had told Darling to do this, but circumstance points strongly to Urquhart. Pearson's view of Darling may be divined from his description of him as the only general to have suffered two mutinies of troops under his command, these being the 1st Battalion in 1944 and the 13th Parachute Battalion after the war in the Far East.

'a pretty funny state of affairs!!': Darling Papers, IWM Docs 13223.

'a "straight from the shoulder" talk on what he wants done . . .': 1st Parachute Battalion War Diary, NA, WO 171/1236.

a mutiny in one battalion of the 7th Armoured Division: the 5th Royal Tank Regiment, the CO of which was also sacked following a mutiny. See my book *The Tank War: The Men, the Machines and the Long Road to Victory* (Little, Brown, 2013) for chapter and verse.

'They believed in a lot of discipline and blacking boots and polishing buttons': Holmes, IWM Audio 9120.

200 men refused to draw their parachutes . . .: ibid.

2nd Battalion was stood by to put their comrades in the 1st under close arrest: ibid.

Hearing about the situation, a brigadier from the local headquarters appeared . . .: ibid. Holmes does not name Lathbury, their own brigadier, so possibly he was elsewhere.

'too much spit and polish': ibid.

A promise was given that these complaints would be heard . . .: ibid. The details of the company commander and Gale meetings are from the 1st Battalion War Diary, NA, WO 171/1236. It should be noted that two passages in that official record have been obliterated with black ink, presumably owing to sensitivity about these events and the regiment's reputation.

'I have a perfectly clear conscience . . .': Darling Papers, IWM Docs 13223.

'they thought they knew all the answers . . .': this comes from Darling's obituary in *Pegasus Journal*, June 1999.

'a great blow to some': Frost, *A Drop Too Many*.

'the men were so jealous of the newly formed 6th Division . . .': Vlasto, Ryan Papers.

'the only thing to do was to go and get tight . . .': ibid.

He had a particular way of dealing with disciplinary issues . . .: Brooks, IWM Audio 18265.

'capable of maintaining discipline with an element of training . . .': ibid.

'we were a new battalion': Priestly, IWM Docs 4214.

'after a couple of months with him . . .': Robert Peatling, IWM Audio 18728.

'a consuming hatred of Germans': Vlasto, Ryan Papers.

Maybury had transferred from the signals to 89 Field Security Section . . .: biographies of Maybury on both the Military Intelligence Museum and Airborne Assault Museum (ParaData) websites note the details of his transfer.

'*an empire builder*': Major General Ray Baker, US Army, quoted in Mead, *General 'Boy'*, which is a good source on both American disdain for Browning and the many cancelled operations of the summer of 1944.

Browning threatened resignation: this is well covered ibid.

'*there were already signs of that dangerous mixture of boredom and cynicism . . .*': Urquhart quoted in John Baynes, *Urquhart of Arnhem: The Life of Major General R. E. Urquhart, C.B., D.S.O.* (Brassey's, 1993).

'*at long last*': Browning Papers quoted in Mead, *General 'Boy'*.

'*a wooden cross or a Victoria Cross*': Waddy, IWM Audio 21036.

'*the Brig. has promised me this, that the 2nd Battalion . . .*': Vlasto, Ryan Papers. Frost's desire to ensure a plum role for the battalion, then to trumpet it to his subordinates, will be familiar to anyone who has accompanied the British Army on operations.

'*it did seem like rather a complicated method of committing suicide*': ibid.

'*How's the war going? . . .*': this exchange is related by Bloys in his IWM Audio 17273.

'*General Boy said he thought it was possible . . .*': Walch Papers, IWM Docs 9487.

'*Not one brigadier or unit commander spoke*': Polish brigadier Stanisław Sosabowski related this in his memoirs, quoted by Mead, *General 'Boy'*.

'*we were all infected with this feeling of impatience, intense impatience*': Hibbert, IWM Audio 21040.

'*I think really, if we'd been asked to drop in the middle of Berlin . . .*': ibid. The force of Hibbert and Urquhart's 'we would have gone anyway' arguments is a potent counter to many of the theories about Arnhem debated since the war, notably the one about the late discovery of German armour in the area and whether that would have made any difference if known about sooner.

'*We couldn't take it seriously at first*': Vlasto, Ryan Papers.

'*one couldn't help but be pessimistic*': Lewis, IWM Audio 4833.

'*not so many, pro rata, as the officers*': Holmes, IWM Audio 9120.

'*They'll be back in an hour's time, with another weekend's leave!*': Vlasto, Ryan Papers. Vlasto also detailed Grayburn's breakfast in his diary. Sadly, Grayburn himself did not complete his journal in the couple of months before Arnhem.

'*I certainly did not anticipate much difficulty . . .*': Frost, *A Drop Too Many*.

Sergeant Lewis was fretting about getting a tracking shot . . .: Lewis, IWM Audio 4833.

Just nineteen of the almost 500 men loading up with the 2nd Battalion that morning . . .: research by Bob Hilton using the aircraft stick lists for the two operations. Two additional Bruneval veterans were jumping with other units that day, and six coming with the sea column.

'transparent insincerity of their smiles . . .': Frost, as so often in *A Drop Too Many*, makes an acute and unsentimental observer.

Chapter 19: The Bridge

Early reports had started coming . . .: see Robert Kershaw, *It Never Snows in September* (Crowood Press, 1990). Kershaw's work is the peerless English-language history of the German Market Garden battle.

'It was a spectacle that impressed me deeply . . .': Student later wrote about the war, and this translation on Market Garden is in the Liddell Hart Archive in Chester Wilmot's Papers 15/15/50.

'just like an exercise in England, unbelievable': Peatling, IWM Audio 18728.

'This is all quite fantastic, to be walking along the main Arnhem road . . .': Vlasto, Ryan Papers.

'a victory parade, the civilians are quite delirious . . .': ibid.

'With due respect, he was right; we had taken far too long . . .': Priestly, IWM Docs 4214.

'brings me down to earth with a jolt': Vlasto, Ryan Papers.

soldiers from one of B Company's platoons were caught by the viaduct . . .': details of B Company's battle were painstakingly assembled by local historian David G. van Buggenum in *B Company Arrived* (R. N. Sigmond, 2003). As with Kershaw, I make no apology for drawing on it repeatedly.

the 2nd Battalion CO hardly needed reminding . . .: Frost's version in the Ryan Papers.

'We thought, we're nearly there': Brooks, IWM Audio 18265.

Killick was hoping to find German secrets . . .: from his subsequent report, Airborne Assault Museum ParaData website.

'a grand military cock up': Dover, *The Silken Canopy*.

'bodies were flung in all directions': ibid.

'seems extremely happy': Vlasto, Ryan Papers.

'All hell seemed to be let loose after that': Frost, Ryan Papers.

'We were hit straight away, I lost two officers in about ten minutes': Timothy, IWM Audio 17182.

Lathbury and Urquhart vanished as far as their HQs were concerned . . .: there are various versions of this tale, including from the protagonists, but Iain Ballantyne's *Arnhem: Ten Days in the Cauldron* (Agora Books, 2019), is a good recent general history of the battle and has much on Urquhart's place within it.

Among them were Maybury and Craftsman John Watkinson: the identity of the two men wounded and other interesting detail here is from Friends of the Airborne Museum Society (of Oosterbeek) Newsletter No. 77, February 2000, accessed via the ParaData website. Ms Schouten's role is described in the *British Medical Journal*, 23 September 2004.

its possession would be his downfall: some Dutch sources maintain that Dr Zwolle's subsequent fate resulted from his having helped the British and cast doubt about the existence of the list. However, the Military Intelligence Museum page on Maybury refers to his carrying the 'Black List' of Nazi members, and, since it was compiled by the Intelligence Corps, we must assume its accuracy.

The orders coming from corps headquarters were clear . . .: Kershaw, *It Never Snows in September* is very good on this.

There were four 6-pounder anti-tank guns at his disposal . . .: some sources say five, initially. This is from Frost's Ryan Papers interview.

'You'll be no bloody good in the Army . . .': Dover, *The Silken Canopy*.

'Only those who have had to make such a decision to surrender . . .': ibid.

'hit on the idea that we would lob a couple . . .': Brooks, IWM Audio 18265.

The first four armoured cars drove undamaged across mines . . .: Frost in Ryan Papers.

'All hell broke loose': SS Corporal Mauga, quoted in Kershaw, *It Never Snows in September*.

'our most enjoyable battle': Frost in Ryan Papers.

'anybody who seems to move up there, they're getting hit': Steve Morgan, ex-machine-gun platoon, interviewed on the bridge in 2014, www.youtube.com/watch?v=JUoza3parRE and www.youtube.com/watch?v=kG1TVzjp7GE.

For much of the route, dubbed 'Hell's Highway' . . .: Antony Beevor, *Arnhem: The Battle for the Bridges, 1944* (Viking, 2018).

He had brought eight tanks from a training base in Bielefeld . . .: Kershaw, *It Never Snows in September*.

'I was about to open up when there was a tremendous explosion . . .': Ted Cleverly, B Company, quoted by Van Buggenum in *B Company Arrived*.

'each hit seemed to pulverize the masonry . . .': Frost, *A Drop Too Many*.

'Where are you going? . . .': Lieutenant Patrick Barnett of the Brigade Defence Platoon, Ryan Papers.

'we are just the first instalment': Frost, Ryan Papers.

'They were fantastic marksmen': SS-Sturmmann Horst Weber, quoted in Van Buggenum, *B Company Arrived*.

As McDermont cleared the ground floor and headed onto the stairs . . .: Corporal Graham Scopes, IWM Audio 18750.

'I have never seen anyone so nonchalantly brave': Lieutenant John Blunt, Ryan Papers.

'One sergeant did go quite berserk . . .': Scopes, IWM Audio 18750.

'they shot him straight away . . .': Peatling, IWM Audio 18728.

'I would like to know if this is worse . . .': Frost, *A Drop Too Many*.

'Well, Freddie, I'm afraid it's not been a very healthy party . . .': ibid.

Frank had come to the view that further defence was pointless . . .: Steve Morgan (who was with this group), YouTube.

'firing a pistol with his left hand . . .': ibid.

'Goodbye, dear boy': ibid.

'It's going to be every man for himself here': Bloys, IWM Audio 17273.

'If I'm still here and if you can still get back': Lieutenant Pat Barnett, Ryan Papers.

'then ordered all opposition . . .': Frost, *A Drop Too Many*.

'Well, Doug': ibid.

Chapter 20: The Cauldron

Late on the afternoon of 17 September, Sergeant Mike Lewis . . .: details of Lewis's battle come from his IWM Audio 4833 interview, his daughter Helen's PhD and her subsequent book, *The Dead Still Cry Out*.

So, the newly arrived men quickly took heavy casualties . . .: 4th Parachute Brigade War Diary, NA, WO 171/594, and associated accounts from the units involved.

'I mocked that up': Lewis, IWM Audio 4833.

'We are completely surrounded and our perimeter is becoming smaller . . .': this letter is attributed to Sergeant Dennis Smith in the IWM note attached to image BU 1121, the famous image of paratroopers near the Hartenstein Hotel. There are many questions posed by this 'letter', not the least of which is, if it is attached to a photo that is, in fact, by Mike Lewis, was it also written by him? Also, it may have been more in the manner of a diary entry, since a letter like this could never have been sent uncensored.

'Fighting intense and opposition extremely strong . . .': quoted by Mead, *General 'Boy'*.

three SS Kampfgruppen, with six or seven battalion strength sub-units . . .: Kershaw, *It Never Snows in September*.

Of the Allied planes bringing in supplies that day, twenty-one were shot down . . .: for excellent detail on the RAF operations, see Ben Kite, *Undaunted: Britain and the Commonwealth's War in the Air 1939–45*, Vol. 2 (Helion, 2021).

'My thought was how could I write to my father . . .': Peatling, IWM Audio 18728.

'The SS men were very polite and complimentary . . .': Frost, *A Drop Too Many*.

'I'm going to give you a brandy, you fought well': Bloys, IWM Audio 17273.

leading Timothy to conclude that some of the men captured on that raid had talked: Timothy, IWM Audio 17182.

Bill Bloys was only mildly embarrassed . . .: he confesses happily to the larceny in his IWM Audio 17273.

'Well fought, Tommy . . .': Private James Sims, Ryan Papers.

when two paratrooper officers leapt from a lorry carrying prisoners, the SS guards opened fire . . .: Peatling pulls together much interesting information on this incident in his book *Without Tradition*. Hibbert's own account can be heard as IWM Audio 21040.

Sergeant Ernest Ballinger from the 2nd Battalion noted in his diary . . .: Sergeant Ernest Ballinger, IWM Docs 25746.

Dr Jan Zwolle, the doctor who had tried to save Arthur Maybury's life . . .: unsurprisingly this has been written about more in Dutch than in English but a brief account appears in the *British Medical Journal*, 23 September 2004.

They were among forty locals killed by the Germans in such acts of vengeance: Ballantyne, *Arnhem*, who gives some details, for example about the British doctor murdered at the hospital.

'They were burning us out, house by house': Lewis, IWM Audio 4833.

'the Red Devils still fought back and battled for every room . . .': Möller's quote comes from his correspondence with Kershaw, cited in *It Never Snows in September*.

At one point a Sturmgeschütz III tracked assault gun . . .: the eyewitness was SS Corporal Wolfgang Dombrowski, cited ibid.

'the most gorgeous sound I'd ever heard': Lewis, IWM Audio 4833.

'annihilate them as soon as possible': an order from the II SS-Panzer Korps commander Wilhelm Bittrich, cited by Kershaw in *It Never Snows in September*.

captured four battle-weary paratroopers walking towards him . . .: Helen Lewis did some detective work on the AFPU 'dope sheets' in attributing this photo and cites also a Dutch article on how it was taken, including the line about other soldiers calling out abuse. Her dissertation can be found at http://hdl.handle.net/10453/36977.

'No one could speak at that . . .': Lewis, IWM Audio 4833.

'all ranks now exhausted . . .': Mead, *General 'Boy'*, is very good on the decision-making to withdraw the remnants of the 1st Airborne Division.

'suddenly there were an awful lot of wounded around . . .': Lewis, IWM Audio 4833.

Urquhart's division took 11,500 men to war . . .: these figures include the Poles and the Glider Pilot Regiment men.

One respected analysis suggests they took around 2,500 casualties . . .: Kershaw, *It Never Snows in September*.

'was shaming, like being a malefactor, being no longer free': Frost, *A Drop Too Many*.

139 men to return to Allied lines in October under Operation Pegasus . . .: I am very grateful to John Howes for sharing his research on this. In

terms of published work, there's a good summary account of Pegasus in Ballantyne, *Arnhem*.

'If in the coming years a man says, "I fought at Arnhem" . . .': in Wood's despatch for the *Daily Express*, 24 September 1944.

Chapter 21: Lessons Learned

'was probably a good thing in the end': Pine-Coffin, letter to Kathleen Lang, 26 September 1944.

'in the event of my getting bumped off': ibid.

'He is really the only expense I have . . .': ibid.

'I shall be glad when the war is over . . .': ibid.

The litany of failures discussed by the airborne men . . .: such discussion can be found in many memoirs and recollections, including Gale, *Call to Arms*, Frost, *A Drop Too Many*, and Dover, *The Silken Canopy*.

'was in no position to exercise command in the field': Gale, *Call to Arms*.

'the very presence of the Airborne Corps HQ was nothing but a nuisance': Frost, *A Drop Too Many*.

'it is the command structure that fixes responsibility': Gale, *Call to Arms*.

the enemy's ability to bring in forces from across the Netherlands . . .: the idea that failing to spot the SS armour near Arnhem sealed the mission's fate is one of the more tendentious theories about Arnhem. Urquhart and others have made clear that it wouldn't have altered their decision. Keep in mind also that II SS-Panzer Korps didn't actually have many tanks, being heavily depleted post Normandy. Also, there were a great many other units a little further afield that could, and did, send tanks to the battle. Well-led men with Spandaus and mortars were what put the 1st Airborne Division into major difficulties well before the forty-eight hours for which they were meant to hold out were up.

'my plan was designed for and could only have succeeded against weak opposition . . .': letter of 2 February 1951 from Gerald Lathbury to Chester Wilmot, in file 15/15/50 of Wilmot's papers at the Liddell Hart Archive.

'not now my battle but a matter for XXX Corps . . .': this letter to Daphne du Maurier is quoted in Mead, *General 'Boy'*.

'*The whole corps, British and American, has done magnificently . . .*': ibid.

'*totally inadequate meeting*': Baynes, *Urquhart of Arnhem*.

'*everyone, from the Supreme Commander downwards . . .*': see Mead, *General 'Boy'*.

'*he was well warned*': Pearson, IWM Audio 21033.

'*perhaps they might be going a bridge too far*': Walch Papers, IWM Docs 9487.

'*Immediately the rumour mongering began . . .*': Lieutenant Ron Hinman's account, via Michael Pine-Coffin.

'*our revered colonel . . . incurred, to the detriment of his own career . . .*': ibid.

'*Within minutes I'd lost a third of my men*': Major Jack Watson, quoted in Woolhouse, *13 – Lucky for Some*, which is by far the best account of what happened in Bure.

'*Mortar bombs rained down . . .*': Private Dennis Boardman, ibid.

'*the Germans were very close, were firing across the street . . .*': Sergeant John Wallace, ibid.

'*[I] waited patiently for the German to stick his head through the door . . .*': remarkable testimony by Cpl John Hutton, who later joined the SAS, also Woolhouse.

'*To everyone's astonishment (including the German troops) . . .*': Tibbs, *Parachute Doctor*.

'*if you don't tickle us we won't tickle you*': Captain Harry Leach, IWM Audio 31554.

Chapter 22: Varsity to VE Day

'*He was determined to take every risk he could possibly take . . .*': Alan Brooke quoted in Brian Gardner, *Churchill in His Time: A Study in a Reputation, 1939–1945* (Routledge, 2021).

'*they're coming! . . .*': this comes from an Alan Moorehead report on the event, quoted in various places, including Gardner, *Churchill in His Time*.

planned to avoid previous pitfalls: stated by many, including Gale, *Call to Arms*. For a good pocket-sized history of Varsity see Tim Saunders, *Operation Varsity: The British and Canadian Airborne Assault* (Pen & Sword Battleground, 2007).

'*the men were in the air for a long time*': Pine-Coffin journal.

'*we descended into hell*': Ken (Nobby) Clarke, article in 7th Parachute Battalion newsletter.

'*it was like walking through a butcher's shop*': Private Gordon Elliott, 7th Battalion. Gordon and his wife Joan sought out and collated many accounts of the 7th's Varsity campaign. These typescript records are now held by Michael Pine-Coffin, but I will refer hereafter to Elliott Papers in reference to them.

'"*have you seen my battalion?*" . . .': Lieutenant Ellis 'Dixie' Dean of the 13th, in Woolhouse, *13 – Lucky for Some*.

'*He kept that gun firing and did an immense amount of damage*': Pine-Coffin journal.

'*caused a considerable diversion of enemy artillery fire . . .*': Nigel Poett quoted in Saunders, *Operation Varsity*.

'*on fire in the air . . .*': Tibbs, *Parachute Doctor*.

'*we simply had to glue ourselves to the ground*': Claffey letter, Claffey Papers, IWM Docs 22646.

'*gliders were crash landing all around us*': Private Harry Clarke, quoted in Saunders, *Operation Varsity*.

'*the most successful airborne operation carried out to date*': ibid.

'*The worry was that after all that had gone before one could still get hit . . .*': Lance Corporal David Robinson, quoted in Woolhouse, *13 – Lucky for Some*.

'*don't bloody talk like that, man*': Tanner, IWM Audio 11448, attributes these words to Sergeant Cherry.

'*in a week or so we all had as many pistols . . .*': Elliott Papers.

'*most of the Germans are servile in the extreme*': letter of 6 April 1945, Clark, IWM Docs 43120.

'*I've never seen lorries cleared so fast*': Tanner, IWM Audio 11448.

'*Everyone with bayonets, fix 'em!*': ibid.

'*Nobby, let's get the bastards!*': Elliott Papers.

'*I went over backwards with this sledgehammer blow . . .*': ibid.

'*[We] were much too far forward to control the battle . . .*': Pine-Coffin journal. His description of this episode gives a hint of his dry wit.

'*had to be done on foot and was very unpleasant*': ibid.

'*They're going to get me, they're going to get me*': Tanner, IWM Audio 11448.

'*none of them got out alive*': ibid.

'*the mood of the chaps was: kill 'em . . .*': Ibid. Tanner gives a vivid description of the Jamieson episode.

'*humanized the situation*': Bramwell, IWM Audio 9542.

'*there's nothing to this*': Elliott Papers.

'*All the men knew there was a risk that the bridge might blow up . . .*': Gush in Elliott Papers.

'*The place was sheer carnage*': ibid.

'*We looked around on a scene of utter destruction . . .*': ibid.

'*You could hear the cries of the wounded*': Tanner, IWM Audio 11448.

'*I find it impossible to express my appreciation in words . . .*': Pine-Coffin journal. This statement might seem like CO's boilerplate stuff, but it shows the degree to which Pine-Coffin valued his medics as an ingredient of the battalion's wider success and gives some idea of why he tried doggedly to get decorations for them.

'*eating us up with their eyes*': Lewis, IWM Audio 4833, which is the source of all of his quotes in the Belsen passage.

'*Our general attitude to the Germans changed to their disadvantage . . .*': Claffey Papers, IWM Docs 22646.

He felt the evil of Belsen prompted theft from German civilians . . .: Clark, IWM Docs 43120, in a letter home: 'we began to take watches, binoculars, cameras, from soldiers and then civilians . . . some boasted openly of how many watches they'd stolen'.

members of the 7th Battalion intervened to stop Russian soldiers . . .: Ronald Follett, 7th Battalion, IWM Audio 12402. He says soldiers from the unit stopped the Russians 'terrorizing' some fleeing German women they'd detained while cycling along a road into nearby woods.

'*I am sick of tales of rape of all sorts and kinds . . .*': Clark, IWM Docs 43120, letter to his mother dated 11 May 1945.

Writing to the commander of the 6th Airborne Division . . .: Gale letter to Bols, marked 'Secret', 5 April 1945, Gale Papers, Airborne Assault Museum.

Chapter 23: Every Man an Emperor

In a photo snapped outside the palace . . . .: IWM Photograph H42042.

'*I soon realized that nobody was going to be able . . .*': Frost, *A Drop Too Many*.

It had lost 188 officers and 2,004 other ranks killed in action : figures compiled by Hilary St George Saunders for *The Red Beret*, an excellent book as a source of reference. In addition, ten officers and 128 other ranks of the 1st Canadian Parachute Battalion fell while it was serving under the British 3rd Parachute Brigade.

it had 200 men killed in action and lost nine during training accidents: Roll of Honour reproduced in Peatling, *Without Tradition*.

men who ended up as prisoners of war: more than 800 : ibid.

By way of comparison, one of the 7th Armoured Division's tank battalions . . .: this is the 5th Royal Tank Regiment, detailed in my *The Tank War*.

'the best planned operation of the lot': Forsyth, IWM Audio 18780.

'You are the elite of the British army': Airborne Ethos card, Airborne Assault Museum.

Even in May 1944, a photograph of officers of the 2nd Battalion . . .: reproduced in Frost, *A Drop Too Many*.

'they proved magnificent material and easy to mould when in good hands': Brigadier James Hill's foreword to James, *A Fierce Quality*.

'The very act of arriving on the battlefield by parachute . . .': Pine-Coffin journal.

'they have "jumped" from the air and by doing so have conquered fear': Montgomery's foreword to Saunders, *The Red Beret*.

'they managed to eliminate some of the weaker elements . . .': Urquhart, IWM Audio 21034.

soldiers parading barefoot on Netheravon airfield . . .: Hancock, IWM Docs 21756.

Browning's obsessions set up constant tension . . .: this view comes from several NCOs in the early regiment, including Bill Aldcroft quoted in Johnston, *Churchill's Warriors*.

'I am a very busy farmer and have not the time . . .': Frost's letter of 4 October 1977 to Douglas Thres, Airborne Assault Museum.

'I do not believe that anything like the scale . . .': Gale, *Call to Arms*.

'There has never been a really properly thought out appreciation of the airborne forces . . .': NA, AIR 2/7913, Air Member for Personnel to D. S. D. 6 March 1947.

28,000 serving with airborne forces in Europe . . .: Saunders, *The Red Beret*.

Brayley *was given a knighthood, then a peerage by Wilson in 1973* : *Dictionary of National Biography* (Oxford University Press, 2004). Salacious allegations about Brayley are made by Joe Haines in *The Politics of Power* (Coronet, 1977).

'believe me, it hurt' : Forsyth, IWM Audio 18780.

'We shall miss him terribly' : her letter is quoted on the school website: https://oldshirburnian.org.uk/lieutenant-j-h-grayburn-sherbornes-a-bridge-too-far-hero/.

but he had achieved other things in his thirty years too : Maybury's *Parachutist* was published in December 1944, the announcement being carried by the *Birmingham Daily Gazette* on the 15th of that month. It followed *Thrills with the Paratroops* and *More Thrills with the Paratroops* (*Nottingham Journal*, 17 November 1944).

'They have the highest standards in all things . . .' : foreword to Saunders, *The Red Beret*, which gave the regiment its great 'Every Man an Emperor' rubric.

Index

He just wanted a decent book to read ...

Not too much to ask, is it? It was in 1935 when Allen Lane, Managing Director of Bodley Head Publishers, stood on a platform at Exeter railway station looking for something good to read on his journey back to London. His choice was limited to popular magazines and poor-quality paperbacks – the same choice faced every day by the vast majority of readers, few of whom could afford hardbacks. Lane's disappointment and subsequent anger at the range of books generally available led him to found a company – and change the world.

'We believed in the existence in this country of a vast reading public for intelligent books at a low price, and staked everything on it'
Sir Allen Lane, 1902–1970, founder of Penguin Books

The quality paperback had arrived – and not just in bookshops. Lane was adamant that his Penguins should appear in chain stores and tobacconists, and should cost no more than a packet of cigarettes.

Reading habits (and cigarette prices) have changed since 1935, but Penguin still believes in publishing the best books for everybody to enjoy. We still believe that good design costs no more than bad design, and we still believe that quality books published passionately and responsibly make the world a better place.

So wherever you see the little bird – whether it's on a piece of prize-winning literary fiction or a celebrity autobiography, political tour de force or historical masterpiece, a serial-killer thriller, reference book, world classic or a piece of pure escapism – you can bet that it represents the very best that the genre has to offer.

Whatever you like to read – trust Penguin.